Chemistry, Energy, and Human Ecology

Chemistry, Energy,

HOUGHTON MIFFLIN COMPANY   BOSTON

and Human Ecology

FRED KABBE   LOIS KABBE
Central Michigan University

Atlanta   Dallas   Hopewell, New Jersey   Geneva, Illinois   Palo Alto   London

Library of Congress Catalog Card Number: 75-27126
ISBN: 0-395-19833-X

Cover photo from Stock, Boston.
Title page photo courtesy of The Carter Oil Company.
Line art by Mark Mulhall.

To Cathy, Shana, Nancy, Laura, Angela, Jeff, and Sharon

Contents

13. Human Egoism and Ecology   401

Preface

The authors believe that some knowledge of chemistry is necessary to understand oneself and one's relationship to science, technology, and the environment. The text is intended for nonscience majors. It avoids the complicated mathematical development required for professional chemists, but it provides the chemical basics needed for intelligent discussions and decisions. Readers should see how chemical principles are useful means for solving ecological problems.

The book is intended to be used in one-semester or one-quarter courses. It is devoted to the basic principles underlying all ecological and chemical action. Atomic and molecular structure is developed in Chapter 2. Other concepts of chemistry are explained later as needed to provide insight into the consequences of our technologies. The text repeatedly shows the interrelationship between a chemical problem and other chemical and/or biological concerns. Since no problem can be solved in isolation from other concerns, a broad picture of the ecosystem is developed.

Apparently technology can improve human welfare tremendously; but energy used for technology brings with it lots of chemically related problems. This theme is important throughout the book. Modern chemicals that affect our well-being may have the face of faithful servants, but also can confound us by the environmental problems they cause. Thus the book shows how chemicals have their limitations as well as their promises.

Another theme is that chemical reactions can be made to occur when necessary substances are available in the environment. The text carefully examines the resource bases of water, land, and clean air as well as of minerals and raw materials essential to an industrial society. Thus an ecology of chemical materials is also seen as human ecology.

An important discussion in the latter part of the book treats human psychology, social and political organizations, and individual perceptions of ecological and environmental matters. This theme is suggested in Chapter 1, supports key points in many places throughout the text, and is discussed more fully in Chapter 13.

The authors were helped with prepublication reviews by James Espenson of Iowa State University, James E. Huheey of the University of Maryland, Oliver Seely of California State College at Dominquez Hills, and Robert Carr of the College of Alameda in California. To all of these people we extend our deep thanks.

Charles W. Huever of the University of Minnesota contributed valuable information on the dangers of the LWR nuclear reactor; E. J. Hoffman of the

University of Wyoming has shared data on the efficiency of the nuclear fuel cycle; and Friends of the Earth have given freely information about the California Water Project.

Colleagues at Central Michigan University also have helped with their understanding and patience as this project developed. Special appreciation is due to H. Malcolm Filson and Paul D. Cratin, and to our expert library staff, especially Caroline Baker and Yvonne Wezensky. In addition, several members of our family have helped with reading, reference work, and typing. They are Carl and Cynthia Kabbe, Janet and Jon Kabbe, Connie Kabbe, and Stephen Osborn. Especial thanks are due to Marilyn Osborn who worked day and night to help meet a particularly difficult deadline.

Fred Kabbe
Lois Kabbe

1 Basic Principles of Ecology

No one decided as a deliberate matter to poison our polluted and dying waterways.

No one decided as a deliberate matter to destroy millions of acres of productive soil through erosion, salination, contamination and the intrusion of deserts. . . .

We did not intend to do this, but this is what we did.[1]

Hon. Maurice F. Strong

Every organism affects its environment and in turn is affected by it. The sum of these interactions is the ecology of that organism. Such ecological relationships are the workings of nature's laws which also apply to man. There is an ecology of man.

A boy trapped skunks on his father's farm. Later, ducklings disappeared from the farm pond. The farmer, deprived of a pleasure, asked a biologist friend to investigate. The biologist found that the skunks had preyed upon the turtles by eating their eggs. After the numbers of skunks had been reduced, the turtles had experienced a population explosion and consumed the baby ducks. The relationship of ducks, turtles, skunks, and man may be viewed as an ecology of ducks, an ecology of turtles, an ecology of skunks—or an ecology of man.

A simple action caused unexpected, unintended, and unwanted effects. In this case, the original action boomeranged and caused the final unwanted consequences to affect the originator of the action—man himself.

These events demonstrate the principle stated by John Muir that when you take hold of anything you find it is hitched to everything else in the universe.

STEADY STATE, SIMPLIFICATIONS, AND STABILITY

Before the skunks were trapped, a steady state existed; that is, the population of the skunks, turtles, and ducks changed very little from year to year. If at some time the turtles laid more eggs than usual, the larger number of eggs would be more easily found and eaten by the skunks. By consuming the "excess" eggs, the skunks would effectively prevent a population explosion of turtles. On the other hand, if the turtles laid a smaller number of eggs, these would be more difficult to find, and a somewhat larger proportion of eggs would hatch to produce turtles. Under these circumstances, the turtle population would tend to increase and become a greater threat to the ducks. Regardless of the number of turtles present in the beginning, the skunks would force the system to come to a steady state with respect to the population of turtles.

After the skunks were trapped, the restraint on the population of turtles was removed. As a consequence, the duck population was destroyed. In addition, the farmer lost the pleasure given to him by the ducks. The ecosystem had been made simpler; it was less stable and drastic changes in the balance of organisms became possible.

It is unlikely that a more complex and well-balanced ecosystem would be subject to the dramatic changes shown by the man-skunk-turtle-duck relationship. There would be other predators, mink, otter, fox, raccoon, that would compete with and aid the skunks in keeping the turtles under control. Under such a complex system of predators, the removal of one of them would not upset the overall balance, because the remaining predators would merely eat a little better. However, if the predators were removed progressively, one by one, the ecosystem would become progressively simpler and less stable at each step in the simplification process. Eventually, when the last remaining mechanism, in this case skunks, was removed, catastrophe would follow.

1. Honorable Maurice F. Strong, Secretary-General of the United Nations Conference on the Human Environment; from the opening statement at the first plenary session of the conference, Stockholm, Sweden, 5 June 1972.

SIMPLIFICATION BY
DOMINANCE A lion would consider it a "good" if he could kill at will. If this were possible, lions would become the dominant organism on earth. However, their success would be short-lived unless there were some restraint upon their population and/or activity. Without such restraints, the lions inevitably would increase without bound and consume all possible food resources. They would be the victims of their own unchallenged success and indirectly through their destruction of food supply would cause their own extinction.

Syphilis is a serious and very infectious disease which is almost always contracted through sexual contact with a person who has the disease. The syphilis spirochete (any of a group of slender, twisted microscopic organisms, many of which cause various diseases) is so fragile that it cannot live for long at temperatures other than the normal human body temperature. However fragile it may be, it is very damaging to the person having the disease. In the final stages of the disease, it may attack the central nervous system, the spinal cord, valves of the heart, and the blood vessels. As a result, a diseased person may develop an uncoordinated gait, general paralysis, and/or a general debility. The usefulness and prospects for survival of such persons are very poor.

The prevalence and survival of the syphilis species depends upon a continuing chain of infective transmission from one person to another. In spite of its fragility and its dependence upon human foibles, syphilis manages to prosper. Presumably the syphilis spirochete would be more likely to survive if it could live outside the human body and at temperatures different from those of the human body. Thus the disease could be transmitted by contact with an infected object or any bodily contact. Because syphilis infection is often not recognized, the disease could go unnoticed in the general population. If this were to occur in the absence of an effective method of detection and treatment, the human race could die from it.

The hypothetical extension of the strength of the lion and the hypothetical relief from its fragility on the part of the syphilis spirochete would in each case lead to disaster for the species. Restraints are not necessarily undesirable.

THE ECOLOGY OF PEOPLE The ecologies of skunks, turtles, ducks, lions, and syphilis are interesting and help to establish an understanding of the ecological principles which apply to all organisms including man.

Man's relationship to his environment has gradually changed since the first man appeared on the earth. As a hunter-food-gatherer, man's impact upon the environment was not greater than any other species. He was not strikingly dominant over other species, nor did he transport appreciable amounts of material from place to place. On the average, the materials which he took for his use in one place were returned to the place from which he took them. Essentially, in the early stages of man, a biological and chemical steady state existed.

Early man learned to use fire and began to change his surroundings. Scientists have speculated that the Great Plains of the United States may have been covered with forest until prehistoric man burned the area to help kill game. Later he domesticated animals and learned to till the soil, thus stripping it of its natural growth. Certain plants and animals were encouraged at the expense of others. Natural, complex ecosystems were replaced by simple systems which better served man's needs and/or desires. Eventually the discovery and use of energy, especially coal and oil, made possible industrial communities, where large human populations gathered in small areas and put heavy burdens upon the air, the waters, and the land. In his attempts to improve the amenities of life for himself, man has created conditions which affect him adversely from a broad ecological point of view.

Man, with his large brain and aggressive personality, has used science, the study of natural phenomena, and technology, the application of science, to circumvent the restrictions imposed by nature. He can change living conditions so that life is possible at the equator, on the south polar ice, in outer space, or in the depths of the oceans. He has been able to increase crop yields, recover valuable minerals from lean sources, and transport large amounts of material great distances. In short, man has attempted to conquer nature (Figure 1–1).

SCIENCE AND TECHNOLOGY

Figure 1–1. Photo © Norman Cousins.

(Vladimir Rencin)

Most of these accomplishments have been due to the use of chemistry. The desirable affluence which chemistry has brought us has also brought many problems. An understanding of these problems and their possible solutions requires a comprehension of chemical principles in order to understand the behavior of man-made materials in the environment, the pollutants caused by their production, the resources needed to produce them, and the possible supply of these resources.

The visible environmental difficulties are often placed at the door of science, and more especially technology, when the basic underlying cause is to be found outside science in what Dr. Alvin Weinberg, former director of Oak Ridge National Laboratory, calls transscience. Decisions are made on the basis of greed, intellectual blindness, *status quo,* arrogance, ignorance, nationalism, carelessness, religion, and even compassion.

For example, compassion for people caused the use of the insecticide DDT to kill mosquitoes in a village in Borneo. Cockroaches, living in the houses, built up DDT in their bodies without themselves dying. Geckos (small lizards) ate the cockroaches, became sick and slow, and were eaten by cats who then died. Without the lizards, caterpillars were uncontrolled and chewed the thatched roofs of the houses until they collapsed. In addition, with the cats gone, disease-carrying rats moved into the village. Just as in the case of the skunk-turtle-duck episode, man caused inadvertent consequences in Borneo.

The difficulties of the village in Borneo were the ecological price of using DDT at that time and in that place. For too long, actions have been undertaken without the price being known until it was paid. Science may be able to furnish definitive information about the results of a proposed action. Then it may be assessed in terms of risk-benefits. Questions are asked: Who receives the benefits? Who suffers the risks? Which is more important? Who shall decide? The answers must include all those who benefit or suffer risks and not just the obvious ones. These questions are fundamental ones that must be asked over and over.

The proposed action may be discussed as a trade-off. An example might be the question of using agricultural land to build a road. Here the trade-off is mobility for food. Is the desirability of mobility important enough to lose the food grown on the land used for the road? Who will use the road? Who will be hurt: the farmer or the consumer? Who will decide? Is the road a local road or is it part of a major cross-country route? Does it matter? Is there a more desirable way to furnish the mobility? There are no easy answers. There will be honest differences of opinion. The question might be asked: What is a trade-off of a road vs. food doing in a chemistry book? Every change which occurs on earth involves chemicals and chemical reactions; that is, it involves the composition and structure of matter and the way it behaves.

The production of food from the land involves many chemical reactions: production of fertilizer, pesticides, seeds, use of energy by the farmer, and the growth of plants. Chemical reactions are also involved in the building and use of the road: the use of energy to build and use the road, the production of the materials needed to build and maintain the road, the changes in the composition of the soil because of the land disturbance necessary to build the road, and the pollutants that wash off the road. Even a change which does not occur because of lack of materials may be important. For example, removal of lead from gasoline would change the chemicals in the air along the road. Chemistry can be focused on the smallest particle of matter, or it can be as wide as the universe.

The choice between two actions is especially difficult when scientists differ on the risks involved. Scientists, like other persons, can be influenced by their beliefs and associations. When the background of a particular scientist is known, the reason for his statements may be explained. However, there are many cases where the pertinent information about a scientist is not known. In many cases there are honest differences in interpretation of data. In other cases sufficient data does not exist. For these cases, Senator Mike Gravel suggests the use of what he calls the "doctrine of comparative consequences."

If we assume Experts "A" are *right* and we follow the policy they support, what will be the consequences if they turn out to be *wrong*?

If we assume Experts "B" are *right* and we follow the policy they support, what will be the consequences if they turn out to be *wrong*?[2]

Science and technology are not to be summarily dismissed as unimportant. Science and technology will be sorely needed in the years ahead. They will be necessary, but not sufficient. How they are used will be equally as important as the developments themselves. Here an informed public must take part in making decisions.

This text is an attempt to show the chemical basis of the environmental problems of mankind. In the future more information will become available about some of the material used in this book. The implications may be strengthened or weakened. However, if the basic chemical concepts are known, any change can be understood. An informed public is necessary.

It is not enough for the public to be informed. In addition, everyone must make their opinions known to those who decide the future direction of the country. Write letters "to the editor", to the governor of your state, to the mayor of your city, to the president, to your congressmen, to secretaries of governmental agencies, and to anyone whom you wish to encourage, chastise, or from whom you seek help. In writing your reasons for believing a certain way, you will clear your own thinking, and if your thinking is clear it is entirely possible that you may transfer an important idea to another important person.

Take an interest in your future. You're going to spend a lot of time there.[3]

Rev. "Dub" Nance

2. *Newsletter Mike Gravel*, 28 September 1973, p. 2.
3. *Chem Tech,* March 1971, p. 164.

KEY CONCEPTS

1. Meaning of ecology.
2. Effects of simplification on a steady state.
3. Limitations of dominance.
4. Assessment of the possible effects of science and technology.

QUESTIONS

1. Describe the *material* basis of life you would like to have in 10 years. Be specific. Keep your description until after Chapter 13. Are your desires the same?
2. List the factors in modern society which may degrade the environment. After you have read chapter 13 revise the list. Should some items be removed?
3. In the text, the effects of spraying a village in Borneo to prevent malaria carried by mosquitoes was used to illustrate how compassion may cause unexpected results. Give an example of several of the other subjective factors which may cause inadvertent results.

BIBLIOGRAPHY

The following is some suggested reading describing environmental problems in general. Specific suggestions will be given for each chapter.

Books

1. Committee on Resources and Man of the National Academy of Science/National Research Council, *Resources and Man,* San Francisco: W. H. Freeman & Co., 1969. Discusses the limitations of the exploitables and the nonexploitables. The book is a report of a study, but unlike most such reports it is interesting to read.
2. Dorst, J., *Before Nature Dies,* Baltimore: Penguin Books, Inc., 1965. Translated from the French. Sometimes slightly awkward construction but always interesting.
3. Ehrlich, P. R. and Ehrlich, A. H., *Population, Resources and the Environment,* San Francisco: W. H. Freeman & Co., 1970. A well-written, broad picture of man and the environment. The emphasis is on the population crisis. The authors demolish the idea that an increase in the affluence of the people of developing countries will automatically result in a decrease in the rate of population growth.
4. Leopold, A., *A Sand County Almanac,* San Francisco: Sierra Club/Ballantine Books, Inc., 1949. A classic by a great natural historian. He writes of the joy and beauty found by a way of life which protects the environment.
5. Rienow, R., and Rienow, L. T., *Moment in the Sun,* New York: Ballantine Books, Inc., 1967. A popularly written, exposé-type book about man's abuse of the environment.
6. Swatek, P., *The User's Guide to the Protection of the Environment,* New York: Friends of the Earth/Ballantine Books, Inc., 1970. The consumer has more power through his purchases than does the voter. This book shows how to make every purchase a vote for the environment.

BASIC PRINCIPLES OF ECOLOGY

1. *Science and Public Affairs,* published monthly by the Education Foundation for Nuclear Science. Technological developments reported as related to political and economic fields. Concerned with the use of scientific information for the benefit of mankind on a world-wide basis.

2. *Chemical and Engineering News* (weekly) and *Environmental Science and Technology* (monthly), published by the American Chemical Society. Generally reflects industry's viewpoint, although guest editorials and letters to the editor give counter opinions. Short announcements give an indication of trends. *Environmental Science and Technology* has some technical articles but most of the material is understandable by the layman.

3. *Ecologist,* published monthly by Ecosystems Ltd. (London). Articles on all phases of man and his surroundings. Believes society must be reorganized. Occasionally the use of British idiom makes it difficult to understand but it is usually amusing. Every issue contains articles of wide interest.

4. *Environment,* published 10 times a year by the Scientists Institute for Public Information (SIPI). Articles usually reflect the viewpoint that faulty technology is the basic cause of man's environmental problems.

5. *National Wildlife* and *International Wildlife,* both bimonthlies published on alternate months by the National Widlife Federation. Articles are usually about wildlife and related problems. Very easy reading. Publishes a prestigious yearly EQ (Environmental Quality) Index on water, wildlife, land, minerals, air, and population. Excellent color illustration.

6. *Organic Gardening and Farming,* published monthly by the Rodale Press, Inc. Special interest in organic food production with practical farm and garden tips, but has broadened into working for an ecologically sound way of life.

7. *National News Report,* published weekly by the Sierra Club. A weekly digest of federal actions in the environmental field.

8. *Not Man Apart,* a twice-monthly newspaper published by the Friends of the Earth. Worldwide reports of environmental news with special emphasis on the United States and affairs of the Friends of the Earth. Contains editorials, informative articles, and book reviews. Covers more news than other publications.

9. *Audubon,* published bimonthly by the National Audubon Society. *Living Wilderness,* published quarterly by the Wilderness Society. *National Parks Magazine,* published monthly by the National Parks Association. *Sierra Club Bulletin,* published 10 times a year by the Sierra Club. Generally wildlife-recreation-wilderness-conservation information but include other related areas. These periodicals present current news on conservation measures and governmental actions. Superb photography.

10. *Stockholm Conference Eco,* published at irregular intervals by the Friends of the Earth with the help of other organizations. When an important environmental group meets, the *Eco* starts reverberating. The writing is spritely, the cartoons unusual, and the topics timely.

11. *Technology Review*, published 11 times a year by the Alumni Association of Massachusetts Institute of Technology. Wide range of technological and energy problems. Letters to the editor aid in presenting all viewpoints.
12. *Ambio*, published bimonthly by the Royal Swedish Academy of Science. Most articles are easily read by those with limited knowledge of the sciences. Articles discuss recent work in environmental fields.

2   Chemistry

A society that blindly accepts the decisions of experts is a sick society on its way to death. The time has come when we must produce, along side specialists, another class of scholars and citizens who have broad familiarity with the facts, methods, and objectives of science, and thus are capable of making judgements about scientific policies. Persons who work at the interface of science and society have become essential simply because almost everything that happens in society is influenced by science.[1]

Dr. René Dubos

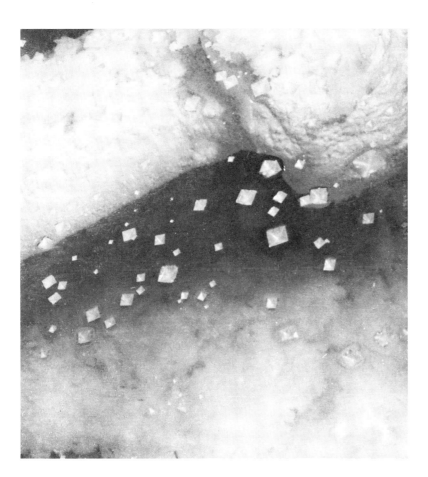

The various pollutions and ecological disorders which now concern us are the result of man's exploitation of the biological and mineral resources of the earth. From the production of the raw material to its incorporation in the final product and its ultimate disposal, each stage in the processing or use of a material has a potential for damaging the environment or disturbing the ecology somewhere on the earth. These damages result from chemical inputs that come from the works of men.

Scientists of all kinds, chemists, physicists, astronomers, sociologists, psychologists, political scientists, and others, seek to correlate accumulated facts under a generalization or "law." The use of generalizations reduces the burden of memorization otherwise necessary and makes logical thinking processes possible. Without prior knowledge of a specific situation, a generalization makes it possible to say: "if such and such is true, then necessarily something else is, or should be, true."

If a generalization accurately predicts the behavior of a previously unknown, but related, system, then the generalization is confirmed and for the time being can be regarded as a "law of nature." However, if the generalization does not accurately predict the behavior of a newly examined system, scientists propose a new generalization which will encompass the new data along with all past data on comparable matters.

In order to aid the thinking process, scientists often develop a hypothetical model of a system which visualizes the system and correlates and "explains" the observations which have been made upon the natural system. The model helps scientists to understand the structure and workings of a system that may not be observable directly.

There is nothing particularly permanent or sacred about "natural laws" written by man. Models and statements of principles are ephemeral products of the mind. As such they are constantly being revised to include new information as it becomes available. The changeable character of the useful generalizations discovered by man is particularly true of chemistry.

MATTER—SOLIDS, LIQUIDS, AND GASES

Matter is anything which occupies space and has weight. It occurs in the form of solids, liquids, and gases. Solids and liquids are easily observed and measured. In contrast, the gases of the air seem to be "nothing at all." Winds may buffet us, but it requires some intellectual effort to realize that each cubic meter of air actually contains about as much matter as is found in a liter of water; gases contain much more "empty space" than do liquids or solids.

Solids may be melted to form liquids and liquids may be vaporized to form gases. Conversely, gases (vapors) may be condensed to liquids, and liquids may be solidified. Frequently, solids, such as ice, carbon dioxide, and paradichlorobenzene (moth crystals), may pass directly from the solid state into the vapor state. The reverse is also true—vapor may pass directly to solid, as, for example, in the formation of snow and frost crystals. In all cases, the matter which was present in the solid or liquid is present in the "nothing at all" state

1 The Bulletin of Arthur D. Little, Inc., January–February, 1971, quoted in *Chem Tech,* August 1971, p. 501.

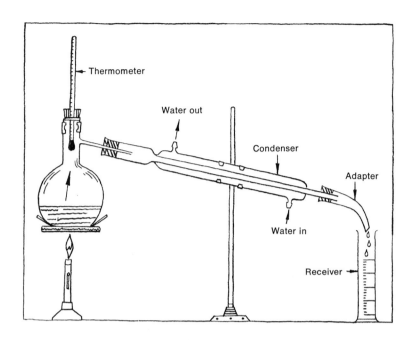

Figure 2-1. Distillation apparatus.

of gases. As much matter can be condensed from the vapor state as was originally vaporized.

There is an extremely large number of different substances on earth. Chemistry is the science of the composition, structure, properties, and reactions of these substances. In the following pages the chemistry of matter will be developed through the use of a few familiar materials: water, ink, table salt, sugar, copper, air, iron, ammonia, and alcohol. In addition, a few unfamiliar substances such as sulfuric acid and nitric acid will also be used. A study of these materials will establish general principles which are applicable to all other matter. In the process some chemical separation and analytical procedures will be discussed.

Pure Substances Scientists use several processes to separate a single substance from a mixture of two or more substances. If a single substance is separated from all others, it contains only one kind of material, all the particles of which are alike. Such a material is said to be pure. In actual experimental practice, purity is a matter of degree and rarely absolute. Each pure substance has a unique set of properties which serve to distinguish the substance from all others. Experimentally, even the smallest fraction (portion) of a pure substance has properties which do not differ from those of any other fraction.

DISTILLATION   In distillation a liquid is changed into a gas (by heating) and subsequently condensed (by cooling) to re-form a liquid (Figure 2–1). In the distillation process, the more volatile (boil at lower temperatures) materials are separated to some extent from the less volatile substances. The closer the boiling points of the components of a mixture are to each other, the less satisfactory is the degree of separation which is attainable by distillation. Conversely, the larger the difference between the boiling points of the components, the better the separation of the substances will be.

A general test for the purity of a distillable substance can be made by comparing the properties of the first portion of the liquid which distills over with the properties of the last portion of the liquid which remains in the flask as distillation proceeds toward completion. If these two portions differ in any way, the original material was impure. If the two portions have exactly the same properties, then the original liquid was a pure substance. There are exceptions to this rule, but it is not appropriate to discuss these here.

Industrially, distillation is used on a large scale to separate crude oil into various boiling-point fractions: gasoline, kerosene, fuel oils, and residual oils (Figure 2–2). On a global scale water vaporizes from the salty, undrinkable water of the oceans, moves overland, and falls as relatively pure water in the form of rain.

Figure 2–2. Baytown oil refinery.
Courtesy of Exxon Corporation.

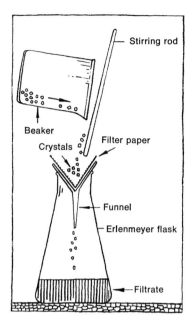

Figure 2–3. Filtration apparatus.

CRYSTALLIZATION The most important substance in table salt is sodium chloride. Table salt, pure or not, is more soluble in hot water than it is in cold water. If a sample of salt is dissolved in just enough pure water to cause all of the salt crystals to dissolve at the boiling point of the solution, a saturated solution of the salt is produced. As the solution cools, crystals of salt will appear and can be separated from the solution by filtration[2] (Figure 2–3). Crystals of sodium chloride tend to separate out as a pure substance, leaving the impurities in the filtrate (the solution that remains after the crystals are filtered out).

The filtrate can be reboiled and evaporated until a saturated solution exists, that is, crystals just begin to form. When the solution has been cooled thoroughly, the crystals can be collected. This process can be repeated until the quantity of remaining solution becomes very small. The last portion of the solvent, in this case water, is boiled away and the residue of salt crystals compared with the first set of crystals obtained. If it is found that the first and last crops of crystals have identical properties by whatever test is made upon both sets of crystals, then the original salt sample was a pure substance. On the other hand, if the properties of the two sets of crystals differ in any way, then the original salt sample was a mixture.

Sometimes, in order to produce a pure substance, many recrystallizations must be performed. In the preparation of the first sample of a radium compound,

2. Filtration is the process of pouring the mixture through a porous paper which catches the crystals but allows the liquids to pass through.

CHEMISTRY

Madame Curie dissolved one tonne of a mineral called pitchblende and, through a laborious series of 2000 recrystallizations, finally obtained 0.2 gram of a radium compound. A weight of 0.2 gram is about one-tenth the weight of a dime.[3] The actual weight of radium in the final sample was about one-ten-millionth as much as the weight of the pitchblende ore. By comparison this corresponds to the monetary value of a dime compared with the monetary value of one million dollars. Persistence produced a new pure substance.

Madame Curie paid for the discovery of radium by dying from cancer induced by exposure to radiation from the radium.

Table sugar is a substance called sucrose. Commercially, sucrose is produced in larger quantities (tonnes) than any other pure substance. It is extracted from sugar beet slices by allowing hot water to flow over the slices which are held in tanks. Undesired solids and colors are removed, the clear colorless liquid concentrated, and pure crystalline sugar filtered from the solution.

CHROMATOGRAPHY   There are many forms of chromatography: paper, column, thin film, gas. All work on the same basis. A sample is adsorbed (held in a very thin layer) on the surface of a finely divided solid called an adsorbent. Different substances are held with different degrees of firmness by the adsorbent. A fluid (liquid or gas) flows over the adsorbent and tends to sweep the adsorbed substances along with it. The less firmly adsorbed particles are swept down stream in the direction of the fluid flow at a more rapid rate than are the more firmly adsorbed particles. Eventually a mixture of substances may be separated into packets of particles which may be collected separately.

Chromatography is capable of separating very small samples (smaller than microgram quantities) of mixtures into recoverable fractions. The rapidity of the movement of a particular substance with the fluid depends upon the substance, the adsorbent, the fluid flow, and the temperature. By means of a chromatograph it is possible to identify the components of a complex mixture and to measure their relative and absolute amounts. Chromatography is also a rapid method of determining whether a given material is a pure substance or not. If only one fraction appears during an appropriate chromatographic process, the sample of material may be considered to be pure.

Gas chromatography is used routinely in oil refineries to monitor the operation of the plant. It has also been used to "fingerprint" oils from various sources. Figure 2–4 shows that gas chromatography is capable of resolving (separating) a very complex mixture.

EXTRACTION   Sometimes substances are so dispersed in water that it is difficult to test for them in the raw water. Often they can be concentrated by extracting (collecting from) them from the water with a solvent which is insoluble in water

3. The terms gram (abbreviation g) and metric ton (tonne) refer to metric units. A dime weighs about 2 g. A tonne is slightly larger than a ton (1 tonne = 1.1 ton). A complete discussion of all metric units together with their relationship to English units will be found in Appendix C.

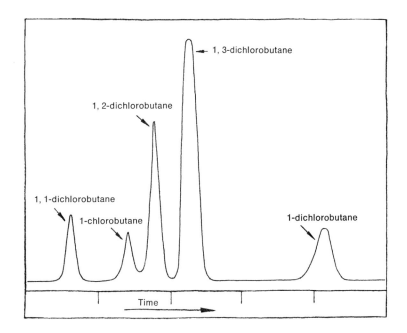

Figure 2-4. An example of a gas chromatograph.

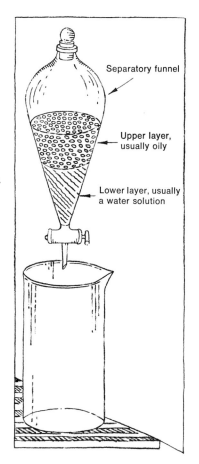

Figure 2-5. Extraction apparatus.

(i.e., does not dissolve in water). Substances which are more soluble in an organic (i.e., a carbon compound, like gasoline or ether) solvent than in water tend to be extracted from the water into the immiscible organic solvent. After separating the solvent from the water layer (Figure 2–5), it can be evaporated. In this way, the concentration of the extracted substances will then be great enough for other tests to be made.

DDT can be extracted from water in this way. Similarly, oil slicks tend to extract DDT and other organic materials out of the water and to concentrate these in the oil films.

If a rotten egg is broken in a room, it soon becomes obnoxiously clear that a rotten egg has been opened. An ersatz ''egg'' in the form of a little iron sulfide and an acid is a good substitute for a rotten egg. Both the egg and the ersatz egg demonstrate that a small amount of matter can be dispersed throughout a large volume of space.

Similarly, a small amount of colored matter may impart a color to a large volume of water; table salt dissolved in water may be tasted in every portion of the water. The progressive changes from solid to liquid to gas, and the apparent interpenetration of a substance (*solute*) which dissolves in another substance (*solvent*) to form a homogeneous (i.e., uniform in composition throughout) mixture of two or more substances, are best explained by a particle concept of matter.

Chemical reactions also indicate that matter is composed of discrete particles. When substances react with each other to form a new substance, they react in definite proportions by weight. The particles of each reacting substance are exactly alike, and the particles of each product are exactly alike. A definite number of particles is required to form a particle of product. This is analogous to combining dimes and nickels to form piles of coins worth 25 cents, in which two dimes are required for one nickel. Instead of dimes and nickels, scientists frequently use ball and stick models (Figure 2–6) to help them represent and visualize particles of substances. No matter how imaginative or ''wild'' the model may be, it must have some of the same critical limitations that the natural system has. The dimes, nickels, and balls as model systems for matter meet these conditions.

Molecules and Elements

The production of pure sucrose from sugar beet was described under purification through a crystallization process. When pure sucrose is heated strongly it decomposes into water and a black crumbly substance, carbon. The weight of the carbon plus the weight of the water exactly equals the weight of the original sample of sucrose, and the weight of the carbon is always the same percentage of the weight of the original sucrose. Obviously, carbon and water are simpler substances than sucrose. The smallest particle of sucrose, a *molecule,* must be composed of a definite proportion of whatever substances that are to be found in carbon and water.

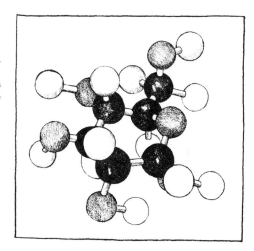

Figure 2–6. Glucose model. The black spheres are carbon atoms; the white spheres are hydrogen atoms; the others are oxygen atoms.

Sucrose belongs to a family of compounds called *carbohydrates*. These compounds decompose into definite proportions of carbon and water; thus it was assumed that they were carbon hydrates, i.e., carbohydrates. The cellulose of wood and cotton, the starches of grains and their flours, and all sugars belong to the family of compounds known as carbohydrates. All can be decomposed into carbon and water. These compounds are among the most abundant compounds in living systems and constitute a large proportion of the food and fiber which we use.

The black crumbly mass of carbon from the decomposition of sucrose cannot be further decomposed into simpler substances. Under all conditions carbon can react to produce only a new substance which weighs more than the original sample of carbon. Therefore, carbon is an elemental substance, an *element*.

On the other hand, water is not a simple substance. Under certain conditions, water can be decomposed into hydrogen and oxygen by passing an electric current through it. Therefore, water is a *compound* and not an element.

Under no circumstances can a given quantity of hydrogen react to form a new substance which weighs less than the original quantity of hydrogen. Similarly, oxygen cannot react to form a new substance which weighs less than the original sample of oxygen. When either of these substances reacts completely to form a new substance, the weight of the product substance will always be greater than the weight of the sample of the substance from which the new substance was formed.

Through processes similar to the analysis of sucrose, scientists have found about 90 elements which occur in nature. Another 15 elements have been made by man in the past three decades. All other pure substances are compounds which are made from various combinations of the elements.

The elements are listed alphabetically in a table in Appendix A. Each element has been assigned a *chemical symbol* to facilitate the description of chemical substances and their compounds. Symbols for a few common elements are one letter, e.g., O for oxygen, H for hydrogen, C for carbon, N for nitrogen. All other elements are designated by two letters; the first letter is capitalized, e.g., Ne for neon, As for arsenic, Pt for platinum, and Zn for zinc. Some of the symbols are derived from Latin or other foreign languages, for example, Na for sodium from the Latin word natrium, Pb for lead from the Latin word plumbum, Au for gold from the Latin word aurum, and W for tungsten from the German word wolfram.

It is customary for the first group of scientists who identify a man-made element to have the honor of naming it. Most of these elements have been made by American scientists working in California, hence the names californium, berkelium, and americium. They have named others after famous scientists, e.g., curium (after Madame Curie, the discoverer of radium), einsteinium (after the scientist Einstein), and fermium (after Fermi, who helped to build the first atom bomb). One new element was first reported by United States, English, and Swedish scientists and was named nobelium after the founder of the Nobel Prizes. Neither the Russians nor the California scientists could repeat the discovery. Later, the United States group finally identified the new element but they chose to retain the name. The difficulty of identifying a new man-made element is understood when one appreciates that only one atom of the element may be produced every 20 hr and that half the atoms will last but a few seconds at most and some last even a hundred times less long.

Students need to know only the symbols for the elements which are being discussed. With a little effort and general use you will be able to associate the elements with their symbols.

The ultimate particles of the elements are the *atoms* of these elements. A definite number of atoms are combined in a definite way to form each molecule, e.g., sucrose or water. The sucrose molecule and its *formula* are rather complicated. Chemists have determined that each molecule of sucrose contains 12 carbon atoms, 22 hydrogen atoms, and 11 oxygen atoms. In formula form this is $C_{12}H_{22}O_{11}$. The subscripts give the number of each kind of elemental atom in the molecule.

SUMMARY   Several new terms have been introduced in the above discussion. These may be reviewed by the following definitions:

1. *Atoms* are small discrete particles of matter which cannot be further divided by chemical reactions. They are sometimes called the building blocks of matter.

2. *Elements* are those substances whose atoms are of only one kind.

3. *Molecules* are pure substances made up of various combinations of atoms. They always have the same definite composition. They can be broken down by chemical reactions.

4. *Compounds* are those substances whose molecules are of only one kind.

Matter is composed of electrically charged particles. The evidence is as close as combing your hair, shuffling over a carpeted room, or stripping masking

Charged and Uncharged Particles

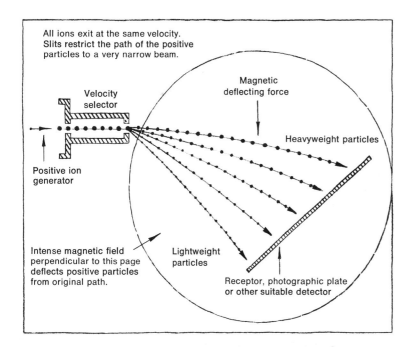

Figure 2-7. Principle of a mass spectograph.

tape from a roll. Opposite charges (+ and −) are formed in each of these cases and attract each other: lint and hair are drawn to a charged comb, a spark and a shock may be delivered from the fingers to another person, and a dim light is produced at the point where the tape is leaving the roll (try the tape experiment in a very dark room). Most matter normally is in an uncharged state. Rubbing, scuffing, and tearing operations cause opposite charges to be produced. Negatively charged particles are removed from one object and collected in quantity on a second object.

Electrons are the negatively charged particles in atoms; *protons* are the positively charged particles. An equal number of protons and electrons are present in a neutral atom. The tiny, heavy protons are found in the small *nucleus* of the atom. The electrons, about 1/1800 as heavy as protons, have an indefinite size. The electrons move constantly through all parts of the outer space of the atom and thus completely occupy it just as molecules of gases or liquids completely fill a given space.

With the exception of one form of hydrogen, the protons do not account for the total weight of the atom. The remainder of the weight of the atom is provided by *neutrons* which have approximately the same weight as protons but carry no electrical charge.

Modern scientists determine the relative weights of atoms of elements by use of an instrument called the mass spectrograph.

The mass spectrograph operates on the principle that, if various atoms and molecules move at the same velocity and are acted on by the same force, the lighter particles will be deflected by a greater amount than the heavier particles. Assuming constant speeds and a constant deflecting force, an object of given weight should always follow the same path and arrive at the same place on a collecting panel (Figure 2–7). However small the difference between the weights of the particles, the mere fact that they do differ in weight would cause them to be collected at different places. Furthermore, if the weights of the objects vary approximately by integral (whole number: 1, 2, 3, 5, . . .) amounts of some weight unit, there should be empty spaces between the specific points at which particles do collect. In this case, if the weight of one or more of the objects is known, it is possible to specify and relate the weights of all of the objects.

The mass spectrograph does this for the invisible individual atoms and combinations of atoms. If a general mixture of substances is introduced into a mass spectrograph a series of uniformly spaced lines appears on the receptor. No particles are recorded between these sharp lines. (Argonne National Laboratories have an instrument which separates the lines representing two consecutive atoms by more than an inch.) The discontinuity of matter is abundantly evident. If pure samples of elements are introduced into the instrument, a limited section of a strip chart might show the lines indicated in Figure 2–8. The numbers show the relative masses. They are called *mass numbers.*

Surprisingly, the element hydrogen is composed of two kinds of atoms, one with a mass number of 2 and the more common kind (99.5% of the total) with a mass number of 1. An atom of a given weight and kind is said to be an *isotope.* Hydrogen, therefore, has two isotopes as it occurs in nature, one called hydrogen and one called deuterium (D).

Each element has a different number of protons. The number of protons is also the *atomic number* which fixes the order of the elements with respect to each other. The difference in the weights of two isotopes of the same element

Figure 2–8. An example of mass spectrograph data.

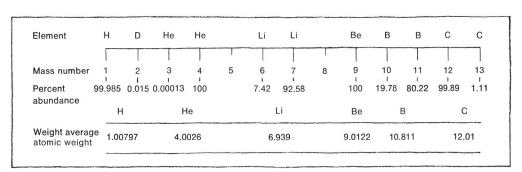

Element	H	D	He	He		Li	Li		Be	B	B	C	C
Mass number	1	2	3	4	5	6	7	8	9	10	11	12	13
Percent abundance	99.985	0.015	0.00013	100		7.42	92.58		100	19.78	80.22	99.89	1.11

	H		He		Li		Be		B		C
Weight average atomic weight	1.00797		4.0026		6.939		9.0122		10.811		12.01

is due to the difference in the number of neutrons in the nuclei of the two isotopes; the number of protons is the same for the isotopes of a given element. Hydrogen has one proton in its nucleus, giving a mass number of 1. Deuterium has one proton (it is also a form of hydrogen) and one neutron in its nucleus, giving a mass number of 2. There is a third isotope of hydrogen called tritium (T) with two neutrons in its nucleus and a mass number of 3. These isotopes along with some other atoms are shown in Table 2–1.

The mass numbers are approximations of the actual weights of the atoms. They are useful, but not accurate enough for scientific work. The actual weights of the atoms are too small to be conveniently used, e.g., an atom of hydrogen weighs 1.67×10^{-24} g ($\times 10^{-24}$ means that the decimal must be moved 24 places to the left). A scale was devised in which the isotope of carbon with a mass number of 12 was assigned a value of 12 atomic mass units (amu). All other weights are calculated relative to carbon-12. On that basis, a hydrogen atom weighs 1.0078 amu. These weights are called *atomic weights* and can be measured in any convenient unit. Weight in grams is most often used for scientific work, but pounds, kilograms, or tons can be used equally as well.

All elements are thought to have been made from hydrogen many eons ago. This process is still going on in the sun.

Atomic weight values compare the weights of an equal number of each of the kinds of atoms. For example, at the atomic level, 12 amu of carbon is equivalent to 1.0078 amu of hydrogen. If the atoms of each are mutliplied by the same number, the ratio remains the same, 12 carbon to 1.0078 hydrogen. If the number of atoms is increased until there are 12 g of carbon, an equal number of hydrogen atoms will weigh 1.0078 g. The atomic weight measured in grams is called, obviously, the gram atomic weight. One gram atomic weight of carbon or any other element contains 6.02×10^{23} atoms. This large number is called Avogadro's number (602 billion trillion) and is the number of particles in one *mole* of a substance. Therefore, the gram atomic weight of any element is the weight of one mole.

The unit mole is not limited to 6.02×10^{23} atoms. It may be used for any kind of particle—molecules, protons, electrons. It could even be used as the number of grains of sand, if that much sand could be found.

Elements do not exist in nature in quantities of isolated single isotopes. Most elements have at least two naturally occurring isotopes. A few have many more, e.g., tin has 10 isotopes. Chemists need a scale which expresses atomic weights for the natural isotope mixture of the elements. The weights found in Appendix A are those the chemist uses. For example, chlorine has two common isotopes, one with 18 neutrons and the other with 20 neutrons. The isotopes are called chlorine-35 and chlorine-37 to represent the mass numbers. About 75% of naturally occurring chlorine is chlorine-35 and 25% is chlorine-37. Thus, the atomic weight of the natural mixture of chlorine isotopes is 35.5.

TABLE 2–1. Atomic Structure of Some Small Atoms.

Element symbol	H	D	T	He	Li	Be	B	C
Mass numbers (from Fig. 2–9)	1	2	3	4	7	9	11	12
Protons (+ charge) (atomic number)	1	1	1	2	3	4	5	6
Electrons (− charge)	1	1	1	2	3	4	5	6
Neutrons (excess weight over protons)	0	1	2	2	4	5	6	6

The two isotopes of chlorine are chemically very similar. However, the most common isotopes of both calcium and argon have a mass number of 40. The atomic weights of the two elements are 40.08 for calcium and 39.95 for argon. Even though the atomic weights are very close these elements have very different properties. The different properties are due to the different numbers of protons in the nucleus of the atoms of the elements.

Removing Electrons from Atoms—Ionization Energies

When elements are subjected to electrical energy (measured in electron volts), electrons may be removed from the atom, that is, they are ionized. When an electron is removed, the remaining electrons are bound more tightly because the number of protons has not changed and the repelling force of the removed electron is no longer present. Consequently, greater amounts of energy are required to remove the second, third, and subsequent electrons. Eventually, it becomes relatively difficult, if not impossible, to remove tightly bound electrons.

When the *ionization energies* are obtained for the elements in order of their atomic numbers, a periodic change is observed in them and in the number of electrons which can be easily removed from an atom. If the elements with the same number of easily removed electrons are grouped in columns, the periodic pattern shown in Table 2–2 becomes apparent. Table 2–2 shows that a dramatic increase in ionization energy appears at the level given by the heavy line. The number of electrons above that line increases regularly from left to right as follows:

```
1  2
1  2  3  4  5  6  7  8
1  2  3  4  5  6  7  8
```

These numbers represent the number of *valence electrons,* i.e., those electrons which can be involved in chemical activity. Each row represents a *shell.* The nucleus and shells beneath the outside valence shell is called the *kernel* of the atom. Each shell ends with an inert elemental gas, after which a new shell is begun. If the above pattern is continued until all the elements are included, the elements would be arranged in the *periodic table* (Appendix B). The number of electrons in successive shells of the periodic table is 2, 8, 8, 18, 18, 32, 32, ... (Figure 2–9).

Elements which have the same number of valence electrons have similar properties. Such elements arranged in columns in the periodic table are called families (see periodic table and Table 2–2).

The first periodic table was published by Dimitri Ivanovich Mendeleev in 1871. He arranged the elements in order of their atomic weights except for the few where that order destroyed the pattern of similarity of properties. There were only 63 known elements at that time. He left gaps in the table where there were no elements to fit the pattern. He predicted the properties of the elements which would fill the gaps in his table. The elements were discovered later and found to have properties very nearly those predicted by Mendeleev.

Lithium, sodium, potassium, rubidium, and cesium constitute the *alkali* metal family of elements. What is known about the properties of one of these elements can be applied, to a degree, to all other members. There is a gradation of properties between the members of a family (column) but the differences are not as great as the differences between the families of elements.

FAMILY CHARACTERISTICS The members of the alkali family are all silvery metals which are good conductors of electricity and heat. They are so soft that they can be cut with an ordinary knife. They react violently with water to produce a gas and much heat. At times the gas may burst into flames.

The next family is the *alkaline earth* family whose members are harder and denser with higher melting and boiling points than the members of the alkali family. They also react with water to produce a gas, but the reaction is slow.

At the right-hand side of the table are the *noble gases.* These gases are generally unreactive toward other elements. However, xenon and krypton at least react with fluorine and oxygen to form several stable compounds.

Figure 2–9. Arrangement of electrons in shells.

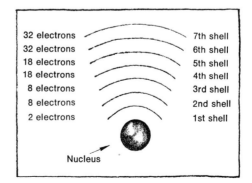

32 electrons	7th shell
32 electrons	6th shell
18 electrons	5th shell
18 electrons	4th shell
8 electrons	3rd shell
8 electrons	2nd shell
2 electrons	1st shell

Nucleus

TABLE 2–2. Table of Ionization Potentials.

	1	2	3	4	5	6	7	8
Shell I	H 13.5							He 24.5 54.4
Shell II	Li 5.4 75.3 121.8	Be 9.28 18.0 153 217	B 8.3 25 38 258 329	C 11.2 14.3 48 64 390 490	N 14.2 21.5 47.4 77 97.4 552 667	O 13.5 34.7 55 77 113 137.5 740 871	F 17.3 34.8 62.4 67 113.7 156.4 184 958	Ne 21.5 41.0 63 97 126 157.9
Shell III	Na 5.12 47 72 99 138 172 208 264	Mg 7.64 15 80 109 141 186 224 266	Al 6 19 28 120 154 190 241 285	Si 8 16 33 45 166 205 246 303	P 10.5 20 30 51 65 220 263 309	S 10.36 23.4 35 47 72 88 281 329	Cl 13 24 40 53.5 68 97 114 348	Ar 16 28 41 60 75 91 124 143
Shell IV	K 4.318	Ca 6.09	Ga 5.97	Ge 8.0	As 10.5	Se 9.7	Br 11.8	Kr 13.93
Shell V	Rb 4.16	Sr 5.67	In 5.76	Sn 7.3	Sb 8.5	Te 8.96	I 10.6	Xe 12.8
Shell VI	Cs 3.87	Ba 5.19	Tl 6.07	Pb 7.38				

The *halogen* family, second column from the right-hand side of the table, are colored to some degree: fluorine, pale-yellow gas; chlorine, greenish-yellow gas; bromine, reddish-brown liquid; iodine, grayish-black solid. They do not react with water to produce a gas.

Atoms combine to form *molecules.* The way they combine and the number that combine are determined by the atomic structure of the combining atoms.

MOLECULES AND COMPOUNDS

For the lower atomic number elements, scientists envisage an atomic structure which assumes that there are four *orbitals* (places) which the valence electrons can occupy. Four equivalent orbitals would be logically equally distributed over a sphere so that each one is equally distant from the others (a tetrahedral

Filling Electron Orbitals

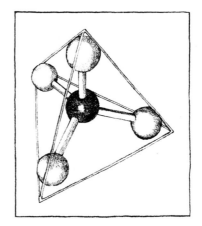

Figure 2–10. Tetrahedral carbon model.

structure) (Figure 2–10). For convenience, the orbitals may be represented on flat paper for the second-row elements of the periodic table (Figure 2–11). The known number of electrons, represented by dots, is placed in the orbitals, shown by rectangles. The symbol for the elements represents the kernel of the atom.

The same pattern of orbital filling is repeated in the third-row elements from sodium to argon, except that a kernel of electrons corresponding to the element neon underlies the third-row valence electrons (Figure 2–12).

Electrons and Chemical Bonds

The attraction of the positively charged nucleus of an atom for the electrons of another atom makes possible the formation of compounds. The nucleus tries to attract enough electrons to fill the four orbitals of the outer shell. The compound formed by sodium and chlorine is an example. The periodic table shows that sodium has one electron in its outside shell; that is, it is one electron above the unreactive electron state of neon. The table of ionization energies shows that this electron is easily removed. Chlorine has seven electrons and is one electron short of the unreactive state of argon. Chlorine easily removes the single valence electron of the sodium atom and both atoms go to the electron state of an unreactive element. This arrangement tends to be very stable. Thus, the attraction of one element, chlorine, for the electrons of another, sodium, makes possible the formation of the compound sodium chloride.

The nucleus of one element may attract the electrons of one or more elements in the attempt to fill its valence shell and attain the electron arrangement of an unreactive element. The attractive force is the ''glue'' which holds the atoms together. The linkages between atoms are called *chemical bonds.* The differences in the numbers of protons in the nucleus of atoms and, thus, the differences in the forces of attraction results in two types of chemical bonds, ionic and covalent.

An *ionic bond* is formed by the attraction of a positively charged particle (*positive ion*) for a negatively charged one (*negative ion*). The ionization energies for the valence electrons given in Table 2–2 were obtained by subjecting the atoms to outside physical sources; i.e., a voltage force from electrical power sources or its equivalent in ultraviolet light radiation. After an electron or electrons are removed from the atom, a positive ion will remain. An ion can also be formed from an element by a chemical reaction, in which an electron or electrons are lost by one neutral atom to another originally neutral atom. The atom losing the electrons will become a positive ion and the atom gaining the electron will become a negative ion. Whether the electron is removed by physical or chemical action, the effects upon the atom are the same. The unlike charged particles attract each other and form an ionic bond (Figure 2–13).

Ions have great freedom of movement in a solution or when fused (melted). The only limitation is that the number of positive and negative charges must balance at all times. A water solution of a compound with an ionic bond or the fused compound will conduct an electric current. If the compound of sodium and chlorine (NaCl) is fused and subjected to a direct current, chlorine gas will appear at the positive electrode and sodium metal is formed on the negative electrode (Figure 2–14). The positively charged sodium ion migrates through the liquid material to the negative electrode where it acquires an electron and becomes sodium metal. The negatively charged chloride[4] ion migrates to the positively charged electrode where it gives up an electron to form chlorine.

4. A single-atom, negatively charged entity is named by using "ide" as an ending; e.g., chlor*ide* ions from chlorine, brom*ide* ions from bromine, iod*ide* ions from iodine, ox*ide* ions from oxygen, sulf*ide* ions from sulfur.

Figure 2–11. Representation of the orbitals of the second row elements.

Figure 2–12. Relationship of valence electrons and the kernel of an atom.

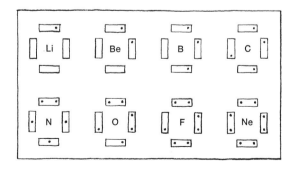

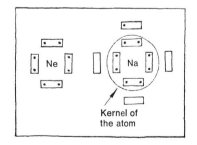

Kernel of the atom

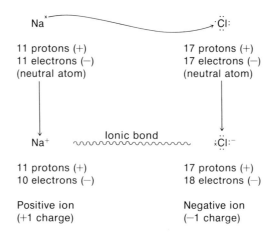

11 protons (+)   17 protons (+)
11 electrons (−)   17 electrons (−)
(neutral atom)   (neutral atom)

11 protons (+)   17 protons (+)
10 electrons (−)   18 electrons (−)

Positive ion   Negative ion
(+1 charge)   (−1 charge)

Figure 2–13.   Representation of an ionic bond.

The possibility of the formation of an ionic bond is greatest between the members of the alkali metal and halogen families. Compounds such as sodium iodide (NaI), potassium chloride (KCl), and lithium bromide (LiBr) are formed.

Na ⤵ :I: K ⟶ ·C̈l: Li ⤵ ·B̈r:

Na⁺   I⁻   K⁺   Cl⁻   Li⁺   Br⁻

Nal   KCl   LiBr
sodium iodide   potassium chloride   lithium bromide

Members of the alkaline earth family also form ionic bonds with members of the halogen family. However, the members of the alkaline earth family, such as magnesium, will give up two electrons, but a member of the halogen family can only add one to its valence shell. Therefore, two atoms of chlorine are needed to remove the electrons from the magnesium atom to form magnesium chloride (MgCl₂).

Mg ⟶ ·C̈l:
   ⤷ ·C̈l:

Mg²⁺   2Cl⁻
   MgCl₂
magnesium chloride

CHEMISTRY

Other formulas of compounds of alkaline earth metals and halogens are $CaBr_2$ and SrI_2.

The members of the third family from the right (the oxygen family) need two electrons to make their valence shells like those of the unreactive elements; for example, formulas of compounds of sodium and calcium with sulfur are sodium sulfide (Na_2S), and calcium sulfide (CaS).

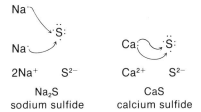

$2Na^+$ S^{2-} Ca^{2+} S^{2-}

Na_2S CaS

sodium sulfide   calcium sulfide

COVALENT BONDING   A covalent bond is formed by the sharing of a pair of electrons between atoms. In this case, both atoms use the shared electrons to fill their empty orbitals. The protons of each element attract the same pair of electrons. This attraction holds the molecule together.

In the elemental state, the atoms of hydrogen and the halogen family elements are bonded together through a single covalent bond to form the diatomic elemental molecules H_2, F_2, Cl_2, Br_2, and I_2. One electron is supplied by each

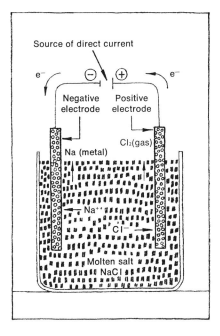

Figure 2–14. Electrolysis of fused sodium chloride (NaCl).

atom to the electron pair that is held in common. Similarly, two nitrogen atoms share three pairs of electrons to form the elemental nitrogen molecule, N_2.

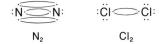

$$N_2 \qquad Cl_2$$

There is a gradation in the electron holding power of the elements across the periodic table. The elements of the right-hand side of the table hold electrons much more tightly than those of the left-hand side. It is possible for chlorine to take an electron from sodium, but it can only make oxygen or nitrogen share an electron. In general the elements clustered to the right of the stairstep line from boron (B) to astatine (At) on the periodic table form covalent bonds with each other. The force of attraction of the nucleus for electrons tends to increase as the atomic number increases within a row. Therefore, the elements on the right are more likely to form covalent bonds than the elements on the left. Within a family, this attraction tendency is somewhat overcome by the shielding of the nucleus by additional shells of electrons. This is the reason for the stairstep character of the line showing the trend toward covalent bonds.

There is no definite place as the elements progress across the periodic table where it can be said that an element forms an ionic bond with a halogen but the element next to it forms a covalent bond. The situation is similar to trying to establish the exact second night appears. It cannot be done. Compounds are said to have 5%, 10%, 50%, or 90% ionic character or covalent character. Probably no compound is completely ionic or covalent.

The elements may combine by covalent bonds to form a compound, that is, a neutral molecule such as carbon tetrachloride (CCl_4), or the gases carbon dioxide (CO_2) or carbon monoxide (CO). The elements may also be bound covalently to form an ionic particle such as the environmentally important nitrate ion, NO_3^- or nitrite ion, NO_2^-.

Compounds formed by covalent bonds are usually named by using the names of the elements. If there are only two elements involved, the more negative element ends in "ide" and often shows how many atoms of that element are present, for example, sulfur dioxide (SO_2) and nitrogen trioxide (N_2O_3).

Compounds with covalent bonds are very common. In fact, the tissues of the human body are held together by covalent bonds. The molecules may be very large and complex, they may serve many different functions, and they may undergo many chemical reactions, but it is the attraction of the protons in the nucleus of one atom for the electrons of another which makes the atoms of the molecules remain together.

WRITING FORMULAS The relationship among the members of families of the periodic table can help in writing correct formulas for compounds. The members of the alkali metal family all form similar compounds. Lithium, sodium, potassium, rubidium, and cesium form similar compounds with other elements.

The pattern of formulas formed by combination of one element with the elements in a row across the table is illustrative of the way elements combine.

Sulfide (S)	Chloride (Cl)	Phosphide (P)
Li_2S	LiCl	Li_3P
Na_2S	NaCl	Na_3P
K_2S	KCl	K_3P
Rb_2S	RbCl	Rb_3P
Cs_2S	CsCl	Cs_3P

If we consider the combination of hydrogen with the row of elements from helium to neon the following is obtained.

He	Li	Be	B	C	N	O	F	Ne
no compound	LiH	BeH_2	BH_3 (B_2H_6)	CH_4	NH_3	H_2O	HF (H_2F_2)	no compound

The elements of the next row combine with bromine to form the following compounds.

Ne	Na	Mg	Al	Si	P	S	Cl	Ar
no compound	NaBr	$MgBr_2$	$AlBr_3$	$SiBr_4$	PBr_3	SBr_2	BrCl	no compound

A look at the subscripts for the H and Br entities shows the following series of numbers.

$$0 \quad 1 \quad 2 \quad 3 \quad 4 \quad 3 \quad 2 \quad 1 \quad 0$$

and

$$0 \quad 1 \quad 2 \quad 3 \quad 4 \quad 3 \quad 2 \quad 1 \quad 0$$

Since bromine and hydrogen can only form one bond each, the number of atoms of these elements which combine with other elements specifies the number of bonds which the elements can form. The bonding information can be applied to writing formulas for various combinations of the elements.

A formula with covalent bonds such as H_2O can have two meanings other than the number of atoms combined. A formula for a substance with covalent bonds shows the number of atoms combined in a molecule. The formula H_2O means that two atoms of hydrogen combine with one atom of oxygen to form a molecule of water. The molecular weight of water can be found by adding the atomic weights of the components of the molecule: two atoms of hydrogen and one atom of oxygen:

2 atoms hydrogen	$2 \times 1 = 2$
1 atom oxygen	$1 \times 16 = 16$
1 molecule of water	18 (molecular weight of water).

The formula H_2O can also mean one mole of molecules of water that were formed from two moles of hydrogen and one mole of oxygen atoms. Just as the weight of a mole of atoms was the gram atomic weight, so the weight of a mole of molecules is the gram molecular weight. The gram molecular weight of water is 18 g.

Compounds with ionic bonds do not form molecules. The ions are held together in a solid by the attraction of the opposite charges. For example, in sodium chloride, NaCl, each sodium ion is surrounded by six chloride ions and each chloride ion is surrounded by six sodium ions.

$$Na^+ \ Cl^- \ Na^+ \ Cl^-$$

$$Cl^- \ Na^+ \ Cl^- \ Na^+$$

$$Na^+ \ Cl^- \ Na^+ \ Cl^-$$

There is no group of atoms which can be called a molecule. Therefore, the simplest ratio of the atoms is used to find *molecular weight,* sometimes called formula weight.

Chemistry of Carbon Compounds—Organic Chemistry

Carbon compounds are called organic compounds because scientists originally thought only living organisms could make them. Although today many tonnes are manufactured annually, they are still called organic compounds.

Green plants remove carbon dioxide from the air and convert it to the huge complex molecules which constitute living organisms. Animals change plant tissue compounds into energy and into their own body structures. Some of the carbon compounds collected in ages past were deposited as coal, oil, and natural gas. These stores of carbon compounds have been used to make useful articles such as plastics, fuels, pesticides, medicines, and paints.

In the discussion of distillation earlier in this chapter, the process of refining petroleum was described. One of the products of the process is propane, a constituent of both natural gas and bottled gas. It has the formula

$$\begin{array}{ccc} H & H & H \\ H\!:\!\!\overset{..}{\underset{..}{C}}\!:\!\!\overset{..}{\underset{..}{C}}\!:\!\!\overset{..}{\underset{..}{C}}\!:\!H \\ H & H & H \end{array}$$

It is inconvenient to detail all of the electrons which may be involved in even as simple a compound as that of propane. The structure may be simplified by using straight lines to represent a single bond between a pair of atoms. Thus, the *structural formula* of propane becomes

$$\begin{array}{ccc} H & H & H \\ | & | & | \\ H\!-\!C\!-\!C\!-\!C\!-\!H \\ | & | & | \\ H & H & H \end{array}$$

Since hydrogen is present in overwhelming quantities and since it is singly bonded in compounds, the symbols for hydrogen can be eliminated and only

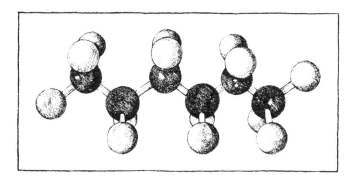

Figure 2–15. Model of straight chain hexane (C_6H_{14}) and the structural formula.

the bonds between the carbons retained. On this basis, the structure for propane becomes C—C—C. In this structure all bonds to carbon not specifically used for other elements are assumed to be occupied by hydrogen atoms.

Carbon has a greater tendency than other elements to bond to itself to form extensive chains or other groupings.

decane

2,2,6 trimethylheptane

cyclopentane

cyclohexane

Structures written on a flat page can only approximate the actual molecular structures. Figure 2–15 shows a six-member straight-chain compound and a photograph of a molecular model for the same compound. The model shows that the molecule may have a zigzag structure: ⌇⌇⌇.

The fact that carbon can bond with itself makes it possible for large molecules to be formed in a multitude of variations. When two or more substances have the same molecular formula, the atoms may be arranged differently to form isomeric compounds, that is, compounds which have the same number and kinds of atoms but are arranged in different structures.

The three structures possible from the molecular formula C_5H_{12} are shown below. The compounds are called *structural isomers.* A different kind of isomerism will be discussed in Chapter 6.

	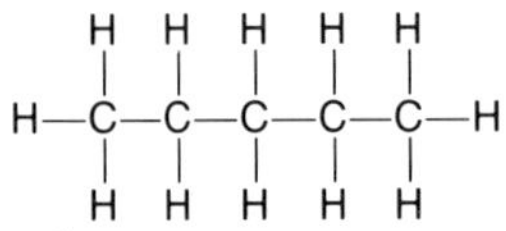	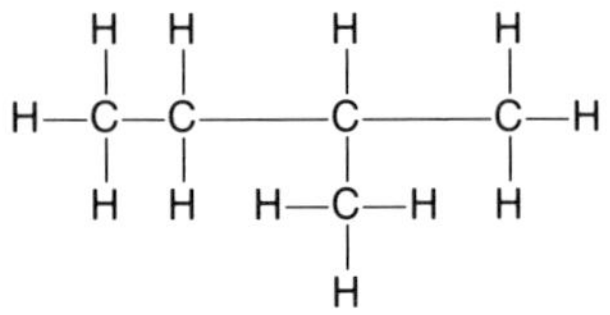	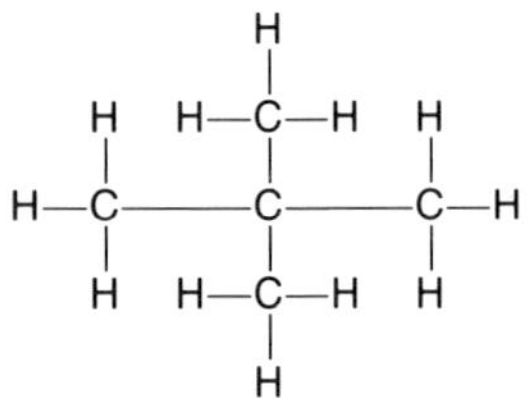
Melting point	−130 °C	−160 °C	−20 °C
Boiling point	36 °C	28 °C	9.5 °C
Density	4.3 g/ml	0.62 g/ml	0.61 g/ml

A second example is that of compounds having the molecular formula $C_4H_8O_2$. Many possible structures can be written for this formula. Only two will be considered here.

	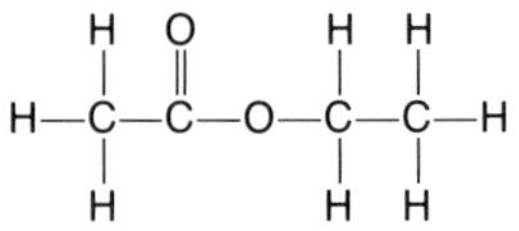 ethyl acetate	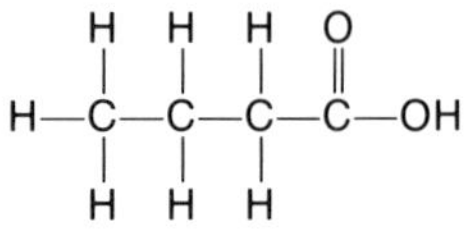 butyric acid
Boiling point	77 °C	163.5 °C
Melting point	−84 °C	−4.26 °C

The boiling and melting points are very different but the effect that the two isomers have on the nose is outstanding. Ethyl acetate has the odor of fresh apples; butyric acid has the odor of rancid butter!

If a molecular formula contains a large number of carbon atoms, the number of possible isomers with that formula becomes extremely large. The theoretical number of possible isomers for the formula $C_{20}H_{42}$ would be 366,310. If the formula $C_{30}H_{62}$ is considered, the number of possible isomers is 4.11 billion. If a single chlorine atom is substituted in each possible position, the number of different compounds is beyond comprehension.

Writing structural formulas looks complicated and forbidding, but really is no more complicated than working a jigsaw puzzle or a crossword puzzle.

Try it. The trick to writing structural formulas is to be careful to use exactly that number and only that number of bonds that the elemental atom is capable of making. Straight lines may be used to represent a bond but, if confusion develops, fall back upon careful detailing of the number of valence electrons possessed by a neutral atom in the elemental state. Then properly pair these electrons with electrons from other atoms. Not only can an atom of carbon form single bonds with other carbon atoms or with many other atoms, but it can also form double bonds and triple bonds with other carbon atoms or with any other atom which needs two or three electrons to fill its orbitals. Examples of such bonds are shown below.

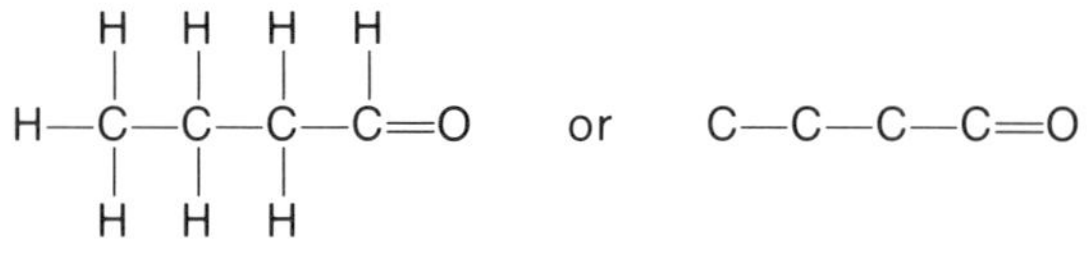

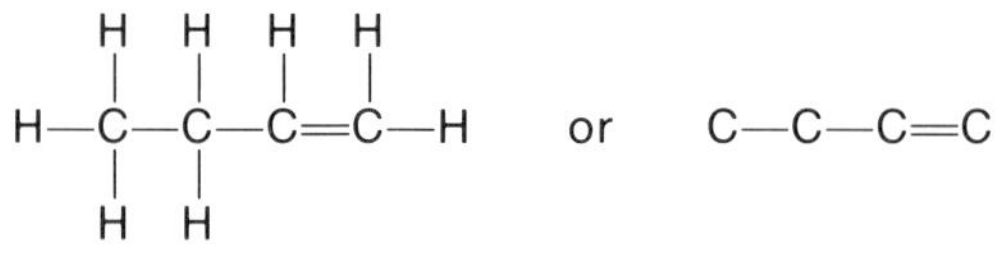

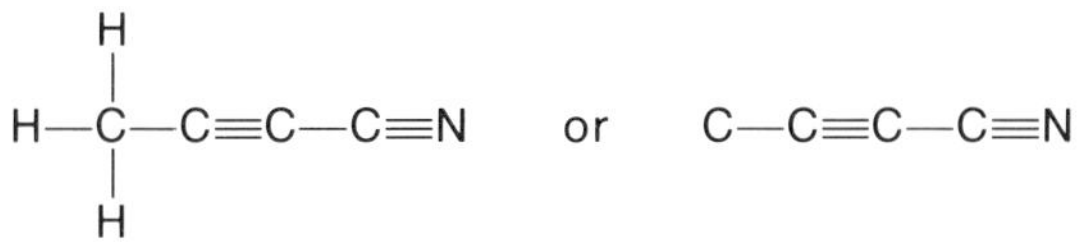

Carbon compounds with only single bonds are said to be saturated, while those with double and/or triple bonds are said to be unsaturated. The term "polyunsaturated" refers to the presence of many double bonds in the compound. This term is often used to describe fats and oils.

The term fat usually refers to a solid while oil refers to a liquid. Both have the general formula

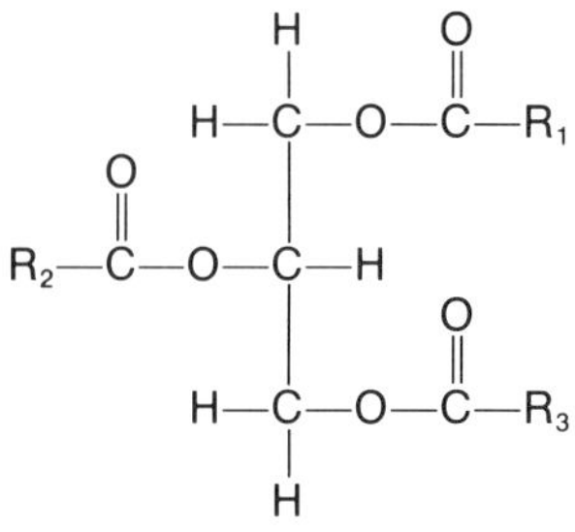

fat or oil

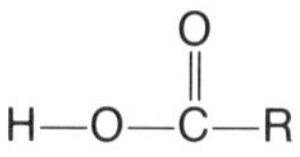

fatty acid

The symbol R generally refers to any carbon group—straight chain, branched chain, or ring. In this case, it refers only to straight chains which may or may not be saturated. For saturated fatty acids R might be $C_{11}H_{23}$ (lauric), $C_{17}H_{35}$ (stearic), or $C_{15}H_{31}$ (palmitic); for unsaturated fatty acids it might be $C_{17}H_{33}$ (oleic) or $C_{17}H_{31}$ (linoleic). The more solid a fat is, the more saturated it is. Tallow fat from beef is almost completely saturated. Butter is less saturated than beef fat but is more saturated than "soft" margarine, which in turn is more saturated than corn oil.

Fats are usually animal products, butter from cows, lard from pigs, and tallow from beef. Oils are usually from plants, olive oil, corn oil, soy oil, peanut oil, and cottonseed oil. In the past animal products tended to be more expensive than those from plants. Therefore, a method was found to make saturated fats from unsaturated fats by combining hydrogen atoms across the double bonds. The hydrogenation of an essential oil, linoleic acid, to stearic acid, a hard fat, illustrates the process.

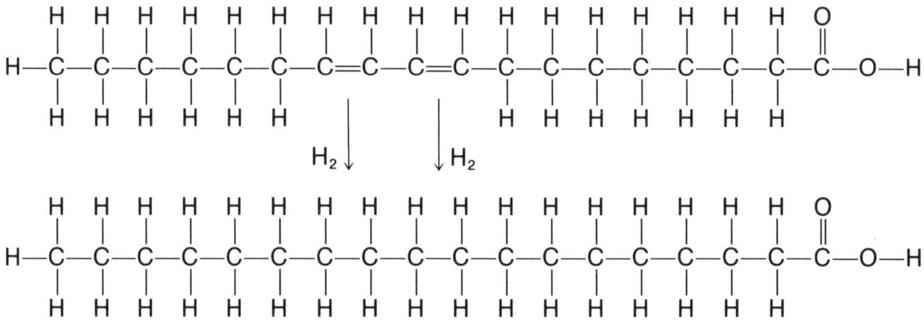

The essential fatty acid, linoleic acid, is a component of many vegetable oils (70.1% of safflower oil, 50.7% of soybean oil). The hydrogenation product of linoleic acid, stearic acid, naturally constitutes about 30.5% of mutton tallow, a hard fat. Platinum or palladium is needed as a catalyst for the reaction. The catalyst helps the reaction to occur but it is present in the same amounts after the reaction as before.

Linoleic and linoleneic acids are two of the fatty acids which must be included in the diet, that is, they are essential because the body cannot make them. When fats are hydrogenated to make margarine and solid cooking fats, the essential fatty acids are destroyed. Today, the oils are only partially hydrogenated when used to produce soft margarines.

Another class of carbon compounds is the ring compounds. One ring, a six-membered ring with three double bonds, is especially important. This structure, the benzene ring, is written by several symbols:

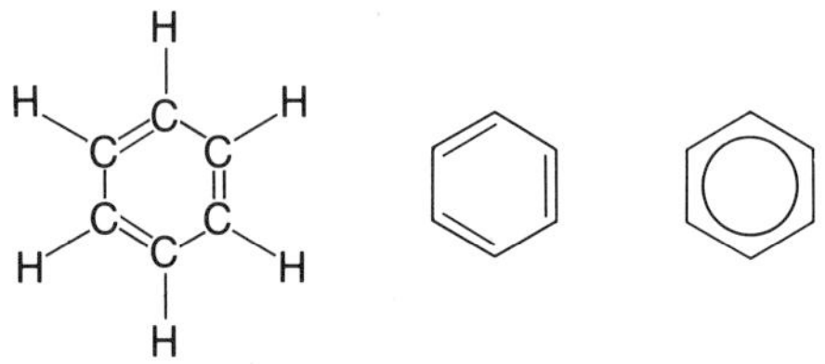

C_6H_6

Carbon compounds containing benzene ring structures are called *aromatic compounds*. The name results from the fact that several of the first compounds known to contain these types of rings had pleasant odors. The following structures illustrate this point.

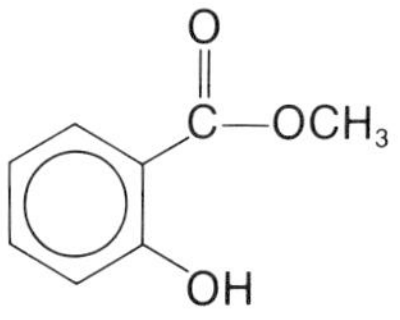

methyl salicylate
(wintergreen)

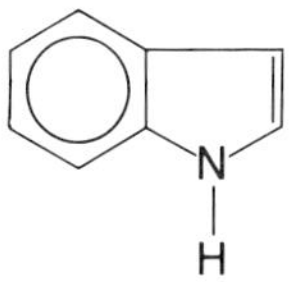

indole
(fecal odor)

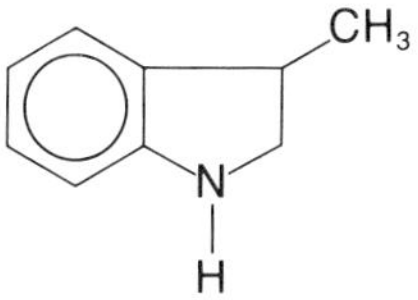

skatole
(fecal odor)

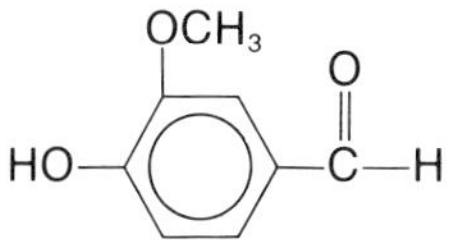

vanillin
(vanilla)

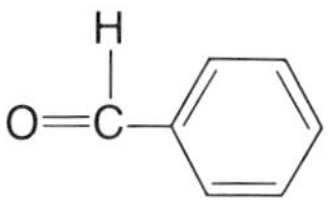

benzaldehyde
(almond)

Carbon compounds are particularly important to our civilization and to life itself. We use these compounds to produce electricity, to fuel our cars, to warm our homes, and to power our industries. We eat carbon compounds, take them as drugs, wear them as clothes, and build and furnish our homes with them. The tissues of the human body as well as those of other life forms are composed of carbon compounds.

Simple molecules are limited by the number of electrons which may be lost, gained, or shared by the atoms which compose them. Some elements that form compounds by sharing electrons have one or more pairs of electrons that are not shared with another element. Examples of unshared electrons are as follows.

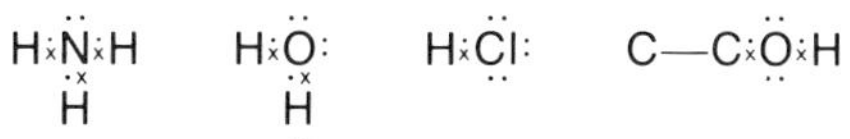

Activity of Unshared Pairs of Electrons

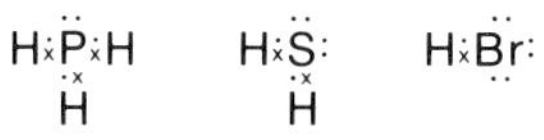

The elements holding these unshared electrons have a full valence shell of eight electrons and can hold no more. However, another atom may not have a complete set of eight electrons. Therefore, it may attach to an unshared pair in order to fill its valence shell. An elemental oxygen atom lacks two electrons. It has a strong attraction for electrons and may be satisfied by a pair of electrons on some other atom. This may be rationalized by taking some liberties with the distribution of electrons in a free oxygen atom. An empty orbital on oxygen could be created by shifting one of the single electrons into the orbital that contains the other single electron.

oxygen atom with two
single electron orbitals

empty orbital

A pair of electrons can enter the resulting empty orbital and thus fill the valence shell of the oxygen atom. Under proper conditions, an oxygen atom can acquire a share of an unshared pair of the electrons from another atom. A bond where both electrons are furnished by one atom is called a *coordinate covalent bond.*

The structure of a number of substances can be rationalized on this basis. In the structures below the rectangles indicate the empty orbital of the oxygen atom and the crosses (×) indicate electrons on the other atom.

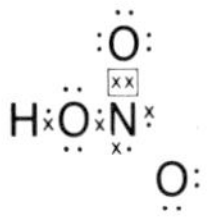

HNO₃
nitric acid

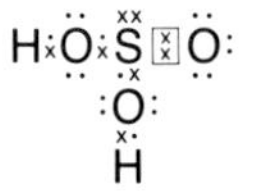

H₂SO₃
sulfurous acid

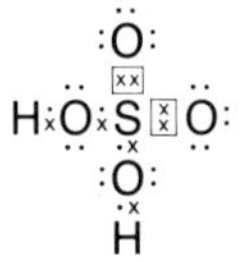

H₂SO₄
sulfuric acid

HOCl
hypochlorous acid

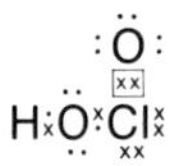

HClO₂
chlorous acid

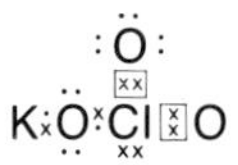

KClO₃
potassium chlorate

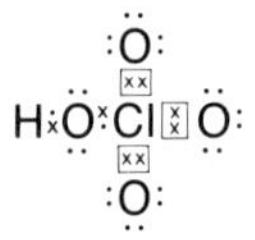

HClO₄
perchloric acid

NH₄⁺
ammonium ion

All of the unshared pairs need not be used; for example, the structures for SO_2, $KClO_3$, and H_2SO_3.

Oxygen will not fill an empty orbital with electrons from another oxygen, as for example:

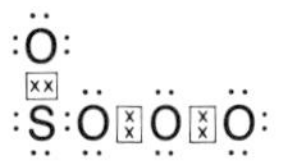

**Acids and Unshared
Pairs of Electrons**

An *acid* is conventionally understood to be a substance which donates protons (hydrogen nuclei) to another substance called a *base* which supplies electrons to the protons.

Most "proton-donating" acids are found associated with water. The water acts as an electron supplier to the protons of the original acid. In water solution, some or all of the protons of an acid may transfer to water molecules as illustrated below.

(a) 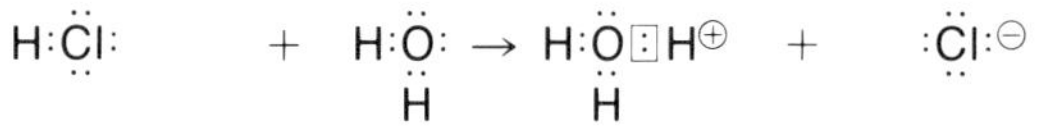   H:$\overset{..}{\underset{..}{Cl}}$:   +   H:$\overset{..}{\underset{H}{O}}$: → H:$\overset{..}{\underset{H}{O}}$:H$^\oplus$ +   :$\overset{..}{\underset{..}{Cl}}$:$^\ominus$

  HCl   + H_2O → $H_3O^\oplus$ + $Cl^\ominus$

hydrochloric acid   hydronium ion   chloride ion

(b) 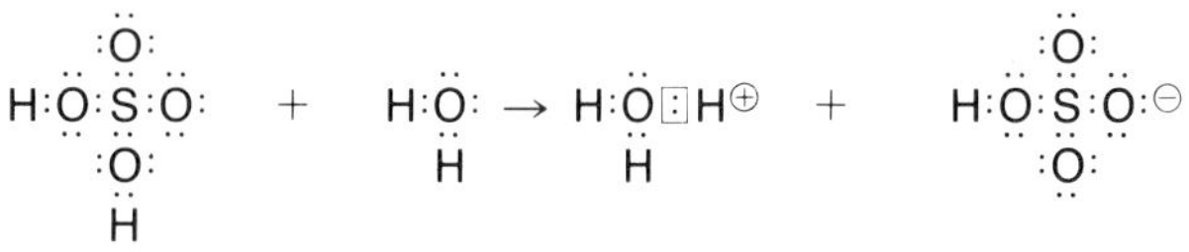   :$\overset{..}{\underset{..}{O}}$:   :$\overset{..}{\underset{..}{O}}$:

   H:$\overset{..}{\underset{..}{O}}$:$\overset{}{\underset{:\overset{..}{\underset{..}{O}}:}{S}}$:$\overset{..}{\underset{..}{O}}$:   +   H:$\overset{..}{\underset{H}{O}}$: → H:$\overset{..}{\underset{H}{O}}$:H$^\oplus$ +   H:$\overset{..}{\underset{:\overset{..}{\underset{..}{O}}:}{O}}$:$\overset{}{S}$:$\overset{..}{\underset{..}{O}}$:$^\ominus$

      H_2SO_4 + H_2O → $H_3O^\oplus$ + $HSO_4^\ominus$

   sulfuric acid   bisulfate ion

(c) 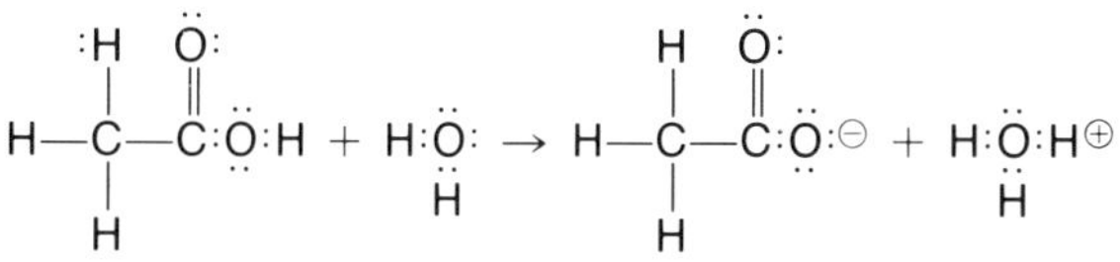   :H $\overset{..}{\underset{..}{O}}$:   H $\overset{..}{\underset{..}{O}}$:

   H—$\overset{\underset{H}{|}}{C}$—C:$\overset{..}{\underset{..}{O}}$:H + H:$\overset{..}{\underset{H}{O}}$: → H—$\overset{\underset{H}{|}}{C}$—C:$\overset{..}{\underset{..}{O}}$:$^\ominus$ + H:$\overset{..}{\underset{H}{O}}$:H$^\oplus$

   $HC_2H_3O_2$ + H_2O → $C_2H_3O_2^\ominus$ + $H_3O^\oplus$
   acetic acid   acetate ion

(d) 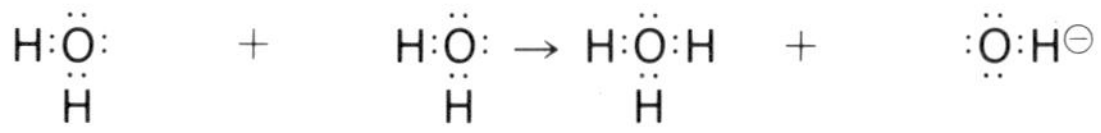 H:$\overset{..}{\underset{H}{O}}$:   +   H:$\overset{..}{\underset{H}{O}}$: → H:$\overset{..}{\underset{H}{O}}$:H   +   :$\overset{..}{\underset{..}{O}}$:H$^\ominus$

   H_2O + H_2O → $H_3O^\oplus$ + $OH^\ominus$
   water   hydroxide ion

In each case, a positive ion is formed along with a negative ion which is itself a base; i.e., it can supply electrons.

The hydronium ion is the acid in water solution which actually provides the protons which attach to the electron pairs of bases. Both HCl and H_2SO_4 are strong acids because protons transfer from these acids to water molecules to a very large extent and produce large concentrations of hydronium ions (H_3O^+). On the other hand, acetic acid transfers only a relatively small number of protons to water molecules. The resulting concentration of hydronium ions is small compared with that produced by an equivalent amount of HCl or H_2SO_4. Acetic acid, therefore, is called a weak acid. Water protonates (transfers protons to) other water molecules to a very slight extent, one ten-millionth of a mole of water molecules per liter. In this case, it should be noted that a water molecule also acts as the receptor (base) for the proton from another water molecule.

A substance which produces OH^- ions in water solution is a base. NaOH is such a substance:

NaOH → $Na^+ + OH^-$

The hydroxide ion of the base will react with the hydronium ion of the acid to produce water:

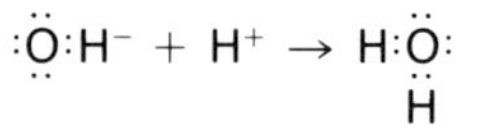

$$:\overset{..}{\underset{..}{O}}:H^- + H^+ \rightarrow H:\overset{..}{\underset{..}{O}}:$$
$$H$$

The overall equation would be

$$NaOH + HCl \rightarrow HOH + NaCl$$
base   acid   water   salt

Salt (NaCl, sodium chloride) is the major ingredient of table salt. However, the word *salt* is a general term which denotes ionic compounds produced by the reaction of a base with an acid.

SULFUR TRIOXIDE AS AN ELECTRON ACCEPTOR   Some compounds with double-bonded oxygen can act as electron acceptors of unshared pairs from other atoms. For example,

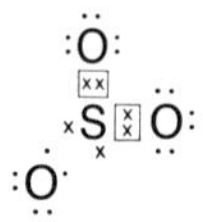

SO_3
sulfur trioxide

If the double-bonded oxygen atom should pull a pair of electrons away from the sulfur atom, an empty orbital would be created on the sulfur atom. The empty orbital could accept an unshared pair of electrons from some other atom, e.g., from the oxygen atom of water:

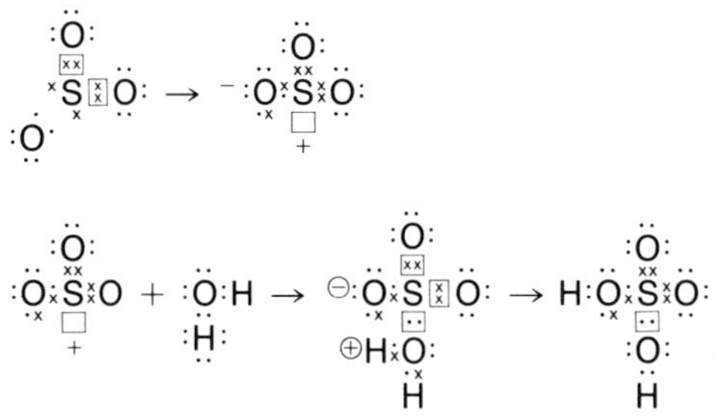

H_2SO_4
sulfuric acid

Sulfur is used in many of the illustrations of oxygen attaching to an unshared pair of electrons. Sulfur is an environmentally important element. It is an essential for life. When living organisms become oil, gas, or coal, the sulfur is still present. When the fuel is burned, the sulfur forms oxides which are very destructive to metals, fabrics, and living tissue. This will be further discussed in Chapter 3.

STRENGTH OF ACIDS   There are many substances which can supply protons in a way similar to the case of HCl. The concentration of protons is measured in terms of moles per liter. For example, carbonated drinks have a hydrogen ion (proton) concentration of 0.001 moles per liter even if carbonic acid itself were present in the mole quantity or more per liter. For less than mole quantities per liter, the hydrogen ion concentrations are more conveniently written in terms of exponents of 10:

$$0.001 = \frac{1}{1000} = \frac{1}{10^3} = 1 \times 10^{-3}$$

$$0.0000001 = \frac{1}{10,000,000} = \frac{1}{10^7} = 1 \times 10^{-7}$$

The negative exponents of 10 are known as *logarithms* of the number they represent. For convenience in representing the concentrations of hydrogen ions (protons), the *pH scale,* which describes the concentration of the ions, has been defined as the negative logarithm of the hydrogen ion concentration, a positive quantity. A negative of a negative quantity is a positive quantity. The pH values of the above hydrogen ion concentrations are

$10^{-3} = $ pH of 3; pH $= 3$

$10^{-7} = $ pH of 7; pH $= 7$

The pH's of several common substances are given in Table 2–3. It should be noted that the lower the pH, the higher the hydrogen ion concentration and

TABLE 2–3.   The pH of Some Common Substances.

Ammonia	11+
Milk of magnesia	10.5
Seawater	8.5
Pure water	7.0
Eggs	7.6–8.0
Human milk	6.6–7.6
Cow milk	6.3–6.6
Rainwater	6.2
Urine	4.8–8.4
Potatoes	5.6–6.0
Tomatoes	4.0–4.4
Cherries	3.2–4.0
Oranges	3.0–4.0
Carbonated water	3.8
Apples	2.9–3.3
Soft drinks	2.0–4.0
Vinegar	2.8
Lemon juice	2.3
Gastric juice	2.0

the acidity that is present. A pH greater than 7 is said to be more basic than water and less acidic than water, e.g., an ammonia solution has a pH of about 11. A pH smaller than 7 is said to be acidic with respect to water whose pH is 7. The pH value is often used for reporting concentration of acids in pollution studies.

EFFECTS OF ACIDS Acids tend to protonate any available pair of electrons. The atom groups which may be affected can have some of the following atom to atom connections as a part of the huge molecules which constitute fabrics and body tissues.

Protons may attach to any of the unshared electrons on any of the oxygen or nitrogen atoms in these structures. However, if the electrons at the ∗ positions are attached by protons, the electrons about that atom will be drawn in the direction of the ∗. Consequently, the bond to the carbon atoms will be weakened. At the same time, if a water molecule approaches the carbon, as indicated by the arrow in each case, the bond may be broken and the molecule may be separated into two parts. As the electrons are pulled away from the carbon, the empty orbital which would be formed is immediately filled with an unshared pair of electrons on the oxygen of the water molecule. The accompanying break in the fiber destroys its strength and its usefulness.

A similar action occurs between acids in air and marble statues or the calcium carbonate ($CaCO_3$) in rocks. The statues of Rome survived in good condition for hundreds of years. Recently, they have been badly damaged, if not destroyed, by the acids of modern air pollution. Marble is chemically calcium carbonate. Simplistically, it can be considered to have the following crystal structure as $CaCO_3$.

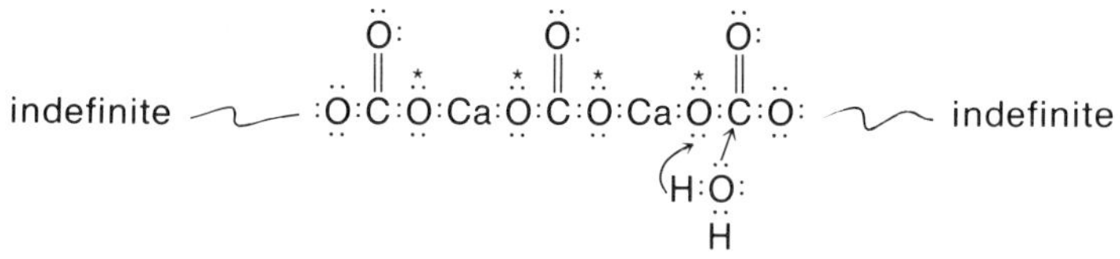

indefinite $\sim$:O:C:O:Ca:O:C:O:Ca:O:C:O: $\sim$ indefinite

Calcium ions bind fairly firmly to the carbonate groups

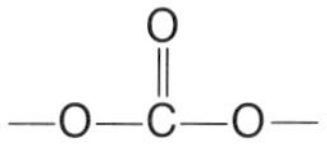

to bind the whole mass together in the form of a water-insoluble solid. However, if protons (H^+) attach to the electrons (indicated by $*$), electrons are withdrawn from the calcium entities (Ca^{2+}), and these are attacked by water molecules and floated away. At the same time the carbonate entity

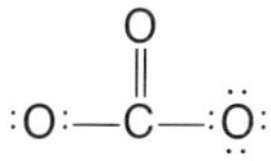

hypothetically is protonated to

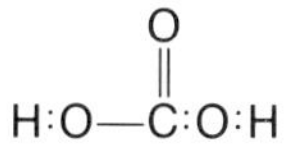

which promptly decomposes into carbon dioxide gas, CO_2, and water:

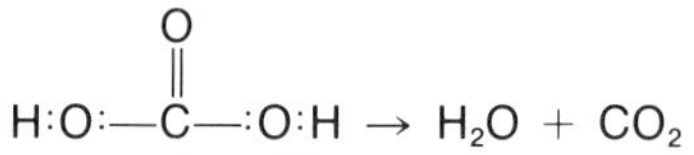

$$H:O:\!\!-\!\!C\!\!-\!\!:O:H \rightarrow H_2O + CO_2$$
carbonic acid

The same type of reaction occurs when acids in the soil dissolve the limestone ($CaCO_3$) material in the soil. As will be shown in Chapter 5, the loss of calcium from the soil by action of acid rain may be a serious matter.

All reactions depend upon competition between atoms or groups of atoms for electrons. Reactions can occur only when particles come together on a molecular, atomic, or ionic basis. Statistically, many contacts may be needed before a reaction does occur. However, if the necessary particles come together under the precise conditions required, a reaction may occur and new substances may be formed.

There is a maximum to the amount of product which can be produced from a given amount of starting material. The formation of tin dioxide from metallic tin is an unimportant reaction but it is easily described. When metallic tin is heated in an excess of air, it forms tin dioxide (SnO_2) according to the equation:

$$Sn + O_2 \rightarrow SnO_2$$

From the atomic weights and formulas of the compounds, it is possible to calculate the molecular weights of the compounds involved in a reaction. The atomic weight of Sn is 118.7 and that of oxygen is 16.0. Since oxygen molecules have the formula O_2, the *gram molecular weight* (gMW) of oxygen would be 32 g of oxygen. Likewise, the formula weight (gram molecular weight) of tin dioxide (stannic oxide) is 118.7 g Sn $+ 2 \times 16$ g oxygen, or 150.7 g of SnO_2.

$$Sn + O_2 \rightarrow SnO_2$$
$$118.7 \quad 32 \quad 150.7$$

On this basis, a maximum of exactly 150.7 g of SnO_2 can be produced from 118.7 g of tin. Thus 118.7 g of Sn is equivalent to 150.7 g of SnO_2 and to 32 g of oxygen. These are the theoretical quantitative relationships which can be derived from the equation of the reaction.

If ten times as much tin is heated in an excess of air, then ten times as much SnO_2 will be produced and ten times as much oxygen will be consumed. Similarly, if one-tenth as much tin is used, only one-tenth as much SnO_2 will be formed.

From the theoretical weight equivalences (atomic and molecular weights) it is possible to calculate the weight of any of the substances in the equation that is equivalent to any specified quantity of one of them; for example, what weight of Sn is required to produce 1.68 g of SnO_2?

$$Sn + O_2 \rightarrow SnO_2$$
$$118.7 \text{ g} \quad 32 \text{ g} \quad 150.7 \text{ g}$$

$$? \text{ g Sn} = 1.68 \times \frac{118.7}{150.7} \text{ g Sn}$$

(See Appendix D for unit approach to calculations.)

The equation quantities (weights) become more complicated for more complicated equations. For example, for the reaction of iron (Fe) with oxygen to produce ferric oxide (Fe_2O_3), writing the formulas of the substances into equation form gives:

$$Fe + O_2 \rightarrow Fe_2O_3$$

The same number of atoms of each of the elements must appear on both sides of the equation. Starting with the oxygen atoms, which are most unbalanced, the least common multiple between O_2 and O_3 is six. Therefore, three O_2 are required for two O_3. The partially balanced equation then becomes:

$$Fe + 3O_2 \rightarrow 2Fe_2O_3$$

It is then a simple matter to find a prefix number for the Fe and the completely balanced equation becomes:

$$4Fe + 3O_2 \rightarrow 2Fe_2O_3$$

The same general procedure may be used to balance most ordinary equations. The important point in balancing an equation is to make sure that there are just as many atoms of each element on one side of the equation as there are on the other side.

Sometimes entire groups appear on both sides of the equation. For example:

$$2NaOH + H_2SO_4 \rightarrow 2HOH + Na_2SO_4$$

It was pointed out earlier that the OH^- group is an ion. The bonding between the oxygen and hydrogen atoms is covalent:

:Ö⋮H⁻

hydroxide ion

The group as a whole has one more electron than it has protons and therefore has a negative charge. The covalent bonding does not break easily. Thus, the group appears on both sides of the equation.

Other covalently bonded groups behave in the same manner:

$SO_4^{\ominus}$	$NO_3^{\ominus}$	$NO_2^{\ominus}$
sulfate ion	nitrate ion	nitrite ion

$NH_4^{\oplus}$	PO_4^{-3}
ammonium ion	phosphate ion

Rates of Chemical Reactions

The rate of a chemical reaction may depend upon the following.

1. Whether the compounds are ionic or covalent: (a) ionic reactions are normally very rapid because the bond-making electrons are exposed to attack by an electron-demanding particle, for example:

$$Na^+ + :\ddot{C}l:^{\ominus} + Ag^+ + NO_3^- \rightarrow Ag:\ddot{C}l: + Na^+ + NO_3^-$$

(b) reactions involving covalent bonds are usually slower because a bond must be broken, most often during the formation of a new bond,

$$H-\overset{\overset{\displaystyle H}{|}}{\underset{\underset{\displaystyle H}{|}}{C}}-\overset{\overset{\displaystyle H}{|}}{\underset{\underset{\displaystyle H}{|}}{C}}-Cl + :\ddot{O}:H^{\ominus} + Na^{\oplus} \rightarrow H-\overset{\overset{\displaystyle H}{|}}{\underset{\underset{\displaystyle H}{|}}{C}}-\overset{\overset{\displaystyle H}{|}}{\underset{\underset{\displaystyle H}{|}}{C}}-\ddot{O}H + NaCl$$

2. Higher concentrations (molecules, ions, or atoms per unit volume) of substances react more rapidly than lower concentrations of substances. A few molecules of natural gas (methane, CH_4) can be present in the air in a room with no danger. If the concentration of methane in the room increases it may become high enough to explode when ignited.

3. Gases react more rapidly at higher pressures than at lower pressures (greater concentration of gases).

4. Most reactions proceed more rapidly at higher temperatures. A general rule of thumb is that a reaction rate doubles or triples for each $10\,°C$ rise in temperature. The addition of energy to molecules in the form of heat increases the velocity of the molecules. The increased velocity increases the chances of the reacting molecules coming together and increases the force with which they will come together. Both factors increase the likelihood of a reaction occurring.

5. The greater the degree of subdivision (small particles), the greater the rate of reaction. An iron bar may completely oxidize (i.e., form rust (Fe_2O_3)) over a long period of time. However, if the iron is very finely divided into powder, it will burn and produce light when sifted into the air.

6. A *catalyst* is a material which affects the rate of a reaction without itself apparently being changed. Many reactions will not occur unless some water is present. Acids (particularly protons) increase the rate of a reaction. The action here is like that given for the breakdown of fibers and tissues (see Chapter 6). Platinum, nickel, and other metals may be used in hydrogenating fats and in producing certain types of gasoline. Metal oxides in smoke catalyze the formation of SO_3 and H_2SO_4 from SO_2.

Implications

The principle of limited reaction between substances applies to all reactions. There is no possibility of getting something from nothing. There are limitations which apply to availability of materials and the products that can be obtained from them.

Many potentially harmful substances are released to the environment. The risk of harmful substances is not completely removed by any amount of dilution. Dilution may not prevent a given reaction but it can statistically reduce the probability that the reaction will occur. However, in view of a limited earth the capability to dilute substances and disperse substances is limited.

KEY CONCEPTS

1. Use of generalizations, laws, and models.
2. Relationship of solids, liquids, and gases.
3. Meaning and separation of a pure substance.
4. Atoms, molecules, elements, and compounds.
5. Structure of an atom.
6. Relative weights of atoms.
7. Mass numbers.

8. The mole.
9. Ionization of atoms.
10. Periodic relationships of the elements.
11. Chemical importance of electrons.
12. Methods of representing chemical bonds.
13. Chemistry of carbon compounds—organic chemistry.
14. Chemical properties of unshared pairs of electrons.
15. Acids and their properties.
16. Chemical equations—weight relationships.
17. Rates of chemical reactions.

1. What is the maximum number of electrons that can be in the valence shell of the elements of the first three rows of elements in the periodic table?
2. How can a pure substance be recognized?
3. Protons and neutrons each weigh one atomic mass unit. Electrons weigh so little that their weight can be ignored. Each atom of any given element has the same number of protons. How is it possible for some elements to have nonintegral atomic weights?
4. What do formulas (such as CaF_2, $AlCl_3$, and CO_2) mean?
5. What is the relative size of the atom (extent of electron sweep) compared with the size of the nucleus?
6. Using Table 2–1, determine the number of valence electrons held by each uncombined element in the first three rows of elements.
7. What is the trend in the ionization potential of the first removable electron of the first three rows of elements—across the row and in the vertical column (families of elements)?
8. In general, what combinations of elements are likely to form ionic compounds? Give two specific examples.
9. In general, what combinations of elements are likely to form covalent molecules? Give two specific examples.
10. What does the electrolysis of LiF show about the composition of the so-called compound LiF?
11. A certain compound does not conduct an electric current under any conditions. What type of compound is it, covalent or ionic?
12. Draw electron structures similar to those shown on page 40 for the compounds (a) $HCCl_3$ and (b) NCl_3.
13. Why are so many carbon compounds possible?
14. What causes elements to form compounds with other elements?
15. Why is it possible for water (H_2O) to react with sulfur trioxide (SO_3)?
16. What are the reactivity properties of unshared pairs of electrons on nitrogen, oxygen, and similar atoms?
17. What is the action of hydrogen ions which can cause insoluble calcium carbonate ($CaCO_3$) to become soluble in water?

18. How do acids act to destroy the fibers (or molecular molecules) of cotton, nylon, and polyesters? The cotton polymer is bound together by

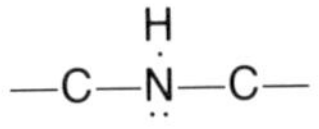

$$-C-\overset{H}{\underset{..}{N}}-C-$$

bonds; nylon by

$$-\overset{\overset{..}{O}:}{\overset{\|}{C}}-\overset{H}{\underset{..}{N}}-C-$$

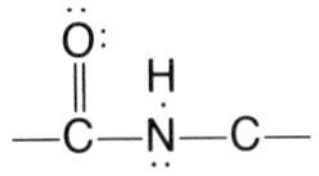

bonds; and polyesters by

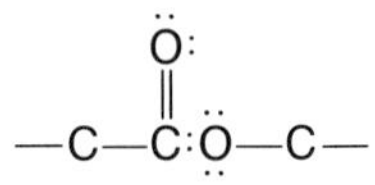

$$-C-\overset{\overset{..}{O}:}{\overset{\|}{C}}:\overset{..}{\underset{..}{O}}-C-$$

bonds.

19. Fill in the chart with the formulas of the compounds formed by combination of the elements listed at the top of the chart with the elements in the column at the far left of the chart.

	Li	B	C	O	F	Ne
Cl						
P						
N						
S						
As						

BIBLIOGRAPHY

1. Asimov, I., *A short history of chemistry,* Garden City: Doubleday & Co., 1965.
2. Dinga, G. P., The elements and the derivation of their names and symbols, *Chemistry* 41:20–22, Feb. 1968.
3. Hofstadter, R., The atomic nucleus, *Sci. Am.* 195:55–68, July 1956.
4. Lambert, J. R., The shapes of organic molecules, *Sci. Am.* 222:58–70, Jan. 1970.
5. Pauling, L. C., *The architecture of molecules,* San Francisco: W. H. Freeman & Co., 1964.
6. Sienko, M., and Plane, R., *Chemistry,* New York: McGraw-Hill, 1971.

3 The Air Around Us

Fly the rank city, shun its turbid air;
Breathe not the chaos of eternal smoke
  and volatile corruption. . . .
This caustic venom would perhaps cor-
  rode
Those tender cells that draw the vital air
While yet you breathe.[1]

Dr. John Armstrong

Polluted air may cause materials to disintegrate, retard the growth of plants or kill the plant, or it may increase the incidence of respiratory disease and death among humans. The pollutants produced, usually directly or indirectly by combustion processes, are of many kinds:

1. *Particulate matter* is finely divided solids or liquids which can range in size from the larger dustfall particles to particles which are invisible. Particulate matter in the atmosphere may form a *smog,* a word derived from smoke and fog. A smog now refers to any visibility-reducing mixture of liquid and solid particles and gases. The type of smog depends on the particular components in the atmosphere.

2. *Sulfur oxides* (SO_x; x is either 2 or 3) are gases which make themselves known in combustion by their odor of burning sulfur. They can be dangerous to living things, alone or in combination with other materials. When sulfur dioxide is present in smoggy conditions, a "London"-type smog is formed.

3. *Carbon monoxide* (CO) is a colorless gas. It has no odor but is dangerous to animal life when present in small amounts.

4. *Carbon dioxide* (CO_2) is a colorless, odorless, tasteless gas which is a normal component of the atmosphere and of the air which is expelled from the lungs in the normal breathing process. It is produced in all combustion processes.

5. *Nitrogen oxides* (NO_x; x is either 1 or 2) are produced from the reaction of the nitrogen and oxygen in the air during high-temperature combustion.

6. *Photochemical smog* is formed under certain weather conditions of reduced visibility because of chemical reactions triggered by light energy.

7. Various *lead compounds* are formed from the burning of ordinary anti-knock gasolines.

The effect of each of these factors upon the environment and living organisms will be discussed in the following sections.

Particulate matter can be seen in a smoke plume, but there are also many particles present which are too small to be visible. Those particles having a diameter greater than 10 μm (ten micrometers, see Appendix C) settle out rapidly. The very small particles gather to form larger particles. The resulting size range is between 0.1 μm and 10 μm in diameter. Ten million billion particles 10 μm in diameter could be placed side by side in a one-square-centimeter area. The size of the particle determines its behavior in the human body.

PARTICULATE MATTER

The damage to the body as a whole takes place through the respiratory system and depends upon the following factors: (1) the structure of the respiratory system; (2) the sizes and amounts of the particulate matter reaching the respiratory system; (3) the clearance methods in the respiratory system; (4) the chemical nature of the inhaled particulate matter or gaseous pollutants.

Particulate Matter and the Respiratory System

1. John Armstrong, *The Art of Preserving Health,* 1744.

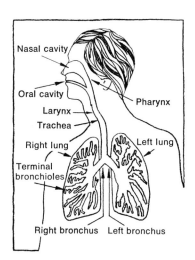

Figure 3–1. The major features of the respiratory system.

STRUCTURE OF THE RESPIRATORY SYSTEM   The respiratory system is divided into three sections (Figures 3–1 and 3–2): (1) the *nasal* system, the nose; (2) the *tracheobronchial* system, tubing or passageway from nose to lungs; and (3) the *pulmonary* system, the lung tissue where oxygen and carbon dioxide are exchanged between respired air and the blood.

The function of the nose and bronchial structures is to supply clean air to the lung tissue and as nearly as possible to protect the *alveoli* of the lungs from foreign particulate matter.

SIZES OF PARTICLES AND THE RESPIRATORY SYSTEM   When particulate matter enters the respiratory system, a fraction of different-sized particles is removed at each section. The nose is a complex of narrow passageways which removes essentially 100% of all particles larger than 10 μm and many of those between 2 μm and 10 μm in size. However, the nose is almost useless for removing particles smaller than 1 μm in diameter. The tracheobronchial system, a set of relatively large connective tubings, traps very few of the particles which can pass through it.

Although each alveolus sac is from 150 to 400 μm in diameter, the total lung area varies between 30 and 80 square meters which corresponds to areas from 10 ft by 27 ft to 10 ft by 72 ft. These areas are much larger than those exposed in the nose or bronchial system, and thus catch and retain more of the particles which reach the alveoli.

Both the nasal and tracheobronchial systems are protected by *mucus* and small, hair-like projections called *cilia* which move back and forth to move the mucus with its trapped particulates toward the exit points. The accumulated matter may be removed from the nose or mouth, or it may be swallowed and passed through the gastrointestinal system. Certain kinds of particulate matter

THE AIR AROUND US

can interfere with the action of the cilia and the cleaning action will not take place.

There is no mucus or cilia in the alveoli but the surfaces must be cleaned if life is to continue. Cleaning of the alveoli is a slow and complicated process. Consequently, continual exposure to pollutants may lead to a build-up of material in the lungs.

Figure 3–3 gives the size ranges of a number of materials and provides a frame of reference for particle sizes and the properties of small-sized particles. It should be noted that most of the smaller particles are man-made. The nose and tracheobronchial systems have not had time to adapt to them.

CHEMICAL NATURE OF INHALED PARTICULATE MATTER The original particle can attract substances different from itself. Water collects on the surface of mineral particles and may completely coat the surface. The resulting droplet, at least on the surface, has the properties of water. In a similar way, practically all other kinds of molecules are capable of being adsorbed (i.e., attached to a surface to form a layer that is only one molecule thick) upon the surface of a particle which is already formed. Thus, substances may be transported as particles of concentrated adsorbed poison or chemical. When the poisoned particles settle upon a surface, there is great potential for harm to the surface.

Adsorption of SO_2 upon an inert particle concentrates the SO_2 and thus increases its potential for harm. If the SO_2 becomes oxidized to SO_3 and this is converted to H_2SO_4 (sulfuric acid, see Chapter 2) the potential for harm is magnified. Either SO_2 or the particle alone may cause harm, but together the harm they may do is greater than the sum of the damage they would do separately. When the effect of two or more substances is greater than the sum of the effects of the separate substances, the result is said to be a *synergistic effect.*

Figure 3–2. Terminal bronchial and alveolar structure of the lung.

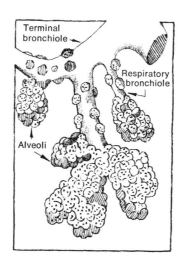

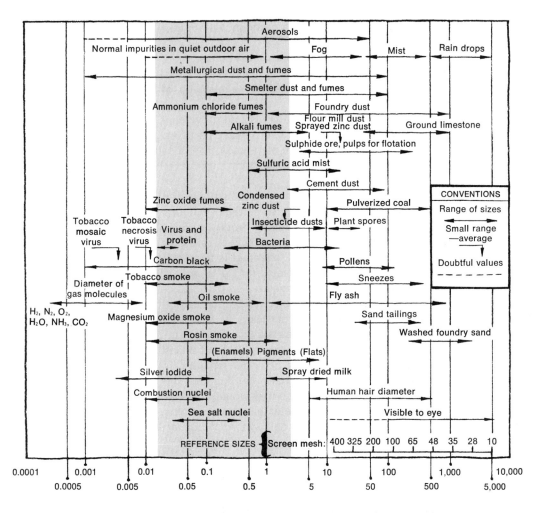

Figure 3–3. Sizes of airborne particles (μm). The screen mesh reference sizes indicate openings per square inch. The shaded area represents the range of particles that are most likely to reach the lung tissue and cause damage to the lungs. Courtesy of Mine Safety Appliance Co., Pittsburgh, Pa.

The resulting poison may merely irritate the tissue, destroy the tissue, or cause the tissue to become cancerous.

Size of Particles
The body has developed means to protect itself from the large particles; the small ones are extremely dangerous. Therefore, it is relevant to determine how the particles are formed and the relationship of the various sizes of particles.

AGGREGATION When two gaseous molecules collide, they are likely to rebound in a perfectly elastic manner and do not form a permanent aggregation or particle. If vapor molecules do not form particles, how can smoke particles and fine sea-salt particles be formed?

Combustion of fossil fuels[2] and certain high-temperature industrial processes produce large amounts of very small particles. These particles are composed of material with relatively high melting points. In coal, minerals are thinly dispersed throughout the coal mass. When coal burns, fine sections of the mineral matter are spattered out of the coal into a hot gaseous stream which may be hot enough to melt the mineral. The very small sections of material draw together to form a more or less spherical structure. When the gas cools, the mineral solidifies and is carried to the stack as smoke. In a similar manner, in a high-temperature industrial process, such as a basic oxygen furnace, thin films of oxides can be broken into very small portions by the violent gassing action taking place. Small sections of the film can be carried out of the molten mass and borne into the hot gases above the liquid. The gases will cool and the small droplets of oxides or other mineral matter solidify.

When a hydrocarbon vapor decomposes and/or is incompletely burned, part of the material may be converted to a more or less pure carbon mass with a very high melting point. Since the original particles of fuel vapor are relatively widely separated from each other, there is little tendency for two separate carbon masses to come together to form a larger mass. As a result the particles of carbon black approach molecular size (see Figure 3–3).

Sea-salt particles are also very small. Seawater is broken into mist droplets by wave actions. When the water portion of the droplets evaporates, the mineral matter (e.g., salt) remains and forms crystalline salt particles which can be very much smaller than the original droplets of sea water.

Water is a vapor at relatively low temperatures and does not readily form aggregations with its own kind even at rather high vapor pressure. However, water and other vapors will collect on particles which already contain several tens or hundreds of molecules. In this case, some of the energy of collision is absorbed by the larger mass. The rebound effect is less elastic and the probability that the incoming particle will remain attached to the larger particle is much increased. The reduction of the rebound allows attractive forces to take over. The new molecule coming into the particle can be held firmly, and the original particle thus becomes larger.

SIZE VS. WEIGHT OF PARTICLES The fact that the larger particles are also heavier seems obvious but its importance is often ignored. A particle 50 μm in diameter is visible and would fall within a few minutes. If the same weight were discharged as particles with diameters of 0.2 μm, the resulting 10 billion invisible particles could remain aloft for years, depending on the area where they were

2. Fossil fuels are fuels which were formed from organisms that lived millions of years ago. The organic matter changed into oil, natural gas, oil shale, tar sands, and coal.

TABLE 3–1. Analysis of Sizes of Particles in a Sample Taken from Discharge of a Mineral Wool Furnace.

Size range (μm)	Total count	Percentage by number	Percentage by weight
45–75	10	0.5	75.0
15–45	10	0.5	10.0
7.5–15	40	2.0	14.5
1–7.5	100	5.0	0.5
1	2000	92.0	0

Source: J. L. Spinks, "Mineral wool furnaces," *Air Pollution Engineering Manual*, J. A. Danielson (ed.), Washington, D.C.: U.S. Department of Health, Education and Welfare, 1967.

discharged. As the number of particles per given weight is increased, the surface area available for poisons to be adsorbed is increased even more.

Particles discharged from a stack will be a mixture of particles with various diameters. Table 3–1 gives an analysis of the size of particles in a sample taken from the discharge of a mineral wool furnace. Ten of the largest particles accounted for 75% of the weight, while the total weight of the 2000 smallest particles was nil. Thus, weight is of little use as a measure of particulate air pollution. However, measurements of particulate matter in air are usually reported in micrograms (see Appendix C) per cubic meter. Even the air quality standards which set limits for the quantity of particulate matter which may be present in the atmosphere are given by weight (Table 3–2).

TABLE 3–2. Air Quality Standards for Particulate Matter to be Met by 1975.

Air quality standards*	Primary	Secondary
Annual mean	75 μg/m³ (geometric mean)	60 μg/m³ (a "guide")
Maximum (not to be exceeded more than once a year)	260 μg/m³ (24 hr)	150 μg/m³ (24 hr)
	Respirable fraction	Total dust
Occupational standard (annual geometric mean of inert or nuisance dust)	5000 μg/m³	15,000 μg/m³

* Primary standards are for the protection of public health. Secondary standards are for the protection of public welfare such as preservation of buildings and vegetation.
Source: Annual mean and maximum standards from *Federal Register,* Title 40, Chapter 1, Section 50.7, p. 61. Occupational standards from *Federal Register,* Title 29, Chapter 17, Section 1910.93, p. 196.

The common method for measurement of particulate loadings (quantities of particulate matter present) is by use of an air filter (a flat piece of fabric similar to the filter discussed in Chapter 2 for filtering precipitates). When air with average loadings is measured, particles smaller than 0.2 μm are not collected. When air with heavy loadings is measured, the large particles tend to fill the openings of the filter and more of the tiny particles are trapped.

It should be noticed that the standard to protect public health allows a higher loading than the standard set to protect public welfare, such as the preservation of buildings and vegetation. The rationale for this is that man has recuperative powers which are not available to inanimate objects and vegetation. The *occupational standards* allow about 66 times as high a particulate matter loading as the *primary standard.* This standard applies to supposedly healthy adults who are exposed for only an 8-hr work day. The primary standard must be set for infants, the old, and the ill.

Another difficulty with measuring air pollution in general is the necessity for averaging the results from several stations in an area. Normally the more heavily polluted areas are monitored first (i.e., checked regularly to collect certain data). As the program expands and more and more stations are added, they must be placed in the less polluted areas. An average result will thus show a decrease in pollution whether or not such a decrease has occurred. Sometimes reports give the best and worst results from an area or the improvement shown at certain sites. This type of report is more easily evaluated.

Other Effects of Particulate Matter

Atmospheric particulate matter can cause (1) dustfalls, (2) corrosion of metals and destruction of paint and textiles, (3) reduced visibility, (4) reduction of the amount of sunlight that reaches the earth's surface, and (5) physiological harm to plants.

DUSTFALLS   The heavier particles fall as dust close to their source. Whether or not they are dangerous depends on their chemical composition, but they always have nuisance value. Dustfall in an area increases with increased human and industrial activity (Figure 3–4). It is usually measured in tons per square mile. A locality may have as much as 100 tons per day per square mile falling on it. This would be enough to coat any object outdoors and to seep into buildings.

CORROSION OF METALS AND DESTRUCTION OF PAINT AND TEXTILES   The concentration of particles in the air, the closeness to polluting sources, and the direction of the wind affect the amount of damage produced by pollutants and/or the frequency of maintenance such as cleaning and painting.

Heavier falls of particulate matter and adsorbed substances may cause metal to corrode more rapidly than the same metal exposed to lesser falls. When metal test panels in a rural Pennsylvania area were exposed to a particulate loading of 60 μg per cubic meter, the secondary standard for particulates, some loss occurred. However, when the loading was increased about three times, the loss on the test panels was thirty times as great.

Figure 3-4. **"Do hurry, darling, otherwise I shall have to wash the salad again."** © 1970 Punch (Rothco).

Sites downwind from a source of pollution suffer greater damage from particulate matter and pollution in general than do more favorably located sites. At a test site downwind and near a smokestack at Halifax, Nova Scotia, Canada, the rate of corrosion was ten times as much as that at State College, Pennsylvania, a rural setting.

REDUCED VISIBILITY   Everyone has experienced or has seen pictures of the haze or smog which reduces visibility in urban areas. The reduction in visibility is due to the scattering of light by small particles suspended in the air. When light strikes these small particles some is reflected or scattered in directions different from the original direction of the light beam. Particles larger than 1 μm in diameter scatter light in this way. On the other hand, particles smaller than 0.1 μm in diameter behave like molecules and do not scatter light. Over the range 0.1–1.0 μm, the scattering effect changes from no scattering to the scattering common to large objects. Figure 3–5 shows that the decrease in visibility is especially rapid for the first small amounts of particulates.

CLIMATIC EFFECTS   The scattering of light reduces the amount of sunlight that reaches the earth by about 5% for each doubling of particle concentration. By reducing the solar radiation reaching the earth, particulate matter may cause local climatic changes.

PLANTS AND PARTICULATE MATTER Particulate matter may carry deleterious pollutant substances to leaf surfaces and thus damage or kill the leaves. Dust may directly block leaf stomata (openings on the bottom surface of the leaf through which leaves exchange the gases CO_2 and O_2) or coat the leaves so that sunlight is prevented from reaching photosynthetic sites within the leaf. In any case, the plants may be damaged and growth reduced.

It is desirable to remove as much of the particulate matter as possible from emissions of all kinds. There are four types of removal methods shown in Figure 3–6. A description of each type follows.

Removal of Particulate Matter from Emissions

Fabric filter collection equipment operates very much like an ordinary household bag vacuum cleaner. Various means are used to shake dust from the bags so that it can be collected. The fabric that composes the bags depends on the temperature of collection and on the size of the particles being removed from the gas stream. Baghouses are relatively large and expensive. The efficiency is good; it ranges from 100% for large particles to 99.7% for those under 5 μm.

Mechanical cyclone collectors are the least expensive and the least efficient. The particles swirl to the outside wall of the collector and slide to the bottom. The cleaner gas escapes from the upper central opening. The efficiency increases with increase of gas velocity and decrease of cyclone diameter. There are many kinds of cyclone collectors. Their efficiency is 90–100% for large particles but only 7.5–63% for particles smaller than 5 μm.

Scrubbers trap dust particles in liquid droplets and allow clean gas to escape from the unit. Scrubbers are relatively efficient devices; however, the dust cannot be recovered, and the scrub water may pose a water pollution problem. All types of scrubbers are 100% efficient for large particles; the different types have a range of 94–97.5% for particles under 5 μm.

In an electrostatic precipitator unit, there are two sets of electrically charged plates or tubes called *electrodes.* One set of electrodes is grounded; that is, it

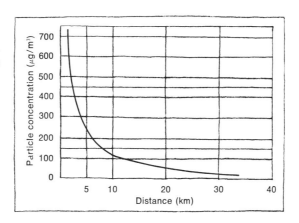

Figure 3–5. Relationship between visibility and particles in the atmosphere.

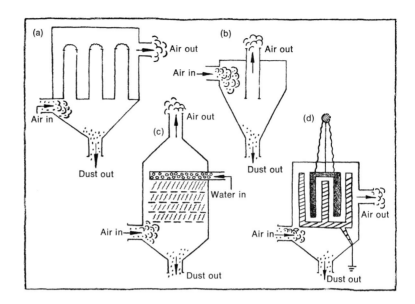

Figure 3–6. Methods to remove particulate matter from the atmosphere: (a) fabric filter collection equipment, (b) cyclone collectors, (c) scrubbers, and (d) electrostatic precipitators.

is in the same charge condition as the earth or ground. The other electrode set has a high voltage with respect to the ground and the other electrode set. The large voltage difference causes a condition similar to that which makes a spark occur at a sparkplug of a car, or on a grand scale, to that which causes lightning between clouds or between a cloud and the ground. As the gas stream passes over or between the electrodes, the particulate matter acquires a charge and is drawn to the grounded electrode. It collects on the electrode and loses its charge. The collected matter, which is loosened from the collecting electrode by a vibrating or hammering action, falls onto the grounded cone, from which it is periodically removed for disposal. The precipitators are very efficient; they remove all the large particles and 97–99% of those under 5 μm.

The efficiencies of the different types of collectors tend to give a somewhat optimistic view of the possibilities of removing particulate matter from emissions. The type of fuel burned changes the efficiency of the collector. Particles from low-sulfur coal cannot be collected as efficiently as the particles from coal with more sulfur. The addition of sulfur to low-sulfur coal has been proposed to improve the collection of particles. All collectors are more efficient with the larger particles. If a collector can remove 99% of the particles smaller than 5 μm in diameter, many more than 1% of the very smallest particles, especially those less than 1.0 μm in diameter, will remain in flue gas. The very particles the collector does not remove from emissions are the ones which are most dangerous. The electrostatic precipitator, which seems very efficient, especially when new, breaks down easily. The charging wires tend to break due to the vibration inherent in the process. Removal of particulates is not a simple efficient process.

Sulfur oxides cause respiratory distress in the young, the old, and the ill. They cause metals to corrode and fabrics to deteriorate, they reduce plant growth and yield, and they affect visibility.

SULFUR OXIDES (SO$_x$)

The burning of sulfur-containing fuels by public utilities, industry, and commercial and residential buildings accounts for about 70% of the total national emissions of sulfur oxides. Industrial processes, principally smelting (a process whereby ores are separated into metallic constituents by melting, often producing sulfur oxides) and refining of metals such as zinc, copper, and lead, account for most of the remainder.

Sources

There are many well-documented health disasters involving particulates and gases from combustion processes and stagnant, highly humid air masses.

Health Hazards

Location	Year	Effects
The Meuse Valley, Belgium	1930	60 dead, hundreds injured
London, England	1948	300 dead
Donora, Pa.	1948	17 dead, 40 ill
London, England	1952	4000 deaths, 100,000–200,000 ill
New York City	1963	300 excess deaths
Eastern coastal U.S.A.	1966	80 dead (New York City only)

These episodes resulted from smoggy conditions. When winds blew the smog out of the area, living conditions improved and it became safe to breathe again.

The Environmental Protection Agency (EPA) has set primary and secondary standards for sulfur oxides as shown in Table 3–3. As in the case of the standards for particulate matter, the primary standard for sulfur dioxide allows a higher concentration to be present than does the secondary standard. Again, the occupational standard is much higher than either the primary or the secondary standard.

The human senses are useless to detect dangerous levels of sulfur dioxide. Most people can taste the gas at concentrations somewhere between 0.3 and 1 ppm (parts per million) in air. The odor becomes noticeable at 3 ppm and is definitely disagreeable at 10 ppm. The gas has no color. Therefore, the human senses of sight, taste, and odor cannot detect sulfur dioxide until the concentration becomes much higher than the primary standard, but the odor and taste of the gas would be apparent at the occupational level.

TABLE 3–3. Air Quality Standards for Sulfur Dioxide to be Met by 1975.

Air quality standards	Primary	Secondary
Annual mean	0.03 ppm	0.02 ppm
Maximum (not to be exceeded more than once a year)	0.14 ppm (24 hr)	0.10 ppm (24 hr) or 0.5 ppm (3 hr)
Occupational standard (8-hr average)	5.00 ppm	

Source: Annual mean and maximum standards from *Federal Register,* Title 40, Chapter 1, Section 50.5, p. 61. Occupational standard from *Federal Register,* Title 29, Chapter 17, Section 1910.93, p. 196.

CHRONIC DANGERS It is more difficult to link stack emissions with chronic illnesses which may result from exposure to less concentrated amounts of pollutants than those which occur in well-developed smogs. Studies have shown that both children and the elderly experience increased frequency and severity of respiratory disease when the level of sulfur dioxide is only slightly higher than the primary standard. This is especially true of patients with bronchitis. It would be extremely difficult, if not impossible, to determine whether the bronchitis was caused by past exposure to air pollutants. On the other hand, monkeys and guinea pigs have been exposed to levels as high as 5 and 10 ppm respectively with no detrimental effects. Unquestionably, smog has killed people at concentrations far lower than these values. The resolution of this discrepancy is to be found in the chemistry of smog (see Figure 3–7).

Figure 3–7. "It *can't* be sundown, so it must be air pollution." Drawing by Alan Dunn; © 1965 The New Yorker Magazine, Inc.

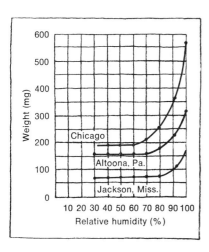

Figure 3-8. Effects of relative humidity on the weight of atmospheric particles at 24°C.

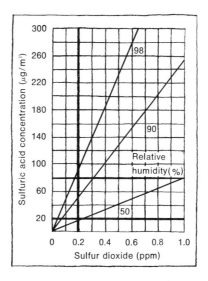

Figure 3-9. Relationship of sulfuric acid to sulfur dioxide concentrations at different relative humidities.

Emissions from combustions contain particulate matter, sulfur dioxide, and a host of other chemical pollutants. The particulate matter tends to adsorb and thereby concentrate vapors from its surroundings. The components of the particulate matter may also catalyze reactions between substances collected on the particles. A dry, solid particle would merely immobilize any adsorbed substance and few chemical changes in the substance would be possible. On the other hand, a particle in humidities greater than 70% acquires an appreciable amount of water and increases in weight (Figure 3-8). The water layer provides an efficient medium where the metal ions can catalyze reactions between other substances.

Sulfur dioxide can react at the particle surface to form sulfur trioxide which can react with water to yield sulfuric acid. Figure 3-9 shows that, as humidity increases, relatively more sulfur dioxide is converted to sulfuric acid. For a 0.2 ppm concentration of sulfur dioxide, if the humidity increases from 50% to 98% the concentration of sulfuric acid increases from 20 μg to 80 μg per cubic meter.

Experiments show that, in the absence of precipitation, as wind speeds increase from 4.5 miles/hr to 9.0 miles/hr, the ratio of sulfuric acid to sulfur dioxide decreases from 0.9173 to 0.068. The speed of the wind cannot affect the rate of reaction. However, wind at the lower speed moves the smog from the emission location to the monitoring point at a slower rate. As a result, more sulfur dioxide has an opportunity to react to form H_2SO_4 before it reaches the monitoring location.

Tremendous weights of SO_2 and H_2SO_4 can be produced by the burning of sulfur-containing fuels. A ton of coal containing 1% sulfur will burn to form 40 lb of SO_2 which in turn may be converted to 60 lb of H_2SO_4. A ton of 3% sulfur coal could be converted (assuming 100% conversion) to about 180 lb of sulfuric acid (pure basis), or nearly 10% of the weight of the original coal before combustion.

If the amount of water vapor is just large enough to form misty droplets that do not fall as rain and there is no wind, a tremendous amount of H_2SO_4-bearing mist may be trapped in a limited industrial area. Since the droplets are so small, this also means that the number of droplets per cubic meter is extremely large. The extremely large number and the smallness of the diameters of the H_2SO_4 mist particles leads to a very stable and persistent smog in which the visibility range is near zero. The small size of the smog droplets allows them to penetrate the defenses of the respiratory system and, finally, to lodge on the delicate tissue of the alveoli where the clearance mechanism for removal of foreign bodies is very slow. The H_2SO_4-containing particle may remain on the lung tissue for relatively long periods of time. The potential for harm from H_2SO_4 is great. If H_2SO_4 destroys cellulose and nylon, it certainly is capable of destroying lung tissue (see Chapter 2).

This emphasizes the fact that SO_2 alone in air, even at concentrations of 5 or 10 ppm, may not be seriously damaging, while 1 ppm or less in a smoggy atmosphere may be extremely damaging. The real damage is due to the H_2SO_4 which is present; a measurement of SO_2 may merely forecast the future potential for the production of the H_2SO_4 and the harm which it may produce.

Danger to Plants
Sulfur dioxide definitely affects plant life. A considerable area downwind from the smelter at Sudbury, Ontario, Canada, is devoid of vegetation. The area has the bare rock appearance of a "moonscape." Sudbury's two nickel smelters emit 2 million tons of SO_2 annually. This is equivalent to a yearly production of 3 million tons of pure H_2SO_4. In view of the strong acidic properties of H_2SO_4, it is understandable that downwind areas would be seriously affected by the effluents from such intensive sources of SO_2. A similar condition exists near smelting operations in Montana and Tennessee.

Most lichens are extremely sensitive to SO_2 and cannot survive where it is present. These simple plants may offer an easy way to monitor air pollution.

Sulfur dioxide can cause effects long distances from its point of production. Acid air pollutants from the Ruhr region in Germany and from industrial regions of England have lowered the pH of rainfall over Scandinavia (Figure 3–10). Records show that the hydrogen ion concentration has risen by a factor of 200 in a period of 18 years (see p. 43); pH values as low as 2.8 have been found.

The entire effect of acid rain is not known. In Scandanavia it is thought to slow the growth of the forests. Streams in Norway have become so highly acid that salmon eggs do not hatch. Buildings are being destroyed. Finally, there is the possibility that the fertility of the soil may be lessened when strong acids formed by air pollutants increase the rate of the leaching of minerals such as

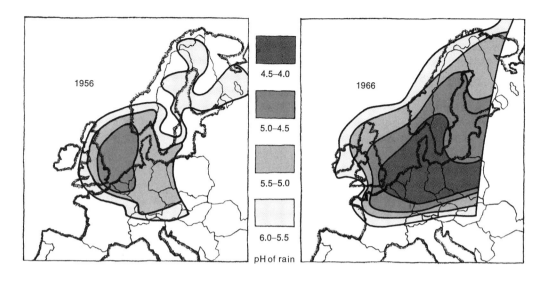

Figure 3–10. Increase of acid rain in Europe. The figures indicate the pH of rain—the smaller the pH, the greater the acidity. Adapted from Gene E. Likens, F. Herbert Borman, and Noye M. Johnson, "Acid rain," *Environment* 14(2):36, March 1972. Copyright © Committee for Environmental Information, 1972.

Ca^{2+} from the soil:

$$CaCO_3 + H_2SO_4 \rightarrow CaSO_4 + H_2O + CO_2$$

insoluble   soluble   gas

Other insoluble materials could be affected in a similar manner.

The situation in the northeastern United States is similar. Between 1965 and 1970 various studies in New York and New Hampshire showed the pH of rain to be between 4 and 4.5. There are no values for comparison before industrialization. However, on the West coast, where the air mass comes from the Pacific Ocean and the acidity is due only to natural effects, the pH is between 5.4 and 6.8, the acidity of carbon dioxide and water. Presumably this should be the pH of the rain over the Northeast. No adverse effects have been noticed in the northeastern states as yet, but studies are needed to determine any ecological price of the acid rain.

Sulfur oxides damage alfalfa growth and thus reduce the production of the plants. The longer the period of exposure and the higher the concentration of SO_2, the greater is the damage (Figure 3–11). At the concentration of the secondary standard, little if any damage would be done. However, exposure to concentrations equal to the occupational standard would result in heavy damage. Even exposure to a lower concentration than man can detect by his sense of smell would result in considerable damage.

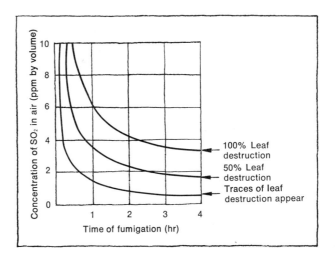

Figure 3–11. Relationship of sulfur dioxide concentration and length of exposure to the damage of alfalfa leaves.

Fossil Fuels and SO$_x$

Seventy-five percent of the sulfur oxides come from the combustion of fossil fuels and most of the remainder from smelting or other industrial processes.

The energy content of fossil fuels becomes available only when the fuel is burned. In this process any sulfur in the fuel is converted to noxious sulfur dioxide. The production of the sulfur dioxide may be reduced by several methods: (1) the use of low-sulfur fuels; (2) the removal of the sulfur before the fuel is burned; (3) the prevention of the build-up of sulfur oxides in the atmosphere after they are produced.

USE OF LOW-SULFUR FUELS   The easiest method of reducing the production of sulfur oxides is to use low-sulfur fuel. These fuels fall into three categories: (1) clean natural gas; (2) low-sulfur oils; (3) low-sulfur coal. At best these solutions must be temporary expedients in view of the expected short lifetime of world petroleum resources (Chapter 9).

Coals contain from about 0.5% to more than 6% sulfur. Low-sulfur coal is relatively abundant in strippable deposits in the states west of the Mississippi, especially in Montana and Wyoming. These coals may contain only about 1% sulfur but they are low-grade coals of the subbituminous[3] or lignite type. Their energy content runs a little above 50% of the energy content of bituminous coal. The net comparison results in the subbituminous coal being equivalent, on an

3. Subbituminous coal has a lower heating value than bituminous coal primarily because of its 25% water content. Lignite with 50% water content has an even lower heating value. See Chapter 9 for an explanation of the various types of coal.

THE AIR AROUND US

energy basis, to a 2% sulfur bituminous coal. This somewhat closes the gap between the two types of coal as sulfur oxide polluters.

The coals of the eastern and western parts of the United States cannot be used in the same type of furnace. The Tennessee Valley Authority (TVA) shipped low-sulfur coal from west of the Mississippi to use in its plants in the Tennessee Valley. The coal "gummed" the furnace until it had to be shut down for cleaning.

Low-sulfur coal makes the collection of particulate matter more difficult (see p. 61).

REMOVAL BEFORE USE   Sometimes it is possible to reduce the sulfur content of a fuel before it is burned. Each fuel must be treated by a different method. Whatever the method or methods used, the process is expensive and requires additional energy to perform the removal process. This, of course, means additional fuel must be burned to furnish the extra energy.

Oil   Raw oil, which usually contains 2–3% sulfur, may be desulfurized by hydrogenation (a process whereby hydrogen reacts with the sulfur in the oil) to give H_2S and a processed oil which contains only 0.375% sulfur. The process, costing the consumer about one-and-a-half cents per gallon (1968 prices), would leave 0.375% sulfur to be burned along with the rest of the fuel and add 15,000 tons of SO_2 to the atmosphere per day at the present rate of United States consumption. Burning untreated fuel oil containing 2–3% sulfur would yield six to nine times as much SO_2.

Natural gas   At the wellhead, natural gas may contain as much as 75% H_2S but usually much less. However, the H_2S is relatively easily extracted and converted to elemental sulfur. The value of the sulfur helps to defray the cost of its removal.

Most (as of 1967) existing hydrogen sulfide extraction plants use either hot (110 °C) potassium carbonate solution or mono- or diethanolamine solution to absorb the H_2S. The potassium carbonate ($2K^+ + CO_3^{2-}$) is used to illustrate the process:

$$K_2CO_3 + H_2S \rightarrow K_2S + H_2O + CO_2$$

or

$$\rightarrow KCO_3H + KSH$$

Hydrogen sulfide can be regenerated from the above product salts by passing CO_2 gas through the salt solutions. The CO_2 reacts with water to form the acid H_2CO_3 which, in turn, donates protons to the S^{2-} ion or the HS^- ion to re-form gaseous H_2S:

$$K_2S + H_2CO_3 \rightarrow K_2CO_3 + H_2S$$

or

$$KHS + H_2CO_3 \rightarrow KHCO_3 + H_2S$$

Some of the H_2S gas can be burned to form SO_2 and H_2O:

$$2H_2S + 3O_2 \rightarrow 2H_2O + 2SO_2 + heat$$

Then approximately two volumes of H_2S are mixed with one volume of SO_2 and reacted to produce sulfur:

$$2H_2S + SO_2 \rightarrow 2H_2O + 2S.$$

Very little H_2S is left in the processed natural gas, and very pure sulfur (99.9%) is produced by this process. The process produces usable, clean natural gas, pure sulfur, and heat.

The removal of sulfur from natural gas has had a great impact on the sulfur industry. If recovery processes from stack gases in other combustion and industrial processes make it economical to recover sulfur, more sulfur could be recovered than is presently used in the United States. Recovery of sulfur from copper smelting alone would more than satisfy all demands. No sulfur wells would be needed.

Coal desulfurization Most coal consumers must use coal having a sulfur content greater than 1%. The average for electrical utilities is about 3.5%. As oil and low-sulfur coal become increasingly scarce, coals of higher sulfur content will be used. If coal consumption grows at a compounded 6% (as of 1970) rate, the amount of coal consumed and the potential for emissions of sulfur oxides would be as shown in Table 3-4. The table should not be taken as what will happen in the future. It is given to illustrate what would happen if the present trends in the use of energy continue and sulfur emissions are not controlled. It is also assumed that coal will take up the energy burden as oil and natural gas become less available. There is difficulty with SO_2 emissions now; an increase by a factor of 10 in 40 years would not be tolerable. Some adjustment must be made.

Sulfur occurs in coal as part of an organic compound or as lumps of an iron-sulfur compound called *pyrites*. There is no way to remove organic sulfur short of changing the coal to a gas. Pyritic sulfur leached into the coal seam after it was formed and was desposited in lumps which are randomly distributed throughout the coal deposit.

TABLE 3-4. SO_2 Emissions from Coal Containing 3% Sulfur Projected at a Recent Rate of Increase (6%).

Year	Coal consumed (million tons)	Sulfur content (million tons)	SO_2 emissions (million tons)
1970	600	18	36
1980	1080		
1990	1920		118
2000	3440		212
2010	6170	185	370

The pyrites lumps are denser than the organic portion of the coal. If the coal is crushed to small-sized particles and floated on a dense liquid (density 1.6 g/ml), coal will float on top and the pyrites will sink to the bottom. If the coal is crushed to smaller particles or if the process is repeated, more pyrites may be removed. About half of the sulfur in coal occurs as pyrites and about half of the pyritic sulfur may be removed. Consequently, coal treatment can remove only about 25% of the sulfur content of the coal.

Coals of reduced sulfur content are prepared primarily for industrial purposes such as the preparation of iron and steel. In December 1970, most coal prices did not make pyrites removal economical for most uses.

Both air and water pollution are caused by processing coal to remove pyrites. After the coal is broken into small particles it must be washed with large volumes of water. Much water pollution results from the efforts to reduce air pollution. After the coal is skimmed off the water, it is dried. During the drying process about 20 lb of particulate matter is lost for each ton of coal recovered.

SULFUR DIOXIDE IN STACK GAS   Stack gases from the combustion of an average coal (3.4% sulfur content) contain approximately 3000 ppm SO_2 and 30 ppm SO_3. The concentration of SO_2 at the ground level is highly dependent upon the number and size of the stacks, the general weather conditions, the temperature of the air, the direction of the wind with respect to a given point on the surface and the stacks, and the velocity of the wind.

Tall stacks are not a method of extracting SO_2 from the stack gases but they do tend to reduce the ground-level concentration of pollutants by injecting them high into the atmosphere. Stacks 400–800 ft high give an average ground-level concentration of less than 0.3 ppm SO_2. The EPA secondary standard is 0.02 ppm for the maximum ground-level concentration of sulfur oxides. If this standard is to be met, some SO_2 must be removed from stack gases.

It is said that 65 ways have been proposed to remove sulfur oxides from stack gases but that none of them are very satisfactory. Whether or not satisfactory methods do exist is a subject of disagreement. A panel representing four Federal agencies thinks there are satisfactory methods. They report that several methods have been developed (1973) for full-scale commercial use in five years. On the other hand, industrial spokesmen point out that, of three processes the EPA thought would be available soon (1967), two have proven unsuccessful. One was a complete failure technically. The second was given up as a commercial installation after the Union Electric Company of St. Louis, Mo., spent 3 million dollars trying to make it work. Industry thinks the risk is too great for widespread application until a method has been tried on a full-scale installation.

Most methods of removing SO_2 from stack gases depend upon converting the SO_2 to the SO_3^{2-} ion by allowing the gas to react with some base. The bases used may be the CO_3^{2-} ion (as $CaCO_3$, $MgCO_3$, or Na_2CO_3), the $:O:^{2-}$ ion (as CaO, etc.), the OH^- ion (as NaOH), or water $H:O:H$ (see Chapter 2).

The product $CaSO_4$, $CaSO_3$, etc., may pose solid waste disposal problems. For example, the Detroit Edison Co. would need 23 installations for its eight power plants. In order to dump the waste, an area a quarter of a mile square would be filled to a depth of 100 ft each year.

Wet slurry of CaCO₃ (limestone) A wet slurry (mud-like mixture with water) of $CaCO_3$ is the cheapest and, currently the most common method. The reaction follows the equation

$$CaCO_3 + SO_2 \rightarrow CaSO_3 + CO_2$$

Dry process In the dry process, another inexpensive method for removal of SO_2 from gas streams, the SO_2 is absorbed by granules of metal oxides such as CaO (calcium oxide) and MgO (magnesium oxide) according to the following reactions:

$$CaO + SO_2 \rightarrow CaSO_3$$

$$MgO + SO_2 \rightarrow MgSO_3$$

However, it is difficult to make these granules porous enough without making them so fragile that they break into fine pieces during the extensive handling which they must undergo. Particles in the gases tend to clog the pores of the granules and make them ineffective. If the absorbent granules are injected into the boiler itself, the particles foul the boiler and reduce the efficiency of the electrostatic precipitator for removing particulates from the gas streams. In general, dry processes seem less promising than wet processes.

Sodium citrate Recently, sodium citrate has been tested for cleaning stack gases. The citrate ion forms a complex with SO_2 (citrate—O—SO_2) which is easily decomposable by reaction with H_2S gas to yield 99.9% pure elemental sulfur. In small-scale tests the process removes 90–95% of the SO_2 from a smelter stack. It would be expected to be less efficient with the lower SO_2 concentrations present in power-plant emissions.

Fluidized bed of activated carbon Gases passing through a granular bed cause the bed to float, that is, be fluidized. The bed can also be fluidized by shaking the charcoal (C) container. The SO_2 adsorbs on the surface of carbon granules. Subsequently, the SO_2 can be driven off by heat and converted to elemental sulfur or sulfuric acid.

Seawater Scrubbing stack emissions with seawater in spray chambers can have a 90% efficiency while a packed column may be 99% efficient.

A packed column is a long, usually vertical cylinder filled with granular matter. Depending on the purpose, the material may be coarse or microscopically fine. The spacing between the granules allows a fluid (in this case a gas stream) to pass through the column. The granules provide extensive surface areas for interaction between materials and regulate the flow of fluid through the column. In the present case, seawater flows downward to a collecting basin while the SO_2-bearing gases move upward through the column. The seawater dissolves the SO_2 and thus extracts it from the gas stream. The cleaned gases escape from the top of the column and the seawater carries the dissolved SO_2 out to the sea.

There is disagreement on the effect on the ecology of seawater. The objections to the method are as follows: (1) the method would lower the pH of the ocean; (2) sulfur dioxide dissolves in seawater to form sulfite which is subsequently oxidized to sulfate using oxygen from the seawater, and thus necessarily depleting the oxygen content of the ocean; (3) high concentrations of sulfur dioxide would occur at the discharge point, because there is incomplete mixing in the ocean in general. The counter claim is that if you want to dump something where it will not cause harm, dump it where it already occurs. The ocean does contain large quantities of sulfate ions; therefore, it can accept small additions. However, the effects of adding sulfate ions and of adding sulfur dioxide may be different. In order to prevent surprises and/or disasters, the ultimate effect on the ocean should be carefully studied.

ASSESSMENT OF SULFUR REMOVAL FROM FOSSIL FUELS   A panel representing four Federal agencies reported that the cost of building a sulfur recovery system into a new plant would range from $30 to $50 per kilowatt of generating capacity. The cost of adding the same system to an old plant would run from $45 to $65 per kilowatt, although it might be as high as $80. These costs compare with a cost for the original generating plant of $250–350 per kilowatt.

Whatever the success of sulfur controls, it is unlikely that the emissions in 1980 will be as low as the levels of 1968 (Figure 3–12). The increase in fuel use will almost immediately replace any amount of sulfur oxides removed by sulfur-control technology.

Figure 3–12. Projected sulfur dioxide emission from power plants (without breeder reactor capability), with and without controls.

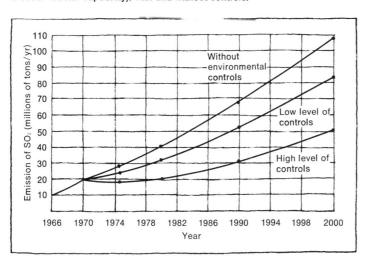

CARBON MONOXIDE, CO

Carbon monoxide is a colorless, odorless, tasteless gas which is slightly less dense than ordinary air and mixes uniformly with air. These same properties are true of nitrogen and oxygen. The question arises as to why carbon monoxide is so poisonous when the other two gases are not. While carbon monoxide may seem very like nitrogen and oxygen in its physical properties, it is very different in its chemical properties.

Oxygen, Carbon Dioxide, and Carbon Monoxide

Whenever a combustion reaction occurs, carbon dioxide, along with some carbon monoxide, is produced. The main reaction can be expressed by the following equation:

$$C + O_2 \rightarrow CO_2$$

A small amount of carbon monoxide may be formed concurrently:

$$2C + O_2 \rightarrow 2CO$$

The carbon may be from coal, from a compound such as C_8H_{18} from gasoline, or it may come from a molecule of food in a tissue of the body. The blood carries the oxygen from the lungs to the tissues where the "combustion" reaction occurs. The blood then takes the carbon dioxide to the lungs where it is discharged to the atmosphere.

EQUILIBRIUM The oxygen in the lungs diffuses through the walls of the blood vessels into the blood, where it is attracted to the slightly positive part of the *hemoglobin* molecule, the carrier of oxygen throughout the body. The resulting change in position of electrons within the hemoglobin molecule causes a proton to be freed. The reaction can be written:

$$HHb^+ + O_2 \rightarrow HbO_2 + H^+ \tag{1}$$

As more protons are freed, they become more available to the negative part of the hemoglobin molecule and force a reverse reaction:

$$HbO_2 + H^+ \rightarrow HHb^+ + O_2 \tag{2}$$

Eventually the two reactions reach a state of *equilibrium;* that is, a state where each reaction is proceeding at the same rate:

$$HHb^+ + O_2 \rightleftarrows HbO_2 + H^+ \tag{3}$$

An increase of oxygen would make the reaction proceed faster to the right until another equilibrium position is reached. Conversely, an increase of protons would cause the reaction to proceed faster to the left until a new equilibrium point is reached. Increasing concentrations of one of the reactants or products of an equilibrium reaction is called putting stress on the reaction. The reaction then changes in such a way as to relieve the stress. Other examples of stress, which do not apply in equation (3), might be a change of temperature, or in the case of gases, a change of pressure.

When the oxygen-carrying hemoglobin reaches the tissues, carbon dioxide from the oxidation of food molecules will dissolve in the blood. Much of the carbon dioxide is changed to the bicarbonate form, HCO_3^-, with the accompanying formation of protons. The protons force reaction (2) in a reverse direction and oxygen is released for use by the tissues. The carbon dioxide is carried to the lungs where it diffuses from the blood into the lungs. This action is also an equilibrium reaction and involves the relative amounts of carbon dioxide and oxygen present:

$$HHb^+ + O_2 \rightarrow HbO_2 + H^+ \tag{1}$$

$$HCO_3^- + H^+ \rightarrow CO_2 + H_2O \tag{4}$$

These reactions occur simultaneously in the tiny blood vessels surrounding the alveoli. The oxygen causes the release of H^+ which promptly releases CO_2 from the bicarbonate ion, HCO_3^-. The net result is that oxygen is exchanged for CO_2 at the lung surface.

When carbon monoxide is present, the equilibrium is changed. This gas can bond to the hemoglobin with a force 200 times that of the hemoglobin-oxygen bond. Here too there is an equilibrium:

$$HbO_2 + CO \rightleftarrows COHb + O_2 \tag{5}$$

The body produces small amounts of carbon monoxide but it has adapted successfully to these constant amounts. Body CO immobilizes about 0.5% of the hemoglobin of the blood. When carbon monoxide is inhaled, the reaction (Equation 5) is shifted to the right and the oxygen carried to the tissue is reduced. The hemoglobin has four sites where it may carry oxygen to the tissues. If one or more of these sites is occupied by carbon monoxide, the oxygen is bound more tightly to the hemoglobin at the remaining sites. Thus, the effects of carbon monoxide are more serious than just displacing oxygen on the hemoglobin molecule.

Treatment for carbon monoxide poisoning consists of exposure to air rich in oxygen which causes equation (5) to be reversed. Policemen directing traffic in Tokyo are required to breathe oxygen from sidewalk supplies every hour to rid their blood of the carbon monoxide attached to the hemoglobin.

If sufficient carbon monoxide is present in the air, large amounts of the hemoglobin will be immobilized and not enough oxygen will reach the cells. Exposure to 0.1% CO for 1 hr will cause immobilization of approximately 50% of the hemoglobin and loss of consciousness. Inhalation of 500 ml of CO is sufficient to produce this state. On this basis it is easy to understand how smoke inhalation kills so rapidly; smoky air in a building may contain much more than 0.1% CO. A concentration of 1% CO can kill in 2–5 min (Table 3–5).

A person made unconscious by CO may have brain cells killed due to the lack of oxygen. Once destroyed, the cells are lost; they do not regenerate. Table 3–5 shows the possible effects of various levels of COHb and the exposure needed to produce those levels. In addition to its effect on the nerve and brain cells, CO

TABLE 3–5. Possible Effects of Carbon Monoxide

COHb levels (%)	Possible effects	Exposure needed* (ppm)	(%)
Less than 0.5	No apparent effect	5 ppm	0.0005%
Less than 1.0	No apparent effect	10 ppm	0.001%
About 2%	Impairment of time-interval discrimination	20 ppm	0.002%
About 3	Impairment in visual acuity and brightness threshold	30 ppm	0.003%
About 5	Impairment in performance of motor skills; changes in cardiovascular system	50 ppm	0.005%
About 35	Loss of consciousness	300 ppm (4 hr)	0.03%
About 65%	Death	750 ppm (4 hr)	0.075%
		1,600–2,000 ppm (1–1½ hr)	0.2–0.16%
		5,000–10,000 ppm (2–15 min)	0.5–1.0%

*The actual exposure needed to produce a particular effect will vary from individual to individual.

may cause degeneration of the arteries. Three Danish scientists found that animals fed cholesterol and exposed to moderate levels of carbon monoxide had two-and-a-half times as much cholesterol deposited in the main arteries of the body as those animals not exposed to carbon monoxide. They also found that young smokers often had defective arteries.

Air Quality Standards The EPA has set the *air quality standards* shown in Table 3–6 to limit exposure to carbon monoxide. Even if these standards are met, continuous exposure would cause 2% of the hemoglobin to be immobilized.

Sources Automobiles are the largest source of the carbon monoxide to which people are exposed. Burning gasoline with insufficient oxygen produces carbon monoxide.

TABLE 3–6. Air Quality Standards for Carbon Monoxide.

Air quality standards	8-hr concentration	1-hr concentration	8-hr average
Maximum (not to be exceeded more than once a year)	9 ppm	35 ppm	—
Occupational standard	—	—	50 ppm

Source: Maximum standard from *Federal Register*, Title 40, Chapter 1, Section 50.8, p. 60. Occupational standard from *Federal Register*, Title 29, Chapter 17, Section 1910.93, p. 192.

THE AIR AROUND US

While the exhaust gases from a car may contain 3000 ppm of carbon monoxide, the levels of CO in air near a highway often exceed 30 ppm and may be higher than 100 ppm. Figure 3–13 shows concentrations in enclosed and open areas. The danger from carbon monoxide produced by the automobile is especially great on windless days, in slow or stalled traffic, and during rush hours.

Another source of carbon monoxide is tobacco smoke. Cigarette smokers inhale air which contains from 200 to 400 ppm of carbon monoxide every time they take a puff. The heavy smoker may cause 15% of his hemoglobin to be bound as COHb. The smoker is in special danger when exposed to other sources of carbon monoxide.

Removal Mechanisms

Carbon monoxide reaches dangerous levels but it does not accumulate, or at least it has not up to the present time. Little is actually known about how the gas is removed, but it disappears.

Figure 3–13. **Carbon monoxide concentrations measured at 54th Street and FDR Drive in New York City to show CO buildup in a completely enclosed area versus that in a partially open area.** Reprinted with permission from Philip C. Wolf, "Carbon monoxide," *Environmental Science and Technology* 5:217, March 1971. Copyright by the American Chemical Society.

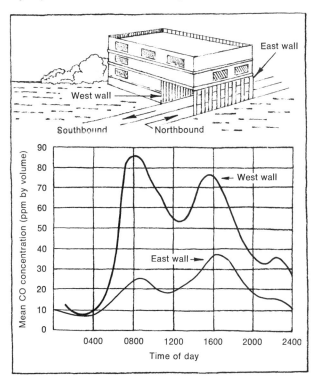

Two investigators, Dr. Robert Inman and Royal Ingersoll of Stanford Research Institute, found that soil bacteria and fungi have the ability to remove carbon monoxide from the atmosphere. However, the efficiency of these microorganisms could be reduced by exposure to moderately high levels of carbon monoxide and to temperatures below $10\,°C$ ($50\,°F$).

Even with removal of CO by soil microorganisms cities will have difficulty meeting the air quality standards. Former EPA administrator William Ruckelshaus has pointed out that, even if automobile manufacturers attain a 90% reduction in CO exhaust effluent by 1975, large cities will have to alter their transportation schemes and commuting habits to meet the standards.

CARBON DIOXIDE, CO_2

Carbon dioxide gas is produced in large quantities from combustion of fossil fuels. The gas is colorless and in the concentration present in air, 0.03%, is odorless and tasteless. As a normal component of air CO_2 is collected by plants and converted into plant tissue by the use of photosynthetic processes. Thus, it is essential for life.

Carbon dioxide poses no immediate problems of poisoning, but in the long run the accumulation of CO_2 in the atmosphere may have a great effect upon the climate of the world. Since CO_2 is only one factor likely to affect future world climate, it will be considered in Chapter 11 along with the other climatic factors.

PHOTOCHEMICAL (SUNLIGHT) SMOG

Many cities awake to calm winds and greet the sun under clear skies. However, as the morning progresses to noon and into afternoon, a haze deepens over the city. Visibility is reduced; eyes smart and breathing becomes a burning sensation; schools may be dismissed and authorities recommend a minimum of exercise. The city is covered by a *photochemical smog,* that is, a smog caused by substances formed by chemical reactions triggered by light energy.

The Villains that Cause Smog

Combustion processes form several substances which react to produce the photochemical smog: (1) *nitrogen oxides* (NO_x refers to the presence of both NO and NO_2); (2) *hydrocarbons* (HC, compounds containing hydrogen and carbon). Hydrocarbons also come from sources other than combustion, for example, the evaporation of gasoline at refineries, loading stations, and gas stations.

Other substances such as carbon monoxide and sulfur dioxide also react, but these are not as important in the formation of the smog as the nitrogen oxides and hydrocarbons.

NITROGEN OXIDES   There are five nitrogen oxides but only two, NO and NO_2, are significant air pollutants. Whenever any fuel is burned in air, the nitrogen and oxygen of the air react to form nitric oxide (NO):

$$N_2 + O_2 \rightarrow 2NO$$

The higher the temperature of the flame, the greater the amount of NO produced. Before discharge to the air, small quantities of NO combine with O_2 to form NO_2 (nitrogen dioxide):

$$2NO + O_2 \rightarrow 2NO_2$$

Once in the air, NO slowly oxidizes to NO_2. In badly polluted air the reaction producing NO_2 is relatively rapid.

Both NO and NO_2 are toxic to plants and animals at high concentrations. At low concentrations, NO is apparently harmless but NO_2 causes respiratory distress. Much study needs to be done on the long-term effects at low concentrations. NO_x fades colored fabrics at concentrations between 0.6 and 2.0 ppm. It is interesting to note that these concentrations of NO_x are found in clothes driers heated by gas.

HYDROCARBONS   Gas and oil are mainly hydrocarbons. When they are burned, most combine with oxygen to form carbon dioxide, water, and small amounts of carbon monoxide, although many other reactions are occurring at the same time. These may produce other hydrocarbons. The newly formed hydrocarbons tend to be very reactive and undergo various chemical reactions in the air to form the extremely harmful compounds of photochemical smog.

Nature produces many hydrocarbons. The blue haze over forests (e.g., the Blue Ridge Mountains of the eastern United States) is probably due to hydrocarbons produced by the trees. With a concentration of about 0.1 ppm, these hydrocarbons are very diffuse.

SECONDARY POLLUTANTS   Secondary pollutants are those formed from the substances discharged into the atmosphere. They are many; some of the most undesirable are ozone (O_3), groups of organic compounds called

aldehydes $\left(R-\overset{\displaystyle \|\atop O}{C}-H \right)$, ketones $\left(R-\overset{\displaystyle \|\atop O}{C}-R \right)$, and

peroxyacylnitrates or PAN $\left(R-\overset{\displaystyle O\atop \|}{C}-O-O-NO_2 \right)$

R may represent a hydrogen atom, a straight or branched carbon chain, or a ring structure.

Ozone, a strong oxidizing agent, is used as a measure of the severity of a developing smog episode. Concentrations of 0.05 ppm cause damage to sensitive plants, i.e., tomatoes, and tobacco. Ozone shortens the useful life of fabrics and is especially damaging to rubber. In humans, the gas causes respiratory distress and eye irritation. The group of substances called PAN produce similar symptoms in man but are not as toxic to plants. Concentrations of 0.2 ppm can damage citrus fruits and pines.

The Federal government has set air quality standards for the components of photochemical smog (Table 3–7).

Formation of Photochemical Smog

The exact pathway for the formation of photochemical smog is not known. The reaction of NO with oxygen to form NO_2 is normally a slow process. Energy supplied by sunlight causes the NO_2 to separate into NO molecules and O atoms:

$$NO_2 + sunlight \rightarrow NO + O \text{ (atomic oxygen)}$$

It should be noted molecular oxygen (O_2) is not formed; oxygen *atoms* are formed. Oxygen atoms are much more reactive than oxygen molecules since the atom lacks two electrons to fill its valence shell. Consequently, atomic oxygen is in an especially energetic state. Two of them might combine to form a molecule of oxygen:

$$O + O \rightarrow O_2$$

The chances are much greater for the atomic oxygen to attack molecular oxygen and form ozone (O_3):

$$O + O_2 \rightarrow O_3$$

The energy content of the atomic oxygen is transferred to an effective degree to the ozone. Normally the O_3 would react with NO to form more NO_2:

$$O_3 + NO \rightarrow O_2 + NO_2$$

The ozone or atomic oxygen O may react with a hydrocarbon to form a free radical RHCO·. (A *free radical* is an element or group of elements which have an unpaired electron which is indicated by a raised period after the formula.)

$$RHC + O \rightarrow RHCO·$$

$$RHCO· + O_2 \rightarrow RHCO_3·$$

TABLE 3–7. Air Quality Standards and Occupational Standards for Some Components of Photochemical Smog

Air quality standards	Hydrocarbons	Oxidants	NO_2
Maximum (not to be exceeded more than once a year)	0.24 ppm (3 hr, 6–9 A.M.)	0.8 ppm (1 hr)	0.05 ppm (annual arithmetic mean)
Occupational standard (8-hr average)	Not applicable	0.1 (ozone)	5.00 ppm

Source: Maximum standards from *Federal Register*, Title 40, Chapter 1, Sections 50.9, 50.10, and 50.11, p. 61. Occupational standards from *Federal Register*, Title 29, Chapter 17, Section 1910.93, p. 193.

THE AIR AROUND US

RHCO$_3$· can react with other hydrocarbons:

$$RHCO_3\cdot + RHC \rightarrow R{-}\underset{\underset{O}{\parallel}}{C}{-}R + R{-}\overset{\overset{O}{\parallel}}{C}{-}H$$

$$\text{ketone} \qquad \text{aldehyde}$$

or it may react with nitrogen dioxide to form one of the substances called PAN:

$$RHCO_3\cdot + NO_2 \rightarrow R{-}C{-}O{-}O{-}NO_2$$

There are many other possible combinations of compounds.

Figure 3–14 shows the relationship of the initiators of photochemical smog during one day in Los Angeles. It should be noted that the peak of NO corresponds to the morning traffic rush. Sunlight causes the NO and oxygen to form NO$_2$ which peaks as the concentration of NO drops to a low value. Again NO$_2$ under the influence of sunlight reacts to produce ozone which reacts to produce other irritants. Although NO is produced throughout the day, its concentration remains low because it is rapidly converted to other substances. The levels of NO$_2$ and O$_3$ also remain low for the same reason.

The complex hydrocarbon irritants are substances with relatively high boiling points which readily form fog-like droplets large enough to scatter light. Nitrogen dioxide is brown so its presence may give the haze a brownish tinge.

Figure 3–14. Average daily one-hour concentrations of selected pollutants in Los Angeles (July 19, 1965).

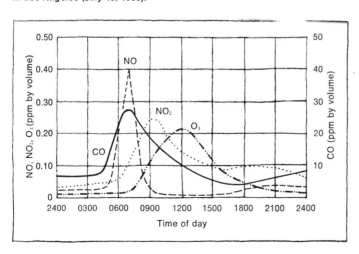

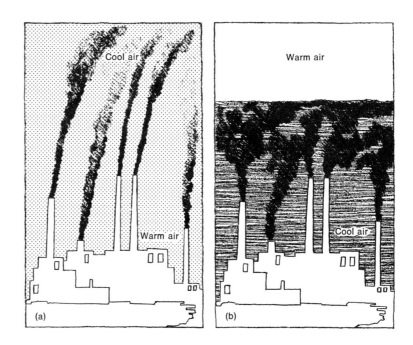

Figure 3–15. (a) Normal air circulation; (b) inversion.

Los Angeles is famous for its smog episodes. It has much industry, myriads of cars, and abundant sunshine to produce the necessary substances and the needed energy for the production of photochemical smog. In addition pollutants may be trapped by *temperature inversions* on about 300 days each year. An inversion occurs when a ground-level layer of cool air is trapped by a higher layer of warm air under windless conditions. Normally warm air rises and carries pollutants with it (Figure 3–15). If the warm air traps a cooler ground layer, the pollutants in the cool air cannot be dispersed. An inversion is characterized by cool, damp, calm air.

Control of Photochemical Smog

It is impossible to control the secondary pollutants. Efforts to control primary pollutants have not been completely successful to date. The fundamental operating principles of the internal combustion engine (common car) make elimination of the nitrogen oxides, carbon monoxide, and hydrocarbons difficult.

The easiest method of control would be to adjust the fuel-to-air ratio in the engine. Figure 3–16 shows the effects of increasing or decreasing the amount of air introduced into the engine. The point where the amount of air is sufficient to burn the gasoline completely to CO_2 and H_2O is the same (*stoichio-*

metric) point at which the maximum amount of nitrogen oxides is produced. Decreasing the amount of air to give a mixture rich in fuel reduces the concentration of NO but increases the amounts of hydrocarbons and carbon monoxide. Increasing the amount of air to the ratio 19 (the intersection of the NO_x and HC curves) gives such a dilute mixture that the operation of the engine becomes unstable. Thus, it is impossible to gain much by adjusting the fuel-to-air ratio.

The exhaust hydrocarbons may be reduced by the use of "catalytic afterburners" in the exhaust system. In this process, additional NO is produced by the catalytic burning of exhaust fumes. In order for the catalysts to work, all lead must be excluded from the fuel. Small amounts of lead poison the catalyst and make it inoperative.

Much controversy has swirled around control devices. Government agencies have said that such devices can be made and must be used, but manufacturers claim it would cost huge amounts in original equipment and maintenance changes. In addition, independent inventors claim that they have inexpensive solutions to the problem.

Recent studies have raised the possibility that the use of afterburners may put particles of the metal catalyst into the exhaust gas. At present, it is not known whether metals such as platinum or palladium are harmful if they are discharged to the air. Much work needs to be done before the answer is found.

Figure 3–16. Effects of air-fuel ratio on exhaust composition.

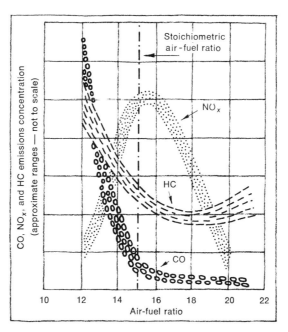

In 1973 the necessity for emission controls for nitrogen oxides to meet air quality standards was doubtful. The EPA may have used an unreliable method for measuring the nitrogen oxides. If the values are too high, only Los Angeles and possibly a few other cities would need emission controls. Without the need for control on nitrogen oxides. reducing hydrocarbons and carbon monoxide will be much easier.

Alternative engine systems have been proposed: external combustion (steam, etc.), rotary (Wankel), turbines, and electric. Each of these has some disadvantages. Any system which operates at a lower temperature or requires a secondary source of energy, such as electricity, will have a lower overall efficiency than the conventional automobile engine.

Another alternative is to use cars less or to use fewer of them.

LEAD POLLUTANTS Ghetto children living in old, run-down housing often contract lead poisoning from chewing lead-paint chips. Recently, elevated levels of lead have been detected in the blood of children from new housing where no lead paints have been used. Blood lead levels were found to be markedly higher near a Los Angeles freeway than they were a mile away in coastal air. Furthermore, the dust of some New York City streets is about 1% lead by weight, a concentration which approaches the amount of lead in many of its ores. Lead in gasoline may be the source of present-day lead poisoning.

Lead and Gasoline The combustion of gasoline in a car engine is a free radical reaction. Since only one electron is required to satisfy the original radical, a secondary free radical is formed as a result of the first radical snatching an electron. Logically, the secondary radical is as electron hungry as the first, and it proceeds to gain an electron from another particle. The reaction then goes on apace as a very rapid chain reaction which may be nearly instantaneous. In an automobile engine gasoline is almost instantly converted into CO_2, H_2O, CO, and hydrocarbon decomposition products. Uncontrolled free-radical combustions occur so rapidly that they produce shock effects similar to those produced by the explosion of dynamite; hence, the sound of a "knock" and the potential for damage to the engine. However, if the chains are branched, the gasoline will continue to burn throughout the stroke of the piston. Under these circumstances no shock waves are created and a much larger proportion of the energy becomes available.

Gasoline is assigned a number called an *octane number* which indicates its tendency to cause an engine to knock. An octane number or rating is found by comparing the gasoline with an arbitrary standard. A smooth burning compound, isooctane, was assigned an octane number of 100 (low-knock potential) and the straight-chain hydrocarbon, heptane, an octane number of 0 (high-knock potential):

THE AIR AROUND US

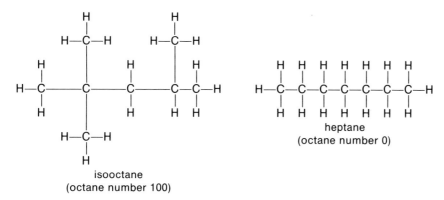

isooctane
(octane number 100)

heptane
(octane number 0)

All other gasolines are judged by comparison. If a certain gasoline burns like a mixture of 91% isooctane and 9% heptane, it will have an octane number of 91 and be suitable for small cars. Other octane ratings are determined in a similar manner.

Straight-chain compounds are the most common components of crude petroleum. These have low octane numbers. The straight-chain compound octane has an octane rating of −19. Branched chain compounds have high octane numbers and ring compounds even higher numbers:

benzene (106) 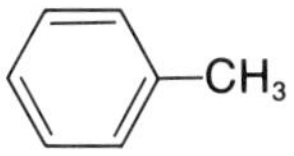   toluene (120)

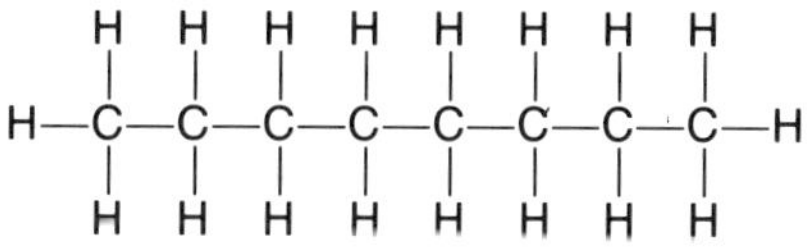

octane (−19)

The addition of a certain quantity of tetraethyl lead into a given gasoline can give the gasoline any desired octane rating.

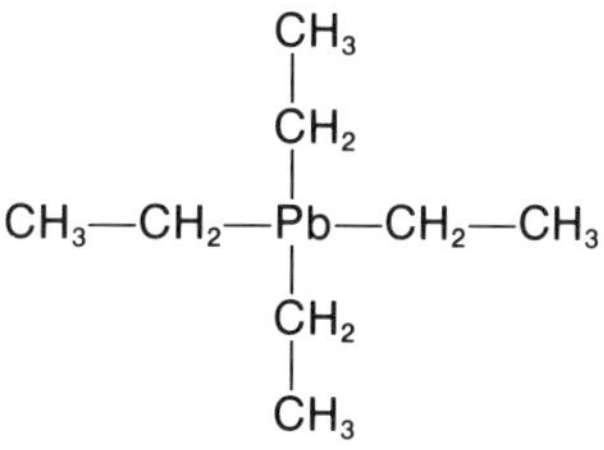

$$CH_3$$
$$CH_2$$
$$CH_3-CH_2-Pb-CH_2-CH_3$$
$$CH_2$$
$$CH_3$$
tetraethyl lead

The tetraethyl groups attached to lead are of the same general nature as the hydrocarbons in gasoline. Therefore, the tetraethyl lead dissolves to give a homogeneous solution. Furthermore tetraethyl lead vaporizes at about the same temperature as gasoline does and forms a homogeneous mixture with gasoline in the vapor state.

When gasoline containing tetraethyl lead burns in an engine cylinder, the ethyl groups burn away and leave the lead atom or a compound of lead dispersed in the combustible gases. Lead atoms or lead oxides have high boiling points and tend to collect in the engine or exhaust system. In order to prevent deposition, dibromoethane (also soluble in and vaporizable with gasoline) is added to the gasoline.

$$
\begin{array}{c}
\quad\ \ H\ \ \ H \\
\quad\ \ | \quad\ | \\
H-C-C-H \\
\quad\ \ | \quad\ | \\
\quad\ Br\ \ Br
\end{array}
$$
dibromoethane

During the combustion the bromine reacts with the lead to form lead bromides which are somewhat volatile and the lead is carried out of the cylinder and exhaust systems as molecular species. On exposure to moist air the lead bromides react with water (*hydrolyze*) to form lead oxide molecules or particles. Since these particles were originally molecular in size in the exhaust gases, it is understandable that the lead particles found in the air will be extremely small (average 0.9 μm). The small size of these particles accounts for their danger to the lungs and their wide transport over the earth. That lead can be found throughout the earth is indicated by its presence in the ice of Greenland (Figure 3–17). This figure also indicates that the use of lead in gasoline correlates with increases in lead deposited in Greenland.

Figure 3–17. Lead content of snow layers in northern Greenland. From D. Bryce-Smith, "Lead pollution—A growing hazard to public health," *Chemistry in Britain*, February 1971, p. 55.

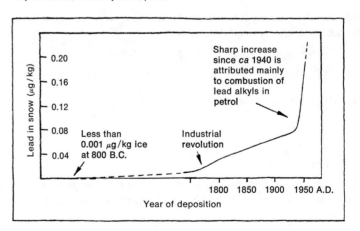

THE AIR AROUND US

The EPA reported that in 1968 98% of the lead emitted into the atmosphere as an *aerosol* comes from lead additives used in gasoline. Gasoline contains 2–4 g of lead per gallon. On the average, each car emits 1.5–3 g of lead for each 15 miles that it is driven. Thus, the thousands of cars along a busy highway can exhaust a large amount of lead aerosols per mile per hour. In the United States, the addition of lead to gasoline amounted to over 500 million lb in 1970 or 2.5 lb per person. Of this, 20% was trapped in the engine and exhaust system, about 40% fell to earth near the highway, and the remaining 40% was swept away into the atmosphere.

There are two ways to adjust the octane rating of a gasoline without using lead: (1) change the mix of products in the gasoline, and (2) find a new additive. The second alternative is the one most used in the United States. Phosphorus compounds have been used but, unfortunately, these belong to a group of which some are carcinogenic (i.e., capable of causing cancer). One compound had to be discontinued as an additive. Addition of a higher percentage of aromatics (see page 39) to gasoline also will increase the octane rating. A few of these compounds are also carcinogens. Protests against their use are countered by the fact that large amounts (20–25%) of aromatics are already present in leaded gasoline. The use of additional amounts to increase the octane rating does not radically change the overall composition of the gasoline.

Lead and Human Health

Scientists have calculated that each year the average man receives about 15 mg of lead from the air, 5 mg from drinking water, and 100 mg from food. Careful washing will remove lead from the surface of foods grown along a highway. There is no way to reduce lead that is part of the food. When lead is ingested with food and beverages, about 95% is quickly excreted. Most of the remaining 5% is absorbed into the blood and later excreted. Small portions are retained in the tissues, usually the bones.

Lead particles from automobile exhausts pose dangers to the body not only because of their lead content but also because 80% have a diameter less than 0.90 μm. Consequently, a large fraction of the inhaled lead reaches the alveoli where it may cause immediate local damage to the living tissue, or where it may be absorbed into the blood and carried to other parts of the body. The threat to the whole body is indicated by the fact that 50% of inhaled lead is absorbed into the blood stream.

Whatever way lead enters the body, the amounts retained become stored lead called the *body burden*. The body burden is stored in various tissues, but especially in the bones. Stored lead in the adult body is usually retained over the lifetime of the individual, although it may be released along with calcium when calcium needs are high, for example, during some drug treatments, old age, or high fevers. The behavior of the body burden of children is unpredictable.

A study of children suggests a relationship may sometimes exist between lead intake and hyperactivity. Hyperactive children are extremely active with short attention spans and are easily frustrated. A study with mice also related hyperactivity and lead intake. The mice reacted positively to the drugs used to treat hyperactive children. The relationship of lead to these conditions needs further investigation.

Stored lead causes little difficulty, so the lead level of blood is an indication of lead poisoning. Although people vary and adults with severe symptoms have had blood levels of 0.40 ppm, the threshold for occupational poisoning (that level below which there is no danger) is 0.80 ppm. The mean blood level is more than a quarter of the threshold for occupational poisoning and even closer to the concentration where some adults have severe symptoms.

Standards Limitations have been placed upon the amounts of lead allowed in the air of various countries:

1. U.S.S.R., 0.7 μg per cubic meter (no lead additives in gasoline);
2. California, 1.5 μg per cubic meter;
3. WHO (World Health Organization), 2.0 μg per cubic meter;
4. U.S.A. (desirable), 2.0 μg per cubic meter (averaged over 90 days);
5. U.S.A. (occupational), 200.0 μg per cubic meter (8-hr weighted average).

In order to achieve the desired air quality, the EPA has set limits on the amounts of lead in gasoline. The limit is the average amount of lead used in grades of gasoline produced by any refinery and is to be met in stages.

1 January 1975	2 g/gallon
1 January 1976	1.7 g/gallon
1 January 1977	1.5 g/gallon
1 January 1978	1.25 g/gallon

These standards are to be met in part by a low-lead gasoline with a limit of 0.05 g of lead per gallon.

CONCLUSION Man's attempt to provide a life of affluence has affected both himself and his surroundings. Physical restrictions (e.g., children not being allowed to play outdoors), illness, and in a few cases death are the personal consequences. In addition, ecosystems are being changed: forests are being destroyed, crops damaged, and stream life changed. Two questions are left to be answered in the future. What are the ultimate effects on man, plants, and animals of continued air pollution? Can controls to limit pollutants be made to work?

KEY CONCEPTS
1. Types of major air pollutants.
2. Small particles—dangers, production, and controls.
3. Effects of particulate matter on the ecosphere.
4. Cause of damage by sulfur oxides—synergism.
5. Methods and limitations of removing sulfur from fossil fuels before combustion.
6. General methods of removal of sulfur oxides from stack gases.

7. Chemical equilibrium and application of equilibrium to the oxygen-carbon-dioxide-carbon-monoxide cycle in the blood.
8. Production of photochemical smog.
9. Methods and limitations of methods to control photochemical smog.
10. Action of lead in gasoline.
11. Sources and build-up of lead in the human body.

1. What is the relationship of air pollution to water, land use, health, energy, and industry?
2. Who will ultimately pay for the cost of the air pollution control devices which industries install? Who will benefit from the cessation of pollution? Explain your answer.
3. Should plants in remote areas be subject to the same standards as industries in urban areas?
4. Industries are threatening to lay off employees and close plants if they are forced to meet air quality standards. What alternatives can you suggest?
5. Is a tax on effluents an adequate way to handle air pollution? If so, how large should the tax be? (Remember that interest is charged on investment money.)
6. Local authorities in London were allowed by law to meet 70% of the cost of changing household equipment to burn smokeless fuel. That 70% of the cost is a subsidy. Should it be paid?
7. Over the years, one company has invested capital to minimize environmental damage. Another similar company has not. If environmental standards are fairly enforced, which company is more likely to survive and be profitable? Explain your answer.
8. Should employers pay workers for lay-offs due to failure of a manufacturer to meet a pollution deadline? Leonard Woodcock of the United Automobile Workers has suggested this. Give arguments for and against the proposal.
9. If you were a city planner, what would you do to eliminate smog in a city like Detroit or Los Angeles?
10. A city needs electricity but has no adequate sites for the utility; a rural area with possible sites objects to the pollution resulting from the production of the electricity for the city (e.g., "Four Corners" dispute). If you were a judge, how would you settle such a dispute?
11. A scientist has commented that if we clean the air to a point where the air quality standards are met and to where visibility is not affected, we shall not have eliminated the harm caused by air pollutants. What is the basis for his comment?

BIBLIOGRAPHY

1. Brodine, V., *Air pollution,* New York: Harcourt Brace Jovanovich, 1973.
2. Craig, P. P., and Berlu, E., Air of Poverty, *Environment,* 13:2–9, June, 1971. (Discusses lead poisoning.)

3. U.S. Department of Health, Education, and Welfare, *No laughing matter, the cartoonist focuses on air pollution,* Public Health Service Publication No. 1561, Washington, D.C.; Government Printing Office, 1966.

4. Agricultural Committee, Air Pollution Control Association, *Recognition of air pollution injury to vegetation: Pictorial atlas,* Information Report No. 1, Washington, D.C.: Government Printing Office, 1971.

5. Schaefer, V. J., The threat of the unseen, *Saturday Review,* 6 Feb. 1971, pp. 55–57. (Discusses particulate matter.)

6. Wise, W., *Killer smog,* New York: National Audubon Society and Ballantine Books, 1970.

4 Water: The Basis of Life

Till taught by pain man really knows not what good water's worth.

Lord Byron, *Don Juan*

W ater is both a valuable and a versatile compound. Not the least of its important properties is its ability to dissolve a wide variety of substances. However, its solvent characteristics not only make it valuable but also make it dirty and polluted. Whether helpful or harmful, the behavior of water depends upon its molecular structure.

On an atomic basis, one atom of oxygen combines with two atoms of hydrogen. An oxygen atom has six electrons distributed between four orbitals (see Chapter 2). The four orbitals are oriented in a tetrahedral direction about the nucleus of the oxygen atom (Figure 4–1). Two of the orbitals contain a single electron. Regardless of which two of the four orbitals of the oxygen atom contain single electrons, the same angle will exist between the hydrogen atoms which share electrons with the oxygen at these positions. Thus, after the reaction between the two elements, the molecule will have the angular shape shown in Figure 4–2.

Since oxygen is the better holder of electrons, the oxygen atom will have a slightly larger share of the shared electrons. Because of the angular shape of the water molecule, even if the electrons were shared equally between the oxygen atom and the hydrogen atoms, the oxygen portion of the water molecule would be relatively negative with respect to the hydrogen atoms. Consequently, the oxygen acts as a center of negative charge and the protons act as centers of positive charge. Since water has this distribution of charges within the molecule, it is said to be a *polar* molecule.

Figure 4–1. Model of orbitals around an oxygen atom (dots represent electrons in orbitals).

Figure 4–2. Model of water molecule. The dots represent electrons in orbitals; the x's represent electrons contributed to the oxygen orbital by the hydrogen.

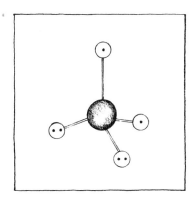

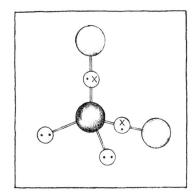

The two unshared pairs of electrons on the oxygen of the water molecule are exposed to attack by any entity which has some positive nature or character. Similarly, the protons of a water molecule are subject to attack by any entity which has an unshared pair of electrons. The molecules of liquid water are very close to each other. It is logical that the oppositely charged parts would attract each other and attach to each other. The numbered protons are used to help follow the direction of the action. A proton thus bonds two entities together. Such bonds are called *hydrogen bonds*.

$$
{}_1 H : \overset{..}{\underset{..}{\textcircled{A}}} :
$$
$$
\overset{..}{H}\,{}_2
$$
$$
\downarrow \qquad\qquad \longrightarrow
$$
$$
{}_3 H : \overset{..}{\underset{..}{\textcircled{B}}} : \quad \longleftarrow \quad H : \overset{..}{\underset{..}{\textcircled{C}}} :
$$
$$
\underset{4}{\overset{..}{H}} \qquad\qquad \underset{6}{\overset{..}{H}} \; {}_5
$$

$$
{}_1 H : \overset{..}{\underset{..}{\textcircled{A}}} :
$$
$$
\overset{..}{H}\,{}_2
$$
$$
{}_3 H : \textcircled{B} : H : \textcircled{C} : \;{}_5
$$
$$
\underset{4}{H} \qquad \underset{6}{H}
$$

The same kind of attachment binds the many millions of simple water molecules which are present in a drop of water, a glass of water, or Lake Superior. If it is assumed that this extended binding together of such a large number of simple molecules is a chemical action, then all of the water in Lake Superior could be considered to be one gargantuan molecule of water.

Water, Acids, and Bases

An incoming positive group which attaches to an unshared pair of electrons of the oxygen will displace all of the electrons in the water molecule in the direction of the newly attached group and effectively withdraw electrons from the protons. As a result, the bond between the oxygen and the protons is weakened and the protons may transfer to electrons on other molecules or ions.

$$
H^{\oplus} \qquad\qquad H^{\oplus} \qquad\qquad H
$$
$$
H : \overset{..}{\underset{..}{O}} : \quad \longrightarrow \quad H : \overset{..}{\underset{..}{O}} : \qquad H : \overset{..}{\underset{..}{O}} :
$$
$$
H \qquad\qquad\quad H
$$
$$
\downarrow \quad \longrightarrow
$$
$$
\qquad\qquad\qquad\qquad H^{\oplus}
$$
$$
H : \overset{..}{\underset{..}{O}} : \qquad H : \overset{..}{\underset{..}{O}} :
$$
$$
H \qquad\qquad H
$$

Similarly, any approach by electrons to a proton of water will drive electrons away from the proton and toward the far side of the oxygen atom, thus making the unshared pairs more attractive to positive entities colliding with the water from that direction.

Thus, if there is sufficient "push" of electrons at a proton position and a helping "pull" at an unshared oxygen electron, the proton may be separated from the oxygen atom of the water molecule.

WATER: THE BASIS OF LIFE

The polar character and the small size of the water molecule make it ideal for dissolving substances composed of ions and other polar entities, for example, common table salt (Na^+ and Cl^-) and ethyl alcohol, the alcohol found in alcoholic beverages.

In the pure state, sodium chloride occurs as a three-dimensional matrix of alternate sodium ions and chloride ions in a cubic crystal (see Chapter 2). When a NaCl crystal is placed in water, the sodium ions are attracted by the electrons of the oxygen atom of water and the chloride ions are attracted by the protons of the water. By the concerted action of water molecules, the bonds between the ions are broken. Thus, the sodium and chloride ions are progressively removed from the crystal and "floated away" to form a homogeneous solution of uniformly dispersed ions in the main body of water.

In a similar manner water dissolves many other substances; for example, ethyl alcohol (ethanol)

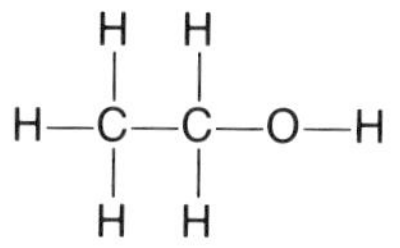

$$
\begin{array}{cccc}
 & H & H & \\
 & | & | & \\
H- & C- & C- & O-H \\
 & | & | & \\
 & H & H &
\end{array}
$$

is soluble in all proportions with water, that is, infinitely soluble in water. The structure in solution has the following character.

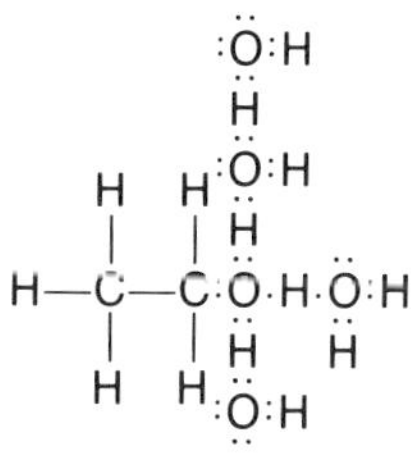

Of course, water molecules surround the

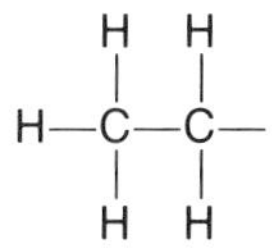

$$
\begin{array}{cccc}
 & H & H & \\
 & | & | & \\
H- & C- & C- & \\
 & | & | & \\
 & H & H &
\end{array}
$$

portion of the molecule but, owing to the fact that carbon allows the protons considerable control over the electrons in the bonds between them, the protons remain firmly attached to the carbon and do not transfer to the electrons of the water molecules in the vicinity. As a result, water merely encompasses the

THE MOLECULES OF WATER

```
      H  H
      |  |
  H — C — C —
      |  |
      H  H
```

part of the ethanol (alcohol) molecule. In fact, the water molecules surrounding the carbon chain of the ethanol try to exclude the ethanol from the mass of water. The effort is unsuccessful because other water molecules are firmly attached to the —OH portion of the alcohol.

The solubility of alcohols in water decreases as the carbon chain becomes longer 1-butanol[1] has a four-carbon chain and is only slightly soluble in water. 1-octanol (an alcohol with eight carbons in the chain) is still less soluble. 1-decanol (10 carbons) is insoluble in water. As the unattractive hydrocarbon chain increases in length, the alcohol becomes less and less soluble. In addition, the longer the carbon chain, the harder it is for the water to find the —OH group which may be deep in the alcohol mass and shielded from the water by unattractive hydrocarbon chains.

In contrast, the unshared pairs of electrons of oxygen and nitrogen entities are available for attachment by protons from water. The solubility of nitrogen compounds parallels the solubility of the alcohols.

A molecule of an organic acid has two oxygens on the first carbon.

```
        O
        ‖
  — C — O — H
```

The solubility for the carbon chain improves slightly because a larger number of electrons are available on the acid groups for attachment of water molecules. Instead of being insoluble, decanoic acid (a 10-carbon chain with an acid group)

```
      H   H   H   H   H   H   H   H   H   O
      |   |   |   |   |   |   |   |   |   ‖
  H — C — C — C — C — C — C — C — C — C — C — OH
      |   |   |   |   |   |   |   |   |
      H   H   H   H   H   H   H   H   H
```

is partially soluble. Logically, all long-hydrocarbon-chain organic acids having more than 10 carbons are insoluble in water.

---

1. The 1 means that the OH group is attached to the end carbon—that is, carbon number 1—the carbons being numbered 4, 3, 2, 1 from left to right.

```
      H   H   H   H
      |   |   |   |
  H — C — C — C — C — OH
      |   |   |   |
      H   H   H   H
```

A substance may have atoms with exposed electrons and yet not dissolve appreciably in water. When the halogens (F, Cl, Br, I) combine with carbon, a single bond is formed between carbon and the halogen. This leaves the three unshared pairs of electrons as possible victims of an attack by some electron-hungry entity. However, the electrons on the halide entities are held so firmly that the protons of water cannot attach very firmly to them, and thus are unable to draw them into the water and disperse them throughout the water mass. Thus, compounds such as carbon tetrachloride (CCl_4) and chloroform ($CHCl_3$) are only very slightly soluble in water.

Substances may not form true solutions. They appear to dissolve but the resulting "solution" is not clear. Stearic acid (Chapter 2) is an organic acid which has a chain of 18 carbons. It is, of course, insoluble in water. If the acid is treated with a base, for example, NaOH, the acid apparently dissolves in the solution. However, a true solution does not result. The solution of an acid in a base has a hazy appearance. The haze is due to aggregation of molecules into very small particles called *micelles.* The micelles are *colloidal* in size, that is, larger than most simple molecules but so small that they cannot be seen through an ordinary microscope. A soap solution is of this type.

Apparent Solutions

Most earth mineral matter is a mixture of metallic oxides. The oxygen atoms are bound in the mineral matrix by covalent bonds. Mineral matter usually is only slightly soluble in water, but the protons of water are attracted to the electrons of the oxygen of the mineral whether or not the mineral dissolves in water.

Attraction of Water to Mineral Matter

Each year an amount of water which would uniformly cover the earth to a depth of 32 in. is evaporated from the seas and oceans and returns to the surface as precipitation. Of the moisture which falls over land, the United States receives about 4200 billion gallons/day. Four-fifths of the water reaching the surface *evaporates* or passes through plants and *transpires* (emits from the surface of the plant) into the atmosphere. Some of the moisture which *evapotranspires* (evaporates and/or transpires) back into the atmosphere may again fall as precipitation before it passes out over the oceans. The remaining approximately 1200 billion gallons/day passes into the soil and becomes ground water and/or provides the runoff (i.e., water which flows over the land) for the streams which return the water to its origin, the ocean.

AVAILABLE WATER

Moisture does not fall equally on all areas of land. The United States receives an average of 32 in. of precipitation each year but the amount varies widely with the location of the land area. Some localities receive more than 200 in. of rain per year while others receive near zero. The amount of rain which falls each year in a given area may vary between 50% and 150% of the average. Figure 4–3 shows the rainfall of the United States.

Mountains cause air pushing against them to rise until the air is cooled, and the moisture in the air falls on the windward side of the mountains (Figure 4–4).

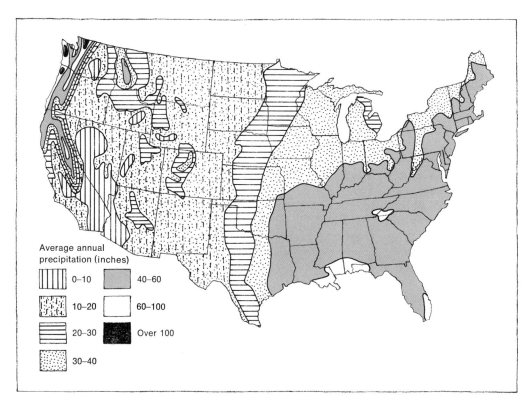

Figure 4–3. Precipitation map of the conterminous United States.

Average annual
precipitation (inches)

‖‖‖	0–10	▦	40–60
░	10–20	☐	60–100
≡	20–30	■	Over 100
⋮	30–40		

As the resulting dry air flows down the lee side it becomes warmer, its water-holding capacity increases, and it removes moisture from the land over which it moves. Thus, if the mountains are sufficiently high, interior deserts are formed.

Figure 4–4. Moisture conditions in air passing over a high mountain.

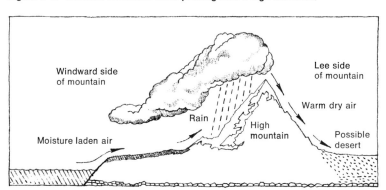

Windward side
of mountain

Lee side
of mountain

Rain

Warm dry air

High
mountain

Possible
desert

Moisture laden air

WATER: THE BASIS OF LIFE

The climate of the state of Washington illustrates the effects of high mountains. Here, moist marine air moves in over a relatively dry coastal area (small cooling effect) and produces very heavy rainfall (more than 60 in. per year) as it rises over the Cascade Mountains. East of the Cascades a desert covers the greater portion of the state.

Forests are important agents for the accumulation and protection of ground water reserves. The water trickles down through the branches and falls gently to the forest floor where it is absorbed by the soil. The stored water moves through the soil and is gradually released. Removal of vegetation increases stream flow after a rain but the stream may cease to flow during periods of low rainfall. Streams from forested areas tend to have a more even flow throughout the year. In general, deforestation tends to increase flooding, erosion, and sedimentation.

Water use can be classified as (1) agricultural, (2) industrial, and (3) domestic. All three types of use withdraw water from both surface resources and drilled wells, consume some, and return the residue to the environment. Agricultural users not only withdraw the most water but they also consume a higher percentage of the water they withdraw. In the year 1965 about one-quarter of the runoff water was withdrawn but only about one-fifteenth was consumed. By the year 2000, one-half of the runoff will be withdrawn and one-tenth consumed.

WATER FOR PEOPLE

The runoff is greatest in spring and lowest during the hot summer. Fall rains cause an increase in runoff but the amount is not as large as the spring runoff. Water demand does not follow these runoff peaks. Industrial water is consumed at a fairly constant rate regardless of season. Domestic and agricultural use both reach peaks during the summer season when the supply is smallest. However, much of the water used by agriculture is stored in reservoirs at times of peak flow.

In the United States an average of 3500 gallons or 15 tons of water are required to produce the daily food for each person. Some examples of water cost are 30 gallons for a slice of bread, 130 gallons for an egg, and 3000 gallons for a pound of beef. The actual figures would vary depending on the season, altitude, and region.

AGRICULTURAL USE OF WATER

Different climatic zones require different minimum amounts of rainfall to sustain a crop. Ten inches of rain is the *minimum* requirement for any agriculture in the temperate regions and at least 20 in. are needed in the tropics. The temperature during the growing season is the critical factor affecting the amount of precipitation needed. High temperatures lead to larger evapotranspiration losses.

In relatively dry areas where there is insufficient rainfall to grow a crop every year, special methods of farming are required.

Growing Crops in Dry Areas

FALLOWING LAND   One of the methods used is fallowing land, that is, leaving the land without a crop in alternate years. The land is cultivated so that no weeds may grow. The method is often used in the western high plains where strips of fallowed land alternate with strips of land growing crops (Figure 4–5). By this means about one-fifth of the rainfall may be saved for the crop grown the next year. However, the land farmed in this way is unprotected by vegetation during the full year that it is fallowed and may be damaged by wind and water erosion.

IRRIGATION   Where there is insufficient water to grow crops by fallowing land or where it is desirable to grow crops requiring more water, it is necessary to supply water for irrigation. Irrigation projects have their own set of problems.

The most serious problem is the accumulation of salts (i.e., any dissolved mineral matter). Rain falling on elevated mountain land dissolves mineral salts out of the rocks and soil as it flows over or through the ground on its way to the streams. When water evaporates from the stream the salts become more concentrated. Water used for irrigation is taken from the stream, allowed to flow over the land, and returned to the stream. Water evapotranspires from the crops so the water that drains back into the stream has a much higher salt concentration than the stream. A river in a humid region may have 200 ppm salts

Figure 4–5. Fallow land in western United States. Courtesy of USDA, Soil Conservation Service.

WATER: THE BASIS OF LIFE

while a river in an arid region may have a salt concentration as high as 1000 ppm. The Colorado River increases in salt content at each point of use on its way to the sea. Concentrations at various stations of the lower river are shown in Figure 4–6. The annual amount of salt carried past Lee's Ferry is 8,500,000 tons. The Mexican part of the Colorado River has become so salty that the President of Mexico has protested to the President of the United States that the cotton lands along the river are being destroyed by the salt content of the irrigation water taken from the river.

The particular salts damaging the crops depend upon the type of land the stream flows through. Generally, the salts are various combinations of the positive ions Ca^{2+}, Mg^{2+}, Na^+, and K^+, and the negative ions CO_3^{2-}, HCO_3^-, SO_4^{2-}, Cl^-, and NO_3^-.

Damage to plants   There are three ways in which plants may be harmed by salts: (1) interference with the process of obtaining water through plant roots, (2) internal derangements, and (3) corrosion of tissue.

In order to understand how water passes into the roots of plants it is necessary to understand the evaporation of water. At all temperatures molecules of water are escaping from the surface of liquid water to become water vapor. The pressure which these molecules exert is called the *vapor pressure* of the water at that temperature. The vapor pressure of water at 25 °C is 25.7 mm of mercury; that is, enough water molecules will leave the surface of the water at 25 °C to support a column of mercury 25.7 mm high. If a substance is dissolved in the water, the new molecules will interfere with the escape of water molecules so that the vapor pressure will be smaller.

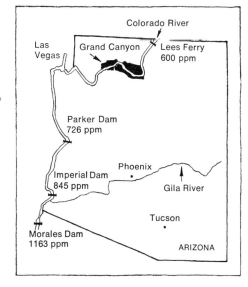

Figure 4–6. Salinity of the Colorado River at various points.

Normally the concentration of salts inside the root of a plant is greater than the concentration of salts outside the plant. Therefore, the vapor pressure of the soil water is greater than the vapor pressure of the plant fluids. Although water molecules will pass through the *membrane* of the cell wall in both directions, more water will pass into the plant than will leave the plant until the vapor pressures are equal.

The process by which fluids pass through a membrane is called *osmosis*. Most cell membranes preferentially allow some ions and molecules to pass through but restrict the passage of others. Such membranes are called *semipermeable membranes* (see page 123).

When the soil water contains large amounts of salts, the vapor pressure of the soil water will be less than the vapor pressure inside the root. A net amount of water will leave the plant. The plant will wilt and, if sufficient water is lost, the plant will die. Salts passing through the membrane into the plant may interfere with the behavior of some vital part of the plant. If sodium carbonate is present, actual destruction of plant tissue may occur. The carbonate ion can attract a proton from a water molecule and leave a hydroxide ion (OH^-) to attack the plant. In turn, the hydroxide ion may pick up a proton from the plant and cause tissue destruction. If calcium ions are present, they combine with the carbonate ions to form insoluble calcium carbonate. The carbonate ion is thus removed from the soil water and no tissue is destroyed.

Sodium ions and carbonate ions change some of the silicate entities in the soil to charged silicate particles which bind more water than before:

$$CaSiO_3 + 2Na^+ + CO_3^{2-} \rightarrow 2Na^+ + SiO_3^{2-} + CaCO_3$$

A jelly-like mass results and the soil becomes impermeable to water. Therefore, the soil becomes sealed and "puddled." If the impermeable layer is below the surface a "hard pan" may be formed. A hard pan layer at shallow depths holds water too close to the surface for the roots to grow properly.

Reducing the harm done by salts Farmers of ancient civilizations were aware of salting problems. They allowed the land to be fallow in alternate years while deep-rooted weeds broke up hard pan and improved drainage. Modern man sometimes tries to grow salt-resistant crops. However, if no other action is taken, soon even more salt-tolerant plants will be needed.

Sometimes no action is needed because winter rains wash (leach) the salt out of the ground. If the natural water table is high or if irrigation waters have raised the water table, there is no place for irrigation water and the salt to go. In such cases wells may be drilled and water pumped out to lower the water table so that the hard pan salts can be washed deeper into the soil.

Modern man also uses drainage ditches to remove the salt. The ditches are 18–40 in. deep to allow the brine, more salty than sea water, to wash out of the soil. The original complex of ditches may occupy as much as one-quarter of the fertile land and the drainage ditches may take up an additional tenth. The produce from arable land is correspondingly reduced.

WATER: THE BASIS OF LIFE

Irrigation water is not only being taken from surface bodies of water but also accumulated ground water is being used in both arid and humid regions of the world. The ground water accumulates, sometimes over centuries, in *aquifers* (underground layers of sand, gravel, or rock which contain usable amounts of water). As the exploitation of ground water increases, deeper and deeper wells are needed to reach the water. In some locations in California, the Union of South Africa, Saudi Arabia, and other areas, wells are so deep that pumping costs are prohibitive. In the state of Texas, the United States Geological Survey (USGS) estimates that it would take more than 100 years to raise the water table the 150 ft it has fallen. Since water is being withdrawn at a greater rate than it is replenished, a continuation of present rates of withdrawal can only lead to the exhaustion of ground water resources. Inevitably, any industry or agriculture which depends upon such water will collapse unless a new source of water becomes available.

In coastal areas seepage of salt water into aquifers as the ground water is reduced has caused at least temporary abandonment of many aquifers. This has happened in Florida, California, Long Island, and New Jersey in the United States as well as in foreign countries. The intrusion of salt water can only be prevented by maintaining an adequate amount of fresh ground water. Then, the flow of fresh water drives the sea water out of the aquifer and back to the sea.

Ground water carries a higher salt content than surface water. Rain picks up carbon dioxide as it falls through the air and as it filters through the soil. The slightly acid solution of carbon dioxide and water attacks the carbonates of calcium, magnesium, and iron found in the underground rocks. These carbonates are insoluble, but carbon dioxide and water convert them into slightly soluble bicarbonates (HCO_3^-) (see Chapter 2):

$$CaCO_3 + H_2O + CO_2 \rightarrow Ca^{2+} + 2HCO_3^-$$

As water passes through the sand, gravel, or rocks of the aquifer it dissolves other substances. Consequently, the variety and quantity of salts in ground water is greater than in surface water.

Ground water aquifers and surface streams are in a state of equilibrium. Many of the world's largest rivers have a large, slow-moving river in the ground beneath them. During periods of high water, ground water is replenished from the river. When the river is low, ground water supplies the river.

Every day United States industry withdraws between 650 and 700 gallons of water for every person, but only a small fraction of this is consumed (Figure 4–7). Water use varies widely from one factory to another; an automobile requires approximately 60,000 gallons, a newspaper 150 gallons, and a barrel of oil 50–200 gallons. Today's demand for water is great and the projected demand for the future is still greater.

Figure 4–7. "What will they do with their money when they run out of air and water?"
Copyright © 1968 The Chicago Sun-Times. Reproduced courtesy of Wil-Jo Associates, Inc. and Bill Mauldin.

Effects of Withdrawal

In addition to water from surface bodies of water, industry withdraws about 7 billion gallons per day from ground water resources. Industry, like agriculture, is withdrawing ground water faster than it can be replenished.

The effect of overpumping may appear dramatically. In Tokyo, Japan, excessive withdrawals of ground water have caused the land to subside at a rate as high as 210 mm (about 8 in.) per year. During World War II, when much industry was moved out of Tokyo, the land rose. Since then subsidence, land designated to be at sea level, property damage, and deaths from typhoons have increased. Dikes have been built along the sea coast to compensate for the subsidence of the land.

Waste Water

Industry may treat its waste water and return it to the environment through its own facilities, or it may dump its waste water into a municipal sewer and have it processed by a governmental agency. Particularly noxious wastes have been pumped down deep wells into permeable rock formations.

DEEP-WELL DISPOSAL Deep-well disposal would seem to have many advantages: (1) permanent disposal of wastes; (2) by pumping salt brines (and other wastes) deep underground fresh water can be protected; (3) toxic fumes can be forced underground to eliminate air pollution; (4) high capacity; for example, a disposal some 50 ft thick and a square mile in area with 20% effective porosity can contain 2.1 billion gallons of waste. Like most technological solutions, deep-well disposal has disadvantages: (1) study of the underground rock structure is very difficult, and flaws and fissures may not appear until pressure is applied; (2) Accidents can and have happened to well equipment such as well casings and cement plugs (Figure 4–8); (3) disposal wells are difficult to monitor. Reputable geologists believe earthquakes have been triggered by wastes forced underground. This may be caused when undetected fissures are forced apart and allow the rocks to slide.

In many places injected wastes have contaminated water supplies. Experts from the EPA report that oil field brines injected into wells have contaminated ground water in Kansas, California, Arkansas, Ohio, Oklahoma, and elsewhere. In Kansas the Public Health Service found that 10 brine-injection failures were reported to the state authorities each year.

Undetected fissures may make monitoring the wells impossible. If observation wells are drilled around a disposal well, the wastes could still seep through cracks between the observation wells or invade an aquifer along a crack between the disposal well and an observation well. If ground water is monitored, the danger would not be known until it is too late to protect water supplies.

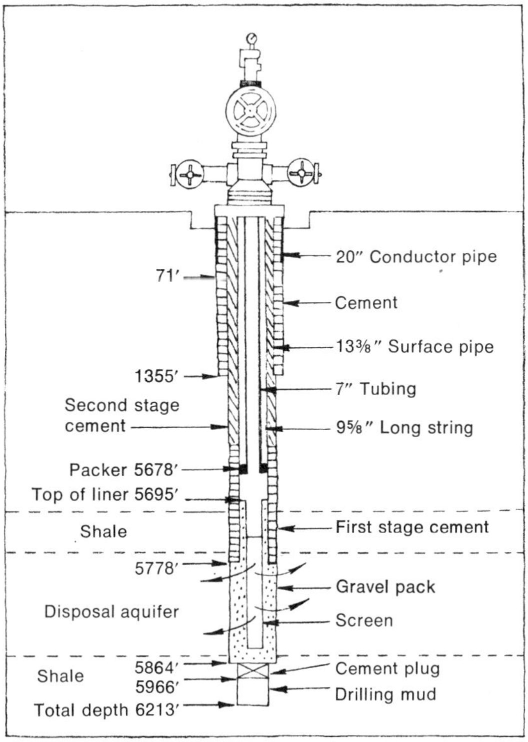

Figure 4–8. A deep disposal well. From statement of John S. Talbot, Dow Chemical Company, to Senate Subcommittee on Air and Water Pollution, 7 April 1971; with permission of John S. Talbot.

Industries sometimes refuse to reveal the composition of the wastes being injected into wells in order to protect their processing secrets. Without such information it is difficult to know what to look for. At present about 10 billion gallons of oil field brines are pumped into 40,000 wells each day. These wells are not regulated. Other industries are rapidly building deep wells to dispose of noxious industrial wastes. In 1972 one million barrels of chemical wastes were pumped into 200 such wells. The EPA wants to restrict their use to the deep disposal of wastes which cannot be adequately treated for surface disposal. These wells are regulated as much as possible.

Dr. R. Allen Freeze of IBM's Thomas J. Watson Research Center has summarized the dangers of deep well disposal (in Special Report: Ecology, 8 May 1972) by saying: "Underground waste won't become a problem for a long time but when it does, there won't be any solution." He believes that there is not enough known about the underground structure and what effects the toxic materials will have on it. He explains: "Pressure injection stresses the underground system and speeds up water flow—but how much? As waste moves with the water, its concentration will be diluted—but to what extent? Chemical reactions will occur between the waste, the water, and the earth material—but what kinds?"

Mining Pollutants
All water problems involving a factory are not in the immediate vicinity of the factory site. For example, if the factory uses coal directly as a fuel or uses electricity derived from coal there are the added difficulties which are associated with coal mines.

Coal is found in layers buried beneath various thicknesses of soil and rock and separated by more rock. In the eastern half of the United States the rock and coal contain pyrites (FeS_2), a compound of iron and sulfur. Natural water circulation has removed the iron sulfide from the soil but, when rock is uncovered during the mining of coal, the pyrites react with air and water, and the products of these reactions change the character of the streams and destroy the aquatic life.

MINING COAL Coal may be mined by underground or by surface mines. If the coal layers are near the surface, the mine is opened by stripping off the *overburden,* i.e., the layers of rock and soil covering the coal deposit. Then the coal is removed. There are three types of *strip* or *surface mines: area mines, contour mines,* and *auger mines.*

Area mines are operated in flat or rolling terrain. A trench is dug along one side of a deposit through the overburden, the coal is removed, and the overburden from the next cut is placed in the previous cut. Rain washes through the broken rock and dissolves the pyrites but the water is trapped by the piles of overburden and does little damage to the streams unless it breaks through the piles of soft rock.

Contour mining is practiced in hilly regions by cutting a shelf or bench into the side of a hill to reach the coal deposit. Additional cuts are made into the hill

WATER: THE BASIS OF LIFE

until it is no longer economical to operate the mine. Rain dissolves various pollutants from the spoil (overburden), which is either stacked on the outer edge of the shelf or pushed off to form oversteep slopes of debris, and from the highwall, the inner edge of the cut.

Auger mining is done to obtain coal from a deposit at the back of a highwall which can no longer be profitably contour mined. Augers up to 7 ft in diameter can bore 200 ft into a seam of coal on a highwall as easily as a screw bores into lumber. The auger holes interfere with normal drainage, provide means for pyrites to be exposed to air and water, and allow heavily polluted water to drain into streams.

WATER POLLUTANTS The water pollution starts with the reaction of pyrites, water, and air. The pyrite is converted to soluble iron sulfate which can be carried away by the runoff.

$$2FeS_2 + 7O_2 + 2H_2O \rightleftarrows 2Fe^{2+} + 4SO_4^{2-} + 4H^+$$

The formation of hydrogen ions lowers the pH of the stream (see p. 43). An investigation of two creeks in the Beaver Creek drainage in Kentucky showed pH ranges of 5.8 to 7.6 for the Helton Branch, which drains an undisturbed area, and 2.5 to 4.2 for the Cane Branch where 10% of the area had been strip mined.

The presence of hydrogen ions causes the chemical composition and quantity of dissolved solids to change. Not only are the dissolved solids in the Cane Branch 12 times those in the Helton Branch, but they are of different kinds. Those in the acidic Cane Branch were composed of the positive ions aluminum, iron, manganese, calcium, and magnesium, with sulfate as the primary negative ion. On the other hand, the ionic content of the Helton Branch was largely calcium, magnesium, and bicarbonate ions. There was also a relatively low concentration of sulfate ions.

Aluminum Aluminum ions of the Cane Branch are produced by the action of the hydrogen ions on the disturbed rock:

$$\underset{\text{(from rock)}}{AlO_2^-} + H^+ + H_2O \underset{pH > 7}{\overset{pH < 7}{\rightleftarrows}} Al(OH)_3 \underset{pH > 5}{\overset{pH < 5}{\rightleftarrows}} \underset{\text{(in water)}}{Al^{3+}}$$

Aluminum occurs in natural earthy materials in the form of insoluble metal salts of the aluminate ion (AlO_2^-), a relatively basic ion. When acid water flows over rock containing the AlO_2^- ion, the AlO_2^- reacts with water and hydrogen ions to form very insoluble $Al(OH)_3$. If the pH of the water is less than 5, the OH^- entities are stripped from the neutral charged $Al(OH)_3$ molecules to form the Al^{3+} ion which would be completely surrounded by water molecules. If the pH of the solution increases above 5, insoluble gelatinous (jelly-like) $Al(OH)_3$ forms. Such an increase in pH occurs at the confluence of two streams when one of them has a pH greater than 5.

Bicarbonate The bicarbonate ion (HCO_3^-) was present in the Helton Branch but not in the Cane Branch. The explanation lies in the equilibrium reaction:

$$CO_2 + H_2O \rightleftarrows HCO_3^- + H^+$$

In the Helton Branch the hydrogen ion concentration was small enough to allow appreciable amounts of the bicarbonate ion to be present. On the other hand, in the Cane branch the high concentrations of hydrogen ions would tend to drive the equilibrium in the direction of carbon dioxide and water.

Iron The iron II[2] ion, Fe^{2+}, from the pyrites is oxidized by oxygen to the iron III ion, Fe^{3+}:

$$4Fe^{2+} + O_2 + 10H_2O \rightarrow 4Fe(OH)_3 + 4H^+$$

The Fe^{3+} ion is soluble only in rather high concentrations of hydrogen ion (i.e., solutions of low pH). When the pH of the solution is increased by dilution with water or by removal of H^+ by a negative ion, for example

$$H^+ + HCO_3^- \rightarrow H_2O + CO_2$$

the Fe^{3+} ion precipitates as the very insoluble $Fe(OH)_3$, a gelatinous reddish precipitate called red or yellow boy.

The Cane Branch drainage was mined in the periods 1955 to 1956 and 1958 to 1959. By 1962 chemical weathering had decreased until it was slightly less than the level of 1957, but little further change in the amount of dissolved solids in the streams occurred between 1962 and 1965.

Effects on flora and fauna The flora and fauna of the Cane Branch were destroyed by the low pH of its water and by the alternate deposition and erosion of sediment. Only a few tiny organisms were found five years after mining ceased.

A study in 1959 seemed to show that trees were growing faster where they were watered with spoil bank or highwall runoff. A possible reason may be the release of essential plant nutrients by the acid water. However, by 1964 trees watered by acid runoff were smaller than those grown in more normal conditions, and reseeding of spoil banks was less well advanced than reseeding of nearby abandoned farms.

Surface mines have been used to illustrate the problems of acid drainage, but underground mines are also exposed to air and water which oxidize pyrites.

DOMESTIC WATER At the domestic level man uses water for sanitation, drinking, cooking, sewage disposal, and perhaps watering his lawn and flowers and washing his car. Biologically he needs about two or three pints a day in temperate climates, but the average American citizen uses about 130 gallons a day. The average western European uses only about half that amount.

---

2. The symbols II and III are used to indicate the number of bonds iron or other positive ions may form.

WATER: THE BASIS OF LIFE

All water is treated before being piped to the nation's homes. Most water is also treated after it is used and before it is dumped into the environment.

There are two crimes against humanity which at their inception seemed like real boons. They are the internal combustion engine and the flush toilet.[3]

Dr. Donald Koons

The dirty water is usually collected in sewer pipes and conveyed to a sewage treatment plant (Figure 4–9), where it may be subjected to various stages of upgrading before release to a stream, lake, or ocean.

1. In primary treatment, the larger solid particles are screened out. Smaller particles settle out in a settling tank. The effluent is sometimes discharged to the environment but is usually discharged to secondary treatment. The solid sludge (a watery solid) is sent to a sludge digester for further treatment.

2. The primary effluent can be sprayed over a trickling filter of stones or it can be treated in an aeration tank (air is bubbled through the effluent). In either case aerobic[4] bacteria and other organisms consume the organic substances before the effluent goes to a settling tank. The effluent from the settling tank may be discharged to the environment after being treated with chlorine to kill the bacteria or it may be processed further. The sludge is sent to a sludge digester.

3. Tertiary treatment comprises a variety of possible processes; for example, phosphates are removed by treating the effluent with iron chloride ($FeCl_3$) from steel industry wastes to form insoluble iron phosphate ($FePO_4$). Odors and remaining organic matter in the effluent may be removed with activated carbon.

The semisolid sludges which accumulate from any settling stage can be gathered and subjected to digestion with bacteria in a heated tank held at 35 °C (95 °F) to decompose the sludge and make it biologically safe. If sufficiently dried, the residue is a crumbly black solid.

Variations of the different treatments are common; for example, the sludge from the secondary settling tank may be returned to the aeration tank to supply the tank with bacteria.

In older systems, drains for storm sewers may empty into sanitary sewers. During storms, extra water may overload the treatment facilities and raw sewage may be discharged to the environment along with treated effluent.

DISPOSAL OF SEWAGE EFFLUENT   The treated effluent may be disposed of on land or, more commonly, is routed to bodies of water. Lakes will be used as an illustration.

3. Dr. Donald Koons, Chairman of the Maine Environmental Improvement Commission, quoted in the *Detroit Free Press,* 11 April 1971.
4. Reaction conditions in which oxygen is present and reacts with other materials. The usual products from aerobic decomposition are carbon dioxide and water and other fully oxidized entities such as sulfate ions.

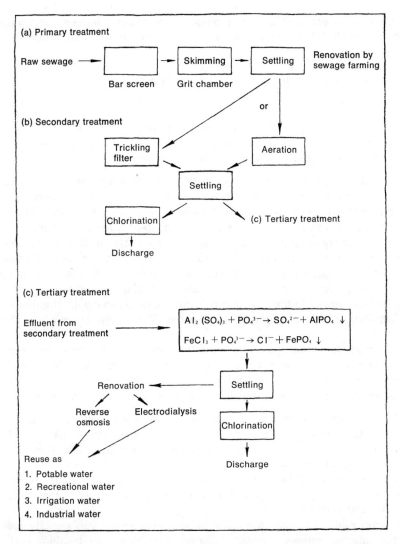

Figure 4–9. Sewage plant: (a) primary treatment, (b) secondary treatment, and (c) tertiary treatment.

In its natural state a lake has a normal cycle which follows the seasons. During summer algae grow on the surface on nutrients washed into the lake. In the fall they die and fall to the bottom. Bacteria break down the algae into nutrients, which are absorbed by the mud which is covered by a thin layer of iron, usually in the form of insoluble iron III hydroxide ($Fe(OH)_3$). The iron also serves to bind phosphate ions as insoluble iron III phosphates. The iron layer prevents the nutrients from escaping back into the water.

Phosphates from detergents and fecal matter can upset the normal cycle by causing algae blooms, huge growths of algae covering all or part of a body of water. This process is known as *eutrophication.* Where the algae die and sink to the bottom, decomposition by bacteria consumes the oxygen of the bottom layer of the lake. Fish die from lack of oxygen and add to the organic layer. The amount of oxygen required by the bacteria to oxidize[5] the organic matter is called the Biological Oxygen Demand (BOD) of the water.

As the amount of organic material increases, the BOD increases until it becomes larger than the available oxygen. When oxygen is exhausted, iron III of the iron hydroxides and phosphates are reduced to soluble iron II phosphate. The protection of the mud layers is gone and phosphates are freed to be used again by plants. Eutrophication is a complex process which is not always reversible.

Not all authorities agree that the main cause of algae "blooms" is the increase in the use of phosphates. Many nutrients are needed to produce the huge growths, and the lack of any one nutrient will limit the production of the algae regardless of the amounts of all other nutrients. If the limiting nutrient, probably carbon, nitrogen, or phosphorus, is supplied, the "bloom" will result. Carbon in the form of CO_2 from air or from decay is always present. Nitrogen fertilizers are very soluble in water and wash from the land into the lakes. Therefore, phosphorus is usually the limiting nutrient.

DETERGENTS—A SOURCE OF PHOSPHORUS   The word *detergent* refers to any substance used for cleaning. Therefore, soap is a detergent. In common usage, detergent refers to those made by man. Here man-made detergents, *syn*thetic *deter*gents, will be called *syndets.*

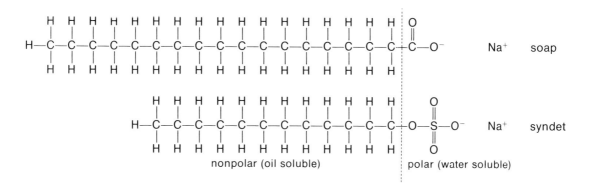

5. To oxidize (the process of *oxidation*) originally meant to combine or react with oxygen. The term oxidation has broadened to mean the loss of electrons. In this case the organic matter lost electrons to the oxygen. The oxygen gained electrons and is said to be *reduced.*

A detergent is usually composed of a long hydrocarbon chain which has a charged end group which will attach to water molecules through hydrogen bonds. Except for the end group, the hydrocarbon chain has negligible attraction for water. However, the long-chain portion of the molecule does mix with materials such as grease or oil which are nonpolar and/or insoluble in water. Dirt is usually covered by a thin film of oil.

Water, a polar substance, is attracted by the charged end group and repels the nonpolar tail. The nonpolar tail and dirt collect as tiny particles suspended in water and surrounded by a negative charge. The relationship of dirt particles, detergents, and water have the generalized character shown in Figure 4–10. Since negatively charged particles repel each other, the particles do not agglomerate to form a massive particle which would be caught and held by the article being "washed." Essentially, the colloidal dirt particle becomes a mas-

Figure 4–10. Diagram of detergent and dirt. The circle represents the dirt, with the detergent adhering to it by the zig-zag carbon chains.

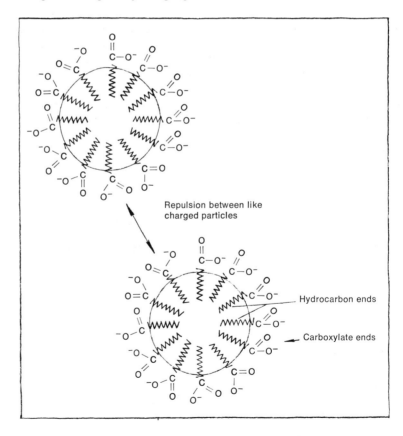

WATER: THE BASIS OF LIFE

sive negative ion the charge of which is balanced by the large number of sodium ions which were a part of the original detergent. The colloidal suspension of dirt is stable as long as the charge remains on the particle. The charge can be destroyed by any positively charged particle or ion which would bind firmly to the negative part of the detergent.

Soap   In the case of soaps

$$CH_3-(CH_2)_{16}-\overset{\overset{\displaystyle O}{\parallel}}{C}-O-Na^+$$

multiply charged ions (Ca^{2+}, Mg^{2+}, Fe^{3+}, Al^{3+}) attach so firmly to the soap ions that the charges on the colloidal particles are neutralized. Consequently, the dirt particles no longer repel each other and tend to form gummy aggregates which cause dirt to adhere to, rather than be removed from, the clothing or article being "washed." Water which contains the multiply charged ions is called *hard water*. Calcium and magnesium ions (Ca^{2+} and Mg^{2+}) are the most common hardness-producing ions.

Water softeners   If the ions which cause hard water are removed or tightly bound, the water is said to be softened.

Frequently, the metal ions are dissolved as the bicarbonates, for example, $Ca^{2+} + 2HCO_3^-$ which exist in an equilibrium state:

$$\underset{\text{soluble}}{Ca^{2+} + 2HCO_3^-} \rightleftarrows \underset{\text{insoluble}}{CaCO_3} + CO_2 + H_2O$$

When the solution is heated, CO_2 is driven off; thus the reaction shifts to the right and the Ca^{2+} is removed. Water from which the hardness-producing ions can be removed by heating is called *temporary hard water*.

When the multiply charged ions are in the form of sulfates ($CaSO_4$ and $MgSO_4$), the water is said to be *permanently hard;* that is, the metal ions cannot be precipitated by boiling the solution.

Several phosphorus compounds, for example, trisodium phosphate ($3Na^+ + PO_4^{3-}$) and sodium tripolyphosphate ($5Na^+ + P_3O_{10}^{5-}$), can supply electrons to the hard water ions Ca^{2+} and Mg^{2+} and form granular precipitates which do not interfere with the action of the soap. Carbonate and silicate ions can also bind the metallic ions in precipitates. Phosphates are harmless to man but sodium carbonate, "washing soda," is too basic for safe use and silicates may cause skin damage. Consequently, both silicates and sodium carbonate are unsatisfactory for use by the general public.

Another way of binding the metal ions is by incorporating them in a ring structure which protects the ion from attack by other ions. This method is called *chelation* after a Greek word meaning claw. One of the most successful chelating agents is ethylenediaminetetracetic acid (EDTA) which has six sites that simultaneously hold the metal ion (Figure 4–11). EDTA is too expensive for general use but it is added to shampoos and soaps to soften the water.

Figure 4-11. Structural formula for the metal chelate of EDTA.

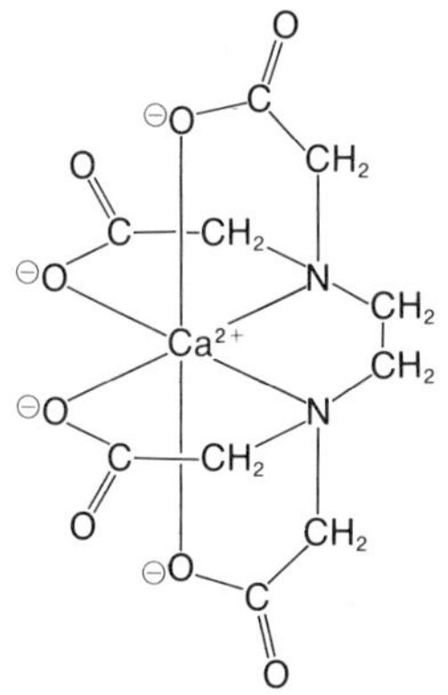

Synthetic detergents Modern syndets, for example

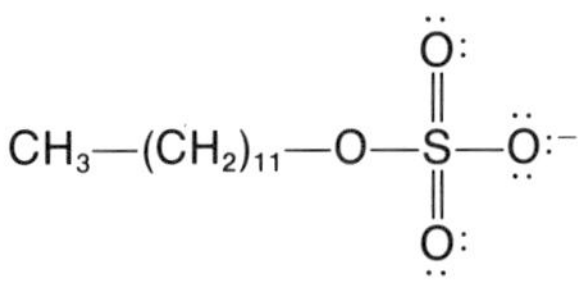

largely avoid "hard water" effects because the negative group holds electrons so firmly that multiply charged ions do not bind together tightly enough to cause the formation of an uncharged particle. As a result, there is no formation of gummy residues and the dirt can be rinsed away. Such action is desirable but the gain has a price.

Syndets are mixtures of substances, not more than 20% are detergent molecules and up to 50% are builders, usually phosphates. Builders have several functions: they are cheap and reduce the cost of the detergent, they keep the solution basic by neutralizing the slightly acidic "dirt," and they bind metal ions which make the detergents less efficient. Phosphates are very efficient builders, and are nontoxic and cheap. However, they have one disadvantage; they can stimulate huge growths of algae on receiving bodies of water.

DISPOSAL OF SEWAGE SLUDGE The sludge from a sewage treatment plant is a jelly-like solid which is difficult to dry. Current methods of disposal are (1) to waterways, (2) to incinerators, (3) to land dumps, and (4) to fields as fertilizer. Sludge adds an increased BOD to waterways with the same effects as sewage effluent.

Currently, most sludge is dumped on land, but incineration is expected to be the disposal method of the future. Incineration causes air pollution, which may be controlled by air pollution control devices, and leaves a residue of ash which must be dumped on land.

WATER: THE BASIS OF LIFE

Several cities are selling dried sludge to be used as fertilizer. Milwaukee markets its dried sludge as "milorganite" to golf courses where its high iron content gives the grass a desirable deep green color. Milwaukee's sludge is particularly rich in iron because much of the organic material comes from breweries where iron interferes with the fermentation process and is removed. A few municipalities continue to try to sell their sludge for fertilizer, but most do not find it economical enough to compete with using a landfill.

SEWAGE FARMING   Sewage farming refers to the use of farm land for disposal of either sewage effluent, or sludge, or both. The practice of using farm land for disposal of human waste has been common in the Orient and Europe for centuries (Figure 4–12). The United States has never used farm land for this purpose because both land and fertilizer were cheap. In the Orient wastes, known as "night soil," were dumped directly on the land resulting in disease and parasitic infection. Industrialized countries use only treated effluent and sludge on the land.

Sewage farming has several advantages: fertilizing materials are returned to the land, waterways are not fouled, water is renovated (i.e., restored to a "clean" condition), and, finally, it may be cheaper than existing methods of sewage disposal. Variations of sewage farming have been tried in a few places in the United States, but usually on an experimental basis.

Figure 4–12. Sewage farming (i.e., sewage water used for irrigation) as practiced in Europe since the mid-nineteenth century. Redrawn from Jonathan Allen, "Sewage Farming," *Environment,* April 1973, p. 37. Copyright © Scientists' Institute for Public Information, 1973.

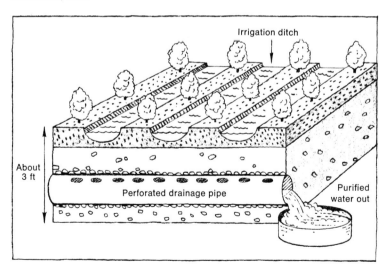

Pennsylvania State University experiment A spray irrigation system for disposal of primary and secondary treated sewage and recovery of potable water was built (Figure 4–13). One to two inches per week were applied at the rate of 1/4–1/6 in/hr, which corresponds to an annual application of about 1600 lb of fertilizer per acre. Fertilizer requirements vary widely with the crop being grown and the soil being planted, but about 400 lb of a similar fertilizer would be a representative amount. The sewage provided several times the amounts a farmer would apply. Control plots receiving fertilizer but no irrigation were planted with forests and crops. The irrigated forests showed an increase in height but no increase in diameter; hay yields increased 300%, corn 50%, and oats 17–51%.

Muskegon, Michigan has built a system patterned after the Pennsylvania State University system. They expect to start spreading wastes on land in 1974.

Sewage wastes have also been applied to strip-mined land with excellent results.

Disadvantages of sewage farming Not all types of soil can be used for heavy application of water. Heavy soils would become water logged and possibly infertile.

The greatest difficulty is the dumping of industrial wastes into municipal sewers where industrial waste water accounts for one-half the volume. Continual application of trace elements from many industrial wastes can harm the soil. Table 4–1 gives tolerances for selected metals in drinking water and

Figure 4–13. Waste water renovation and conservation cycle. Redrawn from R. R. Parizek, et al., *Waste Water Renovation and Conservation,* The Pennsylvania State University Studies No. 23, p. 10, 1967.

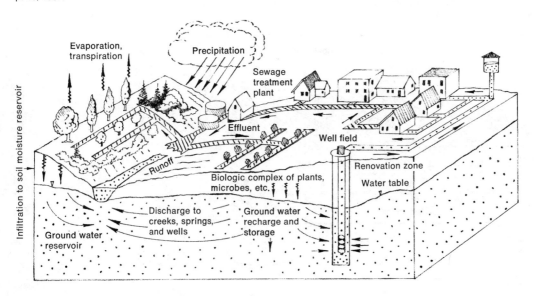

WATER: THE BASIS OF LIFE

TABLE 4–1. Possible Toxic Contaminants of Water.

Element	Digester bottom sludge (ppm)	Tolerance irrigation water (ppm)	Public water supply permissible criteria (ppm)
Cadmium	0.60	0.005	0.01
Copper	0.23	0.20	1.00
Chromium	31.00	5.00	0.05
Lead	0.30	5.00	0.05
Manganese	57.00	2.00	0.05
Nickel	15.00	0.50	
Zinc	58.00	5.00	5.00

Source: Column 2 from testimony of Honorable Austin N. Heller, Secretary of Natural Resources and Environmental Control, Delaware, from information supplied by the Philadelphia Water Department, 10 March 1971. Columns 3 and 4 from Federal Water Pollution Control Administration, Department of Interior, *Report of the Committee on Water Quality Criteria,* Washington, D.C.: Government Printing Office, 1968, pp. 20, 153.

irrigation along with their measured concentrations in the sludge from the industrial city of Philadelphia. Analysis of the table shows that the levels of the metals in a sludge can limit their use as fertilizer.

Tolerance for cadmium is 0.005 mg/liter for irrigation water. On this basis a reasonable application of 5 acre-feet[6] of irrigation water would deposit 5 g of cadmium over an acre of land. The extremely small amount of cadmium which is permissible for this area indicates the extreme toxicity of this metal (Chapter 6). The concentration of cadmium in the sludge from Philadelphia is approximately 0.5 g per ton of sludge. Ten tons of sludge, therefore, would contain as much cadmium as is permissible for the application of 5 acre-feet of irrigation water carrying a concentration of cadmium amounting to 0.005 mg/liter. Some of the cadmium in the water would not be deposited. The full content of sludge applied to the land would remain on the land. In any case, less than 10 tons of Philadelphia sludge is permissible for application to land each year. If heavy metals are absent from the sludge, up to 15 tons per acre may be applied with benefit. Similar arguments can be made with respect to other metals listed in Table 4–1.

It is essential that certain trace elements not be applied to farm land. If the fertilizing materials in sewage are to be used on the nation's cropland, industrial wastes with trace elements will have to be kept out of the sewers. Another option is to use the fertilizing materials on nonfood crops; several communities in Michigan are depositing wastes from municipal sewers and industrial wastes on forest land. If the contaminating elements are allowed to increase enough,

6. An acre-foot is equal to one foot of water spread over an acre. The amount of water applied to farm land depends upon the climate and the crop but amounts of 3–5 acre-feet are common.

the fertility of the land may decrease. The final option is to treat the wastes in the conventional treatment plants and keep all the materials off the land.

THE CLIVUS SYSTEM   The historic pattern of development of sewage treatment was as follows. At first only primary treatment was used. When this was found to be unsatisfactory, secondary treatment was added. Now that this is not sufficient, tertiary treatment is advocated. None of these methods dispose of the sludge. Each method is a *technological fix*. Some scientists are beginning to question the practice of adding technological fix to technological fix. They want to start at the root of the problem.[7]

A Swedish firm has developed a new method of handling sewage from a single family dwelling: the Clivus system, a new type of toilet and water-treatment tank (Figure 4–14). The odor-free system has been used in various places in Sweden, but has not been widely marketed in this country, although it has been recommended for certain ecologically fragile areas.

There are three chambers in the solid waste receiver: (1) excrement chamber, (2) garbage chamber, and (3) storage chamber. During decomposition, heat is produced and warms the air which rises through an outlet which leads from the highest part of the receiver to a roof-type vent. After the second year, humus (decayed organic matter which is a normal and desirable component of soil) can be removed from the storage chamber at the rate of two to four pails per person per year. Only 5% of the original volume of material remains. Health authorities have checked the resulting material and found it safe.

Wash water, called *gray water*, still must be disposed of. Gray water contains 50% of the phosphorus and 10% of the nitrogen of sewage. It also has a high BOD which declines rapidly. Suggested treatment consists of running the water through a filter—a stone-filled box four feet on a side. As the water passes through the filter, the larger particles are trapped and broken up by the action of bacteria. The effluent water is then safe to be dispersed into the ground where the phosphates will be trapped (see Chapter 5).

The system has numerous advantages: all of the fertilizing materials are recovered (the only other system which recovers all fertilizing substances is sewage farming); the streams are kept clean; the toilet is aesthetically acceptable. The cost of the Clivus system is about $2000 (1972). Mass production should bring the price to about $1000, a price which compares favorably with a conventional toilet and sewer system.

The Swedish technology may not be the best answer. However, the idea of trying to find a completely new solution may help to solve this problem and many others.

Potable Water   Man needs *potable* water for drinking, food preparation, and personal clean-

7. The use of technological fixes is common not only in the area of sewage disposal but in other environmental or ecological situations. Air pollution control devices are examples of technological fixes. This is not meant to imply technology is not important.

WATER: THE BASIS OF LIFE

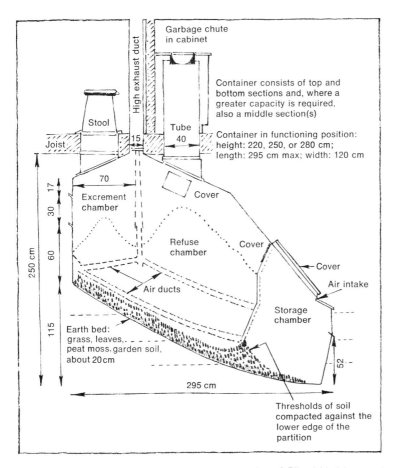

Figure 4–14. A Clivus toilet. Redrawn with permission of Rikard Lindstrom and Clivus Multrum U.S.A.

liness. He uses potable water for these uses and for sewage disposal, watering lawns, washing cars, and other domestic needs.

Some of the desert cities have the highest per capita use of potable water in the nation and close to the record for the world. Those who move to these areas from the more humid areas because they like the climate tend to want to take their surroundings with them. Green grass, flowers, a green golf course, air conditioning, and swimming pools all require large quantities of water.

CONVENTIONAL TREATMENT   Water withdrawn from surface resources must be given various treatments to make it suitable for human consumption (Figure 4–15). Different methods are listed on the next page.

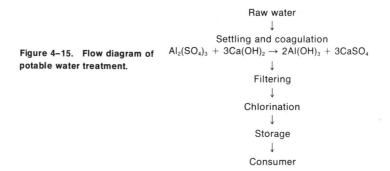

Figure 4–15. Flow diagram of potable water treatment.

Raw water
↓
Settling and coagulation
$Al_2(SO_4)_3 + 3Ca(OH)_2 \rightarrow 2Al(OH)_3 + 3CaSO_4$
↓
Filtering
↓
Chlorination
↓
Storage
↓
Consumer

1. Chemicals such as aluminum sulfate ($Al_2(SO_4)_3$) and calcium hydroxide ($Ca(OH)_2$) can be added to form gelatinous aluminum hydroxide ($Al(OH)_3$) to collect suspended matter and make it easier to filter such matter.

2. The water can be sprayed into the air while exposed to sunlight, an operation which kills bacteria and removes substances which contribute obnoxious tastes or odors to the water.

3. The water can be passed through an activated carbon filter (activated carbon has an uncontaminated surface ready for adsorption of a layer of impurities from a liquid or gas). Carbon adsorbs organic substances and objectionable inorganic substances such as H_2S. The carbon can be reused after heating to a high temperature in a stream of steam.

4. Finally, sufficient chlorine is added to kill the remaining bacteria and have chlorine remain in the water until use.

The success of the treatment process is shown by the fact that few people die of water-borne diseases. Industrial society has brought a different type of problem. Before water reaches the modern treatment plant it may have been used by a municipality or industry which may have added biorefractories or inorganic salts. Biorefractories are organic compounds which are not biodegradable; that is they cannot be broken down by bacteria or other microorganisms.

ADDITION OF ORGANIC COMPOUNDS   Little is known about the organic compounds discharged by the chemical, petrochemical (i.e., one that uses petroleum for raw material), and related industries. Such substances are nonbiodegradable with low molecular weight and low volatility. One of the compounds known to be discharged into the Mississippi at St. Louis, Missouri, is still found in the drinking water at New Orleans. Some of the compounds may cause noxious odors or taste; some have been found to taint seafoods. Several hundred substances, their exact formulas, their effects on man and other life, and the quantities present in water need to be investigated.

Presently, chemical complexes along the lower Mississippi River, the Houston ship channel, and the Cuyahoga River are discharging biorefractories which are found downstream. Biorefractories are expected to be found in other places with a concentrated chemical industry.

INORGANIC SALTS IN WATER   The concentration of salts in the effluent water from a city is usually about double the concentration of the salts in the raw intake water. Even if the added salts are nonpoisonous, the salt concentration may become large enough to exceed the standards set by the Public Health Service.

If the salts could be removed or reduced sufficiently, it should be possible repeatedly to recycle the waste water into potable water. Physical and/or chemical processes for reducing or removing salts from water are complex and expensive. Consequently, the usefulness of these processes for renovating water is limited. Complete demineralization of water can be accomplished by (1) distillation, (2) freezing, or (3) ion exchange. Reduction of mineral content can be attained either through electrodialysis or through reverse osmosis. All of these methods require extensive plants and large inputs of energy.

In distillation, the water must be evaporated to a gaseous form and then recondensed to liquid water. The salts do not vaporize at the boiling temperature of water and remain behind in the distillation chamber. A concentrated brine remains and is discharged to waste (see Chapter 2).

In the freezing process, water freezes into a mass of pure ice which progressively excludes the salts. Again a concentrated salt solution must be disposed to waste.

An ion exchange desalination process operates on the same principle as the home water softener. The water softener contains a mineral called zeolite (NaH_6AlSiO_7). When hard water is passed through the zeolite, calcium ions at any one "site" on the zeolite become more concentrated than sodium ions. The calcium ions displace sodium ions. When most of the sodium ions are displaced, the system can be regenerated by adding a concentrated solution of sodium chloride. On an equilibrium basis, the sodium ions displace the calcium ions from the zeolite. The zeolite water softener is not satisfactory for purifying water for drinking purposes because the water still contains sodium ions which adversely affect people with heart problems. To eliminate all ions, a high-molecular-weight organic-ion-exchange compound is used. Positive ions and negative ions are removed in separate exchangers. Only small amounts can be purified by this method. The resulting pure water is costly.

In electrodialysis (Figure 4–16), the mineralized water is passed between two membranes. Outside one of the membranes is a chamber or cell which contains an *anode* (positive electrode). Outside the second membrane is a cell which contains a *cathode* (negative electrode). A direct current is passed between the electrodes. As the water passes between the electrodes, the positive ions are pulled into the cathode chamber and the negative ions are

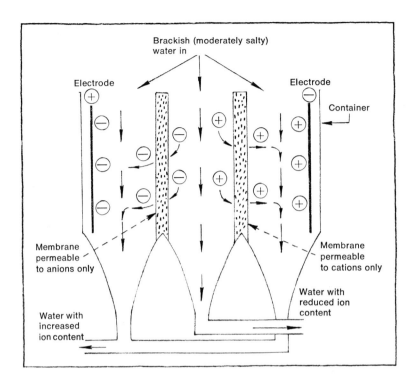

Figure 4–16. Electrodialysis of brackish water.

pulled through the membrane into the anode chamber. Partially purified water is taken from the central chamber. The equivalent of a concentrated brine collects in the electrode cells and must be disposed to waste.

Osmosis (see page 102) occurs when water from a less concentrated solution passes through a semipermeable membrane into a more concentrated solution. If the concentrated solution were placed in an enclosed container inside a membrane, pressure would be built up. When the osmotic pressure of the concentrated solution equals the osmotic pressure of the less concentrated solution, the process stops. Conversely, pressure can be applied to the concentrated solution so that the pressure of the concentrated solution is equal to or greater than the osmotic pressure. Under these circumstances fluid flows out of the more concentrated solution into the less concentrated solution. In this way, a purer water can be obtained from a salt solution. The process is called *reverse osmosis* (Figure 4–17).

Any of the physical or chemical processes which are used to purify or partially purify water requires large inputs of energy. Therefore, the usefulness of these processes depends heavily upon energy economics. Arid urban areas

WATER: THE BASIS OF LIFE

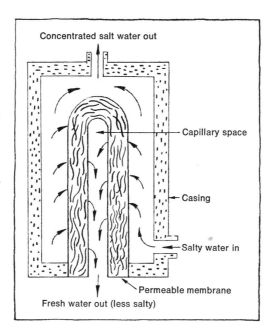

Figure 4–17. Simplified diagram of reverse osmosis. Instead of having only one hollow, permeable fiber, the space is filled with a large mass of hairlike, hollow, permeable membranes.

Concentrated salt water out

Capillary space

Casing

Salty water in

Permeable membrane

Fresh water out (less salty)

may be able to afford the cost of water from such processes but they are too costly for use in agriculture.

STANDARDS FOR DRINKING WATER   The Public Health Service Drinking Water Standards list 20 chemical parameters (factors) for drinking water, but only nine serve as absolute grounds for rejecting the water as unsafe for human consumption. The USSR includes about 300 parameters in its list and more are being discussed. The difficulty is that there is not enough known about what substances are to be found in surface water and what effect they will have on each other and man.

An exotic is something which is not natural to its present location. Wild burros left by western prospectors are exotics. Water transported from one region to another can be considered an exotic.

EXOTIC SOURCES OF WATER

The California Water Project started as a complex plan and then became even more complicated. A dam was built on the Feather River near Oroville and the water transported across the Sacramento River Delta to the southern part of the state for irrigation and urban use. Plans were then made to dam the wild rivers in the extreme northern part of the state for use in the southern areas. A huge canal was to be built around the Sacramento Delta to transport

California Water Project

the water. Finally, a drainage canal would be built to carry the highly saline, polluted irrigation water from the San Joaquin Valley to San Francisco Bay.

San Francisco Bay is a large estuary with a balance between the salt water of the ocean and the freshwater flow from the land. Some of the water which normally would flow into the Bay is now being transported south. The proposed dams and the canal would reduce the freshwater flow even more. At the same time, drainage from the San Joaquin Valley would add an extra salt input to the Bay. The resulting balance of fresh and salt water would upset the ecology of the Bay.

A surprising result of the use of water from northern California for irrigation in the southern part of the state is the change in the structure of the soil. The chemical components of the imported water cause the chemical structure of the soil to become unstable and has caused landslides when the irrigation water has been applied to slopes.

NAWAPA

The North American Water and Power Alliance (NAWAPA) is a plan to collect the waters of Alaska, the Yukon, and British Columbia and pump them over the mountains to the Rocky Mountain Trench, a natural basin. An alternative proposal is to cut huge tunnels through the mountains. Through a system of canals the water could be distributed throughout the midwest and southwest of the United States and Mexico, as well as the prairies of Canada. The canals would also be used for transportation, including an inland waterway from Vancouver, British Columbia, almost to Duluth on Lake Superior.

The effect of such a gigantic system of moving water is unknown. Cold, nutrient-laden fresh water would no longer flow north. Food for aquatic life would be reduced. Without the cold fresh water flowing into the Arctic Ocean, warmer salty water from the south would flow north. The Arctic would become warmer. How much warmer it would become and the ultimate effect on world climate are unknown. The dams and reservoirs would occupy much wild land and the homes of several tribes of Indians. Farther to the south the reservoirs would occupy valleys of productive land.

Use of Ice

Icecaps and glaciers constitute 75% of the globe's freshwater resources. Because ice is a pure form of water, plans have been suggested for its exploitation. Icebergs might be towed to the large cities such as New York City or Los Angeles where they would be melted into fresh water. The members of the Rand Corporation think an iceberg could be towed from Antarctica to California in 10 months.

An iceberg 900 ft high, 1 mile long and 2 miles wide would provide 51,000 acre-feet of water at $65 an acre-foot. This would be enough water for a city the size of San Diego (population 700,000) for a year. Iceberg water might be attractive for agriculture but piping the water to the desert regions would require the use of large amounts of energy. If the use of the ice is limited to that which breaks off into the ocean, the resource can be considered to be renewable.

Only certain amounts of water move over the land in the atmosphere. Water which is naturally or unnaturally removed at one place cannot fall at another. "Unnatural" rains caused to fall at a given place may cause a compensating deficiency at a different place, or the rains may appear at a location down range from the artificially induced rainfall. Knowledge of weather relationships is so rudimentary that much controversy and many lawsuits will occur before the success or failure of this attempt to increase or redistribute water supplies is settled. Seeding hurricanes has been a routine method to slow the winds but the cost is more rainfall. However, seeding hurricanes has been discontinued until more information can be collected.

Desalination of sea water has been suggested as a way in which to make the deserts bloom. Alvin Weinberg, former director of the Oak Ridge National Laboratory of the Atomic Energy Commission, has proposed a large number of groups of nuclear plants (nuplexes) which would produce electrical energy and desalt sea water for use in nearby irrigated farms. Huge amounts of energy would be needed for desalinization (see Chapter 8).

Huge amounts of energy would be required to pump the water up onto the land. Falling water is often used to produce electrical energy. The net amount of energy required to lift a given quantity of water 150 ft above sea level is exactly the same amount that theoretically could be produced by the water if it should fall to sea level from that height. For example, at Niagara Falls water falls 150 ft from the upper river to the rocks below. Much more energy would be required to lift the water up and over the crest of the falls than the water could possibly supply by falling to the lower river because energy would be lost to friction in the pipes and pumps.

Each United States citizen now uses directly or indirectly about 3500 gallons of water per day to produce his food. If his entire supply were obtained from desalinated water, about one-quarter of a ton of salt would be accumulated each day. Desalination of enough ocean water to supply all of New York City's needs for one year would result in the production of 67 million tons of salt, about 10 tons per person. If the water needed for New York City for one year were to be used for agricultural irrigation it would supply 3 acre-feet for about 60,000 acres which would feed 30,000–240,000 people, depending on the level at which they wished to eat.

Where would the salt be put?

1. It could be piled on the ground, a solution only feasible for desert regions.
2. It could be injected into brackish water wells or into disposal wells.
3. It could be dumped into the sea. If the salt is dumped in massive quantities in one place, it would adversely affect sea life in the dump area.

If water for a city were to be desalinated and the salt dumped in the ocean near the mouth of a stream naturally draining the city, the effect on the ocean would be minimal. However, if the water were used for irrigation, much would be lost by evapotranspiration and only relatively small amounts would be returned to the ocean. Thus, more salt would be returned to the sea than corresponds to the amount of water returned. Therefore extra salinity would be created at the discharge point.

OIL AND WATER

An industrial society runs on oil, and oil is spilled. An oil-polluted beach and an oil-soaked bird have become a symbol of oil spills.

What Happens when Oil Is Spilled?

When oil is spilled the water-soluble fractions of the oil immediately dissolve in the water. These fractions are the ones most immediately toxic and also the more stable fractions. The lighter fractions slowly evaporate and leave the heavy parts as tarry lumps, which are found over the globe. Lumps up to 49 cm (16 in.) in diameter occur along the coast of Japan, in the stomachs of surface swimming fish, and in large areas of the Atlantic Ocean (Figure 4–18).

Oil destroys much of the aquatic life wherever it is spilled, shore, tidal river, or marsh, but in a short time the organic matter decays and leaves only a few shells. A worm, *Capitilla capitata,* usually appears in large numbers where it is usually present in small numbers.

Oil may be ingested by fish and shellfish. Once incorporated as part of the body of an animal, it is protected from degradation and passed from predator to predator. Even if the contaminated animals are kept in clean water for an extended period of time, the oil may be detected by liquid-gas chromatography, although not by taste or odor.

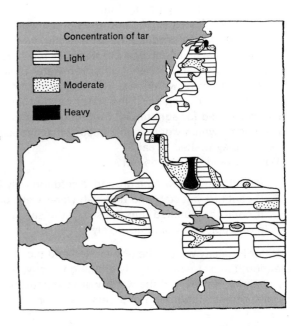

Figure 4–18. Oil-tar lumps found by the National Oceanic and Atmospheric Administration in the Atlantic Ocean. Redrawn from Sierra Club, *National News Report,* 16 February 1973, p. 2.

WATER: THE BASIS OF LIFE

Birds are usually the most obvious casualty of an oil spill. Actual counts of dead birds range from a few hundred to several thousands, but even these large numbers may be only a fraction of the actual kill. Oil-soaked birds may be eaten by predators and not counted. The feathers of birds are covered with a protective coating of a waxy substance similar to crude oil (Figure 4–19). Thus the crude oil is able to spread rapidly over the feathers and mix with the coating. Until recently it was thought that washing to remove the crude oil also removed the protective coating from the feathers. Thus the birds had to be housed and fed until they grew new feathers. Two recent studies have shown that, if the detergent is completely removed, the feathers do not lose their waterproofing. It is possible to release the birds after three days to two weeks.

The area contaminated by oil expands for a considerable period of time but eventually fractions of the oil are degraded and organisms slowly return. However, the oil that is part of the food chain is protected from changes.

The spectacular spills are caused by tanker accidents or offshore drilling, but even more oil may be dumped by small continuing spills.

What Is the Source of Oil?

TANKERS   The *Torrey Canyon,* the wreck of which in 1967 alerted the world to the danger of oil spills, was only a 117,000-ton tanker. Today there are at least four 327,000-ton and one 477,000-ton supertankers in use, and even larger ones on order. Oil carried by a 550,000-ton tanker would fill 110 trains of 100-tank cars each. (Figure 4–20). The large tankers cannot unload at most harbors so they will need "superports" offshore. Whether these will increase or decrease oil spillage is controversial. The huge tankers are slow to react. One of the tankers planned for the transport of Alaskan oil will need 10 miles to stop.

After a 300,000-ton tanker has unloaded, the vessel may have as much as 1500 barrels of oil in its tanks. This may be flushed out with high-pressure water sprays and pumped overboard, or the cleaning water may be collected in a

 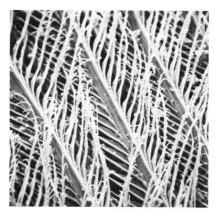

Figure 4–19. Bird feathers, clean and coated with oil. Courtesy of Research Unit on Rehabilitation of Oiled Seabirds, University of Newcastle-upon-Tyne, U.K.

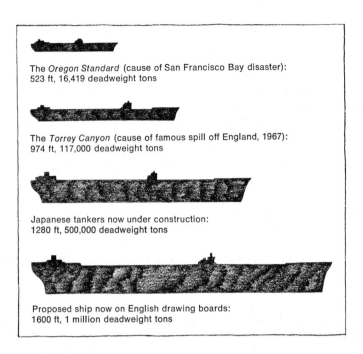

The *Oregon Standard* (cause of San Francisco Bay disaster):
523 ft, 16,419 deadweight tons

The *Torrey Canyon* (cause of famous spill off England, 1967):
974 ft, 117,000 deadweight tons

Japanese tankers now under construction:
1280 ft, 500,000 deadweight tons

Proposed ship now on English drawing boards:
1600 ft, 1 million deadweight tons

Figure 4–20. Increasing size of tankers. Courtesy of Friends of the Earth.

special tank where it spontaneously separates or is mechanically separated. The water layer will be pumped overboard. Little actual oil may be discharged but the water will contain the water-soluble fractions. This system is called the load-on-top system, and only larger tankers can afford the space for the separate tank.

The maritime nations have tried to set up standards to stop the pollution of the seas. The agreements have not been signed by several countries including Liberia, Greece, and Japan who provide "flags of convenience," that is, they register tankers but do not require the high standards of equipment and personnel that most countries do. A few countries who provide "flags of convenience" do not even participate in the meetings. In any case, the agreement is almost impossible to enforce. If enforcement and convictions were possible, the maximum fine is $2500.

OFFSHORE DRILLING An increasing proportion of crude oil is coming from the continental shelf. Any accident causes oil to be spilled on the ocean. Often natural oil leaks and continual pollution from the wells makes it impossible to determine what effects the spill had on the environment.

WATER: THE BASIS OF LIFE

Now that drilling off the North Atlantic coast is beginning, icebergs may increase the potential for oil spills. Icebergs have been known to dig 30-ft furrows in the ocean floor.

SMALL, CONTINUING SPILLS   Every time the oil in a car is changed, the used oil is likely to be dumped down the nearest drain. Gas stations have been returning this oil, about a half billion gallons each year, to a rerefinery to be made into oil for oiling roads, fuel oil, and lubricants, but the rerefinery business is disappearing for the following reasons: (1) rerefined oil once had an excise tax subsidy which it no longer has; (2) the Federal Trade Commission (FTC) requires that the oil be labeled "rerefined" which implies second-rate; (3) many additives added to motor oil to increase the time between oil changes interfere with the rerefinery process.

The outboard motor is a surprisingly large source of water pollution. Up to 30% of the lubrication oil added to the gasoline for outboard motors is spewed into waterways.

Industrial discharges and inadvertent leaks contribute a large quantity of oil to the nation's waterways. Oil may be mixed with water and discharged without separating. A leaky valve, an underground leak, a rusted pipe, broken bolts, or a valve left open all may cause oil to collect and foul streams. Some of these are accidental spills; some are due to carelessness; some are deliberate. Sometimes it is cheaper to let the oil or gas leak than it is to make repairs to prevent the leak.

Methods of Cleanup

"It is as difficult to get oil off the water as it is to get smoke back in the smokestack. There are no fancy, ingenious methods."[8] The water-soluble fractions cannot be removed from the water. The relative success of collecting the remaining oil depends on the location of the spill and the weather. The oil may be dispersed, sunk, burned, absorbed, or skimmed off the water.

A dispersant may be toxic to sea life, and, even if it is not toxic itself, it introduces toxic oil compounds to a region where they are more accessible to marine life. Oil treated with sand and other fine materials may sink and destroy feeding areas, cover marine life, and lead to a large build-up of oil residues. New methods make it possible to burn the oil, but even under the best conditions 15% of the original oil will be left in the form of tar lumps. Absorbents do not work on the open sea but there is no better way to clean a beach or prevent oil from reaching the sand; however, it is an expensive method involving much hand labor.

Bacteria destroy petroleum naturally. By selecting and improving these bacteria it has long been hoped that they would provide an efficient method of degrading oil naturally. When needed, the bacteria, mixed with phosphate and nitrate fertilizers, would be dusted on the spill by an airplane or helicopter.

8. Joan Arehart-Treichel, "Oil on the waters: modest progress in cleanup technology," *Sci. News,* 102:250, 14 Oct. 1972.

An Israeli scientist, Professor Eugene Rosenberg, reports that he has developed a fast-multiplying strain of bacteria to clean a tanker's storage compartments.[9] After emptying the vessel, sea water, fertilizer, air, and bacteria are introduced into the tank. When the tanker reaches its destination, a small amount of recoverable oil, clean water, and an increased quantity of bacteria have been produced. The bacteria can be used for animal feed. The usual cleaning by high-pressure hoses causes a build-up of static charges which may cause fires. Cleaning by bacteria eliminates this danger. If the method works as well when used routinely as it has on a small scale, oil pollution on the ocean could be greatly reduced.

NATURAL BODIES OF WATER

Surface waters and the biological systems connected with them are often adversely affected by man's manipulation of these resources.

Streams

Streams are affected by any event that occurs in the entire watershed. Sedimentation of a stream is increased by logging, mining, road building, overgrazing, cropping, and building construction. Wastes dumped from industrial plants and washed from fields may increase the loading of dissolved solids as well as the oxygen demand.

Estuaries

The flow of fresh water from the land carries nutrients to the estuaries and continental shelves. There organisms create time-honored conditions for the growth and breeding of ocean inhabitants. At least three-quarters of the animals in the ocean spend an essential portion of their life in an estuary or are dependent on those organisms that do.

Presently, most of the streams reaching the ocean are polluted with domestic and industrial effluents of all kinds. The oceans and the estuaries are the ultimate dump. Twenty-two of the world's 32 largest cities, including the four largest, Tokyo, London, New York, and Shanghai, are built on estuaries. All or parts of many estuaries have been destroyed, for example, the Hudson River, Chesapeake Bay, San Francisco Bay, the Mississippi River, and the Rhine River. Industrialization, residential developments, and irrigation have eaten into the nation's estuaries and damaged important food resources and recreational areas.

The importance of clean, fresh water to an estuary is shown by the conditions in Galveston Bay in Texas. Like other estuaries, Galveston Bay is a brackish body of water which, in general, becomes less salty toward the head of the Bay where there is an inflow of fresh water from tributary streams. The Bay waters are enriched by nutrients brought in by tributaries or flushed out of the shallow water and marshes by tidal action. This accounts for the abundance of marine life which this and other estuaries support. A dam at the head of Trinity Bay off Galveston Bay prevents fresh water from entering the bay and

9. Eugene Rosenberg, "Oil eater," *Time*, 21 May 1973, p. 60.

WATER: THE BASIS OF LIFE

prevents tides from washing over marshes. This effectively eliminates 20,000 acres of wetlands and ponds, almost all prime shrimp and fin fish nursery. The Houston ship channel passes through the Bay and up to Houston, the third largest port in the United States. The ship channel and part of the Bay are covered in places to a depth of 2 ft with domestic and industrial solid wastes which make it almost impossible for aquatic organisms to survive. Most species require clean, brackish water and a clean bottom for breeding grounds where eggs are deposited; decaying debris consumes oxygen and may physically smother the eggs. The Bay is still able to support commercial and sport fishing but the production has been reduced. Fishing biologists are worried that pollution and man-made changes in the Bay will cause the Bay's productivity, and thus the fish population in the Gulf of Mexico, to decline still more.

Oceans

The oceans cover 70% of the surface of the earth. They have been regarded as a storehouse of food: fish, whales, and shellfish. As a last resort it was, and is, assumed that man could directly harvest plankton (very small organisms in water which provide the ultimate food base for all of the larger animals in the water) and make nutritious food preparations from them. Now fish species are being overfished, whales are on the verge of extinction, and shellfish are disappearing in many areas because of polluted water, but plankton have proven to be elusive. It costs more in energy to catch them than they provide in the way of food.

OXYGEN IN THE OCEAN   The oceans are vast, complex reservoirs where chemical reactions are constantly occurring. The greatest biological activity takes place in the coastal estuaries where the oceans receive a continual enrichment of minerals and contaminants from land areas.

Everywhere at the surface between air and water, interchanges of material are constantly taking place. The ocean absorbs gases from the atmosphere and returns gases to the atmosphere. Carbon dioxide is one of the gases that the ocean absorbs from the air.

It is generally assumed that the ocean supplies an appreciable amount of oxygen to the atmosphere, but, unless the undecayed or partially decayed organic matter is deposited in the ocean in appreciable amounts, the oxygen produced from photosynthesis is completely consumed by decay processes. Thus, no net gain of oxygen can occur in the water or be transferred to the atmosphere. Bizarre as it may seem, whales and other sea mammals may contribute to increasing the supply of oxygen in the seas. Phytoplankton release oxygen to the ocean when they grow. If they die and fall to the bottom without decaying, that oxygen will represent an increase in the oxygen content of the ocean. If the phytoplankton are eaten by a predator which uses them for growth, the oxygen released by the phytoplankton will not be used. Eventually a whale may eat some predator which has the molecules made by the phytoplankton. If the whale metabolizes the phytoplankton for energy, it uses oxygen of the air for the process. The result is an increase of oxygen in the ocean and a reduction of oxygen in the air. If the whale uses the food for growth, dies, and falls to the bottom without decaying, the oxygen originally produced by the phytoplankton will be a net increase for the ocean.

Conversely, any oxygen-consuming material which is added to the sea will be a net consumer of sea oxygen. The material may be sewage, oil or other organic substances, or even sulfur dioxide. Heavy dumping of such materials may upset the delicate oxygen ecology of the ocean. Once oxygen is reduced to low values, life in that area of the ocean is diminished or destroyed.

DUMPING IN THE OCEAN   The ocean has been used for dumping wastes since prehistoric times. To those who lived near it, it was convenient; it was so large it was incredible that any harm could be done. However, the huge amounts of wastes produced by modern man are overwhelming the ocean in places. Ocean dumping is worldwide. England and Japan pipe low-level radioactive wastes far out to sea. The countries of Northern Europe have barged wastes into areas agreed upon for ocean dumping.

In the United States ocean dumping has increased as industry and population have grown. Between 1964 and 1968, the average yearly amount dumped into the ocean (7.2 million tons) was almost as large as the total dumped in the four years between 1949 and 1953 (8.5 million tons). The total waste dumped between 1964 and 1968 was almost four and a half times that dumped between 1949 and 1953. These figures do not include dredge spoils, military explosives, or radioactive wastes. Both industrial and domestic dumping have increased since 1959, but industrial dumping increased by 114% while domestic dumping increased by 61%.

The EPA has approved 118 sites for ocean dumping. Three sites, off Delaware Bay, Massachusetts, and Los Angeles, are for the disposal of toxic wastes. Certain materials are not allowed to be dumped anywhere in the ocean: radioactive wastes (see Chapter 10); materials containing more than trace amounts of mercury, cadmium, and their compounds; oils; organic compounds similar to the pesticide DDT.

The site off Delaware Bay is typical; it is 6 miles in diameter and 6000 ft deep. Fishing is not allowed there. Fishermen complain that dumping is not confined to the designated site and is spoiling other fishing areas. Sewage sludge from Philadelphia accounts for the largest amount of material, followed by acid wastes from various industries.

For a long time, New York City has dumped its sewage sludge and garbage 20–30 miles out from the harbor in an area called the New York Bight. Investigations have shown that the central site is completely devoid of normal sea life and that fish near the Bight are diseased. Experience at the New York Bight shows that, although no damage was apparent for many years, damage was being done. In a relatively short time the sea life was gone.

In addition to bacterial pollution, heavy metals can contaminate organisms that are used as food. Not only industrial wastes but also sewage sludge contain metals (see page 117). Many shellfish concentrate metals far above the

TABLE 4–2. Trace Metal Enrichment Factors for Shellfish Compared with the Marine Environment.

Element	Oyster	Soft-shelled clam
Cadmium	318,000	800
Chromium	60,000	10,400
Copper	13,000	2,000
Iron	68,000	41,000
Manganese	14,000	3,350
Nickel	14,000	4,250
Lead	14,000	3,400
Zinc	110,000	1,700

Source: B. H. Pringle, et al., Trace metal accumulation by estuarine mollusks, J. Sanit. Eng. Div., Amer. Soc. Civil Eng., 94 (SA 3), June 1968.

concentrations present in water (Table 4–2). For example, the concentration of copper in oysters is 13,000 times the concentration in the water around the oysters. Copper salts are green or blue. Green oysters are an indication of copper ions in water. Copper is an essential element in the biochemistry of oysters. Natural uncontaminated waters contain very little of the essential copper. Consequently, oysters have developed very efficient methods of extracting copper from water and retaining it jealously. Industrial and domestic effluents contain chlorine. The chlorine frees the copper from the soil so that the concentration of copper is higher than that of natural streams. Oysters do not know that copper is now available in relatively large amounts and continue to hoard the ion; thus, green oysters are obtained. Other metals are concentrated by oysters to an even greater degree than copper.

FOOD FROM THE OCEAN The estuaries and the tidal marshes provide the nurseries for sea life. The continental shelves and banks (elevations of the bottom of the ocean where the sea is relatively shallow) provide food for the growth of fish. Some of the most productive areas of the sea are the "fishing banks." Thus, the relatively shallow seas supply the nutrients necessary for the growth of plankton, "the grass of the sea." The production of plankton is declining; the reason is unknown, but efforts are being made to determine the cause.

The deep oceans are biological deserts and cannot be expected to produce an appreciable amount of food. Fish production from various parts of the ocean is given in Table 4–3 which emphasizes the relative sterility of the open ocean and the great productivity of the coastal upwelling areas where nutrients are brought to the surface from cooler nutrient-rich levels. Certainly it is in our enlightened self interest to protect the coastal areas, but these are the very places which we are destroying.

Biological food chains follow a 10:1 ratio for each step. For example, to gain 1 lb a man needs to eat 10 lb of tuna which indirectly needs 1000 lb of plankton

TABLE 4–3. Fish Production from the Ocean

Area	Percentage of ocean area	Area in square kilometers	Annual fish production (metric tons)
Open ocean	90.00	326,000,000	160,000
Coastal zones	9.90	36,000,000	120,000,000
Coastal up-welling areas	0.10	360,000	220,000,000
Total annual fish production			240,160,000
Annual fish production available for sustained yield			100,000,000

Source: From "Open sea vs. coastal zones," *Saturday Review,* 4 April 1970, p. 64. With permission of *Saturday Review/World.*

(Figure 4–21). Tests have shown that in some places the ocean may produce 4000 tons of plankton per square mile in a year. If 100% biological efficiency is assumed, each square mile of the most productive ocean can produce 4 tons of tuna each year. However, such high efficiency of use and fishing is unlikely and tuna has competitors for the available food, so the actual catch would be much less than 4 tons. A square mile of land could produce about 2 tons in the arid high plains and about 10 times that amount on very fertile land.

Figure 4–21. Quantity relationships in a food chain.

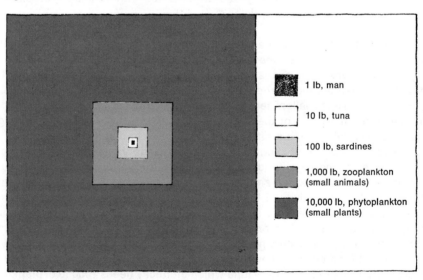

1 lb, man

10 lb, tuna

100 lb, sardines

1,000 lb, zooplankton (small animals)

10,000 lb, phytoplankton (small plants)

If fish are caught or die naturally at the same rate that fish are hatched each year, the sustained yield is harvested. Many fish species are overfished. Haddock stocks, once the mainstay of the Massachusetts fishing industry, have been declared a resource disaster. Herring and yellow tail flounder are on the verge of commercial extinction. Cod, mackerel, and lobsters are threatened. On the Pacific Coast hake and pollack, once considered worthless, are being fished in huge amounts. The catch of these scrap fish was previously made into protein meal, but now hake is being used for the table.

Various techniques have been developed to increase the fish catch. If the mesh of the fish nets is reduced from 3 in. to 1 in., small and immature fish are caught, but fish size makes little difference if it is to be converted into fish meal. However, the removal of small fish will lead to an early destruction of the fishery. Another technique is the location of fish by airplanes or electronic devices. The fish can be driven or attracted into nets by sound or light. Electric currents can drive fish toward the nets. Fishermen of the United States are not allowed to use these sophisticated techniques.

Fisheries are declining for a number of reasons. It is pertinent to consider fisheries by analogy with the extinction of the blue whale.

If the blue whale had been kept at the optimum level of around 60,000 individuals, they could have supplied mankind with a sustainable yield of some 6000 blue whales a year . . . The story of modern whaling is a tale of . . . miscalculation, short-sightedness, and disregard for scientific evidence. It should have been comparatively easy to control the cropping of whales and to have implemented a plan that would have ensured the continuance of this important source of protein.[10]

The tragedy of the blue whale is the reflection of an even greater one, that of man himself. What is the nature of a species that knowingly and without good reason exterminates another?[11]

Each nation sets its own rule for control of its fishing. Whaling is controlled by the International Whaling Commission whose members are the whaling nations. Until recently, the Commission voted down every attempt to limit whaling.

At the 1974 meeting of the International Whaling Commission, the members voted to place an automatic ban on the killing of any whale species whose population falls below an optimum level, which would be established by the Commission's scientific committee. Under this system, fin whales in the North Pacific and sei whales in certain areas would be totally protected. Whether Russia and Japan—the two nations that catch the most whales—will be bound by the limits is another question. Both of these countries voted against the automatic ban and both have said in the past that they would not follow any decisions they did not consider reasonable.

10. Arthur Bourne, book review of *The blue whale* by George Small, New York: Columbia University, 1971, in *Nature* 235: 404, 18 Feb. 1972.
11. George Small, *The blue whale,* New York: Columbia University, 1972, p. 213.

The International underwater expert Jacques Yves Cousteau, speaking at the International Conference on Ocean Pollution on 18 October, 1971 said that, unless drastic measures are taken immediately, ocean life will be gone in 30, 40, or 50 years and that will be the end of everything. During 30 years of diving he has seen the gradual death of hundreds of species of marine life. He said that some scientists are already saying it is too late, but he thinks that drastic programs can save the ocean and the world. He recommended stringent national and international laws to prohibit dumping of any toxic product anywhere. All such products must be kept within the manufacturing plant.

KEY CONCEPTS

1. How water dissolves polar substances.
2. Build-up of salts in irrigation water and the effect on vegetation.
3. Advantages and disadvantages of deep-well disposal of toxic wastes.
4. The action of pyrites when exposed to air and water.
5. Conventional treatment of waste water by a sewage plant.
6. Advantages and disadvantages of sewage farming.
7. Action of soap, water softener, and syndets.
8. Conventional treatment of domestic water.
9. Advantages and disadvantages of exotic sources of water.
10. Cause of oil spills, effect of oil spills, and methods of cleanup.
11. Importance of estuaries.
12. Source of oxygen in the ocean.
13. Effect of using the ocean as a dump.
14. The oceans as a source of food.

QUESTIONS

1. What impurities are apt to be present in ground water and in rainwater?
2. There are bacteria in the digestive systems of all healthy persons. Why is water labeled "polluted" if it contains digestive bacteria?
3. "Water purifies itself by running two miles from the source of incoming waste" is a folk saying. What types of pollutants will be removed from the running water? How will they be removed? What types will not be affected?
4. At what point should pollutants be removed from a body of water? Who should pay for the removal? Does the source of the pollutants affect the decision of who should pay?
5. What level of purity is desirable in a body of water?
6. Some people have recommended dumping sewage in the ocean to produce large numbers of edible fish. Comment for and against this recommendation.
7. Ground water is used for irrigation in Western Nebraska. Comment on the environmental implications.
8. Why not breed crops to limit evapotranspiration?
9. It has been suggested that all forests be removed and the water collected and stored for use. Comment for and against this suggestion.

10. What should be done with municipal sewage sludge? Explain your answer.
11. Assess the potentialities of atomic desalinization nuplexes as suggested by Alvin Weinberg. (Ignore any questions about the advisability of nuclear energy as such at this time.)
12. Along a river, how would you decide who gets the water? Several states are fighting over the use of the Colorado River water. (An example is the desire of Las Vegas for water from a lake that the Pago-Pago Indians feel belongs to them.)

1. Borgstrom, G., *Too many,* New York: Macmillan, 1969.
2. Carr, D. E., *Death of sweet waters*, New York: Beckley Publishing Corp., 1971.
3. Carson, R., *The sea around us*, New York: New American Library, 1961.
4. Cousteau, J., *Oasis in space*, New York: World Publishing Co., 1972.
5. Marx, W., *Oil spill*, San Francisco: Sierra Club, 1971.
6. Marx, W., *The frail ocean*, New York: Coward, McCann, Geohegan, 1967.
7. McLusky, D. S., *Ecology of estuaries*, New York: Hillary House, 1972.
8. Potter, J., *Disaster by oil*, New York: Macmillan, 1973.
9. Small, G. L., *The blue whale*, New York: Columbia University, 1971.

5 Land: The Human Habitat

The earth is our mother.

Iroquois Indian saying

The land as we know it is the result of physical and chemical changes which took place in the past and which are still taking place. In the past, the changes formed the deposits of minerals which are mined today and built the soil which grows food and fiber. Today, chemical changes within the soil make agriculture possible. Chemical reactions in industry make modern farming feasible. Thus, past and present chemical reactions are important for the survival of the human species.

Most of the earth is covered with soil which varies widely in composition from place to place. The soils of the western United States are very different from the soils of the eastern United States. Soils also vary locally although the differences are not so great. Even one part of a field may be more fertile than another. Scattered over the earth are concentrations of minerals which are the basis of mining and industry. Both the formation of soil and concentration of minerals are the result of the changes which occurred over a period of billions of years.

Transformation of Rock

Billions of years ago the outer surface of the earth began to congeal. As the molten mass cooled, the substances with higher melting points tended to separate out of the molten mass as pure crystals of that substance. The resulting basalt or obsidian rock is very fine grained, has a glassy appearance, and is very resistant to the erosive action of water. If the molten rock cooled slowly, the substances with high melting points migrated out of the viscous solution to form large crystals of the various components in the parent *magma* (molten rock). Mineral deposits may be formed in this way. Transparent to translucent quartz crystals (SiO_2) of coarse-grained granite rock were also formed by the slow-cooling rock. Quartz crystals are surrounded by substances called feldspars and micas which are softer and more easily soluble in acid and water. Although granite is more durable than most rocks, it does disintegrate at a faster rate than the glassy basalts. The more soluble materials were removed from around the quartz crystals which became grains of sand (SiO_2, silica). The softer parts of the granite, the feldspars and micas, yielded the finely divided particles which eventually were deposited as shale or clay.

Rock debris from high areas washed into the streams and was carried to the sea by the flowing water. When the streams reached the tranquil waters of the oceans, they slowed their pace and dropped their load in graded sizes and densities. The sorting process was similar to chromatography (see Chapter 2). Sands collected in one area and clays in another. Mineral matter was also concentrated into ores. Sea organisms intermingled their remains with the river effluent material. Eventually the sediments consolidated under large pressures to form sedimentary rocks. During certain periods, sea organisms provided the major contribution of material to the deepening sediments and often formed massive deposits (500 ft or more deep) of limestone ($CaCO_3$), dolomite ($MgCO_3CaCO_3$), and chalk ($CaCO_3$). Later, ocean deposits were lifted above sea level and again were subjected to erosion and the formation of new rocks under the ocean. The lifting process bent and twisted the sedimentary rocks. The erosion and lifting process was repeated many times. Thus, the great variations in deposition guarantee that even the basic minerals would differ in different soils.

Algae and fungi are primitive plants which were and are important in the production of soil particles from massive rock. Both organisms respire to produce CO_2 and organic acids which speed the dissolution of the rock surface, the release of nutrient minerals, and the formation of soil colloids. When enough soil is formed, higher plants may take root in the soil. Their roots extract minerals and water from the soil and supply these to the parts of the plant above ground. The roots respire to produce acid-forming carbon dioxide and other acids and dissolve minerals which are supplied to other parts of the plant. The photosynthetic (i.e., light-absorbing) part of the plant uses the minerals, CO_2, and H_2O to manufacture food which is supplied to the roots.

Humus   Humus, the crumbly black material in the upper layer of soil, is the result of the action of microorganisms on dead plant and/or animal matter. The microorganisms obtain a food supply for themselves and at the same time free the contained minerals for use by by other organisms.

The fresh vegetable residue which eventually becomes humus decomposes rapidly in the early stages of decay. Two-thirds of fresh rye grass debris is decomposed in a period of six months. Thereafter, it decomposes at a rate such that one half is consumed in four years, i.e., a *half-life* of four years. During each subsequent four-year period half of the remainder will be consumed. Thus, at the end of eight years, one quarter will remain, at the end of twelve years, one-eighth will remain, and at the end of sixteen years, one-sixteenth will still be present. The black residue is particularly difficult to decompose. This material has a half-life of 25 years and thus is an exhaustible component unless continuously replenished by fresh inputs of organic matter.

In the process of decay the carbon of the debris is largely changed to CO_2 and water; the nitrogen-containing materials are rearranged and incorporated into the bodies of the fungi and bacteria. A portion of the nitrogen is converted to nitrate or ammonium ions which are the forms of nitrogen which can be used by the higher plants. Depending upon soil conditions, some of the nitrogen may also be converted to NO_2^- and thence to N_2 gas which returns to the air (Figure 5–1).

The number of different microorganisms found in humus is huge, and their relationship is complex and little understood. The number of compounds is also large and little understood. An idea of the complexity may be seen in the following molecule, which is only suggestive. Actual molecules may be many times as large as the one shown.[1]

Several groups of atoms in the molecule are especially important (the groups are shown in boxes on the molecule).

1. L. M. Thompson and F. R. Troeh, *Soils and fertility,* New York: McGraw Hill, 1973, p. 125.

LAND: THE HUMAN HABITAT

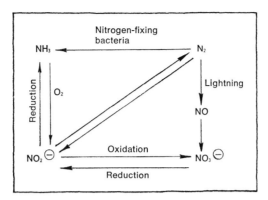

Figure 5–1. Nitrogen cycle in the soil.

1. Acid groups, COOH: the hydrogen can be removed leaving a negative site which can attract any positive ion, that is, it can store positive ions such as K^+, Ca^{2+}, or Mg^{2+} for later use by a plant.

2. Phenol group (a benzene ring with an OH group on one carbon): the hydrogen may be removed by ionization but less easily than the hydrogen from an acid group. Again, a storage site for a positive ion becomes available.

3. An amine group, NH_2: when the nitrogen atom is combined with three other atoms (the two hydrogen atoms and a carbon of the molecule), it has a pair of electrons which can attract a positive particle (see Chapter 2). Thus the amine group may act as a storage site for positive ions. However, if the pair of electrons attracts a hydrogen ion, the site will become positive and act as a storage site for negative ions.

Ion Exchange

Plants obtain the required metal ions from the soil through ion exchange processes (see p. 121). Colloids on the surface of the roots are in contact with soil and humus colloids so that exchange of materials is simple. By the process of respiration, the plant root uses oxygen and produces carbon dioxide which collects inside the root as hydrogen and bicarbonate ions. The hydrogen ions are exchanged for relatively large amounts of Ca^{2+}, Mg^{2+}, K^+, and NH_4^+ as well as for small quantities of the "micronutrients" Cu^{2+}, Na^+, Zn^{2+}, Mn^{2+}, and several other substances which are needed by plants. If the exchange of hydrogen ions for metallic ions is continued for long enough, the supply of metal ions will become depleted, the soil will become acidic, and the plants will grow poorly. The small hydrogen ions do not fit the sites as well as the metallic ions and the structure of both the soil colloids and humus may be destroyed.

Although both the soil and humus colloids have storage sites for ions, humus is able to store two to ten times as many ions for a given weight of material. Most of these sites are negative, that is, they store only positive ions. Negative ions (Cl^-, NO_3^-, and SO_4^{2-}) are found in soil solution where they are easily washed away.

Phosphates (usually $H_2PO_4^-$ and HPO_4^{2-}) are ions needed in large amounts by plants, but, if aluminum or iron ions are present, they bond so tightly to the phosphate ions that these essential ions are not available to plants. The addition of a chelating agent (see p. 113) frees the phosphate by binding iron and aluminum ions. Phosphates are also released by the chelating action of certain organic acids such as oxalic, malonic, and tartaric acids which are formed during decay of organic matter in the soil.

$$
\begin{array}{ccc}
& & \text{COOH} \\
& & | \\
& \text{COOH} & \text{H—C—OH} \\
& | & | \\
\text{COOH} & \text{CH}_2 & \text{H—C—OH} \\
| & | & | \\
\text{COOH} & \text{COOH} & \text{COOH} \\
\text{oxalic acid} & \text{malonic acid} & \text{tartaric acid}
\end{array}
$$

Each of these substances is capable of enclosing a metal ion in a five- or six-member ring in a manner similar to EDTA.

A chelating agent can also make a positive ion available by chelating it and carrying it into the plant structure. For example, iron is not available in alkaline soils even if present in huge amounts and the addition of iron does not prevent deficiency symptoms. However, adding iron and a chelating agent is usually successful. In one case the addition of 10–50 g of iron per tree in the form of FeEDTA complex was more effective than adding 1000 kg of iron sulfate per tree. *Legumes* (plants whose roots have colonies of bacteria which change atmospheric nitrogen into a form usable by the plant) secrete chelating agents which form complexes with insoluble iron, thus making it available to themselves and nearby plants.

Effect of pH   Although plants grow best on soils which are nearly neutral, that is, near a pH of 7, the pH of most cultivated soils varies from 4 to 8. That the pH can affect the availability of ions is shown by the behavior of phosphoric acid (H_3PO_4):

LAND: THE HUMAN HABITAT

$$H_3PO_4 + HOH \leftrightharpoons H_2PO_4^- + H_{(aq)}^+$$

$$H_2PO_4^- + HOH \leftrightharpoons HPO_4^{2-} + H_{(aq)}^+$$

$$HPO_4^{2-} + HOH \leftrightharpoons PO_4^{3-} + H_{(aq)}^+$$

Thus, phosphoric acid is present as four entities: H_3PO_4, $H_2PO_4^-$, HPO_4^{2-}, and PO_4^{3-}. The H_3PO_4 form is always present, although in very small amounts at high pH. Below a pH of 6.7, $H_2PO_4^-$ is the dominate entity. Above a pH of 6.7, HPO_4^{2-} is more important. Above a pH of 9.0, the PO_4^{3-} ion becomes more prevalent but it never reaches a concentration equal to that of HPO_4^{2-}. From this, it is apparent that any reactions involving the essential element phosphorus are highly dependent upon the pH of the soil.

If the pH is much higher than 8, the soil is alkaline with sodium and/or potassium ions attached to the colloid particles. If excess sodium ions are present, the soil is saline. If the excess sodium ions are in the form of Na_2CO_3 (strongly basic), the humus particles become highly ionized and soluble in water. Evaporation of the soil water will precipitate both the white Na_2CO_3 and the black humus particles. The resulting formation is called "black alkali." If the excess sodium ions are in the form of sodium sulfate, the sulfate ion is not as strongly basic and will not attract the positive ions from the humus. When this type of soil dries, the resulting crystals will be white, thus, the term "white alkali."

LAND FOR FOOD

Soil provides the chemical materials required for the production of food; thus soil is essential for the production of food. Is there enough soil to produce food to feed the populations of the United States and the world? What is being done today to increase the food supply? What can be done in the future? There are no simple answers, but there is much controversy.

The battle to feed humanity is over. Unlike the battles of military forces, it is possible to know the results of the population-food conflict while the armies are still "in the field." Sometime between 1970 and 1985 the world will undergo vast famines—hundreds of millions of people are going to starve to death.[2]

Paul Ehrlich

Instead of fearing a world perishing from hunger, we should be on our guard against the opposite danger, of farmers producing surpluses which cannot be sold while people are dying from overeating.[3]

Collin Clark

How Much Food is Needed?

It is difficult to determine the exact amount of food needed by the world's population and the amount that is available. The requirement for protein de-

2. *New Scientist,* 14 December 1967.
3. *Daily Telegraph,* 11 December 1967.

pends upon the size of the individual, while the total requirement for food depends upon the size and activity of the individual. An average consumption is meaningless because many people are consuming far less than the average.

Nutritionists of the World Health Organization (WHO) and the Food and Agriculture Organization (FAO) give general estimates which show that there is enough food in the world to give everyone a barely adequate diet if the food were to be divided evenly. The estimates also show that one third of the world population receives too little food and one half receives too little protein. In any case, there are countries such as India where a large number of people do not get enough to eat and other countries such as the United States where a relatively small number of people do not have enough to eat.

How Much Land is Needed? The amount of land needed to support one person depends on many variables —the fertility of the land, the length of the growing season, the climate, and the type of food the individual desires. On the very best agricultural land, such as some in California, one quarter of an acre may be enough to produce food for one person, while in arid Montana one cow requires 160 acres for pasture. More than one cow would be necessary to supply food for a person for a year. Overall, 2 acres per person may be a reasonable average.

A DENSE POPULATION   The Netherlands, with about 950 people per square mile, is often acclaimed as a model of how a dense population can successfully support itself on a small area. The country has about 0.6 acres of all land per person but only about 0.18 acres of actual tilled land per person. On this, the Netherlands produces about one-quarter of its food supply; of the remainder about 39% comes from the sea and 37% from trade. Other densely populated developed countries follow the same pattern.

The Netherlands imports about 170 lb of two types of protein per person per year: (1) oil-seed cakes (material left after oil is extracted from seeds) and seeds, and (2) fishmeal. Seeds and oil-seed cakes are especially important as protein supplements for animal feeds. Europe imports much of the seeds which enter world trade: peanuts, 70.2%; sunflower seeds, 54.3%; soybeans, 53.3%. The protein from fishmeal is obtained at the expense of other countries. Much of the fish caught off the coast of South America is exported, two-thirds to Europe and most of the remainder to the United States. If all of the South American fish protein were consumed in South America instead of being used to feed animals in the developed countries, it could raise the dietary level of the entire continent to a minimum desirable level.

The United States imports large amounts of animal protein. Most of it comes from undeveloped countries. On the other hand, it exports large amounts of plant protein, primarily soybeans, to other developed countries. Overall, the United States is a net exporter of protein.

UNITED STATES   The United States, with between 2200 and 2300 million acres of land, has enough land to feed its people easily. One-third of these 2200–2300 million acres is federal land such as forests, parks, and military reservations. The remaining two-thirds is the land we live on and which furnishes the lumber, food, and fiber for our civilization.

If everyone had an equal share of the total area of land in the United States, every person would have about 11 acres. Of the 11 acres, about 3.7 acres are federal land, about 0.3 acres is nonfederal public land, and another 0.3 acres is urban land. Of the remaining 7 acres, only about 2.0 acres is suitable for cultivation of food and fiber. About another 2 acres is forested and another 2.3 acres is suitable for pasture and range.

Both the quality and quantity of land available for food production is declining. Sixty-four per cent of the nation's cropland needs conservation treatment (Figure 5–2). Of the 2.7 acres which are available to each person, 1.7 acres needs treatment. If the cropland is irrigated land, 71% needs treatment. Of the 2.3 acres of range and pasture land 1.5 acres needs treatment (Data obtained from the Soil Conservation Service.) In addition huge amounts of topsoil are washed down the rivers every day. The Mississippi River system alone carries about one-quarter of a million tons of silt each day. Not all of the silt carried by the rivers is from land which produces food, but much of the loss is due to poor farming practices.

Not only is land deteriorating in the United States but also all over the world. Table 5–1 shows the deterioration between 1882 and 1952. Not only is the quality of the country's crop land deteriorating, but the amount available for food production is also decreasing. Every year about two million acres of arable land are lost to the building of houses and highways, to industries, to mining, or because irrigated land has become too salty to grow crops. Some of the loss is compensated by the recovery of about one million acres by irrigating new areas of arid soil. One million acres loss per year does not seem like a large

Figure 5–2. Cropland needing conservation treatment (shaded area).

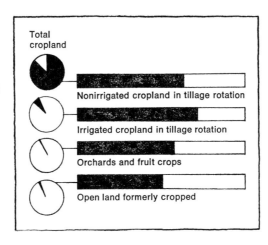

LAND FOR FOOD

TABLE 5-1. Quality Classification of Tilled Land.

	1882 (%)	*1952* (%)
Good	85.0	41.2
Half of original humus lost	9.9	38.2
Marginal soils	5.1	20.3

Source: Robert R. Doane, *World balance sheet,* New York: Harper & Row, 1957, p. 24.

percentage of the nation's cropland. However, much of the land lost is the best in the nation.

When cities were established, they were located on good, fertile land, usually on a river and/or coastal location. The water provided transportation facilities and the surrounding fertile land supplied food for the support of the local urban population. Once established, the area continued to grow. The process is usually irreversible. This relationship of food production and cities is apparent throughout the United States and the world. The growth of cities has been accompanied by the growth of the highway. Each has contributed to the growth of the other. Roads use large amounts of land. There is an average of one mile of road for every square mile of land area. Each mile of freeway uses 24–36 acres of land with 80 acres required for each interchange.

Methods of Increasing Food Production

Modern agriculture, especially since 1950, has tried to increase production on less land by the use of chemicals and by selection and development of improved seeds. The result has been a phenomenal increase in the variety and amount of food available in the United States. However, such abundance has been purchased at an environmental price. The use of huge quantities of agricultural chemicals has disrupted the ecosystem.

FERTILIZER   Ion exchange removes huge amounts of inorganic substances from the soil. For example, four tons of alfalfa may be cut from a fertile field each year. In order to produce this alfalfa, two tons of rock must be weathered to soil. The alfalfa does not use the entire two tons, of course, but the minerals from the two tons of rock are needed—Ca, S, P, Mg, and K (Table 5–2). Some of the minerals are replaced by *fertilizer,* usually as a mixture of water-soluble compounds of potassium, phosphorus, and nitrogen. Small amounts of other essential elements such as B, Zn, Cu, and Fe may be added.

Fertilizer use has grown steadily since 1950 but the increase has been even more rapid since the mid-1960s (Figure 5–3). Interestingly, phosphates were the most important fertilizing element until about 1960 when the use of nitrogen as a fertilizer began to increase. At present nitrogen fertilizer amounts to more than half the fertilizer used on crops.

The importance of the commercial production of fertilizer as an industry is indicated by the quantity of important industrial chemicals used to produce fertilizer. The two substances produced in the largest amounts in the United

LAND: THE HUMAN HABITAT

TABLE 5–2. Rock Needed to Produce Minerals Required for Four Tons of Alfalfa.

Type of rock	Amount needed (lb)
Raw phosphate rock (Ca + P)	148
Gypsum (S + Ca)	134
Dolomite (Mg + Ca)	118
Limestone (Ca)	30
Granite (K)	4000
Total	4430 lb of Agstone

Source: Robert C. Brasted, "Broiled rocks with a side order of baked minerals—the blue plate special," *J. Chem. Ed.*, 48: 456, July 1971.

States are sulfuric acid and ammonia. Slightly more than 50% of the sulfuric acid production and over 70% of the ammonia production goes into fertilizer.

Nitrogen Nitrogen is added to the soil by the use of such nitrogen compounds as ammonium sulfate [$(NH_4)_2SO_4$], ammonium nitrate (NH_4NO_3), urea

$$\underset{\displaystyle H_2—N—C—N—H_2}{\overset{\displaystyle \overset{O}{\|}}{}}$$

and ammonia gas (NH_3) or the gas dissolved in water (NH_4OH). The solid forms are mixed with other materials and sold as bagged or bulk fertilizers. The ammonia solution is injected directly into the soil where it is held by humus and soil colloids.

Commercial nitrogen fertilizers are largely produced from ammonia. The process to produce ammonia was developed in 1910 by a German, Fritz Haber, and named after him. The *Haber process* freed Germany from dependence upon imported $NaNO_3$ found naturally in Chile. As a result, Germany was able to make explosives for World War I,

Figure 5–3. Fertilizer use in the United States. From Norman L. Hargett, *1972 Fertilizer Summary Data*, Tennessee Valley Authority, 1972, p. 14.

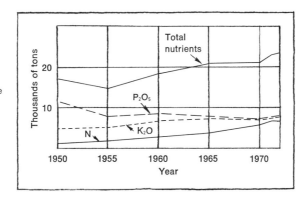

Ammonia is produced from the gases nitrogen and hydrogen at high pressure and high temperature:

$$N_2 + 3H_2 \xrightarrow[\text{catalyst}]{450-600\,°C} 2NH_3 + \text{heat}$$

The synthesis is conducted under pressures of 300–1000 atmospheres (atm) (4500–15000 lb per square inch). Normal air pressure is about 1 atm.

The equation for the production of ammonia shows that heat is evolved when nitrogen reacts with hydrogen to form ammonia. It would seem then that the valuable ammonia fertilizer could be produced and that the energy evolved could serve a useful purpose. However, large amounts of energy are required to operate the plants and to supply the raw materials, hydrogen and nitrogen.

At present, hydrogen is obtained principally from the high-temperature decomposition of natural gas:

$$CH_4 \xrightarrow{\text{heat}} C + 2H_2$$

or

$$CH_4 + H_2O \xrightarrow{\text{heat}} CO + 3H_2$$

If natural gas becomes scarce, a change may be needed in the source of hydrogen. Alternatively, hydrogen can be produced from coal and water according to the equation:

$$C\ (\text{coal}) + H_2O \xrightarrow{\text{heat}} CO + H_2$$

In all of these methods energy is needed for the production of hydrogen. Pure nitrogen is obtained by fractional distillation of liquified air. The resource base is as large as the atmosphere since 79% of the air is nitrogen. However, the nitrogen is not free. Large amounts of energy are required to compress and cool the air to liquid-air temperature which is less than $-180\,°C$. Large amounts of energy are needed in the manufacture of ammonia itself primarily to obtain the necessary high pressures.

When all energies are considered, nitrogen is found to be an energy-intensive industry; that is, an industry which uses large inputs of energy as opposed to large inputs of labor. In order to produce a pound of nitrogen fertilizer the energy equivalent of a pound of coal is needed.

Phosphorus Phosphate fertilizers are prepared from phosphate rock. Phosphate rock has a varied composition. The phosphate combination is $[Ca_3(PO_4)_2]_3 \cdot CaF_2$ which represents a varying percentage of the rock. It can be used as the rock but is usually reacted with sulfuric acid to produce "superphosphate" according to the following equation:

$$[Ca_3(PO_4)_2]_3 \cdot CaF_2 + 7H_2SO_4 + 17H_2O \rightarrow$$
$$3CaH_4(PO_4)_2 \cdot H_2O + 7CaSO_4 \cdot 2H_2O + 2HF \uparrow$$
$$\text{superphosphate}$$

Superphosphate contains about 16–22% phosphate measured as P_2O_5. If the phosphate rock is reacted with phosphoric acid, an even more concentrated phosphate is formed. The equation is

$$[Ca_3(PO_4)_2]_3 \cdot CaF_2 + 14H_3PO_4 + 10H_2O \rightarrow 10CaH_4(PO_4)_2 \cdot H_2O + 2HF \uparrow$$
$$\text{triple phosphate}$$

Because this substance has a phosphate content of 45–48%, or about three times the phosphate content of superphosphate, it is called "triple phosphate."

The mining and processing of phosphate have caused environmental degradation in mining areas in the southern United States. The gaping holes of the open mines are close to urban districts. Processing produces a slime which must be stored in ponds for years. The volume of the slimes is about 50% greater than the original mineral. A mined-out pit is used for storage with dikes and dams to supply extra volume. Fresh water for processing phosphate may be short in the mining areas, notably North Carolina. Western mines are underground mines with a much higher grade of rock phosphate. The environmental damage is not as severe.

Potassium The United States has limited reserves of potassium, which is especially important to the farmer because 95% of the potassium used in this country is used as fertilizer. The most productive mines have only a 6–10-year supply of high-grade ore. There are lower-grade deposits which can be worked if the price of potassium is increased. More ore must be handled so the cost of mining and refining is greater for a leaner (lower-grade) deposit. A price increase is unlikely in view of the extensive high-grade reserves in Canada. A country is considered deficient in a mineral if it produces less than 50% of its domestic demand. The United States produced around 55% of its potassium demand in 1971 and 1972.

The sea is a possible source of the element. Each cubic mile of ocean contains about 1.5 million tons, but current costs for exploitation are several times the 1972 world price. Recovery of this potassium would require large inputs of energy.

It is interesting to note that the United States used about 33 lb of potassium fertilizer per capita in 1968. The world per capita use was only about 5.8 lb. If the entire world used fertilizer at the same per capita rate as the United States, 577 million tons of potassium fertilizer would have been consumed in 1968 and the worldwide cumulative use to the end of the century would amount to 30 billion tons. Even the large terrestial reserves could not fill such a huge demand.

Other fertilizing elements Calcium, magnesium, and sulfur are considered secondary fertilizer nutrients. Additions of Ca^{2+} as lime ($CaCO_3$) and sometimes Ca^{2+} and Mg^{2+} as dolomite ($MgCO_3CaCO_3$) are made to soil to increase the pH. Sulfur is usually present in soil in sufficient quantities to supply growing plants. All superphosphate contains sulfur or it may be added as ammonium sulfate [$(NH_4)_2SO_4$].

Essential nutrients needed in very small quantities are called *micronutrients.* The most important and the most often needed nutrient is Zn^{2+}. Next are boron, iron, manganese, molybdenum, and copper. Some micronutrients are toxic if present in excessive quantities. For example, 0.5 ppm of boron in soil is adequate, but four times that amount (2 ppm) is lethal to a few species. The level needed for toxic symptoms to appear is dependent upon the pH of the soil.

Organic fertilizer vs. mineral fertilizer   There is no disagreement about the necessity of returning to the soil the nutrients which are removed by harvesting the crops. However, not all farmers and gardeners think that using mineral fertilizer is the best method to return the needed nutrients. A small but vocal group believes that all fertilizers should be materials which can be found in the natural state.

Ammonia fertilizers can be changed to nitrites by soil bacteria:

$$2NH_3 + 2O_2 \rightarrow 2H^+ + 2NO_2^- + 2H_2O$$

The nitrite ion is immediately oxidized to the nitrate ion:

$$2NO_2^- + O_2 \rightarrow 2NO_3^-$$

Nitrogen in the form of nitrates, whether applied as nitrate fertilizer or the result of oxidation of the ammonia ion, readily washes off the field and contaminates ground water. A second disadvantage is that the availability of fertilizer is at a peak when it is applied and decreases with time. The plants need the nitrogen most when the weather is hot and the plant growing fastest. A third disadvantage is that experiments have shown that the addition of large quantities of nitrogen fertilizers to certain soils has been followed by a decline in nitrogen-fixing bacteria in the soil.

Fertilizer manufacturers agree that the use of nitrogen compounds does have the difficulties claimed, but they think that they are countering these difficulties. By adding a coating to granules of fertilizer, the fertilizer will be released slowly over the growing season. The manufacturers do not consider the decline in soil bacteria serious; in fact, substances are added to inhibit the bacteria which change ammonia ions to nitrite ions.

Organic farmers believe that nitrogen can best be applied as organic matter which will decay into humus and by planting legumes with their colonies of bacteria which *fix* nitrogen, that is, change atmospheric bacteria into a form usable by the plant. The nitrogen cannot wash off the field and it will be available when the plants need it most.

Organic farmers prefer pulverized rock and organic material such as activated sewage sludge instead of phosphate and potassium fertilizers. They claim that the addition of large amounts of salts upsets the soil life and interferes with the plant's utilization of other essential ions. A recent study indicates that their contention might be true, at least for one type of soil. Several groups of investigators have found that the addition of large amounts of phosphate to the soil decreased the levels of zinc in various parts of the plant. Whether the same situation is true for other soils needs to be determined.

Phosphate salts are tightly bound by aluminum and iron ions, so additional fertilizer must be added each crop year. Organic farmers believe that the yearly addition of huge amounts of fertilizer is unwise because phosphates are a limited resource. Estimates of the lifetime of the resource vary, but most sources give 60–70 years.

Little scientific work has been done to determine the comparative merits of "organic farming" and "chemical farming." Both laboratory and field research is badly needed if decisions are to be made on the basis of information and not feelings or hunches. We may well agree with Dr. Karl Schulze of Michigan State University that the natural vs. chemical fertilizer argument is futile. He said (at the National Conference on Composting-Waste Recycling in Denver, May 20, 1971) that the real essential is humus, a "resource without which it will not be possible in the future to keep the productivity of the soil."

INSECTICIDES

The conclusion that one reaches is that pesticides logically are a basically unsound method of control. At best they should be considered as a stop-gap until sounder methods can be found and should be, as soon as possible, relegated to a secondary role. These considerations apply to all types of pesticides, persistent and non-persistent.[4]

Dr. David D. Peakall

The tragedy is that DDT, while it probably did kill a few birds and fish, never harmed a single human being except by accidental misuse. When the ultimate report is written, it may show that the opponents of DDT—despite the best of intentions—contributed to the deaths of more human beings than did all of the natural disasters in history.[5]

Thomas R. Shephard, Jr.

Pesticides and insecticides are often confused. A *pesticide* is a general term referring to any substance used to destroy plants or animals. *Insecticides* are those substances used to kill insects. *Herbicides* are those substances used to kill plants.

Plants produce their own food and the food for all other life, including insects and man who compete for plant products. Ideally in nature, plants, insects, and insect predators exist in an ecological balance, a steady state.

For thousands of years various mechanisms have held each biological factor in check. Mixed stands of plants force the herbivorous insect to seek out its host and thus reduce the chances of a plant being destroyed before completing

---

4. Senior Research Associate, Section of Ecology and Systematics, Division of Biological Control, Cornell University.
5. Thomas R. Shephard, Jr., "The case against the 'disaster lobby'," *Living Wilderness*, Summer 1971, p. 28.

its cycle of growth. Natural predators, insects, birds, snakes, and toads, help to control the number of herbivore insects so that there will be sufficient food for both the herbivores and the predators. The predators may consume the herbivores directly, they may parasitize the insect in the egg or the larval stage, or they may lay eggs which destroy the herbivore later. At no stage must one element, plant, herbivore, or predator, be too successful in destroying its food supply. Conversely, enough of each element of the system must be destroyed so that the numbers are controlled. The predator must consume enough, but not too much, of the herbivore. If a sufficient number of predators are not available the herbivores may increase without bound, destroy the plant growth, and prevent the plants from reproducing to supply the herbivores with food in later times. On the other hand, if the predators are too numerous and efficient, the herbivore population may be reduced to the point that future food for the predator disappears and the predator population declines.

Even without interference by man the steady state can be upset. A change of climate, whether temporary or permanent, would change the kinds of plants available for the herbivores. This in turn would change the relationship of predators and herbivores. Eventually, if conditions were stable, a new steady state would be evolved.

Man's interference with nature's pattern disrupts the steady state. He plants large areas of the same crop (monoculture). Through carelessness and accident many pests have been introduced into areas where they have no natural controls. For example, the gypsy moth was introduced into Massachusetts in 1869 to investigate the possibility of using it for silk production. It escaped when a wind blew the covering off a bush where it was feeding. Since then it has spread along the Atlantic seaboard and into the mountains of Pennsylvania. Man is not interested in maintaining the natural balance. He tries to tip the balance of the plant-insect-predator system in his favor by using: (1) biological controls, (2) chemical controls, and (3) integrated controls.

Biological controls Organic farmers refuse to use chemical substances to control insects. They prefer to use nature's methods to reduce insect damage. However, they do not believe in *no* controls. They raise or purchase ladybugs, praying mantis, lacewings, and parasitic wasps, and release them in large numbers to control crop-destroying insects (Figure 5–4). Bacteria and viruses may be sprayed on an infested area. The milky spore disease can be used to control the Japanese beetle.

Farming practices may help to control insect pests. Crop rotation will reduce losses due to soil pests and diseases. Planting dates may be shifted to prevent the crop being susceptible at the time the insect is present; for example, wheat-planting dates are chosen to avoid the Hessian fly. Insect damage tends to be less on fertile soil. Mixed plantings may be practiced instead of monoculture. Small fields of different crops may be grown or crops may be grown on alternate strips in the same field. When alfalfa strips are grown in cotton fields, lygus bugs eat the alfalfa instead of the cotton.

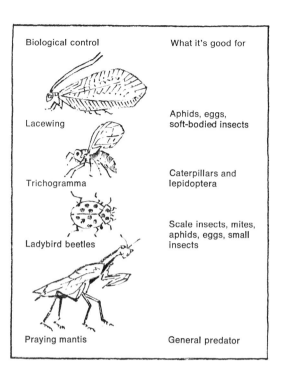

Biological control	What it's good for
Lacewing	Aphids, eggs, soft-bodied insects
Trichogramma	Caterpillars and lepidoptera
Ladybird beetles	Scale insects, mites, aphids, eggs, small insects
Praying mantis	General predator

Figure 5-4. Biological controls for insects. Adapted from *Organic Gardening and Farming*, February 1974, p. 84.

Insects find their mates by odor, somewhat after the fashion of the use of perfume. Scientists have been able to isolate the sex attractant of some insects, determine its formula, and synthesize it. The odor attracts one of the sexes and by trapping these, fertile matings may be prevented. If there are no fertile eggs, there will be no bugs.

Radiation treatment of insects makes them sterile. Large numbers of sterile males are released in the control area to "flood the market." The sterile insects show no loss of interest in sex and are able to convince the opposite sex that it is the real thing. Again there are no fertile eggs and hence no bugs.

Finally, rotenone, a pesticide from natural sources, is used when other biological controls fail.

Chemical controls Natural controls do not always work, or at least not as well as the farmer would like. Chemical controls seem easier to use. Even with no apparent damage, if insects are visible they seem to endanger plants. For these and other reasons, chemical methods have long been used.

The insecticide DDT is a good example of the problems which surround the discovery and use of an insecticide. DDT is an abbreviation for the word *di-chlorodiphenyltrichloroethane* which describes the structure of the substance.

DDT was synthesized in Germany in 1892, but its insecticidal properties were not discovered until the early 1940's. It is persistent, nonspecific, and, initially, very potent. During World War II its use allowed the Allies to attack Rome from the south across malaria-infested swamps. Later it prevented the usual post-war epidemics in Europe.

DDT was so successful at killing insects during the war that it was hoped that agricultural pests could be completely eliminated by its use. However, in a few years disadvantages began to appear. Larger quantities and more applications were necessary to control insects. A few insects had developed an enzyme (a substance which functions as a catalyst in living systems) to convert DDT to a less active form, for example

DDE is one of several routes by which DDT can be metabolized. DDE is persistent but not as potent an insecticide as DDT. Another degradation product of DDT is DDD. It is persistent but not as biologically active as DDT although more active than DDE.

DDT is a broad-spectrum or nonspecific insecticide, that is, it kills a wide range of insects including both predators and herbivores. With the biological controls gone, the surviving species multiply rapidly. The survival of insects after exposure to an insecticide is called the development of *resistance*. Within a few years flies were found that were resistant to DDT. Not all species are affected by DDT. With the predators gone a species which had been a minor pest could become a serious pest.

The persistence of DDT is a help to the farmer because he will need to spray less often, but it also means that it and its degradation products will build up in waterways and the soil. There is some concern that DDT may affect the ability of plankton to carry out photosynthesis. The critical level for observable effects is about 1 ppm. The present level in the ocean is about 0.7 ppm. Phytoplankton is the grass of the sea. If plankton does not grow, nothing will grow in the sea.

DDT is a nonpolar hydrocarbon. It would be expected to dissolve in similar substances such as fat. DDT deposited in the fat of fish, birds, or mammals is not subject to attack and destruction. Microorganisms may ingest and store DDT. The predator which feeds on them will ingest and store DDT from many microorganisms. Each step up the food chain will find more DDT ingested and stored. Those animals at the top of the chain, such as birds, build up high levels of DDT. Birds can lay soft-shelled eggs which break before hatching. These eggs are thought to be formed when DDT affects the hormone balance which regulates the egg-forming cycle and causes the egg to be laid before sufficient shell has been developed.

DDT is thought to be one of the safest compounds known for human beings. However, its effect on other species may cause man great difficulties. There is no doubt that DDT has saved thousands, perhaps millions, of lives besides reducing illness. However, do its advantages outweigh its disadvantages? Will it continue to be effective? Is there another way to control insects, especially in the developing countries? DDT is a very cheap material. Will a more ecologically sound method be too expensive for the poorer countries to afford? Will someone underwrite the research needed to find a better solution? If alternative solutions are too expensive for the developing countries, can some way be found to help them with more ecologically sound controls?

DDT is one of a number of organochlorine pesticides. When scientists find a compound which has certain desirable characteristics, they investigate other similar compounds (Figure 5–5). All of the compounds have carbon rings and chlorine atoms. These pesticides are called "hard pesticides" because they are all persistent.

Figure 5–5. Formulas of several chlorinated hydrocarbon pesticides.

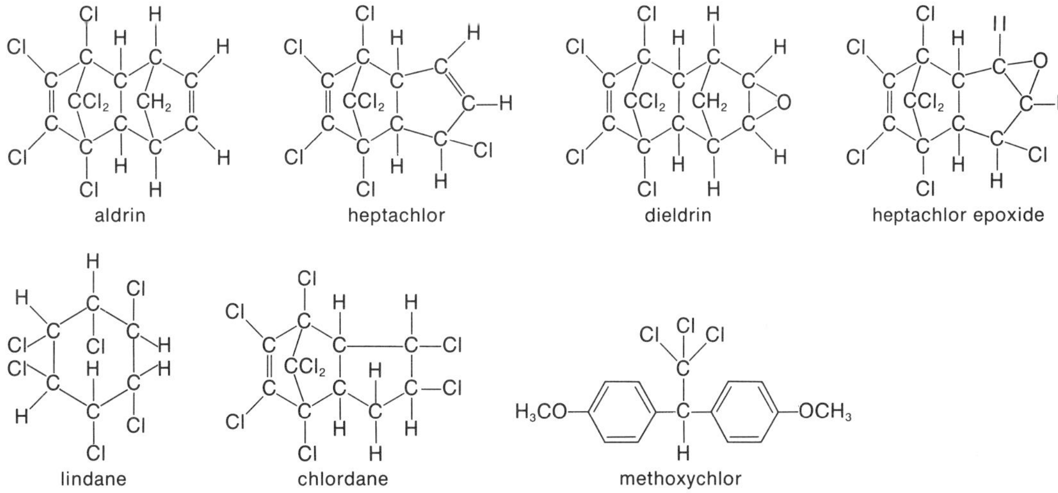

aldrin heptachlor dieldrin heptachlor epoxide

lindane chlordane methoxychlor

Another family of pesticides, the organophosphates, are "soft pesticides," that is, nonpersistent. The key atom in these pesticides is a phosphorus atom which is combined with two atoms of sulfur or oxygen, or one of each (Figure 5–6). These pesticides are not only nonpersistent but also nonspecific and toxic to man. They interfere with the transmission of messages along the nervous system.

An inactive form of a substance called acetylcholine is present at the end of some nerves. When a message reaches the end of the nerve it frees acetylcholine which activates a receptor on a nerve fiber, muscle fiber, or gland. The nerve transmits the message, causing the muscle to contract or the gland to secrete. Immediately an enzyme, cholinesterase, deactivates the acetylcholine on the receptor by splitting it into choline and acetic acid. The stimulus to the nerve, muscle, or gland then stops (Figure 5–7). Organophosphates combine with cholinesterase so firmly that the enzyme can no longer decompose acetylcholine. The acetylcholine continues to stimulate the nerve fiber, muscle fiber, or gland. Hyperactivity, tremors, irregular heart beat, convulsions, and death can result.

Thus, the organophosphates are very dangerous substances. Several hundred deaths a year are reported in cotton-growing Central American countries. California reported 26 deaths from these pesticides in 1970.

Juvenile hormones are expected to be the next big advance in insecticides, the third generation of insecticides (first generation, inorganics; second generation, DDT). The stages in the development of an insect are regulated by substances called *hormones.* If the juvenile hormones are present at the wrong stage, the insect will not complete its life cycle. These chemicals are nontoxic to higher animals and are nonpersistent. Manufacturers have succeeded in making them more persistent and in producing hormones which affect more than one species. Because the chemicals are natural substances used by insects, insects are not expected to become resistant to them. At this time only

Figure 5–6. Formulas of several organophosphate pesticides.

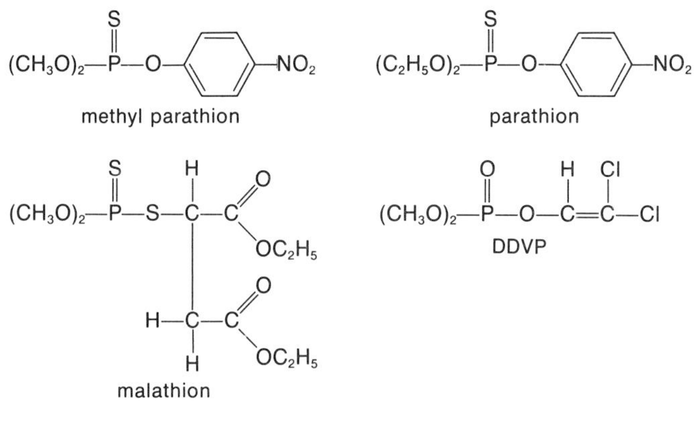

methyl parathion

parathion

malathion

DDVP

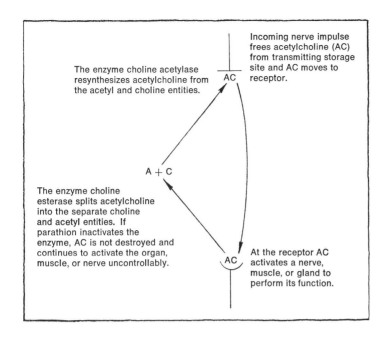

The enzyme choline acetylase resynthesizes acetylcholine from the acetyl and choline entities.

Incoming nerve impulse frees acetylcholine (AC) from transmitting storage site and AC moves to receptor.

AC

A + C

The enzyme choline esterase splits acetylcholine into the separate choline and acetyl entities. If parathion inactivates the enzyme, AC is not destroyed and continues to activate the organ, muscle, or nerve uncontrollably.

AC

At the receptor AC activates a nerve, muscle, or gland to perform its function.

Figure 5–7. Action of parathion to inhibit the destruction of acetylcholine.

one compound is being marketed, but already a laboratory has found flies which are resistant to a hormone.

Some experts are worried about the ultimate effect of broad-spectrum juvenile hormones. They would disrupt the predator-pest relationship just as any broad-spectrum insecticide does. The cost of developing and testing an insecticide is so great that only broad-spectrum insecticides can be economically feasible.

The use of synthetic insecticides may lead to economic chaos in agricultural areas. Outstanding difficulties have occurred in Peru, California, New Mexico, and the Rio Grande valley. In Peru the use of DDT resulted in the usual pattern of resistance and destruction of the cotton crop by resistant insects. In the late 1940s insecticide programs were switched to organophosphates. By the mid-1950s resistance had developed to the organophosphates and some species had become uncontrollable. The Peruvian government introduced natural enemies and other natural methods and used insecticides only as a back-up system, the integrated method. In two or three years, the cotton yields again were high and have remained that way.

Integrated controls   Dr. Robert Van Den Bosch[6] recommends the integrated method. A top executive of an insecticide manufacturer asked Dr. Van Den

6. Division Chairman of the Division of Biological Control, University of California, Berkeley.

Bosch what could be done to stop the problems with pesticides. He answered that it would be necessary to use as little insecticide as possible and apply it as seldom as possible. The executive commented that this was impossible because the parent company insisted upon a certain amount of growth each year.

A few people are using the integrated method in the United States. The method requires continuous examination and supervision of the fields being controlled. The supervisors must be knowledgeable, know what to look for, and what they are seeing. Predator insects are raised artificially in large numbers so that they may flood the area and reduce the pests to low levels. Synthetic insecticides are used only in emergencies when the pests greatly outnumber the predators, and then specific ones are chosen. The supervisors find that they need less and less insecticide once the land has been under their control for several years.

Growers are reluctant to give up a spray system which seems to work for a system which gives less dramatic results. One man who runs an integrated control service told a Congressional subcommittee that it takes courage for a farmer to refrain from spraying cotton when visible insects are eating a crop. However, the cotton plant produces more bolls than can mature and no harm is done if the excess is damaged. The entomologist must be able to decide when the damage will be excessive.

The use of integrated controls is controversial. Secretary of Agriculture Butz claims that it is not possible to grow sufficient food for the world's hungry people without heavy use of insecticides. On the other hand, many research scientists and a growing number of independent operators of control services insist that they have developed integrated methods which will give yields as large as those which use chemical controls. The latter group believes the integrated method should work for thousands of years.

HERBICIDES   Man has long controlled unwanted plants by cutting, burning, and cultivating. The use of herbicides is a recent method which apparently reduces the cost of controlling such plants. One spraying of herbicide may accomplish as much as several cultivations and use less energy by the farmer.

However, the use of herbicides is not without problems. These compounds are biologically active substances which may act on nontarget species. Recent studies show that they kill soil bacteria which produce humus. This, in turn, leads to dead plant materials remaining in the soil and erosion of the soil because of its reduced humus content. Once a herbicide has been used on a field, the field must be planted with that type of crop continuously. If a field is treated to remove broad-leaved plants from corn (a grass-type plant), then it will not grow broad-leaved plants such as soybeans for several years. Such continuous farming increases the need for fertilizers and pesticides.

Many compounds are used as herbicides. The two most common are 2,4-D and 2,4,5-T, two stable and persistent compounds

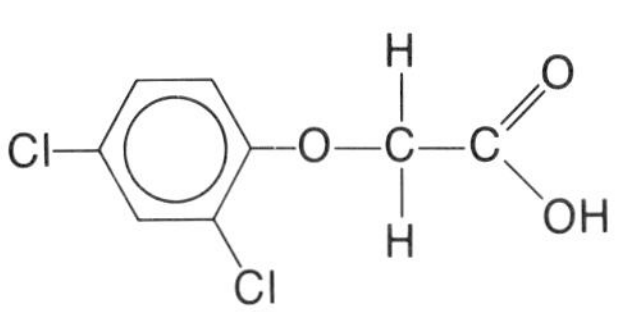

2,4 dichlorophenoxy
acetic acid (2,4-D)

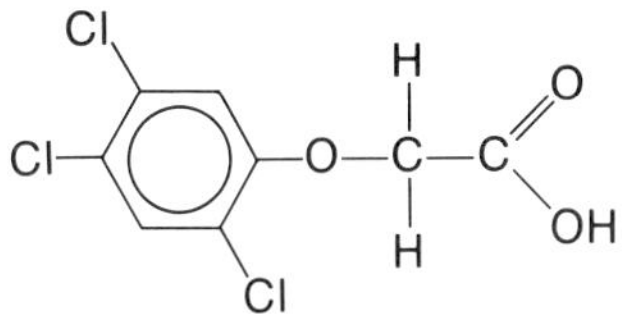

2,4,5 trichlorophenoxy
acetic acid (2,4,5-T)

2,4,5-T, like most other manufactured chemicals, contains impurities. When a factory produces a substance, there are usually several different steps or stages in the process. The process may start with compound A and compound B to produce compound C:

$A + B \rightarrow C$

The result will be a mixture of A, B, and C. Normally each step in a process does not occur as two substances producing a third, but rather as

$A + B \rightarrow C + D + E + F$ (perhaps more compounds)

In this case, compounds A, B, D, E, and F must be removed before substance C can react in the next stage of the process. Making a pure chemical is almost impossible, whether in a laboratory or in a manufacturing plant.

Often isomers are formed along with the desired substance. The two chlorine atoms on the carbon ring of 2,4-D could form different isomers by being attached in different relationships, such as:

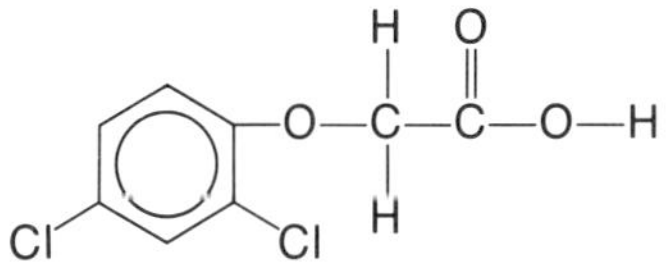

2,4-D

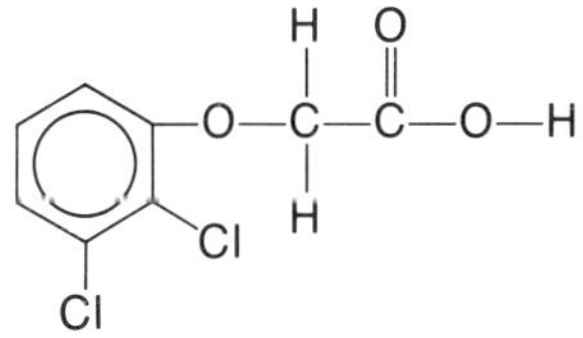

2,3-D

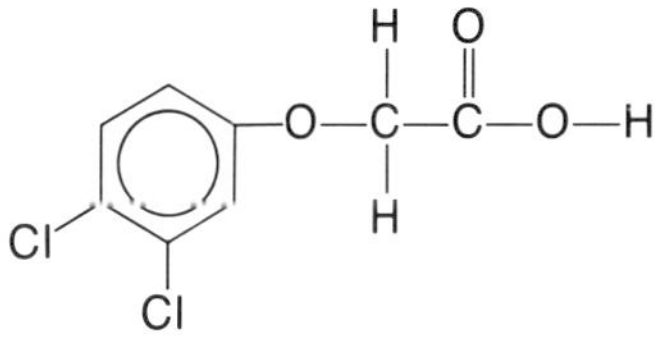

3,4-D

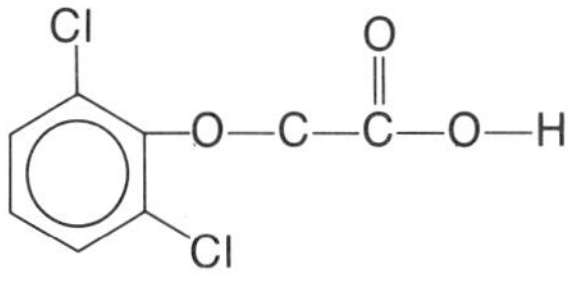

2,6-D

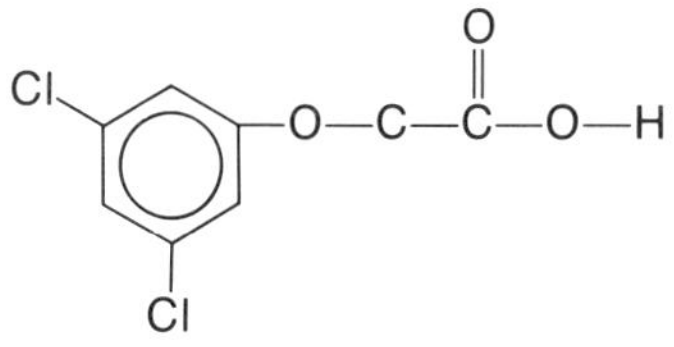

3,5-D

Choice of conditions of manufacture can encourage the formation of one isomer but others will still be present.

2,4,5-T may contain as impurities members of a group of compounds called *dioxins*:

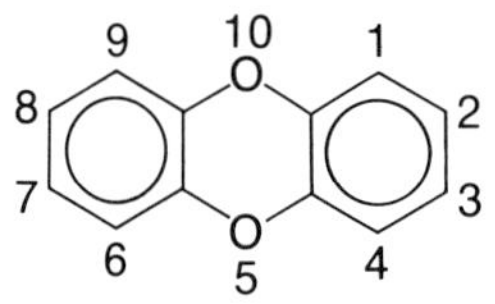

Chlorine may attach to the carbons at various positions; 2,3,7,8-tetra chlorodibenz-p-dioxin (TCDD) is one of the most potent tetratogens (compounds which cause noninheritable birth defects) known. Dioxins appear to build up in the soil but over a period of years they disappear. Sunlight does not seem to affect them. However, one study showed that when 2,4,5-T is heated to a high temperature, 10% dioxins are formed. Therefore, the possibility exists that burning will increase the amount of dioxins.

THE GREEN REVOLUTION   The *Green Revolution* is the name given to efforts to increase the world's food supply by increasing crop yields. The new strains of plants which have been developed do produce greater yields but they also require larger inputs of fertilizers and pesticides.

Native plants in developing countries tend to be long stemmed. If they are fertilized too heavily, the stems tend to break. The new varieties have thick, short stems and thus can be planted more closely and fertilized more heavily. The closely planted stands need more water and usually are irrigated. The damp, thick plants attract insects so that heavy use of pesticides is necessary. If two crops are grown where only one grew before, the use of fertilizers and pesticides is further increased.

The new varieties have increased yields per acre but the percentage of protein is lower than that of native varieties. Hybrid corn grown in the United States is a Green Revolution type of crop. Indian corn has about 15% protein while some commercial varieties of hybrid corn have only 5% protein. The lower protein content makes it difficult for the consumer to have a diet with sufficient protein (see Chapter 6).

Protein is being increased in several crops. Triticale, a wheat-rye cross, has excellent protein quality and quantity but so far farmers have been reluctant to plant it. A gene to improve the protein content of corn has been incorporated into the seed. The new corn has been planted in a few developing countries where it has improved the overall nutrition. Most recently, a gene to improve the protein quality of sorghum was found.

A hidden danger in the Green Revolution is the loss of genetic wealth (the total of the different varieties available) and the threatened loss of more. Wild varieties are destroyed by pesticides and native varieties are supplanted by the new varieties. Such a situation has occurred in corn production in the United

LAND: THE HUMAN HABITAT

States (Figure 5–8). Another subtle danger exists when the genetic base is too narrow. Corn production in the United States can illustrate this difficulty. In 1970 almost every corn variety raised in the United States was grown from seed with only one kind of cytoplasm, T-cytoplasm. Corn leaf blight, a fungus, has always affected a few plants since before the white man arrived in America but no one paid attention to it. Every few years it would mutate and the new strain affected a few plants. Then in 1970 it mutated again and found susceptible plants, those with T-cytoplasm. The weather was favorable for the spread of the fungus, and the United States lost 15% of its crop. In 1971 the weather favored the crop and not the fungus so the crop was saved. Two wet years would have made the corn loss staggering.

Other crops may be in a similar danger. Rice in the southern states is limited to five main varieties, and in California to three varieties. Seventy-five percent of the world's soybean crop is grown in the United States from closely related varieties. Other examples are as follows: potatoes, 69% from one variety; peanuts, narrow base over entire world; sorghum, limited; peas, two germ plasma in commercial peas. Similar limitations exist in most other commercial varieties.

Animals are undergoing the same genetic manipulations as plants. Up until the present, nothing has occurred that would indicate that any harm has been done. However, no one knows what genes are present which might mean increased vulnerability to some disease.

The Green Revolution has had political and social implications in the countries where it has been promoted. Small farmers have been displaced and forced

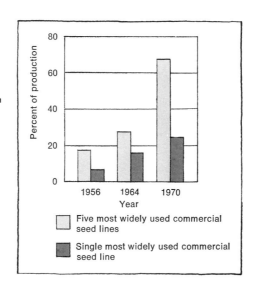

Figure 5–8. Genetic lines in corn varieties in the United States. Reproduced from *Chemical and Engineering News,* 8 January 1973, p. 15, with the permission of the Copyright Office, American Chemical Society.

into the city slums. The increased need for fertilizers and pesticides has made the developing countries more dependent on the industrialized nations.

OTHER SUGGESTIONS

1. The production of protein from petroleum is possible. Great Britain has a factory to produce protein from natural gas by the action of yeast, one-celled organisms which can use hydrocarbons for food and produce carbon dioxide and water. When the yeast dies the protein of the organisms becomes available. The resulting concentrate is to be used for animal feed with plans to produce synthetic meats later. Japan has also built such a plant for food for human consumption. However, it was found that an impurity in the product might be dangerous for man. The product is being sold as dog food. There are two difficulties in this method of obtaining food: first, our petroleum resources are limited (Chapter 9), and second, no petroleum must remain in the final product

2. Yeasts have been used to produce food from other carbohydrate sources: papermill wastes, wood residue wastes, and waste from sugar factories. Some of these products are palatable. Several countries are producing food from yeast but most of the products are being shipped to the industrialized countries for animal feeds.

3. Some of the best agricultural land available is used for nonfood crops such as rubber, coffee, tobacco, cacao, tea, and cotton and other fibers. In the United States nonfood crops use about 250,000 square miles of land, one-and-a-half times the size of the state of California. Two-thirds of the arable land in Latin America is used for such cash crops. In addition, some of the land used for sugar and bananas could be used for more necessary crops. Unfortunately, the production of nonedible food crops is increasing at a more rapid rate than edible food production.

4. Another possibility is to shorten the food chain by having men consume plants directly. There are many difficulties involved in this idea. Some plants cannot be digested by man, and most of them must be processed before use. Plants are a lean source of protein and the protein is usually incomplete for human consumption. As a result, a careful selection and mixture of plant foods are required to give a balanced diet (see Chapter 6).

Men cannot use large amounts of leafy plants such as alfalfa without processing. Animals, however, can convert these to useful food for man either as milk or meat. Thus to depend upon plants alone would deny man the food which can be harvested from pastures by animals. Sixty percent of the feed used for animals throughout the world is not suitable for man. However, in the United States this percentage is much less, as much of the grain grown in this country is used for animal feed. Consumption of animals and plants gives a diversified food system for man, and reducing that diversity unnecessarily limits man's food supply.

5. Possibly the easiest way to increase available food without hurting the environment is to reduce storage loss, which may be as high as 32–33% in de-

veloping countries. In 1965 the storage loss in India was about equal to the amount of food imported.

6. Better distribution is another way to feed the hungry. In developing countries there have been famines in one area while food rotted in warehouses in another part of the country.

In 1900 the average farmer fed about six people; in 1970 the number had increased to almost 40. Part of the increase is due to the large amounts of energy used by today's farmer, and part is due to a misconception of what constitutes a contribution to food production. In 1900 the farmer raised the food, processed what he wanted to sell, produced his own fertilizer, and provided his own source of energy. Today every worker who produces fertilizer, farm equipment, fuel for that equipment, chemical insecticides, or herbicides as well as those who process farm products is as much a part of the food industry as the farmer. The processing of food after it leaves the farm requires three times as much energy as the farmer uses.

A group at the New York State College of Agriculture and Life Sciences of Cornell University headed by Drs. David Pimental and L. E. Hurd[7] found that 1 kilocalorie of input returned about 2.8 kilocalories in the form of corn on the farm. The 1:2.8 ratio applies only to corn production and does not include any energy use off the farm. Another more complete study by Eric Hirst[8] found that 8.2 million calories are required to provide each person with 1.1 million calories of food each year, about a 7.5:1 ratio.

Agriculture in primitive societies returns more energy than is put in, often 10–15 or more times as much; that is, modern farmers are less efficient than primitive farmers when efficiency is measured in terms of yield per unit energy. Dr. René Dubos has said (in a speech to the delegates to the U.N. Conference on Human Environment, June 1972) that the only reason the modern farmer can expend more energy than he receives from the land is that the price of crude oil is less than that of soybean oil.

Various suggestions have been proposed to make modern farming more efficient. A return to the use of horses is often suggested. However, land that grew feed for horses is now used to grow food for people; thus, horses are not the answer. Dr. Hirst notes that substituting vegetable protein for animal protein and using less processed food would make the food industry more efficient. The group at Cornell University made several recommendations.

1. Feedlots for cattle should be moved closer to cropland where manure could be used in place of fertilizer. The manure from one dairy cow or two fattening beef cattle will fertilize an acre of corn at the average of fertilization of 1970.

2. Rotations should be practiced wherever feasible.

7. David Pimental, *et al.*, "Food production and the energy crisis," *Science,* 182:445, 2 Nov. 1973.
8. Eric Hirst, "Living off the fuels of the land," *Nat. Hist.* N.Y., 82:20–21, Dec. 1973.

3. Less herbicides should be used.

4. An increase in the protein content of corn would lead to a decrease in the need for other protein feeds.

5. Inputs and crops should be moved by train instead of by truck.

FORESTS

Forests retain rainwater for later slow release to streams, hold steep soil in place, provide lumber, yield paper and cardboard products and some useful chemicals, offer solitude and recreation for people, and shelter wildlife.

The kind of forest growing in a region is dependent upon the soils and the climate of the region (Figure 5–9). As growing conditions change from region to region so do the problems of lumbering and reforestation. Information about forest-soil relationships in one region may or may not apply to another. A look at these relationships in several regions of the United States will show some of the difficulties associated with cutting lumber and replanting the forests.

Forests and Soils in the United States

Four regions have been chosen to illustrate the differences in forest-soil relationship in the United States. Even within a region soils are not alike and cannot be treated alike. Therefore, the descriptions apply only to the four forests discussed. These particular forests were chosen because of the availability of information.

1. Hubbard Brook Forest in New Hampshire is an example of a forest in a region of sufficient rainfall. Under the entire soil layer is a layer of impermeable rock which prevents water percolation. Two-thirds of the rainfall is in summer.

Figure 5–9. "I think that I shall never see a poem lovely as all those money-making boards." Reprinted by permission of Don Wright.

LAND: THE HUMAN HABITAT

2. An arid Western forest on the eastern slope of the Rocky Mountains in Montana is subjected to dry summers and very cold, dry, snowy winters.

3. The H. J. Andrews Experimental Forest near Blue River, Oregon, is in a region with dry summers and wet winters. The steep slopes are covered by loose soil over porous rock. Continued washing over thousands of years has leached the minerals out of the soil.

4. A forest in the southeastern United States grows on a deep, leached soil in a region with a humid climate. The land is gently rolling.

HUBBARD BROOK FOREST   The forest was clearcut, that is, all growth was harvested, but the timber was allowed to remain where it fell. For two consecutive years the area was sprayed with a herbicide. Although the experiment was designed to study the results of clearcutting the treatment was much more drastic than any commercial clearcut.

When a forest is clearcut, the forest floor is exposed to the sun and the temperature of the soil increases. The life processes of soil bacteria are more rapid at the higher temperature. Humus decomposes faster, free nitrogen is changed to ammonia more rapidly, and the ammonia is quickly converted to the nitrite ion which is oxidized to nitrate ion immediately. The negative ion cannot enter a solution by itself; a positive ion must accompany it. The hydrogen ion from the conversion of ammonia to nitrite releases positive ions such as Mg^{2+}, Ca^{2+}, K^+, or Na^+ from the humus or clay colloids. These ions are displaced from the soil and washed into streams.

Calcium loss increased by 417%, the potassium loss by 1558%, and the nitrate loss by 5600%. In all 97 tons per square kilometer or eight times the expected amount of dissolved solids were washed from the clearcut watershed each year. The water flow increased 30–40% in the first year. Most of the increase was in the summer months. After the third summer vegetation was allowed to grow, but even after 15 years the logged area was losing dissolved solids faster than the control.

A later study of a commercially cut watershed showed increased runoff with increased dissolved solids, but the stream loading never reached the levels of the Hubbard Brook Forest.

ARID WESTERN FOREST   The trees are evergreens which shed needles infrequently so that organic materials do not have an opportunity to build up. The summer is too dry and the winter too cold for biological activity and humus production. The present soil may have been formed during periods when the climate was much wetter than at present. If this is true, the soil is a nonrenewable resource.

Nutrients are removed from the soil with timber harvesting. The annual removal of nutrients from an acre by timber harvest will average 1–3 lb of phosphorus, 10 lb of nitrogen, 10 lb of potassium, and larger amounts of Ca^{2+}. If the limbs and upper parts of the trees are removed the nutrient loss will increase 3.5–4.5 times. Additional losses are caused by leaching after clearcutting, but these losses would not be as large as those at Hubbard Brook as the rainfall is only about one quarter of that in New Hampshire and the soil does not have the store of nutrients which are present in the eastern forest.

WET WINTERS AND DRY SUMMERS   In Oregon small areas were clearcut but measurements did not begin until four years after cutting. Even then the study showed that large amounts of soil were being washed into the streams. The uncut control lost 0.0012 in. of soil, the clearcut without roads lost 3.3 times as much, and the watershed with roads lost 109 times as much. The loss from the clearcut with roads is undoubtedly too large for sustained yield. A study is being conducted to determine whether the soil loss from the second clearcut is being replaced. Little is known about the amounts of dissolved solids. Even if the quantity of dissolved solids lost in the streams was known, the loss to ground water would not be known.

SOILS OF THE SOUTHEASTERN UNITED STATES   These soils tend to be without humus because bacterial action is very rapid in the warm climate and destroys organic matter quickly. Five percent organic matter will make a soil appear black. These soils do not appear black. When humus is absent, iron often determines the color of the soil. Iron may be present in the soil in three different forms, each in a different color: iron III oxide (Fe_2O_3) which is red; hydrated iron III oxide ($Fe_2O_3 \cdot H_2O$) which is yellowish brown; iron II oxide (FeO) which is bluish gray. The particular form of iron, and thus the color of the soil, depends upon the amount of water and air in the soil. If the soil is well drained, enough oxygen will be present for the iron III form to be present and the soil will be red. If the soil is wetter but oxygen is still present, the hydrated form will be present and the soil will be brownish. If the soil is very wet, oxygen will not be present and the soil will be grey.

Future of Forests in the United States

The future of forest land in the United States depends upon who is speculating. Commercial operators and the United States Forest Service believe that with 70–100-year rotations trees can be harvested indefinitely. If trees are planted every year, there will be trees to harvest every year. Others believe this plan is based upon a faulty assumption. They contend that some forest soils are a nonrenewable resource and that not enough is known about other soils to determine whether or not they are renewable or nonrenewable.

With the above plan, forests must be planted immediately after harvest. Currently this is not being done. In the Pacific Northwest region alone there are 2.5 million acres which have either not been replanted or in which the growth has been poor. Overall the Forest Service has at least a 60-year backlog of reforestation. Replanting is not always successful. One clearcut in the Shoshone National Forest has been replanted four times with only marginal success.

The Forest Service has suggested that limitation be made on areas where the land is unstable. Scientists at the Forest Service experiment stations are trying to develop better techniques for harvesting timber in difficult areas. Whether these efforts will be successful can only be answered in the future.

Much of the discussion has centered on public forests. Private forests also need conservation treatment. Earlier in this chapter it was mentioned that the population density of the United States was one person per 11 acres. Of that 11 acres, 2 acres are covered with private forests, and 62% of that area needs conservation treatment (Figure 5–10).

The region around the Mediterranean gives historical evidence to support the concern about erosion brought about by forest harvest. At one time the cedars of Lebanon covered the slopes with luxuriant growth. Solomon cut the trees thousands of years ago, and today the slopes are barren. It is speculated that the rainfall in Israel has decreased since the cedars were felled. In the Golden Age of Greece its steep mountains were covered with luxuriant forests. Today the mountains are largely barren rock.

It must be our responsibility to see that our forests and lands have a better destiny. Studies about soil-forest-water relationships are needed before irreversible decisions are made.

Tropical Forests

In the wet tropical forest 70% of the nutrients are stored in the vegetation. As the vegetation dies and falls to the ground, both microorganisms and large organisms immediately scavenge it and use the nutrients to produce new vegetation. When the trees are harvested, the storehouse of nutrients is removed. Consequently, little is left to regenerate regrowth of the forest.

The land may be cut and burned in preparation for farming. With loss of vegetation, the soil becomes warmer. Cultivation increases the amount of oxygen available to the microorganisms. Organic residues decay rapidly. Heavy rains leach away the released nutrients. Thus the soil usually cannot be farmed more than three years.

Laterites are tropical soils whose surfaces can change to rock under certain conditions. Leaching by heavy rains leaves the soils composed of iron, aluminum, and titanium oxides. If vegetation is removed from this type of soil in hot climates with alternating wet and dry seasons, the surface of the soil will

Figure 5–10. Forest land needing conservation treatment (shaded area).

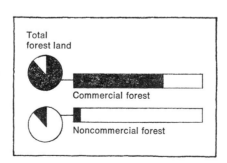

Total forest land

Commercial forest

Noncommercial forest

bake into a rock-like crust. Under the crust the soil is a soft clay. The word "laterite", which is derived from the Latin word for brick, describes the surface.

MINING

The Romans made a desert and called it peace; we make a desert and call it progress.[9]

Hon. John Seiverling

Any mining, whether surface or underground, removes or disturbs the land in the vicinity of the mine. Often huge piles of earth and rock accumulate. Large open pits used for gravel, iron ore, copper, aluminum ore, and other minerals effectively destroy the land surface and leave huge holes when the mine is exhausted.

Coal, especially surface or strip-mined coal, disturbs more land than any other mining operation. Although underground coal reserves are many times larger than the reserves which can be strip mined, strip mining is increasingly used as the method for mining coal. In 1969, 30% of the coal was surface mined while in 1972, 52% was strip mined.

Most coal has been mined east of the Mississippi River, but strip mining is beginning in the West which has tremendous reserves of coal that can be surface mined. The problems of returning the land to usable condition are very different in those two parts of the United States. While much of the strip-mined land has not been reclaimed for some appropriate use, some has been reclaimed by nature so that vegetation holds the soil.

Mining laws in the United States do not require great care to preserve the land. Topsoil is not usually separated from the subsoil and stored. Often only token efforts are made to reclaim the land after the mining operation is completed. At this writing, Congress is working on a bill to force the mining industry to reclaim the land once the operation is finished. They are presently deadlocked on a provision giving the surface owner the right to refuse to allow his land to be stripmined.

In contrast, the mining laws in Europe are very strict. After the mining operation is finished, the land must be covered with topsoil which has been stored and the land returned to agricultural use; this procedure costs at least $4000 per acre. In Europe the flat land does not contain pyrites which form acid water, but broken aquifers are a problem.

In the eastern United States much of the coal contains pyrites which forms acid water (Chapter 4). If the land is heavily limed, fertilized, and covered with topsoil, crops can grow on it. However, if oxygen from the air can reach the pyrites residues, acid water will be formed and the crops or pasture may die. Several years after reclamation, acid water may still be flowing from the reclaimed land or may begin to flow from it. Complete leaching will take several years or even a decade.

9. Honorable John Seiverling, U.S. representative from Ohio, quoted by Harry Caudell, "Strip mining—coast to coast," *Nation*, 212:490, 19 April 1970.

LAND: THE HUMAN HABITAT

In both the eastern and western United States the mining operation may break into an aquifer. When this happens there is no way to stop the water from draining from the aquifer. In the West aquifers may be in beds of coal and may supply many square miles of land.

The soils in the West are very thin with very distinct layers. In arid lands, where the potential for evaporation exceeds that for precipitation, water rises to the surface and evaporates. The water carries dissolved solids which are deposited at various levels in the soil in the manner of chromatography (see Chapter 2). Separation of the 2–4 in. top soil layers by mechanical equipment is impossible. Thus, the top layers will be mixed even if the topsoil is stored for use later. When the layers are mixed, nutrients are released and the land is very productive for a few years. When the nutrients have been removed, the soil becomes much less fertile than undisturbed land. Soil rebuilding would take thousands of years or importation of organic material and water. This is another example of a trade-off. The difficulties in the West may be symbolized by a sticker on a stop sign near one coal mine in Montana: "coal or food."

Chauncey Starr, Dean of the School of Engineering and Applied Science, University of California, Los Angeles, has suggested (in a testimony to the Senate Subcommittee on Science, Research, and Development) that certain areas be set aside as expendable. They would be mined and destroyed. No attempt would be made to reclaim them. However, the following questions can then be asked: What lands? How much? What will be the effect on the surrounding land?

SOLID WASTE DISPOSAL

A fundamental physical constraint is conservation of matter; we can shove wastes all around our environment, manipulate them, decrease their volume, change their state, but we cannot ultimately destroy most of the waste residues. The solid waste problem will not disappear through any technological miracle.[10]

John F. Collins

Americans dump their rubbish in two ways: one is in municipal garbage called solid waste, and the other is by littering along the streets, roads, streams, parks, trails, or wherever they happen to be (Figure 5–11). Only a change of habits of the American people will stop littering. A story is told about an American visiting Switzerland. When he threw his cigarette butt on the sidewalk, it was picked up and politely returned to him. He remarked that it was only garbage. The European commented that in his country they did not throw their garbage on the ground.

Municipal Wastes

In 1968, an average of 5 lb of trash was discarded by each person each day. By the year 1980, not only is the number of people discarding trash expected

10. John F. Collins, visiting Professor of Urban Affairs at the Massachusetts Institute of Technology; testimony to the Senate Subcommittee on Air and Water Pollution.

Figure 5–11. "Yes, sir, we enjoy the highest standard of living known to the world!" Editorial cartoon by Frank Interlandi. Copyright, Los Angeles Times. Reprinted with permission.

to increase, but the amount of trash discarded by each person is expected to increase to 7–8 lb per day.

Past accumulations of solid waste have required large areas for dumping, the most common method of disposal. In the future, the waste may be recycled or reused, or it may be converted to some useful form. At present these developments are mostly in an experimental or pilot plant state. The outlook is bright for at least some of the newer approaches.

LANDFILL   The unsightly dump with burning refuse has been used for centuries. Today it is being replaced by the sanitary landfill where the wastes are covered each day to prevent the spread of disease from the fill and to discourage rodents from feeding on the garbage.

Care must be taken to plan and construct the landfill carefully. Water must not be allowed to leach water-soluble materials and biological contaminants into ground water. Methane (CH_4, the main component of natural gas) produced by anaerobic bacteria must not be allowed to seep into an enclosed area in sufficient amounts to be an explosion danger. The surface must be regraded periodically for several years to alleviate subsidence, the settling of the land surface.

Marshland is often used for landfills for two reasons: the land is useless for development but after being filled it can be used for commercial or residential purposes, and the land is low which makes it easy to dump the waste and cover

LAND: THE HUMAN HABITAT

it. However, the filling of a marshy area destroys the breeding places of many wildlife species which may be directly or indirectly important to mankind.

Many cities are rapidly running out of suitable land disposal sites. Not only are the current sites expected to be filled in a few years but new landfill sites are hard to find.

REUSE AND RECYCLE   Much of the municipal waste load could be eliminated by proper recycling of useful discarded materials (Table 5–3). In addition, use of these materials would save virgin resources.

Paper is the largest component of solid waste. Much of the paper could be recycled (see Chapter 11). Food garbage cannot be reused or recycled, but it can be returned to the land as humus. In order to prevent transmission of disease the food wastes should be composted before being applied to the land. The widespread use of garbage disposers, especially in suburbia, removes the wastes from municipal trash but adds them to sewage. Grass and dirt can be disposed of directly to cropland. Pieces of wood can be reused. Smaller, un-usable pieces can be added to the compost pile with garbage. In composting the volume of the waste would be reduced and a useful fertilizing material produced. Cotton textiles can be reused as wiping rags, made into high-grade paper, or composted for return to the land. Leather can be composted and returned to the land.

Plastics are not biodegradable but some can be recycled. At present there is no satisfactory way of separating plastics from municipal rubbish or of recovering recyclable plastics from other plastics (Chapter 9 includes a dis-cussion of the chemistry of plastics.)

Glass, aluminum, and iron are the materials considered most suitable for recycling. Only a small percentage of each is collected and returned to the consumer market, usually by individual and private organizations. Govern-

TABLE 5–3.   Municipal Trash Components.

Material	Percentage of trash
Cardboard, newspaper, other paper	46
Garbage (food waste)	12
Grass and dirt	10
Wood	7
Textiles	3
Plastic film	2
Leather, molded plastics, rubber	2
Glass, ceramic, stone	8
Metallics	10

Source: Adapted from the testimony of Hon. Robert H. Finch, Secretary of the Department of Health, Education, and Welfare, to the Senate Subcommittee on Air and Water Pollution, 30 Sept. 1969.

mental and industrial sectors have shown little interest. A discussion of paper, glass, steel, aluminum, and other recovered metals is included in Chapter 11.

CONVERSION The organic material in municipal trash may be converted by various processes into useful substances or energy. Conversion may be by (1) pyrolysis, (2) incineration (conversion to energy), (3) hydrolysis and fermentation, or (4) composting.

Pyrolysis Pyrolysis, a process which breaks down organic substances by heating to 590–760 °C (1100–1400 °F) in the absence of oxygen, has been used only on a pilot plant scale for municipal refuse. The process can produce such useful substances as tar, pitch, acids, alcohol, fuel gas, and a residue which represents 3–5% of the original volume. An important advantage of the process is its ability to handle plastic and rubber which cause serious difficulties in other methods. One process turns tires into carbon black, a necessary raw material for more tires.

Incineration All organic matter in trash has some fuel value, about 5000 Btu/lb, which may be recovered. A few cities obtain a portion of their electrical energy by this means.

Incinerators have several disadvantages. Incineration of plastics may produce HCl, but few difficulties have been encountered in this country. Operators of incinerators in Europe, where large amounts of plastics are incinerated, have reported extensive damage to the incinerator and much interference with air pollution devices. Incinerators are expensive to build and operate. A residue of material (about 3–5%) must be added to a landfill.

Much of the heat comes from the high paper content of municipal refuse. If paper is recycled, the fuel value of the waste will be very low and the amount of recoverable energy much reduced. The question has been asked if it is fair to encourage recycling of paper in a city when it would reduce the energy the city could obtain from its wastes.

Hydrolysis and fermentation Trash can be a source of alcohol and protein (Figure 5–12). The protein is higher in price than that obtained from soybeans for animal feed so the market is small. One ton of organic waste would yield about 100 lb of protein, so most of the original material would remain for disposal in a landfill.

Figure 5–12. Yield of protein from trash. From Robert R. Grinstead, "Bottlenecks," *Environment* 14:10, April 1972. Copyright © Committee for Environmental Information, 1972.

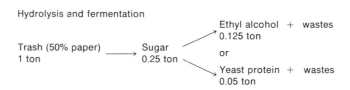

Hydrolysis and fermentation

Composting Composting of organic wastes is common in Europe but is little used in the United States. The difficulties are the same as in the case of composting and marketing sewage sludge. Municipalities keep trying to operate such systems but most are forced to close because of a shortage of markets for their products. Heavy metals and biorefractory organic substances must be excluded from the compost.

COLLECTION OF MUNICIPAL RUBBISH Collection is the most expensive step in waste disposal. If all possible materials are going to be recovered for recycling or reuse, the waste must also be sorted, an expensive process involving much hand labor. Mechanical sorting is being tried, but is only at the pilot plant stage and operates at the cost of large amounts of energy. Just as it is far easier to mine a rich deposit of a mineral than mine a lean deposit, so it is easier to sort refuse at the point where it is in a concentrated form, that is, at the residential, commercial, or retail establishments. These places are resistant to the idea of sorting trash, but the threat of high taxes has motivated the residents of some municipalities to sort their trash before it is picked up by the trash collector. Milwaukee, where consumers segregate 75% of the newsprint used, is a notable example.

Agricultural Wastes

Agricultural and forest wastes are many times the amount of total domestic, municipal, and commercial wastes. The rural wastes do not reach landfills but may destroy the good water quality of aquifers.

Formerly manure was spread on the fields of the farms where it was produced. Today the practice of raising animals in large numbers in small areas makes returning the manure to the land difficult, if not impossible. The expense of hauling manure long distances and the low cost of commercial mineral fertilizer has turned manure into something to be disposed of in any way possible. Sometimes it is burned, producing air pollutants. Manure may be used to produce oil and gas, a proposal which will be discussed in Chapter 12.

KEY CONCEPTS

1. Formation of soils.
2. Relationship of pH, soils, and plants. Relationship of plants and nutrients in the soil.
3. Relationship of people, food, and land needed to grow food.
4. Fertilizer: production methods, types, and problems involved.
5. Controlling insects: methods and problems.
6. Herbicides: advantages and problems.
7. Other sources of food.
8. Energy required by agriculture and food production.
9. Relationship of forests and soil.
10. Difficulties of reclaiming strip-mined land.
11. Methods of disposal of solid wastes; their advantages and disadvantages.

1. Why do hunting and food gathering cause less change in an ecosystem than agriculture?
2. Does the productivity of land always decrease if it is farmed for many years? Explain your answer.
3. Why are naturally occurring organic compounds usually more biodegradable than those devised by man?
4. Pesticides tend to affect the populations of predator insects more than the populations of target pests. Explain this statement.
5. The Green Revolution crop system allows high yield crops to be produced. Evaluate its value for meeting the food demands of the people of the earth.
6. What is the relationship of paint to a forest?
7. What is the relationship of offshore oil to a loaf of bread?
8. What is the connection between urban decay and the price of lettuce?
9. Evaluate the use of marshy, mosquito-ridden land for landfills.
10. Agricultural wastes are ten times as large as domestic sewage. Evaluate the impact upon the environment of these two sources of organic pollutants.
11. What responsibilities should a mine operator have with respect to mined areas?
12. Throughout the history of the earth many species have become extinct. Should great efforts be made to prevent the extinction of animal or plant species? Explain your answer.
13. Is the Swedish law dealing with the disposal of manure from cattle-feeding operations adequate? Explain your answer.
14. Of the 7 acres that are "yours," what is the total amount needing conservation treatment?
15. What is the relationship of land use to water pollution, air pollution, health, energy, and industrial pollution?

BIBLIOGRAPHY

1. Abbey, E., *Desert solitaire,* New York: Ballantine Books, 1970.
2. Borgstrom, G., *Focal points,* New York: Macmillan, 1973.
3. Borgstrom, G., *Too many,* New York: Macmillan, 1969.
4. Caudill, H., *My land is dying,* New York: E. P. Dutton, 1973.
5. Curry-Lindahl, K., *Conservation for survival, an ecological strategy,* New York: William Morrow, 1972.
6. Mowbray, A. Q., *Road to ruin,* Philadelphia: J. B. Lippincott, 1969.
7. Osborn, F., *Our plundered planet,* Boston: Little, Brown, 1948.
8. *Where not to build,* Washington, D.C.: Government Printing Office, 1968.
9. Wood, N., *Clearcut,* San Francisco: Sierra Club, 1971.

Two books with opposing views of the population-food problem:
10. Freeman, O. L., *Worlds without hunger,* New York: Frederick A. Praeger, 1968.
11. Paddock, V. and Paddock, P., *Famine–1975,* Boston: Little, Brown, 1967.

Books with opposing views of the pesticide problem:

12. Carson, R., *Silent spring,* Boston: Houghton Mifflin, 1962.
13. Graham, F., Jr., *Since silent spring,* Boston: Houghton Mifflin, 1970.
14. McInikov, N. M., *Chemistry of pesticides,* New York: Springer-Verlag New York, 1971.

6 Chemistry of Health

The secret of prolonging life is not to shorten it.
Feuchtersleben

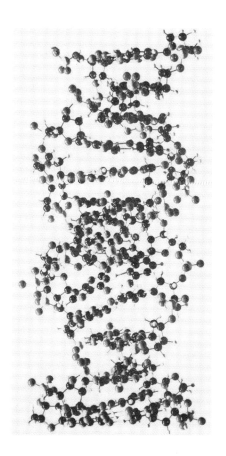

It is obvious that many substances are ingested by, breathed in by, or applied to the human body. Any given chemical substance may be usefully metabolized by the body, rejected by the body, or may harm the body. In order to determine the effects of a change, scientists collect *base-line data,* that is, data which document the conditions which existed before any change occurred. For example, before the forest was cut at Hubbard Brook, scientists spent four years collecting base-line data. In the case of the present deluge of exotic chemicals, there has been no collection of base-line data. The best that can be found is the chemical relationships of plants, animals, and man.

Ultimately, animals and man are almost completely dependent upon and restricted by the chemical substances that plants produce. Plants combine CO_2, water, soil minerals, and sunlight energy to produce a multitude of substances. These give structure to the plant and insure that descendants will carry on into the future. Plants produce the *proteins* of living tissue, *carbohydrates* (starches, sugars, cellulose), and *fats* which store energy for later use. (Cellulose is the major component of the woody tissue of plants.) In addition, they produce other substances necessary for the life of the plant.

Most molecules produced and used by plants and animals have the atoms arranged in a very specific manner in three-dimensional space. Most substances involved in biological systems are compounds of carbon. Carbon atoms most often combine with other atoms by forming four separate bonds which are oriented uniformly about the carbon atom. This results in a tetrahedral distribution of bonds and of the atoms or groups of atoms that are held by those bonds. If four different groups are attached to a carbon atom, that carbon is said to be *asymmetrical* or an *asymmetric carbon.*

In Figure 6–1, the *A, B, D,* and *E* entities may be simple atoms or they may be very large collections of atoms bound together as groups of atoms. The range of possibilities is shown in Figure 6–2.

For simplicity a letter designation is used to represent groups attached to the carbon. Different letters represent an entirely different atom or group from that represented by any other letter. In representing a compound, if all of the letters are different, the molecule is said to be asymmetric. An asymmetrical molecule cannot be split by an imaginary plane in such a way that the portions of the molecule on opposite sides of the plane are mirror images. Two different arrangements of the groups are possible on an asymmetric carbon (Figure 6–3).

Interchanging any two groups on one of the mirror pair of molecules makes that molecule identical with the molecule which originally was its mirror image. Interchanging a second pair of groups in either of the identical asymmetric molecules changes that molecule into the mirror image of its identical molecule. Thus an asymmetric molecule involving one asymmetric carbon has only two different forms. These *stereochemical* relationships are best demonstrated by actually constructing two asymmetric molecules, each containing the same groups and then changing these around as described above. If two of the

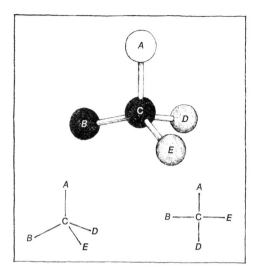

Figure 6–1. Equivalent representations of a simple organic molecule.

attached groups are the same, it is possible to split the molecule by means of a mirror plane into two structures which are mirror images of each other. The molecule is then said to be *symmetrical* rather than asymmetrical. Any rearrangement of the groups does not actually change the structure. Simple rotation of one of the structures would bring it into a position where it can be recognized as being identical with the original structure (Figure 6–4). By slicing the molecule through the plane containing the points *D*, *C*, and *B*, the molecule can be split into mirror-image halves. Such a molecule is symmetrical.

The space properties of the asymmetric carbon atom are extremely important in biological systems. Very often the property of asymmetry alone determines whether or not a substance can be *metabolized* by an organism.

Figure 6–2. C is an asymmetric carbon with four different groups represented by A, B, D, and E.

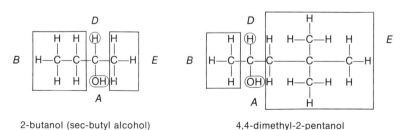

2-butanol (sec-butyl alcohol)   4,4-dimethyl-2-pentanol

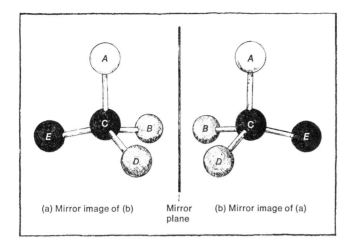

Figure 6-3. The two possible arrangements of groups around a carbon atom.

Enzymes are huge, high-molecular-weight compounds which are a part of or are attached to a protein molecule. Only a small portion of the enzyme molecule actually attaches to a *substrate* molecule (i.e., substance being acted upon) and causes it to change. If chemical action is to occur, certain atoms on the enzyme must attach to certain atoms on the substrate. The attachment is very complex and involves several atoms in both asymmetrical molecules. The points of attachment must match exactly. The situation would be analogous to the model system in Figure 6–5. For simplicity, the assumption is made that like lettered atoms must contact each other.

Figure 6–4. The symmetrical quality of a molecule that has two identical groups attached to the carbon atom.

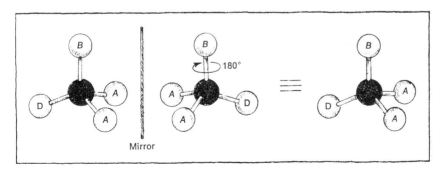

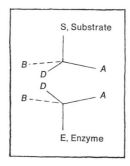

Figure 6-5. Matching of enzyme-active sites with substrate sites.

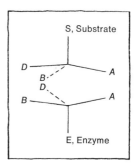

Figure 6-6. Mirror orientations about the active site of a molecule cannot be acted upon by the enzyme for the opposite orientation.

If the substrate and enzyme must meet these conditions, there is no way in which the mirror image of the substrate can be acted upon by the enzyme because the critical atom-to-atom contacts cannot be made (Figure 6-6). Consequently, only molecules which have a certain stereochemical structure can be metabolized by living organisms.

The importance of asymmetric carbons in biological systems is well illustrated by the chemistry of the six-carbon sugars. Although there are 16 possible six-carbon sugars which have the empirical formula $C_6H_{12}O_6$, only a few of these 16 compounds are produced naturally by plants. The most common sugar molecule is called D-glucose, and its structure is represented in Figure 6-7. The two structures α- and β-D-glucose differ only in the orientation of the —OH group on the asymmetric carbon at the top of the molecule. Many of the molecules can join together (*polymerize*) to form starch (the α form) or cellulose (the β form). Most organisms have enzymes which can metabolize starches but do not have the necessary enzymes to metabolize cellulose. The stereochemical orientation about a critical carbon atom makes the difference in the reactivity and usefulness of these two kinds of glucose.

Ruminant animals, for example, cows, sheep, and deer, cannot digest cellulose directly but avoid the restriction somewhat by harboring bacteria in their stomach which at least partially do the job for them. A "postscript" to the conversion is that the β-D-glucose obtained from the cellulose can be converted to α-D-glucose which can then be used by animals.

The specific orientation of the atoms of the enzymes fixes the orientation of the atoms in the product molecules. These have exactly the correct orientation, or *configuration,* of atoms which the consuming organisms can use. On the other hand, compounds produced by strictly chemical means, for example, in

CHEMISTRY OF HEALTH

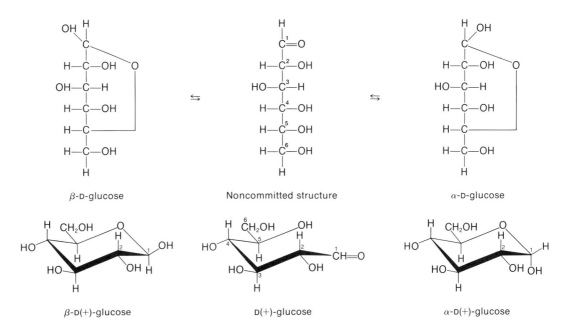

β-D-glucose Noncommitted structure α-D-glucose

β-D(+)-glucose D(+)-glucose α-D(+)-glucose

Figure 6–7. α- and β-D-glucose.

a manufacturing plant, may have asymmetric molecules but will have an equal number of molecules of the two stereochemical forms. Because of the stereochemistry of their enzymes, organisms are able to metabolize only one of the two stereochemical forms. The other form will remain unconsumed and must be excreted.

The complexity of even simple changes on a substrate molecule are indicated in Figure 6–8. The substrate acetaldehyde

$$
\begin{array}{ccc}
& H & H \\
& | & | \\
H - & C - & C = O \\
& | & \\
& H &
\end{array}
$$

is taken one step along the pathway of degradation of glucose to water and carbon dioxide.

The substrate is acted upon by two *coenzymes* in succession. (A coenzyme is a stable, organic molecule which must be loosely associated with the enzyme in order for the enzyme to function.) First the coenzyme lipoic acid combines with it; then the coenzyme CoASH displaces the lipoic acid entity from the acetyl group to form acetyl-CoA. The coenzyme lipoic acid must be returned

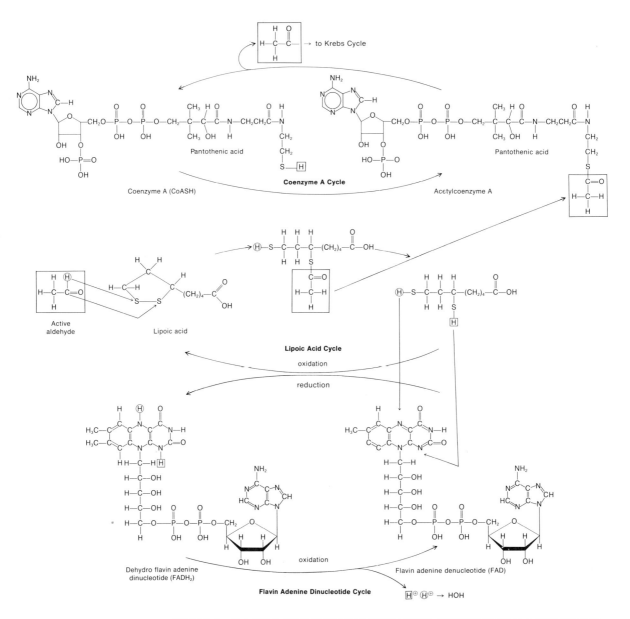

Figure 6–8. One step in the metabolism of glucose where acetaldehyde loses a hydrogen atom. Two hydrogen atoms are traced through several successive reactions. One hydrogen is identified by a circle; the other by a square.

to its original form. Dihydrolipoic acid has two hydrogen atoms removed by another coenzyme, FAD, and active lipoic acid is reformed. The coenzyme

CHEMISTRY OF HEALTH

lipoic acid is now ready to combine with another substrate molecule. In the process FAD becomes $FADH_2$ which must be oxidized to FAD so that it can oxidize more dihydrolipoic acid to active lipoic acid. Thus, both the lipoic acid and FAD entities are "recycled."

The substrate-coenzyme A combination continues to the next step where the acetyl group

$$H-\overset{\overset{\displaystyle H}{|}}{\underset{\underset{\displaystyle H}{|}}{C}}-\overset{\overset{\displaystyle O}{\|}}{C}-$$

is transferred to the Krebs cycle where it is further decomposed and the enzyme is changed to active coenzyme A. Both coenzyme A and FAD have a *vitamin* as part of their structure. A vitamin is a complex organic compound small amounts of which are essential to metabolism. Pantothenic acid is part of coenzyme A; riboflavin is part of FAD. Other coenzymes may have vitamins as part of their structure.

The enzyme must attach properly to the substrate in an exact manner with just the correct amount of firmness. All factors must work precisely. When the desired reaction has been accomplished, the substrate must be released so that it may proceed to the next step in the process which will further change it and bring it closer to the end products CO_2 and H_2O while the enzyme can work on a new substrate molecule.

The complete process of degradation of glucose to carbon dioxide and water may be likened to an assembly line where the substrate is passed along a line while coenzymes cause it to react and change form. Just as an assembly line will operate only with certain parts, so the degradation system of the body will degrade only a particular original substrate.

Any molecule which affects the ability of the enzyme to attach to or dissociate from the substrate molecule may interfere with the metabolic process and prevent a necessary reaction from occurring. For example, parathion, an insecticide, attaches itself so firmly to the enzyme cholinesterase that the enzyme cannot break down acetylcholine (see Chapter 5).

A metabolic step which requires the help of a metal ion may be inhibited by the presence of a different elemental ion which attaches more firmly to the substrate. In addition, an excessive amount of the normally required ions or catalysts can cause a disturbance or stoppage of a particular metabolic step. Conversely, if a required agent is low in amount or missing, the reaction slows or stops. Just as an assembly line must stop if one stage is stopped, so must the degradation process stop if one step halts for lack of substrate, enzyme, coenzyme, or metallic ion.

The entire metabolic process is a sensitive mechanism whose details have been worked out over the eons of time. It is best not to disturb it too greatly.

There are many ways in which the human body may be adversely affected. The most important of these are as follows: (1) *viruses* and *bacteria* which cause infections; (2) *malnutrition;* (3) *toxic* substances (poisons); (4) *mutagens* (affect genes), *carcinogens* (cause cancer), *teratogens* (cause birth defects).

Infections

Bacteria or viruses may enter the body through a body opening or a break in the skin. After an infection occurs, the body defenses, for example, stomach acid, white blood cells, antibodies (substances in blood which act to overcome poisons produced by an infection), may destroy the invaders. If the defenses are ineffective, bacteria multiply and produce chemical poisons which interfere with the metabolic processes of the body. A virus invades a cell and uses the cell material to reproduce its kind.

In order to control disease the following measures can be taken: bacteria and viruses can be prevented from entering the body by *sanitation; vaccination* or *inoculation* can prevent the invading agents from becoming established; the disease can be treated with drugs.

SANITATION Water treatment, personal cleanliness, and cooking practices have improved sanitation since the beginning of the century. However, even today food can be a source of infection. The Federal Center for Disease Control estimates that infections caused by food may be as high as 2–10 million each year. The usual symptoms of infection caused by food, nausea, headache, diarrhea, and fever, are attributed to a "24-hour flu" although there is no such disease.

The Food and Drug Administration (FDA) and the U.S. Department of Agriculture (USDA) are at a disadvantage in their efforts to conduct adequate inspections of food-processing plants. The inspector must present his credentials and ask to be admitted. He may be refused or, if he is admitted, the formalities may take long enough to correct illegal practices in the processing area. Hairnets may appear, rat- and insect-contaminated materials may be hidden, adulterants may be hidden, and the floor may be swept.

Convenience foods, even those prepared by the best of processes, may be another source of disease. These foods require more handling and processing, and thus more opportunity for contamination, and little cooking by the consumer to destroy contamination. In addition bacteria and viruses are slowly developing strains which resist freezing and high temperatures. For his own protection, the consumer should be careful to follow all refrigeration and cooking directions exactly.

VACCINATION AND INOCULATION Vaccination and inoculation have succeeded in reducing the incidence of many diseases. Vaccination is very useful but it is not completely without danger. Children no longer routinely receive smallpox vaccinations. Experience in other countries has shown that, even if smallpox is introduced into a country every five years, prompt vaccination of those exposed and treatment of those who become ill reduces the fatalities to less than the few caused by a routine vaccination.

DRUGS AND DISEASE   After bacteria gain a foothold in the body and have caused symptoms of disease, drugs may be necessary. However, no drug is completely without *side effects,* that is, reactions other than the desired one. The chosen drug must kill the bacteria faster than it causes more changes in the already upset balance in the body (see Chapter 7). Once the bacteria have been killed and the drug discontinued, the body can gradually regain its normal healthy condition. An infection caused by a virus cannot be treated with drugs.

Authorities differ in their use of terms describing the various disorders involving nutrition. In this chapter, malnutrition will refer to any type of poor nutrition. Types of malnutrition are *undernutrition* (lack of sufficient nutrients in general, sometimes called general malnutrition), *overnutrition* (consumption of too much food, obesity), *nutrient imbalance* (one or more nutrients lacking or in excess in the diet).

Malnutrition

EFFECTS OF MALNUTRITION   The ultimate effect of undernutrition is starvation, but much damage can occur without actual death. Children are especially susceptible to damage because the nutrient needs of a growing organism are high and the child cannot consume large quantities of material.

In babies lack of food in general, undernutrition, causes the disease *marasmus* where the infant looks old and wrinkled. Lack of sufficient protein causes *kwashiorkor* where the child has an emaciated frame covered with puffy, watery tissue. Both of these diseases are common in war-devastated areas and during famines. Whether kwashiorkor or marasmus is reversible depends on the age of the child and the severity and duration of inadequate protein exposure. Even if the child recovers, he may never reach his potential in either mental or physical development.

The nervous system of a child is especially sensitive to lack of nutrients. The most rapid growth period of the brain is from three months before birth to about six months after birth. Slower growth continues until about the age of three. For the remainder of his life, the child will have only those cells in his nervous system which he developed during the first three years of his life. A shortage or interruption of nutrients to the nervous system will not only retard growth but may also cause the number of nerve cells to decrease.

Undernourished children are very susceptible to disease. Often deaths are attributed to diseases such as dysentery, measles, or influenza when malnutrition may be the cause or a contributory cause.

Diseases involving nutrition, such as kwashiorkor and marasmus, are expected to be found in underdeveloped countries and war-devastated areas. Surprisingly, these diseases are found in the United States. Between December 1969 and January 1971 a dozen more or less advanced cases of marasmus and seven cases of kwashiorkor were admitted to the University of Colorado Medical Center. For every case admitted to the hospital, there were undoubtedly many others.

Adults can also be affected by a poor diet. A recent study published by the USDA in 1971 shows that a large percentage of almost all chronic disease could be prevented by good, long-term nutrition.[1] Examples of the findings are listed below.

1. A 25% reduction in the 5 million people with definite or suspected heart disease in the period from 1960 to 1962.

2. A 50% decrease in the 16 million people afflicted with arthritis.

3. Fifty per cent of the 3.9 million cases of diabetes either improved or avoided.

4. A 33% reduction in the cases of alcoholism.

5. Twenty per cent fewer incidents of respiratory and infectious diseases.

Other groups go even further in connecting diet and disease. Dr. Emanuel Cheraskin and Dr. W. M. Ringsdorf of the University of Alabama Medical Center believe nutrition is a factor in all disease, including infectious disease.[2]

DIET NEEDS   Essentials for human life include about 40 *nutrients* and 20 *amino acids*.

Each amino acid contains an amine group ($-NH_2$) and an acid group ($-COOH$):

R is a different group for each of the amino acids, for example, H for glycine, $-CH_3$ for alanine,

for phenylalanine. Since the amino acids contain such a variety of groups, they can easily be converted into many vital compounds.

1. C. Edith Weir, *Benefits from human nutrition research,* Washington, D.C.: Government Printing Office, 1971, pp. 4–11.
2. E. Cheraskin, *et al., Diet and Disease,* Emmaus, Pa.: Rodale Press, 1968.

CHEMISTRY OF HEALTH

Amino acids can react together:

$$H-N-\overset{\overset{\displaystyle H}{|}}{\underset{\underset{\displaystyle H}{|}}{C}}-\overset{\overset{\displaystyle O}{\|}}{C}-OH \;+\; H-N-\overset{\overset{\displaystyle H}{|}}{\underset{\underset{\displaystyle H}{|}}{C}}-\overset{\overset{\displaystyle O}{\|}}{C}-OH \;\rightarrow\; H-N-\overset{\overset{\displaystyle H}{|}}{\underset{\underset{\displaystyle R}{|}}{C}}-\overset{\overset{\displaystyle O}{\|}}{C}-N-\overset{\overset{\displaystyle H}{|}}{\underset{\underset{\displaystyle R}{|}}{C}}-\overset{\overset{\displaystyle O}{\|}}{C}-OH \;+\; H_2O$$

The bond is called a *peptide linkage* and the compound a *dipeptide*. The dipeptide still has amino and acid groups which may combine with other amino acids to form a larger molecule. When 50 or more amino acids are joined, a protein is formed. Protein can be found in cell structures, enzymes, antibodies, and hormones. *Hormones* are similar to enzymes in that they control the rate of chemical reactions. However, hormones act only upon reactions already controlled by enzymes. The body can make some of the amino acids out of other amino acids, but eight essential ones must be entirely supplied by food. Two others are not made in sufficient amounts to satisfy the body needs, especially during growth. These, too, must be supplied by food.

Each protein molecule contains a different number of amino acids arranged in a particular order. The number of different proteins is practically unlimited. It is analogous to the number of different paragraphs (or arrangements of letters) which could be made from 20 different letters.

Animal protein (meat, fish, eggs, and milk) contains all the essential amino acids. Vegetable proteins are low in at least one essential amino acid: wheat, corn, and rice lack lysine; corn lacks tryptophane; rice lacks threonine; beans lack methionine. By combining various vegetables a complete protein diet may be obtained. For example, the proteins of corn and beans or wheat and beans supplement each other. Most of the world's population obtain their protein in this way.

All amino acids except glycine contain an asymmetric carbon atom and thus occur in two stereoisomeric forms. Only one of the two forms is produced by plants and only this form can be metabolized by other living organisms. If the amino acids were to be made synthetically, both isomers would be formed.

Minerals are part of the body structure; for example, bones and teeth contain large quantities of calcium and hemoglobin, the oxygen-carrying part of the blood, contains iron. Minerals are also needed in smaller amounts to aid in body processes, for example, potassium and magnesium ions are needed to help catalyze the combination of acetic acid and choline to form acetylcholine (see Chapter 5). Other elements, *trace elements,* are needed in very small amounts. Copper, molybdenum, cobalt, and zinc are essential trace elements; recent research indicates that chromium and tin are also needed, and others may be found in the future.

Essential metallic ions may be toxic when ingested in large amounts. Each ion is needed in rather definite amounts and each has a specific effect. An excess of one metal will not counteract the deficiency of another.

Vitamins are organic compounds which are required by the body in small amounts. Within the body they are incorporated as part of enzymes or coenzymes. Figure 6–8 shows pantothenic acid as part of coenzyme A and riboflavin as part of the coenzyme FAD. Authorities disagree on which substances are vitamins. Biotin and inositol are essential nutrients but may or may not be vitamins. Europeans consider a substance called vitamin B_{15} an essential vitamin; in this country it is thought to be neither a vitamin nor essential.

Surveys of nutritional intakes in developing countries often reveal an extremely low intake of essential nutrients without the appearance of deficiency diseases, that is, diseases caused by nutrient imbalance. Rats fed a diet deficient in niacin will develop pellagra and die in a few weeks while rats fed a diet completely lacking in all the B vitamins will live much longer although they too will die eventually. Thus, the removal of large amounts of nutrients and the replacement of only a few may be shortsighted.

Very little is actually known about the metabolic disturbances which cause a deficiency disease. The function of vitamin A in reducing night blindness is understood. However, the most striking symptoms of pellagra cannot be explained by the lack of niacin or the symptoms of scurvy by lack of vitamin C.

The optimum amounts of the various nutrients are the subject of a controversy which appears in periodicals ranging from popular publications to scientific journals. The amounts of most nutrients needed to prevent the classic deficiency diseases (i.e., scurvy, lack of vitamin C; pellagra, lack of niacin; rickets, lack of vitamin D) are more or less well known. These values, increased somewhat to allow for special cases, are the Recommended Daily Allowance (RDA) published by the FDA. Critics believe that the values are too low for two reasons. In the first place, the RDA was intended only as a guide for institutional diets to prevent deficiency diseases and not as the amount for optimum health. Second, the RDA may not make sufficient allowance for individual differences. Dr. Roger Williams, an internationally known authority on individual requirements of nutrients, has found that daily human needs for certain nutrients may vary by a factor of seven and perhaps more. While the RDA may be sufficient to prevent deficiency disease, the amounts may not be large enought to prevent small breakdowns in metabolism. These may eventually appear as susceptibility to disease.

Vitamin C is a current example of the nutritional controversy. The recommended intake varies from country to country: United States, 70 mg/day; Britain, 20 mg/day; India, 10–15 mg/day. On the other hand, Dr. Linus Pauling, Professor of Chemistry at Stanford University, believes that while the accepted value will prevent scurvy, it is far too low for optimum health.[3] He supports his thesis by an unusual method of reasoning based on studies of the effects of mutations and available nutrients. Man is one of the few animals unable to synthesize vitamin C in his tissues. It is probable that at one time man or a

3. Linus Pauling, *Vitamin C and the Common Cold,* New York: Bantam Books, 1971.

CHEMISTRY OF HEALTH

remote ancestor lost this ability through a mutation. Experiments[4] with a bacterium with the power to synthesize an amino acid and a mutant strain that had lost the ability showed how one of the strains could die out. If the two strains were supplied all needed nutrients except the amino acid, the mutant strain died. However, if they were placed in a medium with a sufficient supply of the amino acid, the original strain died. Using similar reasoning, Dr. Pauling thinks a mutation may have destroyed the ability of man to produce vitamin C at a time when an adequate supply of vitamin C was available. He calculated the amount of vitamin C present in 110 raw, natural plants which would supply an adult 2500 calories of energy. The average amount of vitamin C was 2.3 g or 33 times the RDA. Selecting just the 14 foodstuffs richest in vitamin C, he found the average content of the vitamin to be 9.4 g per 2500 calories. He concluded that the optimum daily intake would range from 2.3 to 9 g. Requirements vary for different persons so the actual amount needed would be somewhere between 0.25 and 10 g.

Dr. Irwin Stone found a similar answer by using a different method, a comparison of the requirements of other animals based on relative body weights.[5] Based on the requirement per kilogram of body weight of a monkey, a man needs 3 g per day; based on the requirements for a guinea pig, man needs 3–11 g per day. Separate calculations for most vitamins give values three times the RDA.

Other authorities believe that such large amounts of vitamin C are dangerous and that they cause kidney problems or a type of diabetes. Dr. Pauling agrees that anyone with diabetes might find such a dosage dangerous but for the average person he contends vitamin C is safer than the usual cold remedies.

There are many individuals in the United States who do not ingest enough nutrients to meet the RDA. If Dr. Pauling is correct, the number of individuals whose diets do not supply sufficient nutrients is even larger.

PREVALENCE OF POOR DIET   The USDA made surveys in 1955 and again in 1965 to determine the prevalence of inadequate diets. Figure 6–9 shows that the quality of diets in the United States declined in the 10 years between 1955 and 1965. Inadequate diets were present in all income groups, all racial groups, and all regions of the country.

A more recent study by the USDA (1968–1970) was an attempt to identify population groups with poor diets and not determine the number of people with inadequate diets. However, it did indicate that no improvement had been made and that possibly a further slight deterioration had taken place.

CAUSE OF POOR DIET   When man was a gatherer of food, his diet had a high ratio of nutrient content to calorie content. Today calories overbalance the

4. S. Zamerhof and H. H. Eichhorn, "Study of microbial evolution through loss of biosynthetic functions: Establishment of defective mutants", *Nature* 216:456, 1967.
5. Irwin Stone, *The Healing Factor: Vitamin C Against Disease*, New York: Grosset & Dunlap, 1972.

Figure 6-9. Comparison of
diets in the United States,
1955 and 1965.

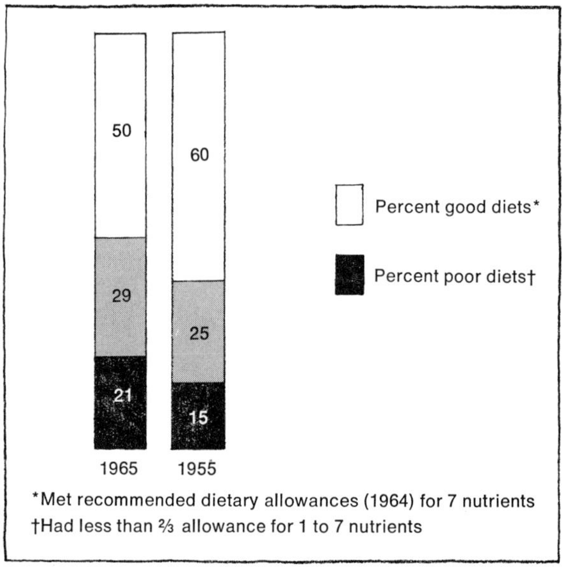

50

60

Percent good diets*

29

Percent poor diets†

25

21

15

1965   1955

*Met recommended dietary allowances (1964) for 7 nutrients
†Had less than ⅔ allowance for 1 to 7 nutrients

nutrient content. The change has been due to breeding of plants, processing, and choice of food by the consumer.

Breeding   The protein content of the Green Revolution foods was found to be less than that of natural varieties. The same kind of loss is found in much of the food commonly grown in the United States, where the plant breeder has neglected nutrition in order to increase such economic factors as yield, shipping resistance, attractiveness of fruits and vegetables, and sweetness of fruit. Table 6-1 compares the nutrient content of food crops consumed in the United States with those of Central America and Mexico. The latter foods are nearly natural.

Recently corn from the Inca civilization was found. The ears were small and crooked and the kernels were misshapen, but the protein content was very high.

Processing   Food has been processed, first by cooking, then by drying, canning, pickling, salting, smoking, and freezing, until today much of man's food little resembles the product harvested by the farmer.

In Southeast Asia progress has meant an increase in the disease beriberi which is caused by lack of thiamine (vitamin B_1) in the diet. Peasants who grow and process their own rice usually obtain enough thiamine to prevent beriberi. When rice mills are introduced into the countryside, the rice is more highly polished and the peasants do not get enough thiamine.

The American diet contains much more processed food than that of the peasants of southeast Asia. Each stage of processing may remove needed nutrient. High temperatures may destroy nutrients or affect the availability of

CHEMISTRY OF HEALTH

TABLE 6–1. Comparison of Nutrient Content of Plant Foods of Central America and of the United States.

	Minimum value as basis of comparison (mg/100 g)	No. of plant foods above minimum value		No. of Central American foods above U.S. maximum value
		United States	Central America	
Nitrogen	2,500.0	8	20	1
Calcium	100.0	12	39	6
Iron	3.0	19	51	10
Carotene	2.0	14	32	3
Thiamine	0.2	16	42	5
Riboflavin	0.2	13	34	1
Nicotinic acid	2.0	13	31	0
Ascorbic acid	75.0	7	48	20

Source: R. S. Harris, "Influence of culture on man's diet," *Arch. Environ. Health,* August 1962, p. 147. Copyright 1962, American Medical Association.

other nutrients. Nutrients may be removed by milling, washing, peeling, or chemical action.

Flour is an example of a food which is highly processed. It is made in a roller mill where the bran and germ are removed and used for animal feed. Much of the protein is lost in the germ and bran; enriched all-purpose flour has 11 g of protein per 100 g of flour while wheat germ contains 25 g of protein per 100 g of wheat germ. The amino acids in the wheat are selectively discarded to the wheat germ so that the wheat germ has a better amino acid balance than the wheat; that is, the quality of the protein in the wheat germ is better and the quality in the flour is poorer than that of the whole wheat. Table 6–2 details the loss of nutrients and shows that four must be replaced while two others may be replaced. The amounts replaced do not equal those removed. Thus, efforts to compensate for losses may lead to imbalances of nutrients in the diet.

Processed food in the diet has increased from 10% in 1941 to 50% in 1971. Whenever processed food is served, the consumer has little control of the nutrient content.

Consumer choice The consumer may choose a poor diet because of (1) inadequate income, (2) inadequate knowledge, and (3) inadequate motivation.

Many people have such low incomes that it is difficult for them to obtain conventional high protein foods. Satisfactory inexpensive high protein foods may be available but, if they are to be eaten, they must be familiar and of a type that is acceptable to the consumer. Superstitions, prejudices, attitudes, and religion affect the desirability of food in any one locality. In Northern European countries corn (maize) is regarded as a chicken feed although in South American countries it may be a prime source of protein. Locusts, mice, and snails are considered delicacies to some but are repugnant to others.

TABLE 6–2. Loss of Vitamins and Mineral Contents of Wheat due to Milling.

Chemical	Study I (% lost)	Study II (% lost)	Enrichment
Chromium	40		
Zinc	78		
Selenium	16		
Molybdenum	48		
Manganese	86	98	
Iron	76	80	Mandatory
Cobalt	89		
Copper		65	
Calcium	60	50	Optional
Sodium	78		
Potassium	77	50	
Magnesium	85	75	
Phosphorus	71	70	
Vitamin B₁ (thiamine)	77	80	Mandatory
Folic acid	67	Greatly reduced	
Vitamin A	Most		
Riboflavin	80	65	Mandatory
Niacin	81	75	Mandatory
Pyridoxine	72	50	
Vitamin D	Most		Optional
Pantothenic acid	50	50	
Choline	30	Greatly reduced	
B vitamins—biotin, inositol, paraaminobenzoic acid		All greatly reduced	

Source: Study I, information from Dr. Henry Schroeder quoted by John Lear, "Flimsy staff of life," *Saturday Review,* 53:53, 3 Oct. 1970. Study II, E. Baker and D. S. Lephorsky, *Bread and the war food problem,* College of Agriculture, University of California, June 1943.

An increase or decrease in income may adversely affect the diet. If too little money is available, cheaper food will be purchased. Cheaper food may have fewer nutrients. On the other hand, if more money becomes available, the consumer may change to more processed foods; for example, from whole grain rice to "socially superior" white rice which has fewer B vitamins than whole grain rice. Unless other changes accompany the use of white rice the deficiency disease beriberi will increase.

Some groups of people cannot metabolize certain foods because their bodies have never developed the enzymes to metabolize the food. For example, many Negroes cannot tolerate milk. They do not produce enough of the enzyme to metabolize lactose, a sugar in milk. They can usually eat cheese, buttermilk, and yogurt which contain less lactose. Lactose is removed during cheese manufacture when it drains off the solid cheese with the liquid residue. Both buttermilk and yogurt are cultured with bacteria which consume much of the lactose.

A few countries are producing concentrated vegetable powders to fortify native foods. The results have been mixed. A cheap protein product, which can constitute up to 30% of the protein in hospital, institution, and school meals, is produced by drying and purifying soy protein. If the protein is heated, extruded through a mesh, and nutrients, color, and flavoring added, a cheap, imitation meat is produced.

In order to be able to choose food properly, the consumer must know what and how much to choose. A family in Colorado had several children with severe clinical symptoms of vitamin A deficiency. At the rear of the house was a trailer full of carrots which were being used to feed hogs but not the family. Carrots are an excellent source of vitamin A.

Food manufacturers are beginning to label foods with nutrient components. Fats, carbohydrates, and proteins are reported in grams per serving, slice, or cup; vitamins, usually A, C, thiamine (B_1), riboflavin (B_2), and niacin (B_3), and minerals, calcium and iron, are reported as a percentage of the RDA. Many nutrients are not listed: pyridoxine (vitamin B_6), pantothenic acid (a B vitamin), folic acid (vitamin B_{12}), vitamin E, choline, inositol, the minerals magnesium, zinc, iodine, sodium, and potassium, and many other substances which may or may not be essential. The assumption is made that if the seven key nutrients are present in the food the other essential vitamins and minerals will also be there. This is undoubtedly true when the food is not processed but, if one or more nutrients have been added to replace those lost in processing, others may have been lost and not replaced. Storage conditions affect vitamin content, for example, high storage temperature means greater loss of nutrients. Canned fruits and vegetables were found to have lost 10% of their vitamin C content during six months storage at 18 °C (65 °F); when stored at 27 °C (80 °F) the foods lost 25% of their original vitamin C. Vitamin C is sensitive and thus will be destroyed by air entering the package. Riboflavin is destroyed by light; milk is an excellent source of this vitamin but storage in clear glass bottles exposed to light may destroy a large percentage of the original vitamin. Nutrient labeling is a help but it is not the complete answer to a good diet. It must be used with care.

Man survived for thousands of·years on the foods available to him in the region in which he lived. In many cases, his life expectancy as an adult was equal to that of modern man. The primitives of the Australian Outback live about as long as the people of the United States if they survive the accidents and diseases of infancy. Today, making a good choice of food from a health standpoint is very difficult. Many different choices are available but most foods are processed, with a resulting loss of nutrients.

Toxic Substances

There are several types of toxic substances. Some are immediately toxic upon ingestion. The insecticide parathion is of this type (see Chapter 5), as are carbon monoxide and a few drugs. The behavior of these substances is well known and usually can be avoided.

The more dangerous substances are those whose ingestion is not immediately followed by clinical symptoms. The substances may be ingested for long periods of time, perhaps years, before damage is apparent.

Mutagens, Carcinogens, Teratogens

Mutagens, carcinogens, and teratogens are substances which act on cellular material. A mutagen changes sperm or egg cells; carcinogens act on the reproduction of other cells; and teratogens act on fetal cells.

MUTAGENS   By acting on the reproductive cells, a mutagen may change the hereditary characteristics of an organism. These characteristics are controlled by the *chromosomes* which are composed of deoxyribonucleic acids (*DNA*) bonded to a protein. The *gene,* the unit of inheritance, is the chemical equivalent of part or all of a particular DNA. There is at least one gene for every enzyme, hormone, and structural protein in addition to the genes which control the development and activity of the cell. Since more than 1100 enzymes are known, the number of genes must be in the thousands.

Genes of all living organisms always have the same general structure, a coiled molecule constructed like a rope ladder (Figure 6–10). The "sides" of the ladder are made of alternating units of a phosphate and a sugar called deoxyribose. The "rungs" of the ladder are composed of four different bases that are of two types: adenine (A) and guanine (G) are pyrimidines; thymine (T) and cytosine (C) are purines. In order to have a rung of the correct length, a pyrimidine and a purine must combine by hydrogen bonding. T can only combine with A; C can only combine with G. Thus, there are four possible combinations, or *base pairs:* AT, TA, GC, and CG. Together they make a molecule called deoxyribonucleic acid or DNA.

During cell division, the ladder splits lengthwise with each rung dividing between the bases (Figure 6–11). The two half-ladders pick up the missing bases with the sugar and phosphate entities to complete both DNA molecules. Each cell now has an identical set of chromosomes.

DNA is a blueprint for cellular materials. When a particular protein is needed by the cell, the DNA splits lengthwise as it does during cell division. This time only one half of the ladder is completed and the parts are slightly different, the sugar ribose replaces deoxyribose and the base uracil (U) replaces thymine (T). Several other bases, mostly derivatives of the more usual bases, are present in small amounts. When the ribose nucleic acid (*RNA*) breaks away, the DNA molecule recombines. Thus, RNA is a reverse mold of DNA.

About 85% of the RNA is ribosome RNA (*rRNA*) which has more variation in its bases than other forms of RNA. rRNA is found in the cell in clumps where protein is made but its exact function is unknown. Messenger RNA (*mRNA*) carries the instructions to make a particular protein. Transfer RNA (*tRNA*) consists of three bases which are the code for one amino acid. When the amino acid is attached to tRNA, it is carried to mRNA. After all the amino acids are

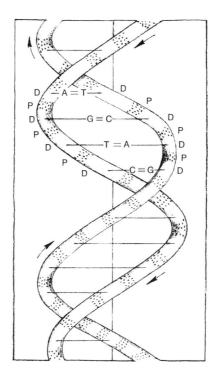

Figure 6–10. Structure of DNA.

lined up along the mRNA, the complete protein leaves to fulfill its function (Figure 6–12). This pattern of RNA and DNA is accepted by most biologists although there are a few who think the theory is oversimplified. An indication of the validity of this view is the existence of rRNA.

A mutagen changes the code. For example, at one of the 300 possible sites on the RNA from which hemoglobin, a protein, is made the code is changed by a mutagen to AAC instead of TAC (the amino acid valine instead of glutamic acid) and this results in the genetic disease sickle cell anemia. This disorder causes the hemoglobin to be fragile and change to a crescent shape when exposed to conditions of low oxygen in the tiny blood vessels. The sickle cells plug the vessels.

Sickle cell anemia is an example of a qualitative change in the code. Other changes may be quantitative. These may range from the addition or elimination of a base pair to the addition or elimination of an entire chromosome. The code may be rearranged without either qualitative or quantitative changes. In this case the chromosomes may break but rejoin in a different order. Most chromosome breaks are repaired without damage but some may not be.

The extent of mutations in man is not known. Dr. James Crow found that mutations are being produced in genetic material faster than they can be eliminated. The human race is being exposed to an increasing number of mutagens, and forces of natural selection have been reduced so that muta-

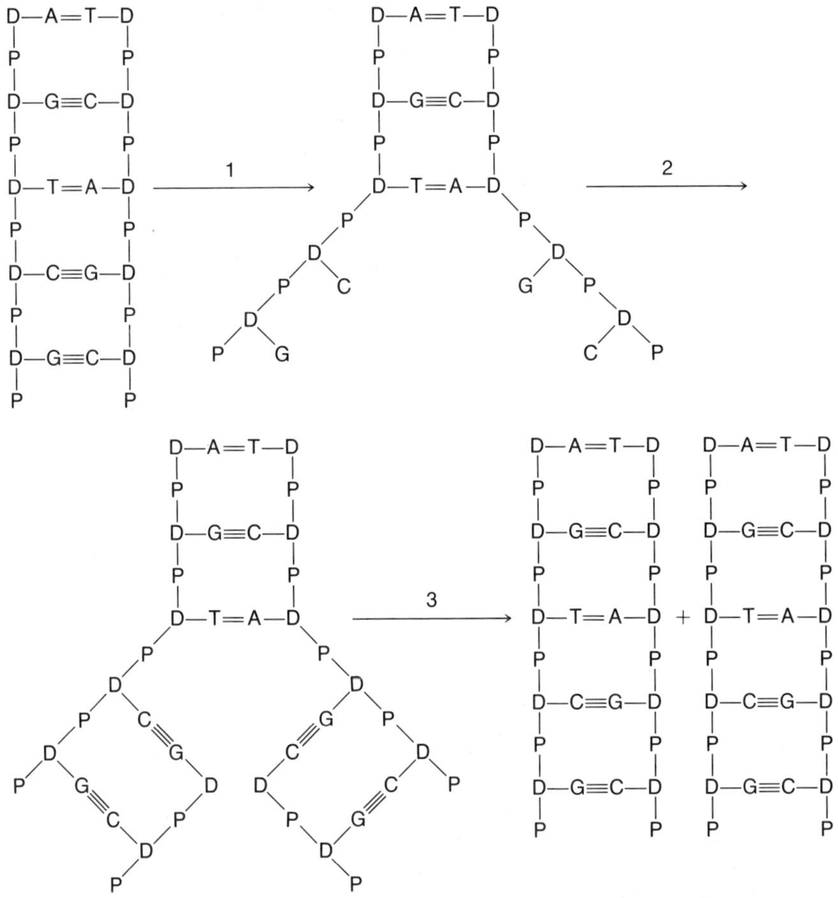

Figure 6–11. Reproduction of DNA. (1) The double helix uncoils. (2) Unattached nucleo-tides consisting of the sugar deoxyribose, a phosphate, and a base (e.g., A—D—P) float in the cell nucleus. Identical ones to those that split-off bond to the separate strands. A poly-merizing enzyme joins the nucleotides together, generating new strands. (3) The process continues until two new double helices are formed.

Figure 6–12. Protein production from DNA. (1) The double helix uncoils. (2) In the cell nucleus, free-floating units of RNA containing the sugar ribose, a phosphate, and a complementary base (the base uracil is equivalent to the base thymine) assemble into place along the separate strands. Information for protein synthesis is copied in a long strand of RNA, the messenger RNA (mRNA). The single-stranded mRNA is released from the DNA template to the cell cyto-plasm. (3) In the cytoplasm, short strands of RNA, the transfer RNA (tRNA), first attach to spe-cific amino acids and then join to the mRNA in a sequence dictated by the mRNA particular to the protein that is being manufactured. (4) The resulting protein molecule is a chain of amino acids. (See page 201.)

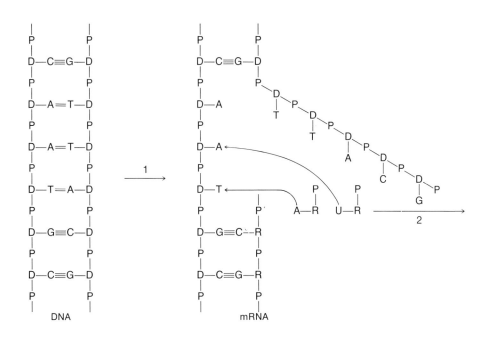

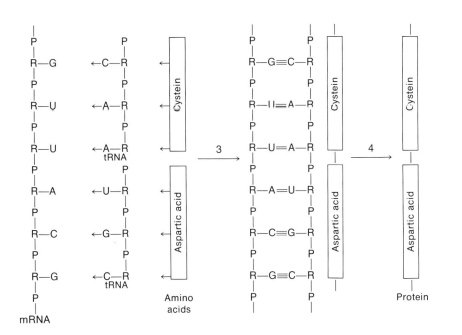

tions are not eliminated as fast as has been the case in the past. He estimated that a mutation in the genetic material will remain for an average of 40 generations; so succeeding generations are more susceptible to genetic damage.

Most mutations are unfavorable, i.e., they do not have survival value. Dr. Barton Childs of Johns Hopkins University reported that 4–20% of all conceived embryos and 0.5% of all births have chromosome abnormalities. Twenty per cent of the pediatric patients admitted to the Johns Hopkins University hospital had chronic diseases in which the action of the genes was the primary cause or a very significant contribution.

Radiation has been the most important source of mutations in the past. Not only is mankind's exposure to radiation increasing but exposure to chemicals which may be mutagenic is also increasing. There is no data on the relative importance of radiation or chemicals as mutagens, but estimates of various values up to 50% have been assigned to chemicals as a cause of mutations.

CARCINOGENS Carcinogens cause abnormalities which are similar to mutations, but the abnormalities are in the *somatic cells,* that is, cells which are not sperm or egg cells and which are not involved in production of sperm or egg cells. There is evidence that all carcinogens may be mutagens.

Cancer cells can spread (*metastasize*) to be bizarre in growth with unusual shapes, sizes, and nuclei. They may be so changed that the origin of the cell cannot be determined. Usually the more *malignant* (deadly), the more the cell has changed from its parent. Malignant cells grow faster than normal cells.

About 610,000 new cases of cancer are found each year. The rate of cancer in men has increased from 280 per 100,000 in 1947 to 304 per 100,000 in 1969 and decreased from 294 to 256 per 100,000 for women in the same period.

TERATOGENS If the chemical acts on fetal cells to cause nongenetic defects it is called a teratogen. The specific chemical and the stage of development of the fetus determines the damage. In general, the younger the fetus, the greater the damage.

Cleft palate may be the result of a teratogen. The chemical may act at a stage of growth when the male fetus is developing faster than the female fetus. The chemical has more chance to act on the female fetus and thus cause cleft palate to be more prevalent in the female.

The registration of birth defects and a blood test of all newborns have been requested by many in the medical profession. Such an action would not prevent birth defects but it would show patterns and help in identifying the cause.

SOURCES OF CHEMICALS WHICH AFFECT HUMAN HEALTH

Modern civilization has increased man's exposure to factors which may interfere with health. They are to be found everywhere: (1) air pollution (Chapter 3); (2) pesticides (Chapter 5); (3) drugs (Chapter 7); (4) food additives; (5) industrial chemicals; (6) radiation; (7) noise.

Food Additives

Many substances are added to food in small amounts to improve the storage

Figure 6–13. "I'd like half a pound of anything you have that doesn't contain tars, resins, pesticide residues, polysupersaturated fats, artificial sweeteners, softeners, foaming agents or chemical additives...." Norris in *Vancouver Sun,* Canada (Rothco).

capability or the acceptance of the food by the consumer. Each person ingests an average of over 3 lb of additives each year (Figure 6–13).

There are many types of additives and many substances for each type (Figure 6–14). Consideration of one widely used additive will show some of the problems related to additives and their use.

BHA/BHT   BHA (butylated hydroxyanisole) and BHT (butylated hydroxytoluene) are two examples of *antioxidants,* substances which hinder oxidation. The names of these compounds are unusual. The common name would contain the term phenol, but phenol has a connotation of toxicity. Consequently, the term butylated was chosen to avoid consumer rejection.

acidifiers	creaming	peeling
air replacement	curing	pesticides
alkalizers	dispersing	plasticizers
anticaking	dough conditioners	preservatives
antifoaming	drying	propellants
antihardening	emulsifiers	refining
antimycotics	enrichment	sequestrants
antioxidants	firming	solvents
antispattering	flavors	stabilizers
antisticking	flavor enhancers	sterilizing
bleaches	foaming	sweeteners
buffers	glazes	texturizers
chillproofers	humectants	thickeners
clarifiers	leavening	waterproofing
colors	maturing	water retainers
color retainers	neutralizers	whipping
container liners	nutrients	

Figure 6–14. Types of food additives and their uses.

Fats in any food will slowly and spontaneously oxidize to compounds which have the bad odor and taste of rancid fat. The first reactions are free-radical reactions started by oxygen with metal catalysts:

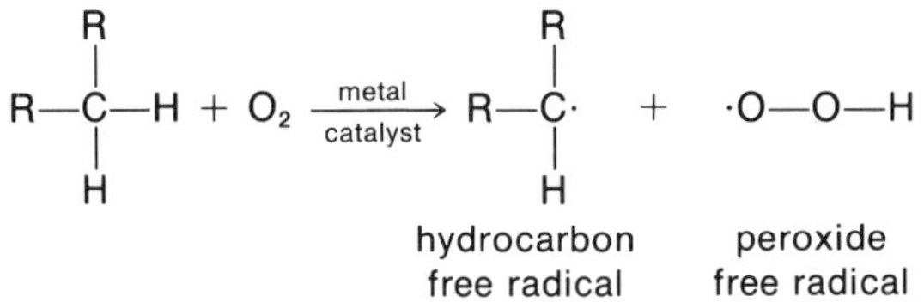

A peroxide has a bond joining two oxygens. Such compounds are unstable and very reactive. The reactive peroxide attacks the double bond on the fatty acid of the fat and forms the mixture of compounds which cause the bad taste and odor. The free radical starts (initiates) other free-radical reactions causing more peroxides to be formed. The antioxidants BHA and BHT can detach a hydrogen atom from the OH group and stop the chain reaction. The extra electron is added to the other electrons of the ring structure and does not start the formation of new free radicals.

BHA and BHT are often used with chelating agents which trap metal ions which catalyze the formation of free radicals. If the number of free radicals is reduced, the antioxidants will be able to stop the chain reactions which occur.

Fats within the body may also undergo free radical reactions. BHA added in small amounts to the food of mice seemed to increase their life span.

CHEMISTRY OF HEALTH

The use of these antioxidants is widespread. They are added to fats and oils to retard spoilage, and thus can be found in any food which contains fat, such as baked goods, fried foods (e.g., doughnuts or potato chips), salad dressings, and dry mixes. Because BHA and BHT are added to packaging materials, they migrate to many other foods.

The difficulty is that allergic reactions to BHA and/or BHT are not uncommon. Since the label does not always indicate their use, it is difficult for anyone to avoid foods which contain these two additives.

REGULATION The protection of food, drugs, and cosmetics is under the control of the Food and Drug Administration (FDA) which was given its authority under the Food, Drug, and Cosmetic Act of 1938. The original act has been amended by the 1954 Pesticide Amendments, the 1958 Food Additive Amendment, and the 1960 Color Additives Amendment. Under the 1958 Food Additive Amendment all additives are to be classified as follows: (1) excluded from food if they cause cancer when ingested by man or animals (the Delaney clause); (2) subject to few restrictions if considered generally recognized as safe (GRAS); (3) subject to intensive testing by manufacturers and excluded from food until proven safe.

Delaney clause The Delaney clause is often criticized because it does not allow the scientist enough freedom in making decisions about possible carcinogens. However, the scientist does have the freedom to devise "appropriate" methods with suitable animals to determine whether a food additive is carcinogenic. If a food additive is found to cause cancer by these methods, then it must be removed from the market. This is what Dr. Alvin Weinberg calls a "transscience decision"—after the scientist furnishes the information, the decision must be made by a political process. Here the decision was made by Congress.

GRAS In order to belong to the second classification, the additive must be "generally recognized among experts qualified by scientific training and experience based on common use in food to be safe." The FDA selected 189 additives to send to 900 scientific experts to comment on their safety. 350 scientists replied and 194 of these responded favorably or without comment. 182 substances were approved as GRAS. Today there is estimated to be about 600 GRAS items.

A few of the additives were selected as GRAS although at least one expert questioned their safety. Some of these have since been removed from the list; e.g., cyclamates, the sweetener removed from the list in 1969.

CONTROVERSIAL ADDITIVES, NO_2^- AND NO_3^- These additives are added to meats in relatively large amounts to retain the color and in small amounts to preserve the meat. Both have been used for a long time in the preservation and coloring of meat.

Sodium or potassium nitrate can be changed to nitrite

$$\text{oxygen receiver} + NO_3^- \rightarrow NO_2^- + \text{oxygen compound}$$

in the infant stomach. Nitrites can cause methemoglobinemia in infants. In this disease the nitrite ion bonds to the hemoglobin of the blood to form a stable brownish compound similar to the compound formed by carbon monoxide (CO) (Chapter 3). Not all children are affected; some can ingest nitrates without harm while others die. Nitrates and nitrites are no longer used in baby food. A baby can ingest these additives only by eating adult food.

Nitrates are not toxic to adults at levels ordinarily ingested; the adult stomach is more acidic and does not reduce the nitrate ions, and adult hemoglobin is not affected by nitrites to the same extent as the hemoglobin of an infant. However, nitrites can combine with secondary amines to form compounds known as nitrosamines; such reactions occur under the same conditions of acidity as present in the stomach (pH about 2). An amine is a compound with a nitrogen atom as a center and three groups attached to it:

H | H—N—R	H | R—N—R	R | R—N—R
primary amine	secondary amine	tertiary amine

Secondary amines are common. They exist in cereals, beer, tea, wine, tobacco smoke, herbicides, insecticides, drugs, and possibly cooked meat.

$$\overset{R}{\underset{R}{\diagdown}} N-H + H-O-N{=}O \rightarrow \overset{R}{\underset{R}{\diagdown}} N-N{=}O + H_2O$$

hydrogen nitrite   nitrosamine

There are many nitrosamines; some are very carcinogenic. Research on their effects is just beginning. A Canadian scientist has found that cats fed nitrites and an amine produced a nitrosamine. A German scientist showed that mice fed nitrites and an amine produced the same type of tumor that was produced when a nitrosamine was fed. Recently nitrosamines have been found in prepared meats treated with nitrites. On the basis of such information, Norway banned the use of nitrates and nitrites in meats after 1 January 1973.

The Delaney clause of the 1958 Food Additive Amendment does not apply to nitrosamines because they are not an additive but are formed from substances in the meat.

THE FDA AND FOOD ADDITIVES   The FDA has been the center of controversy ever since it was formed as the Bureau of Chemistry under the Department of Agriculture.

CHEMISTRY OF HEALTH

One topic of contention is the Delaney Clause of the 1958 Food Additive Amendment. The FDA, the food industry, and some scientists insist that the Delaney Clause is too strict, since a certain amount of a carcinogen (called a threshold) can be ingested with no harm. They believe that the DNA can accept a small amount of damage without becoming uncontrollable. An example may be the hemoglobin molecule, which exists in different individuals in many slightly different forms which may have been caused by mutations at some time in the past. Each type functions with no harm to the individual. Other scientists, just as reputable, believe that whether or not a cell exposed to a carcinogen becomes cancerous is a matter of statistics. From this point of view, any molecule of a carcinogen can cause a cancer. Repeated exposure increases the chances. Little definitive evidence exists to support either contention. This is a situation in which Senator Gravel's questions (see p. 7) should be asked.

Critics of the FDA also claim that the agency is over-receptive to industries' desires without showing a corresponding interest in the needs of the American public. They note that executives pass freely back and forth from high positions in the agency to positions in the food industry and the American Medical Association; this has been called the "revolving door" policy. They think that the FDA is too willing to let industry use any additives it wishes without adequate testing. FDA spokesmen insist that their close relationships with the food industry allows them to accomplish their goals with less difficulty and much more quickly than would otherwise be possible. They insist that their actions are based on scientific studies by their employees and by industry.

In any case the use of additives by the food industry is increasing steadily. Perhaps Dr. Jean Mayer,[6] Professor of Nutrition, Harvard University, has best expressed the problem:

> As for the mess of additives listed on the label, even if one suffers from no particular phobia towards them, the question remains: Why go out of one's way to consume them?
>
> All of us have become used to the concept of "risk-benefit ratio:" if the benefit outweighs the risk that might possibly be involved, we can accept the risk. Let us make sure, however, that with an ever-mounting number of pseudo foods we don't get into a situation where the benefits are the manufacturers' alone while the consumer has all the risk.

There are several thousand additives. Dr. Samuel Epstein of Case Western Reserve Medical School has told numerous Congressional committees that the number of additives could be reduced to less than 100 without affecting the variety of food or the manufacturer's production. The smaller number would allow rigorous testing for safety.

No one wants to eliminate all additives or even all the items on the GRAS list. For example, salt and common spices and flavorings are considered additives and are probably harmless to most people. However, the number of additives

---

6. From Dr. Mayers' column "Food for Thought," "Why go out of the way to consume additives?" *Detroit Free Press*, 25 July 1973.

should be as few as possible and the consumer should have the option of knowing what he is ingesting.

Effluents from Industries

Chemicals are not 'innocent until proven guilty,' they do not have human rights. Unless we treat them as guilty until proven innocent, they will deprive real human beings of the rights to health.[7]

Charles F. Wurster

The Chemical Abstract Service list of 1.7 million chemical compounds grows by 25,000 each year (Figure 6–15). Each year 300–500 new compounds are added to the over 10,000 commercially made synthetic compounds. In addition, many intermediate substances must be produced. In the oil industry alone 15,000 different compounds are known.

Not only are more compounds being made but larger quantities are being produced (Table 6–3). The growth in the chemical industry is expected to continue. The quantity of plastics produced, for example, is expected to increase three-fold from 1969 to 1980, from 17.7 to 50 billion pounds.

All of these compounds must be returned to the environment in some form and at some place. From the twelfth century to the Industrial Revolution in the eighteenth century a person was completely responsible for any degradation to

7. Letter to the editor, *Science,* 175:834, 25 February 1972.

Figure 6–15. "We need a cease-fire between the Industrial Revolution and our environment." Engelhardt in *St. Louis Post-Dispatch.*

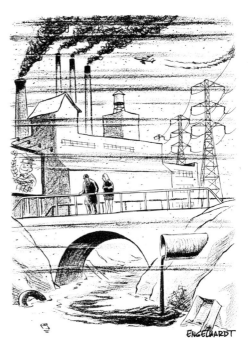

CHEMISTRY OF HEALTH

TABLE 6–3. Production of Synthetic Organic Compounds.

Year	Production (billions of pounds)	Average annual increase (%)
1943	10	14
1953	24	15
1963	61	13
1970	138	

the property of another. During the Industrial Revolution, a person was liable only if the damage was clearly his fault. If the degradation was due to an "accident," the victim had to pay the cost. This practice helped industry to survive. Since the Industrial Revolution, there has been little control over where, how, and in what form chemicals, poisonous or harmless, are dumped. Only the government had authority to question industry's right to dispose of its waste products in any way it wished.

Workers in various industries are often the first to be exposed to dangerous substances. Thus the health of the worker may act as an early warning system for the rest of the population. The number of workers who die each year from occupational disease (100,000) is many times the number who die from industrial accidents (14,000–15,000).

Different types of pollutants are produced by different industrial processes. Among the important pollutants are the heavy metals, inorganic minerals, and synthetic organic compounds.

HEAVY METALS   Heavy metals in general are those five times as heavy as water per unit volume. In the periodic table, they lie between vanadium and germanium, zirconium and antimony, and lanthanum and polonium.

Some are toxic at high concentrations and some at very small concentrations. Since the heavy metals are different chemically, they affect the body cells differently. Mercury, silver, and copper attack the sulfur atoms of body protein where the sulfur is part of the molecule of three of the amino acids. One of these, cysteine, forms a bond to another cysteine molecule through a pair of sulfur atoms, Cys—S—S—Cys, the disulfide bridge. The small mercury atom has a strong attraction for the large negative sulfur atom with its exposed electrons. The disulfide bridge is broken and the protein is no longer capable of performing its function in the cell. Heavy metals can also combine with the sulfhydryl groups (—SH) and interfere with the enzymes or other substances involved.

Other heavy metals combine with the membrane surrounding the cell. Copper, lead, mercury, cadmium, and others thus interfere with the passage of nutrients into and out of the cell. Other heavy metals may combine with various substances in the cell and change the behavior of these substances.

Mercury and cadmium will be studied in detail.

Mercury Mercury has properties which make it unique. Its widespread use is a result of these special properties. It is the only liquid metal although cesium and gallium will liquefy on a warm day. It freezes at $-38.9\,°C$ ($-38.02\,°F$) and boils at $356.6\,°C$ ($673\,°F$). Thus it is well suited for use in thermometers and barometers. Since mercury is a metal, it conducts an electric current, Since it is also a liquid, it has special applications in the field of electronics, for example, in silent switches, rectifiers, electrodes, and thermostats.

Mercury dissolves many other metals; the resulting solutions (liquids or solids depending upon factors such as temperature and composition, as well as the identity of the second metal) are termed *amalgams*. In the refining of gold and silver, mercury dissolves the precious metals out of ores. When the amalgam is heated, mercury vapor is driven off and leaves the gold and silver in a pure state. Amalgams are also used in making mirrors and filling teeth.

Because mercury and its compounds are toxic, they have been used in pesticides. The toxicity to man depends upon the form of mercury that is ingested and the route of ingestion. Mercury vapor is so toxic that mercury from a broken thermometer should never be played with. No one should coat coins with mercury. Several forms are less toxic than vapor but still poisonous. The effects of ingesting liquid metallic mercury, inorganic mercury, or mercury combined with a benzene ring (phenyl group, thus phenylmercury) can be treated. However, if mercury is combined with a straight-chain carbon group, the compound is especially toxic and the condition is untreatable. In this case, the alkyl groups are straight-chain carbon entities which are usually methyl, $-CH_3$, or ethyl, CH_3-CH_2-. The corresponding alkyl mercury compounds are called methyl mercury and ethyl mercury.

The symptoms from the ingestion of a mercury alkyl compound begin with numbness of the extremities and tongue followed by ataxia (inability to co-ordinate voluntary movements), deafness, tunnel vision, and eventually a completely vegetative existence and death. Whether there is a threshold to damage is debatable. There is a threshold below which there are no clinical symptoms. However, it is possible that when brain and nerve cells are damaged by any amount of ingested mercury, other brain and nerve cells substitute for the damaged cells. No apparent damage may appear until substitute cells are no longer available. The symptoms might be attributed to early senility.

There is evidence to indicate that methylmercury may be a teratogen. Babies with defects caused by mercury have been born to mothers showing no symptoms of mercury poisoning. The fetus is especially vulnerable, because animal studies indicate that it is more susceptible to cell damage by mercury than is an adult and because it may be exposed to a higher concentration than the mother. Higher concentrations of mercury have been found in the blood of newborns than in the maternal blood.

Mercury enters the environment when it is used or when it is dumped after use. Table 6–4 shows that every use of mercury decreased between the years 1969 and 1971. Whether the decrease in the use of mercury in the production of

TABLE 6–4. Uses of Mercury in the United States.

Uses	Pounds used	
	1969	1971
Agricultural uses (including fungicides and bactericides for industrial purposes)	203,000	112,000
Industrial uses		
Catalysts	225,000	86,000
Amalgamates	14,000	—
Electrical applications	1,417,000	1,286,000
Preparation of chlorine	1,575,000	932,000
General laboratory uses	156,000	137,000
Industrial and control	531,000	370,000
Paint		
Antifouling	18,000	31,000
Mildew proofing	641,000	623,000
Paper and pulp manufacturing	42,000	—
Pharmaceuticals	55,000	52,000
Other	736,000	175,000
Unknown	85,000	200
Total	6,012,000	3,985,000

Source: Adapted from V. Anthony Cammarota, "Mercury." *Minerals Yearbook,* Washington, D.C.: Government Printing Office, 1973, p. 734.

chlorine is due to new methods is not known. The use of mercury fluctuates widely as chlorine plants close and open.

The largest single use of mercury is in the chlor-alkali cell (apparatus for electrolysis of an ionic substance, Chapter 2) for the production of chlorine (Figure 6–16). An electric current passed through a saturated solution of sodium chloride (NaCl) produces chlorine gas and sodium metal which is very reactive and difficult to handle:

$$2Na^+ + 2Cl^- \rightarrow 2Na + Cl_2$$

The sodium metal dissolves in a layer of mercury which flows along the base of the cell into a second compartment where the amalgam is passed through water. The sodium reacts with the water to form sodium hydroxide:

$$2Na + 2HOH \rightarrow 2NaOH + H_2$$

The spent mercury again flows through the cell. Thus, the overall reaction for the electrolysis of a solution of NaCl is:

$$2NaCl + HOH \rightarrow 2NaOH + H_2 + Cl_2$$

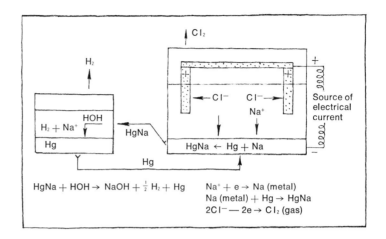

Figure 6–16. A chlor-alkali cell for the production of chlorine, by using mercury as an electrode and by forming an amalgam with sodium.

Brine (concentrated salt solution) is continuously added to the cell to replace that used in the reaction. Eventually, the brine becomes so contaminated by extraneous material, including trapped mercury, that it is dumped and replaced with fresh brine. In the past, no great effort was made to recover the relatively small amounts of mercury lost in this way, since the relatively unreactive mercury was not considered a threat to the receiving body of water. The mercury was thought to fall to the bottom, become covered with sediment, and, therefore, be unavailable to life.

In 1956, 42 cases of a "new" disease appeared around Minamata Bay in Japan. The symptoms became known as Minamata disease. It was traced to the mercury dumped from chlor-alkali cells into the Bay, where anaerobic bacteria acted on the mercury metal and changed it to methyl mercury. Mercury poisoning was not "new"; it had been known previously as an occupational disease for hatters. Felt for hats was treated with mercury as part of a preparation process. What was "new" was the surprising discovery that mercury metal dumped on the bottom of a body of water could be changed to a poisonous form. Minamata disease sparked a worldwide hunt for places where mercury might be found as a pollutant. In the United States, chlor-alkali plants around Lake St. Clair and Lake Erie were found to be dumping huge quantities of mercury in the lakes. The dumping has been stopped and mercury residues are being stored in underground salt mines. There is another type of cell which can be used for the electrolysis of salt, but it does not work as efficiently as the mercury cell.

Methylmercury and ethylmercury, as well as phenylmercury, have been used as fungicides on seeds before planting. Deaths of Swedish birds were traced to mercury seed treatments; mercury concentrated in the new seed crop which was ingested by animals who further concentrated the poison. When the use of such seed treatments was discontinued, residues in meat and eggs fell to one-third and one-quarter respectively of their previous values. The deaths of wild birds declined. Use of methylmercury and ethylmercury seed treatment has been stopped in the United States, and use of phenylmercury has been reduced. There are other substitutes for the seed treatments but they are more expensive than mercury compounds.

The paper and pulp industry has stopped using mercury as a fungicide because the FDA no longer allows paper produced from factories treated with mercury compounds to be used for food wrappings. A compound called pentachlorophenol (PCP) has been substituted for the mercurial fungicides. PCP has its own set of problems; it has the same impurities, dioxin compounds, as its relative 2,4,5-T (see Chapter 5).

Paints often contain a mercury fungicide. A recent investigation found such paints to be a common source of mercury in homes.

It is estimated that it will take a lake 10–100 years to clean itself by flushing the mercury through its outlet and, eventually, into the ocean. Examinations of ocean fish in museums have indicated that mercury has been in fish for centuries. However, this is not the issue. Mercury does damage nerve tissues; the issue is to prevent such damage.

Cadmium Cadmium lies below zinc in the periodic table and thus belongs to the same family of elements. Logically, it is found in zinc ores.

The Japanese have had the most experience with the toxicity of cadmium. High cadmium intake causes painful decalcification of the bones causing them to break easily, even on turning in bed. Most of the cases were elderly women with large families, but some were men and young women. All cases were near a zinc mine or smelter.

There is evidence that cadmium may be mutagenic, teratogenic, and carcinogenic. These effects may be related to zinc deficiencies which are known to produce abnormal fetuses in animals. Since it takes 20–50 years for carcinogenic effects to appear, a cause-effect relationship is difficult to determine.

The average man of 50 years of age and weighing about 150 pounds has a body burden of about 30 mg of cadmium. In the United Kingdom and Sweden, levels are 15 and 20 mg, respectively.

The largest amounts of cadmium in the environment come from refining ores, mostly copper and zinc. Steel is often coated with cadmium; when the scrap steel is heated to high temperatures, cadmium vaporizes and is lost to the atmosphere. Cadmium is used as a catalyst in the making of plastics; when the plastics are burned, cadmium is vaporized. Coal and petroleum contain cadmium which is released when the fuel is burned.

Refining of grain changes the ratio of zinc to cadmium in the flour. Zinc is present in greatest amount in the bran and germ of the grain berry while cadmium is present in greatest amount in the starchy part of the berry. In refining grain for the production of flour, the removal of the bran and germ may remove much of the contained zinc while removing little of the cadmium contained in the starchy part which eventually becomes flour. In effect, the cadmium becomes more concentrated as a result of the refining process.

Each cigarette produces tobacco smoke which contains 1.4 μg of cadmium, mostly in the form of cadmium oxide which is the more immediately toxic form of cadmium. Smoking 10–20 cigarettes per day adds 1–4 μg to the body burden. The body burden of the nonsmoker will increase if he is exposed to cigarette smoke.

Little is known about the effect of cadmium on the molecular level. Symptoms may be due to interference with the enzymatic roles of zinc and copper. Since the body burden of the people in the United States is rising and damage is known to have been done by cadmium, research should be done on the effects of cadmium on the human body.

ASBESTOS, A MINERAL   Asbestos is a mineral which is very stable; it is fireproof and resistant to attack by chemicals, and it separates rather easily into fibers which may be spun and woven into fireproof clothing and curtains. These properties which make it useful are the same properties which make it a problem in the environment.

In the home, curtains, rugs, potholders, and ironing board covers are made from asbestos. In building construction, it is sprayed on walls as a fireproofing material, and put into plaster, wallboard, paints, and floor and roofing tile. It is used as a filter in the manufacture of beer, medicine, and fruit drinks. It is found in brake and clutch linings, mufflers, and sealants in every car, truck, tractor, airplane, and ship. It has even been found in baby powder' since talc beads sometimes contain asbestos fibers.

When asbestos fibers enter the lungs and fall on the lung surface, they stay there and become coated with a yellow-brown substance. These are the yellow bodies commonly found in the lungs of industrial workers. Asbestosis, a disease of the respiratory system, has been common among workers and miners in the asbestos industry. As the death rate from this disease is cut by industrial controls, the workers live long enough to die of cancer which is asbestos related. Cancer deaths among asbestos workers are increasing.

Dr. Irving J. Selikoff and Dr. Cuyler Hammond studied the deaths of asbestos workers from information given them by the labor union. The records of 632 men who had worked at least 20 years in the industry showed that lung cancer was about seven times greater for the asbestos worker than expected. Intestinal cancer was three times greater than expected. An apparent synergistic effect between smoking and the effect of asbestos was found in another study. The smoker had a 90% greater chance of cancer than his fellow nonsmoking workers.

Japan has one of the highest rates for cancer of the stomach in the world. A possible relationship may exist between these cancers and asbestos. Rice, a staple of the Japanese diet, is dusted with talc which may contain asbestos fibers.

Asbestos bodies are being found in the lungs of people who have never worked near an industry that uses asbestos. In 3000 consecutive autopsies in New York City in three different hospitals, 48.3% of the cases had asbestos bodies in their lungs.

The current standard for the general public is that each milliliter of air may contain no visible fibers. For the occupational worker the standard is not more than 2 fibers, each not more than 5 μm long, per milliliter of air. However, in every milliliter of air with 2 long fibers, there may be 10–100 times as many short fibers (see Chapter 3 for a discussion of the danger of small-sized particles.)

PCB, AN ORGANIC SUBSTANCE   PCB is the abbreviation for the group of extremely stable compounds whose family name is polychlorinated biphenyl. Theoretically there are 210 possible isomeric substances formed by replacing one or more hydrogen atoms by chlorine atoms in various positions on the molecule.

All of the compounds have high boiling points, low solubility in water, high solubility in a wide range of organic solvents, and electrical insulating qualities. The commercial isomers, liquids or resins, are stable to heat, acids, bases, and oxygen. These properties make them useful, but they also make them persist in the environment.

PCBs act as electrical insulators and as a heat-transfer medium. The good electrical insulating properties of the PCBs make possible the compact commercial transformers and capacitors which electrical power companies use. Without these substances, it would be necessary to make these essential instruments 50% larger at considerably greater cost.

The desirable properties of PCBs have caused them to be used extensively in large amounts. Some of these materials have been discarded or have leaked into the environment. As has been the case too often with pollutants, PCBs have become widely dispersed before it was recognized that they might be causing biological problems.

As in the case of mercury and cadmium, the Japanese have had the most experience with the effect of PCBs on the human body. The only known incidence of poisoning occurred there in 1968. The rice oil disease, so called because oil contaminated with PCBs from a heat-transfer system was the source of the poisoning, affected 10,000 people and caused 60 deaths. The symptoms vary from patient to patient and change as the disease progresses. Few completely recover from the acne-like eruptions, discharging eyes, loss of hair, general fatigue, poor eyesight, vomiting, respiratory distress, loss of appetite, headache, forgetfulness, and loss of ability to concentrate.

Many aquatic organisms, crustaceans, and fish may be injured or killed by levels as low as 1 ppb of PCB in water. The low levels build up in the food chain and eventually reach toxic levels. Birds eating the fish may develop extremely high levels. Several studies have shown that PCBs do not produce eggshell thinning. However, they do affect the hatchability of eggs and they may delay breeding. Chickens hatched from PCB-affected eggs do not develop as fast as the controls. These characteristics may be even more dangerous than eggshell thinning.

Normally, when most foreign chemicals are taken into the human body the activity of liver enzymes increases. Usually the chemicals are destroyed. However, PCBs stimulate the production of the enzymes in animals without being broken down themselves. The enzymes may destroy necessary naturally occurring compounds including sex steroids. In view of these actual and potential dangers, efforts are being made to control their use. Monsanto Chemical Company, the only company that makes these compounds in the United States, refuses to sell PCBs to food-processing plants. For other uses it demands that they be used in closed systems from which, theoretically, they can be recovered. The company has built an incinerator to destroy any PCBs that are shipped to it. However, the incinerator has a capacity of only 1 million pounds annually and between 50 and 60 million pounds are sold each year. There is one other incinerator available for discarded PCBs but most will be dumped in a landfill.

The PCBs may no longer be used in plastics or "carbonless" duplicating paper. Since paper with PCBs is being recycled, the FDA put a limit of 10 ppm on packaging used for human and animal foods.

Although today's use is restricted, the PCBs cannot be removed from waterways. As products that were made with PCBs are discarded, the quantities in the environment may increase. However, if the controls are successful, the level should eventually decline. Only the future can tell.

Research has not given the answers to the final disposition of the PCBs. Do PCBs cause the same kinds of effects in humans as they do in birds and mink? Do pure PCBs cause the disabilities or is the cause an impurity in the product? What are the conditions under which PCBs will produce the contaminating impurity, assuming there is such an impurity? What are the degradation products of PCBs? DDT, PCBs, and mercury are found together in some birds. Is there a synergistic effect?

CONCLUSION The history of each of the above toxic substances has two characteristics, which show that time and lack of awareness trap many people.

1. A short period of exposure may result in damage appearing many years later (asbestos). A long period of exposure at low levels may result in the sudden appearance of clinical symptoms (mercury).

2. Before the cause of the delayed disease was discovered the substance was considered to be harmless and had become widely, perhaps irreversibly, dispersed throughout the environment.

The general public as well as industrial workers are becoming increasingly exposed to ionizing and nonionizing radiation. *Ionizing radiation* is energy or particles of matter which may remove electrons from atoms and/or break bonds between atoms. The energy content of *nonionizing radiation* is too small to cause loss of electrons by atoms or break the bonds between atoms.

Visible white light can be separated into a *spectrum* of many colors. If a body, for example, an iron bar, is heated, it will radiate heat even when it does not glow. Later as it becomes hotter it may glow a dull red, then yellow, and finally white. If the light from a glowing white-hot bar is passed through a set of narrow slits so that a narrow beam is produced and is then passed through a prism, the light becomes spread out into a band of colors from red through yellow to violet. Scientists believe that light is a wave motion that travels at 300,000 km (186,000 miles) per second through space. The waves, called *electromagnetic waves,* vary in length in a manner similar to water waves.

A *continuum* (Figure 6–17) of electromagnetic waves extends both beyond the visible red and the visible violet. Red light waves are longer than violet light waves. *Infrared* light, the longer waves immediately beyond red, is not visible but can warm an object. Progressively in the direction of longer waves are found microwaves, radio waves, and electric current waves. Red light waves are about 80 μm in length, while electric current waves (60 c/sec) are 5000 m (about 3 miles) in length, a tremendous range. In the other direction (beyond violet light), the electromagnetic waves become progressively shorter in going from violet to cosmic rays. (For our purpose rays and waves are interchangeable when describing the transmission of energy by systems similar to light.)

Figure 6–17. An electromagnetic spectrum.

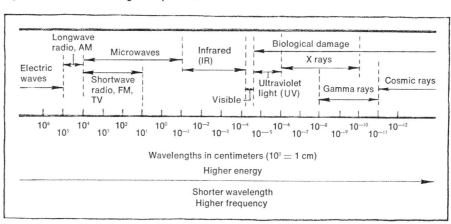

Infrared rays will warm you. Ultraviolet rays can burn your exposed skin or destroy your sight. X rays can penetrate your flesh and give a shadow picture of your bones and other tissues. Clearly, the short-wave radiation is more penetrating and can cause more changes to take place than can the long-wave radiation; short-wave radiation (gamma rays, x rays, and cosmic rays) contains more energy and can cause changes in molecules, that is, ionize them.

IONIZING RADIATION When energetic radiation (particles or rays of energy) removes an electron from an atom, a chemical reaction which forms new compounds can occur. Proteins, enzymes, hormones, or genes may be changed to different configurations. The individual may become ill until his body has time to repair the damage. If the damage is extensive, death results. The damage may be mutagenic, teratogenic, or carcinogenic. The smallest amount of high-energy radiation could be effective if a precise "hit" is made. Statistically, a viable "hit" requires considerable exposure to be achieved.

Any change which occurs as the result of radiation expands its effect during growing processes. Thus young children are 10 times as susceptible to radiation damage as adults, and fetuses are 100 times as susceptible; the younger the fetus, the greater is the potential for damage. For the same reason irradiation of pregnant women or of genital regions poses genetic dangers to future generations.

Atmospheric testing of nuclear weapons and leakage from underground testing have produced large quantities of elements which can produce energetic radiation. Isotopes of strontium and iodine are examples. Iodine-131 will concentrate in the thyroid gland and produce radiation which will damage the surrounding tissues. Strontium-90 is a member of the alkaline earth family. Thus, it may concentrate in bone tissue and irradiate bone marrow. The result may be leukemia. Isotopes of other elements may affect other tissues in the body and produce carcinogenic, mutagenic, or teratogenic effects. A more extensive discussion of sources of nuclear radiation will be given in Chapter 10.

X-ray examination accounts for 95% of all man-made radiation experience. About 130 million Americans had one or more x-ray examinations last year. One x-ray picture may equal the background radiation (radiation from natural sources) received by the average person in one year. The radiation to a patient may be limited by reducing exposure at the time the x ray is taken or by reducing the number of x rays needed. The Bureau of Radiological Health is attempting to do both.

The Bureau is establishing a standard requiring x-ray equipment to follow more closely that of European countries where the patient is exposed to less radiation. The equipment is to be designed to restrict the beam to the size of the film or the fluoroscope screen. This alone would reduce exposure by 65%. The Bureau has also distributed thousands of beam restricters and filters to reduce dental x-ray exposure. They have also improved x-ray measuring equipment.

Another requirement is for equipment to reproduce image quality at definite settings so that retakes are reduced or eliminated. The Bureau is helping to train personnel to use x-ray equipment. Courses at the medical and graduate school level have been improved. A computer project to improve storage and retrieval of x-ray pictures has been initiated. Thus, the number of exposures needed by a patient would be reduced.

NONIONIZING RADIATION, MICROWAVES   Microwaves are similar to radio waves but they are shorter and have a higher frequency. They penetrate below the surface and produce heat.

Industrially, microwaves are both a time-saving device and a method to produce a better product. The radiation can be used to dry products. Potato chip manufacturers heat the potatoes in oil until they are at a desired stage of brownness and contain about 6% moisture. Microwaves are used to reduce the moisture to about 2% without further browning. Paper, ink, photographic film, and lumber are other industries that can use microwaves for drying.

The heat produced by microwaves can reduce the time for a chemical reaction to occur. Food can be cooked quickly for processing and restaurant service. Microwaves can be used to reduce the time needed to "cure" plastics, that is, reduce the time needed for the chemical reaction to occur.

The absorption of microwaves and production of heat in the human body is a complex process. Short-wavelengths are absorbed mostly by the skin; longer wavelengths are absorbed partly by the skin and partly by deep organs. The amount of absorption depends upon the amount of fat present. Fat is a poor absorber of microwaves; tissues with high water content are good absorbers. Microwaves with long wavelengths are absorbed by deep organs.

The skin can absorb considerable radiation without harm because the generated heat is easily dissipated. However, the deep organs, especially those insulated by fat and with a small blood supply, have difficulty in dissipating heat and are likely to be damaged. The organ with the most sensitivity to microwave radiation and the resulting heat is the testes. This organ is normally 2 °F cooler than the remainder of the body. At normal body temperature the testes become sterile, but it is doubtful if the sterility is permanent. Power densities of 5 mW per square centimeter will raise the temperature of the testes of a dog to normal body temperature.

Other effects are athermal because they are produced by energy too low to produce heat. The first reports of such effects came from the Soviet Union, where they found that chronic exposure to low-level microwave energy resulted in a variety of symptoms. The body chemistry can be upset and effects felt in circulatory, nervous, and respiratory systems. Behavioral alterations are common. All of the effects are reversible, although some may take up to two months to disappear after exposure has ended. The Russian scientists theorize that the effects are caused by microwaves acting on the brain or nerves. The Soviet standards reflect their concern about safety in the use of microwaves (Table 6–5).

American scientists are skeptical of the reports because there is no known function of the nerves which would explain the effects observed by the Russian

TABLE 6–5. Various Standards for Exposure to Microwaves.

Agency	Limit for continuous exposure (mW/cm²)
HEW	5.00
Armed Services	10.00
Bell Laboratories	1.00
Russia	0.01

scientists. However, one American scientist, Dr. Allen H. Frey, has made studies which may support the Russian studies.[8]

Two biologists irradiated male fruit flies and found mutations in the next generation.[9] This does not mean that low-energy microwaves will cause mutations in humans, but it does mean that the subject needs to be carefully investigated. Much research is now in progress but it will take years, maybe decades, before the results are obtained. Meanwhile, the use of industrial microwaves is expected to increase many times in the next few years.

In the home, a microwave oven cooks food in one-half to one-eighth the time required in a conventional oven. Hot dogs in buns cook in 1 min, bacon in 4 min, a TV dinner in 5–10 min. However, there are disadvantages. Food does not brown; for example, a cooked hamburger is grey. Metal utensils may not be used because radiation might bounce from the metal to the radiation bulb and damage it. Limits set by the FDA are a presale level of 1 milliwatt (mW) per square centimeter and 5 mW per square centimeter after sale. Part of the cause of excessive leakage is the lack of proper care by the homemaker. If the oven door is not kept clean, it will not close properly and may leak radiation. The only way to determine actual leakage is to have the oven tested.

Water craft equipped with radar devices are an increasing source of microwave radiation for the general public. Excessive leakage has occurred from electronic devices in high school and college science classes. These devices need to be handled properly, and some have had to be redesigned to reduce radiation to acceptable levels.

TESTING   The problem of discovering which substances are toxic, mutagenic, carcinogenic, or teratogenic is a very complex one.

Difficulty of Testing   Until recently, most of the suspected substances have been found by their

8. A. H. Frey, "Brain stem evoked responses associated with low-intensity pulsed UHF energy," *J. Applied Physiol.* 23(6):984–988.
9. G. H. Mickey, "Electromagnetism and its effect on the organism," *N.Y. State J. Med.*, July 1963.

actions on the exposed public, for example, thalidomide and x rays (teratogens), smoking and asbestos (carcinogens), cadmium and mercury (toxic substances). Determination of the dangers of these kinds of substances before human exposure is desirable but difficult.

If thalidomide (a teratogen) had caused an increase of a common defect such as cleft palate or kidney problems, it might never have been identified as the cause of the problem. Similarly, if a teratogen or mutagen caused a lower resistance to disease, a lower IQ, a shortened life span, or decreased fertility, the discovery of the causative agent would be difficult, if not impossible, to determine. Not only would it be difficult to connect the damaging agent and the defect but the agent could be widespread throughout the environment and the population.

A mutagenic defect may appear in the first generation or it may not appear for many generations. In this case the new embryo would need to inherit the characteristic from both parents. Many generations would have to pass before two carriers of the mutated gene would produce a new organism. By that time, the source of the mutagen would be impossible to find.

The effects of carcinogens may be latent for long periods of time. Generally it takes 15–20 years to correlate data which relate a carcinogen to the cancer it causes. A further difficulty is that people are exposed to many substances at the same time. A cancer may be the result of the synergistic action of two or more substances. Birth defects and mutations may also be the result of synergistic actions of several substances.

Testing for drugs (Chapter 7) and food additives is a more or less standardized procedure. Several tests are necessary and others are desirable. A sufficiently large number of animals must be used to ensure statistical validity of the data and the conclusions that are drawn from it. A study must be made of the effects of the substance upon at least two species of animals, one of which is not a rodent. The animals being tested are fed various dose levels of the substance. Blood samples are taken during the feeding period. After the feeding is finished, the animals are sacrificed for microscopic tissue studies. During a long-term study of several generations, animals are sacrificed at appropriate stages in the study.

Methods of Testing

Just recently mutagenicity tests have been required. These tests usually start with simple tests of bacteria and yeasts, and progress through a study of the descendents of a treated male rat. Chromosome breaks are studied, although the relationship between mutations and chromosome breaks is not understood. However, the appearance of chromosome breaks may indicate genetic changes in the future individual.

Not only must the prospective additive pass the tests but the compounds resulting from the metabolism of the compound must be safe. Cyclamates metabolize in one-third of the population to a compound called cyclohexylamine (CHA). The FDA adopted a standard for CHA in 1958 of 10 ppm in boiler feed water in food-processing plants. In that part of the population which converts cyclamates to CHA, the amount of CHA body levels could range from 20 to 500 ppm.

The animal studies must be made at levels higher than that to which man is normally exposed. Because the substance in question may only produce one cancer (in the case of a test for carcinogenity) in 10,000 exposed persons, the chances of detecting this in a limited number of animals (50–100) is very small if the same sensitivity is assumed for the animal species as in man. Therefore, the substance is tested at higher exposure levels than those to which humans will be subjected. Extrapolation from animal experiments to man is usually made by reducing the safe animal dose by a factor of 100.

If a substance is not a carcinogen, it will not cause cancer even at dosage levels that are large enough and toxic enough to cause the death of the individual. The same dosage relationship applies to mutagens and teratogens.

Fertile eggs are frequently used to test for teratogenicity of a substance. A nonteratogenic substance may irritate the embryo and may kill it, but it will not produce teratogenic effects such as three legs, legs attached backwards, or wings attached to the back.

Even with the greatest care animal studies alone will not tell how safe a substance is for man. Thalidomide is not an effective teratogen in animals, but in humans 0.5 mg/kg/day acts as a teratogen.

Reviewing and Retesting

Instruments are becoming more sensitive and people are being exposed to more substances for longer periods of time. An established limit may be judged to be unsafe at a later date. All testing needs to be reviewed regularly.

Testing of Industrial Compounds

The testing program is very inadequate for compounds which are released to the environment or those found in a working environment. Four hundred fifteen standards have been set for only 450 of the 15,000 commercial chemicals produced by the oil industry. The worker is the first to be exposed to any toxic chemical. He is the "guinea pig"—the early warning signal. Studies at the workplace would help the entire community.

KEY CONCEPTS

1. Stereochemistry of molecules.
2. Impact of malnutrition.
3. Essential nutrients.
4. Manipulations of food.
5. Selecting food.
6. Chemical basis of heredity.
7. Food additives in the diet.
8. Interference of heavy metals in body chemistry.
9. Mercury: uses and dangers.
10. Cadmium and the environment.
11. Asbestos: uses and dangers.
12. PCBs: properties, uses, and dangers.

13. Characteristics of ionizing radiation.
14. Characteristics of nonionizing radiation.
15. Testing of suspected substances: difficulties and methods.

1. What guidelines can a nonscientist use to make decisions about topics (e.g., salt, vitamin C, microwave limits, food additives, etc.) when scientists disagree?
2. How much access should the general public have to studies involving decisions by government agencies on the use of food additives, drugs, pesticides, etc.? Would the answer be different if persons with special interests and backgrounds (e.g., lawyers, doctors, and scientists) were involved?
3. Should the same restrictions be placed on exports as on articles for domestic use (e.g., DDT, PCBs, and cigarette labeling)?
4. How much would smoking a pack of cigarettes per day add to the body burden of cadmium over a ten-year period?
5. Should PCBs be allowed if it is known that they affect some living species? Should they be allowed if it is known that they affect only one living species?
6. What are some of the advantages and disadvantages of testing toxic compounds on animals?
7. Repeated ingestion of a substance by rats fails to produce a cancer? Does this mean the compound is harmless? Explain your answer.
8. What are the pros and cons of eating "natural foods" as opposed to eating foods containing chemical additives?
9. Under what conditions should volunteers, prisoners, or mental defectives be used to test suspected substances?
10. Discuss the implications of synthetic meat from the standpoint of health, social, political, and economic consequences.
11. Modern bread is the name of a product in India. It has lysine added to it. What are the implications?
12. Are vitamin and mineral deficiencies a problem in the United States, other developed countries, and underdeveloped countries at this time?
13. How necessary are food colors?

BIBLIOGRAPHY

1. Brodeur, P., *Asbestos and enzymes,* New York: Balantine Books, 1972.
2. Montague, K. and Montague, P., *Mercury.* San Francisco: 1971.
3. Robson, J. R. K. *Malnutrition: its causation and control,* Vol. I and II, New York: Gordon & Breach, 1972.
4. Schroeder, H. A., *Pollution, profits and progress,* Brattleboro, Vt.: Stephen Greene Press, 1971.
5. Tolgskaya, M. S., and Gordon, Z. V. (translated from Russian by B. Haigh), *Pathological effects of radio waves.* New York: Plenum Press, 1973.

The following two books give opposing views on food additives:

6. Bernarde, M. A., *Chemicals we eat,* New York: American Heritage Press, 1971.

7. Marine, G., and Van Allen, J., *Food pollution—the violation of our inner ecology,* New York: Holt, Rinehart, and Winston, 1972.

Two opposing views on the vitamin C controversy are:

8. Pauling, L., *Vitamin C and the common cold,* New York: Bantam Books, 1971.

9. "Vitamin C—a prevention of the common cold," *Consumers Bull.,* September 1971.

7 Drugs as Problem Solvers

In a sense we believe in *magic;* all you have to know is what to ask for at a drugstore or from your drug dealer.[1]

Dr. Arthur Berger

The many accomplishments, both real and fancied, of drugs make it easy to believe in their magic. They are undoubtedly necessary in our modern society. However, their use is not without difficulties. A look at the limitations in the use of drugs and the careless way they may be used does not imply criticism of all drugs; drugs have saved lives and will continue to do so. An understanding of the problems involved may help the consumer to deal with these "magic" substances.

Drugs are those substances used to treat a disease or which enhance, or appear to enhance, physical or mental well-being. The most regulated drugs can only be obtained with a prescription from a medical doctor. Others, the over-the-counter drugs, can be purchased at a drugstore or supermarket. The illegal drugs can only be found at the drug dealer.

The molecular relationship between a drug and its effect on the human body usually cannot be determined by inspection of the formula of the drug.

Benzocaine is a mild anesthetic often used in over-the-counter preparations to be rubbed on the skin. Methyl anthranilate is a perfume used in ointments. These two substances differ only in the position of attachment and in the size of groups but have very different effects.

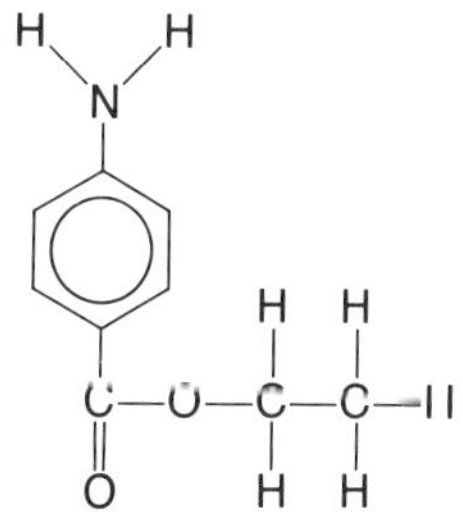

benzocaine

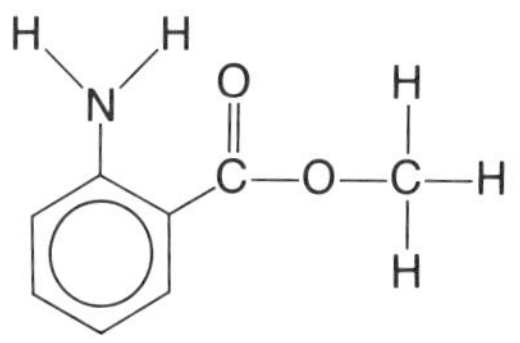

methyl anthranilate

If the

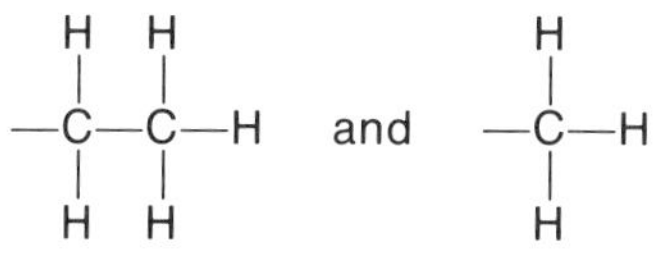

and

groups were exchanged, would the resulting compounds be perfumes, anesthetics, or something entirely different?

Scientists change groups in this manner to try to develop new drugs with desirable characteristics. Penicillin, the most common *antibiotic* (any of a large

1. From a testimony to the Senate Subcommittee on Alcoholism and Narcotics, 18 January 1971.

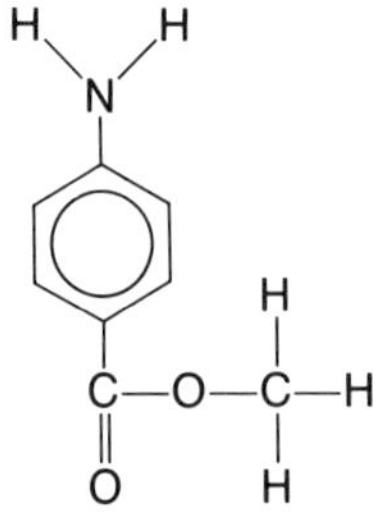

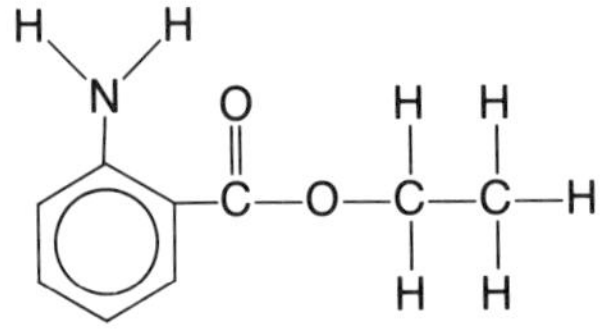

group of substances produced by microorganisms and having the property of destroying other microorganisms), has the following general formula.

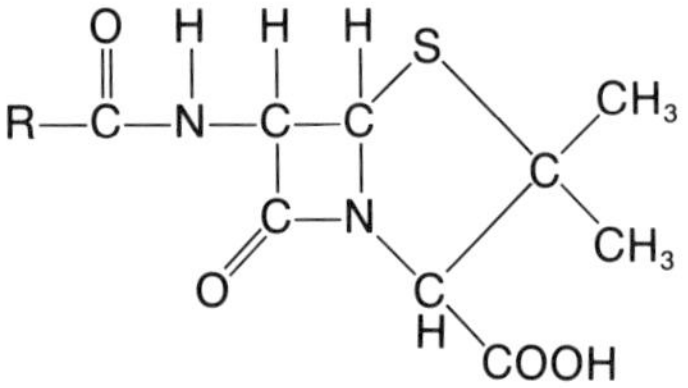

penicillin

By using different groups for R a drug with slightly different properties may be made.

R	Penicillin
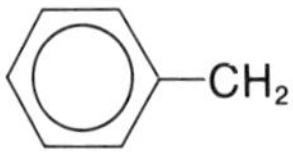 —CH$_2$	penicillin G (most common form)
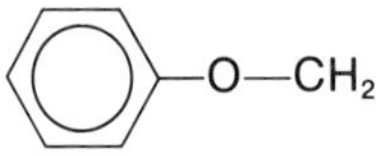 —O—CH$_2$	penicillin V
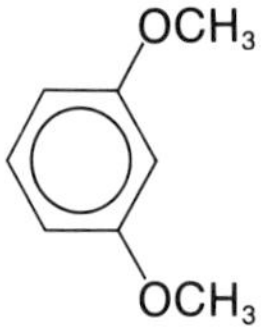	methicillin
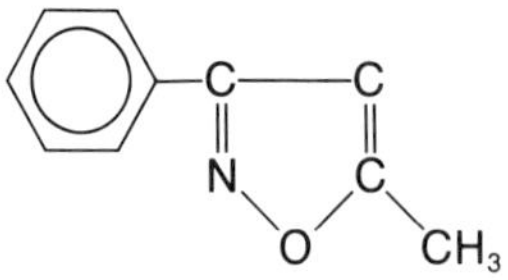	cloxacillin

Another group of antibiotics is the tetracyclines with four six-membered rings. For example, the formula for Terramycin, one of the tetracyclines is

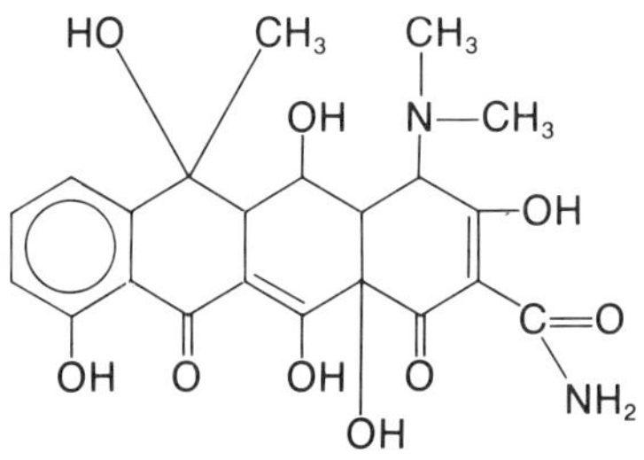

terramycin

There are many other types of antibiotics, each with certain characteristics which make it useful for treating certain conditions.

A drug must help the body destroy invading bacteria if it is being used to treat an infection, or must change the body chemistry of the user to attain some desired physical or mental state.

A drug being used to help destroy a microorganism may act on the microorganism in different ways. Penicillin interferes with the passage of nutrients through the cell walls of bacteria. Bacterial cell walls consist of layers with cross-links. Penicillin interferes with the cross-linkages and, as a result, the weakened cell wall bursts as water enters the cell. Human cells are not constructed with cross-linkages and are not damaged by the action of the drug. A drug may interfere with an essential life process of a bacterium. The drug sulfanilamide, the simplest of the sulfa drugs, has a structure similar to that of the vitamin para-aminobenzoic acid (PABA):[2]

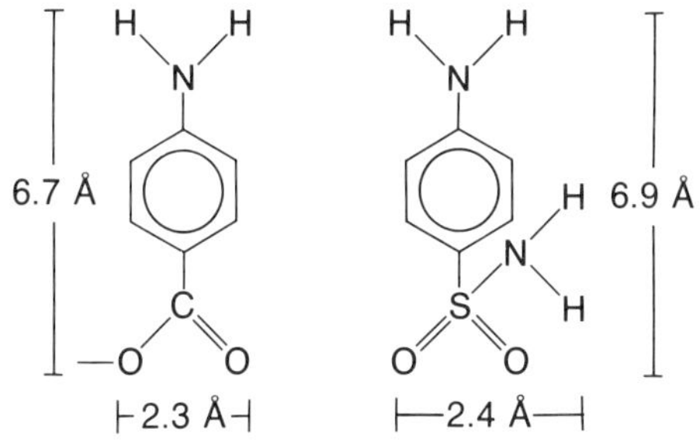

para-aminobenzoic
acid (PABA)

sulfanilamide

Not only are the two molecules much alike but also the sizes of the two are similar. Bacteria are tricked into incorporating the sulfanilamide into an enzyme system in place of PABA. The sulfanilamide-enzyme formation is irreversible and the microorganism does not function properly. The bacteria are then more easily destroyed by white blood cells.

2. Å is the symbol for Ångstrom, a unit of length equal to one-ten-millionth of a millimeter.

All drugs have two disadvantages: they may cause adverse reactions (serious side effects) in some persons, and microorganisms may become resistant to the drug.

Adverse Reactions

The Public Health Service estimates that 1.5 million hospital admissions annually are due to adverse reactions, and their hospital stay is 40% longer than average. Every year 600 people die from allergy to penicillin, the most prescribed drug. Dr. Bernard B. Levine has developed a test to determine whether a patient is allergic to penicillin. If the test is successful after clinical testing, adverse reactions to penicillin may be eliminated.

Since 1966 drug reactions from 11 hospitals have been fed to a computer for recording and correlating. The results showed that one out of every 20 drugs prescribed caused a reaction, but only one in a 100 cases caused an increase in the length of the hospital stay. A nationwide monitoring system should be even more successful at spotting trends in adverse reactions. If such information is available, a doctor can be on the alert for drug reactions.

Resistance

Microorganisms can become resistant to any drug, but we usually think of resistance to antibiotics because these drugs are the type of treatment most frequently used.

Dr. Alexander Fleming discovered penicillin because it had inhibited the growth of a *Staphylococcus* organism. Today *Staphylococci* are notorious for developing strains resistant to antibiotics. Three-quarters of the *Staphylococci* strains found in hospital patients are resistant to penicillin, and one-third to two-thirds are resistant to other antibiotics; e.g., streptomycin, tetracycline, and erythromycin. In 1959, methicillin, a modification of the penicillin molecule (see p. 228), was introduced. By 1960, a resistant strain of *Staphylococci* had been found but, fortunately, the incidence of these strains has continued to be low.

The mechanism of resistance is not understood in all cases. The resistant strain may have been present before the use of antibiotics and may have grown in numbers when other strains were killed. Resistance may be transferred from one species to another. Japanese scientists first discovered this genetic transfer in 1955 when they found dysentery bacilli that were resistant to three or four drugs. They also found that many patients who harbored the resistant dysentery bacilli (one of the members of the genus *Shigella*) also harbored resistant strains of the harmless bacillus *Escherichia coli*. Investigations showed that the two bacteria did not become resistant coincidently, but that the resistance of one species was transferred to the other. Since then the genetic transfer factor has been observed in countries around the world.

The genetic character of drug resistance has led to questioning of the practice of routine feeding of antibiotics to livestock. The practice is common where large numbers of livestock (poultry, cattle, or hogs) are kept in close quarters. The animals develop resistant strains of bacteria which may be transferred to man without his awareness of the transfer. There the bacteria can transfer the

DRUGS AS PROBLEM SOLVERS

resistance factor to microorganisms which normally live in the human body. From these the resistance factor can be transferred to the disease organism. Researchers in England believe that they have traced the deaths of human newborns to resistant bacteria from animals fed antibiotics.

Hospitals by their very nature are collection centers for disease and infections. Labor problems and the ease of treating infections with antibiotics have caused some hospitals to become lax in aseptic techniques. Consequently, disease microorganisms are becoming more resistant to antibiotics.

It is not "inconceivable" that a "super strain" microorganism could develop which would give rise to an epidemic. At the neurosurgical unit at Killearn Hospital, Glasgow, Scotland, routine administration of antibiotics escalated until a new type of bacteria appeared. It soon was found on walls, floors, and even the ceiling as well as in the patients' urine and sputum. The bacterium was sensitive to two particular antibiotics. High doses of these reduced the infections somewhat but not enough. As an alternative to closing the unit, antibiotics were banned for four months. The infection rate fell from 45% to 15%, and urinary tract infections fell from 21% to 8%.

In order to improve the use of prescription drugs in the United States, regulation and use must be improved at all levels: manufacturer, government, physician, and the patient. **Drug Use**

THE PHYSICIAN   Part of the difficulty lies with the doctor who prescribes the drug. Several studies show that there is a surprising amount of iatrogenic disease (doctor-caused disease).

The *Vital Statistics of the United States* gives deaths from "therapeutic misadventure in the administration of drugs or biologicals" as follows.

Year	Cases	Rate per 100,000 deaths
1960	1025	0.6
1965	1328	0.7
1967	1361	0.7

The figures are probably low because most deaths are classified by the organ affected; e.g., heart, liver, etc.

Probably the most celebrated case of drug misuse is the case of chloramphenicol (brand name, Chloromycetin).

Chloromycetin   It was first marketed in 1949 when it was thought to be a very effective, broad-spectrum antibiotic. Sales the first year exceeded $9 million, followed by $28 million in 1950 and $52 million in 1951.

In 1952 use of the drug dropped after it was found to have caused serious blood disorders and deaths. Several times since 1952, Congressional hearings on the drug and stronger warnings on the label caused the use of the drug to decline, but sales always increased again. The FDA did not withdraw the drug because it was necessary in the treatment of typhoid fever, bubonic plague, and a few other disorders. Recently it has become the drug of choice for treatment of resistant strains of gonorrhea. There was no adequate replacement in these cases.

The patents have run out and other companies are making the drug. It is now sold under 46 brand names. The use of Chloromycetin has spread to foreign countries where it may be sold over the counter or advertised as having few side effects.

Causes of drug misuse   The major cause of many faulty drug prescriptions is the lack of a good source of information on drugs. Studies have shown that 50–80% of the information the doctor has comes from the promotional activities of the manufacturer (Table 7–1).

Dr. Charles Edwards (former FDA Commissioner) says that there are about 15,000 detail men, or about one for every dozen or so doctors. Enough is spent on the promotion of drugs to send every doctor in the United States to a year of medical school. T. Donald Rucker (Chief of Drug Studies of the Social Security Administration) estimates the price of the average prescription is raised 25% to cover the money spent on promotion.

The *Physician's Desk Reference* (PDR) is the most common book about drugs for the use of doctors. The book, consisting of advertisements of each drug with the same regulations as the package insert, is a promotional activity and is free to all doctors. Although it contains most of the drugs manufactured in the United States, a few small companies cannot afford to advertise their drugs in the book.

The American Medical Association has published a book which supplies drug information. *AMA Drug Evaluation* has over 90 chapters about different uses of drugs; e.g., analgesics, gout, hypertension. Although the format of each chapter varies, they all contain a general introduction followed by a discussion of specific drugs. Structural formulas, when the drug should and should not be prescribed, adverse reactions both common and rare, dosage, and prepara-

TABLE 7–1.   Sources of Drug Information Used by Physicians.

Source of information	Percentage*
Detail men (salesmen)	58
Medical meetings	35
Journal advertisements	32
Direct mail advertisements	32
Colleagues	24
Journal articles	20

*The totals are more than 100% because some physicians gave two sources.
Source: From the testimony of Dr. Robert Mosher to the Senate Select Committee on Small Business, 20 Feb. 1969.

tions identified by trade name and manufacturing company are included. Two possible disadvantages are that drugs are included that were discontinued after the book went to press, and drugs authorized after publication are not included.

Another reason for unwarranted prescribing is the demands of the patient. Antibiotics have no effect on the common cold but many patients feel they are being poorly treated without a "shot" or a few pills.

A group of physicians in the San Joaquin Valley are attempting to reduce the use of drugs for their patients and at the same time to reduce the cost of medical care. Lay workers were trained to scan and computerize all bills submitted by the physicians. The computer can quickly sort and spot trends. After panels of specialists have reviewed about 15% of the bills, the questionable prescriptions are discussed by the reviewers and the physicians involved. Only about 1.5% of the doctor fees are saved, but cutting down on overutilization of drugs saves 12–15%. Groups of physicians from all over the United States are studying the plan.

THE INDUSTRY   The pharmaceutical industry is responsible for developing drugs and preparing them in sanitary conditions to a labeled strength. It is also responsible for reporting any adverse reactions found for any of their drugs to the government supervising agency, the FDA.

Some companies are not as careful as is desirable. Between 1966 and 1973, the 16 largest companies had 186 recalls of drugs, for an average of over 23 each year. One recall involved 93 different products. Probably the most celebrated recall involved an intravenous solution which had been linked to 50 deaths and more than 200 infections.

The General Accounting Office (the investigating arm of Congress) has reported that firms often delayed reporting adverse reactions involving their drugs by as much as 19 months.

GOVERNMENT REGULATION OF PRESCRIPTION DRUGS   The FDA has the responsibility to regulate drug sales. The type of regulation depends upon the date the drug was introduced and the kind of drug being marketed.

All drugs introduced before 1938 need not be tested for safety or efficacy. If the drug has been on the market for over 30 years, it is assumed that any lack of either safety or efficacy would have been found. All drugs introduced since 1938 have been tested for both efficacy and safety. In addition, each batch of both antibiotics and insulin must be tested for potency.

Before a sponsor can test a new drug on humans he must file a Notice of Claimed Investigational Exemptions for a New Drug (IND). If clinical tests show the drug is safe and efficacious, the sponsor will file a New Drug Application (NDA). Any advertising must be included as part of the NDA because it is considered as part of the labeling.

IND   Any drug entering the market since 1962 undergoes a regulated procedure. The sponsor submits an IND (Notice of Claimed Investigational Exemption for a New Drug). He must supply extensive information about the drug and future testing plans: (1) composition of drug; (2) manufacturing methods to insure identity and uniformity; (3) results of animal studies; (4) plan of clinical studies; (5) qualifications of clinical investigators.

After submission of the IND, the clinical testing may begin. These tests are divided into three parts:

(1) effect on man (often healthy volunteers); (2) effect on a few patients; (3) effect on a large number of patients.

Before using any new drug on a patient, the physician must inform the patient that he is using an untested drug and the benefits and risks involved. If the patient is incompetent (too old, too young, or too ill) some representative close to the patient should be informed. However, there is a loophole; these cases are defined as those in which the investigator could not communicate with the patient or his representative, or where it would seriously affect the patient's well-being.

The consent must be in writing in parts (1) and (2) of the clinical investigation, but oral consent is sufficient for part (3). The degree to which a patient is informed is controversial. Recently (1972) the media have reported a case where terminal cancer patients were treated with whole-body radiation. The question was not whether the treatment was safe, because all the patients were terminal, but, because they were all poor and uneducated, it was questioned whether they understood the side effects of the radiation. In addition to the problems of cancer, the radiation made them ill.

It is difficult to obtain informed consent for use of experimental drugs on children. Parents naturally hesitate to have their children used for experiments. Consequently some potentially useful drugs cannot be tested on children and are therefore labeled "not indicated for children."

The tissue distribution of the drug varies with maturity. Body mechanisms of children are different from those of adults. Immature gastrointestinal systems metabolize and absorb drugs at different rates than mature systems. The enzymatic and excretory systems function differently. Higher water content and the relatively larger surface area of a child's body makes dosage in infants and children difficult to determine.

Some drugs are more toxic to children than adults and others less so. Oxygen in high concentration causes blindness in babies. Phenobarbital and vitamin K are other substances more toxic to the young, while codeine and mercurial diuretics are less toxic.

To add to the problem, children now are getting diseases thought to occur only in adults—peptic ulcer, migraine, ulcerative colitis, gout.

The FDA has the right to stop the testing at any time adverse or dangerous reactions appear. Clinical investigators are obliged to make prompt reports of any such effects as well as a yearly report to the sponsor.

Test results are only as good as the investigators make them. Drug manufacturers have been accused of buying the results they desire (see Chapter 6). Whether or not this is a fact, it is true that doctors have testified to Congressional committees that they have submitted their papers containing their results to the sponsoring company because they wanted the paper to say what the company wanted.

The situation is somewhat different when a drug already on the market is being tested for a new use. An example is methotrexate, an anticancer drug, which is being tested for psoriasis, a skin disease. Any doctor may write a prescription for the drug without knowing the details of its use.

Another problem is follow-up studies on people who have been used to test the drugs under investigation. It is suspected that in most cases there are no medical follow-up tests of any kind.

NDA At the conclusion of the clinical studies, the sponsor files an NDA (New Drug Application) with the FDA. The NDA contains new information from the clinical studies and the labeling the sponsor expects to use. The labeling includes not only the label on the container and box but also the package insert and promotional material. The material submitted to the FDA may be sufficient to fill a foot locker or it may be enough to fill a moving van. The FDA has 180 days to decide to approve, disapprove, or ask for more information. At times there has been a backlog of applications and approval has taken much longer. A member of the FDA staff told a Congressional Committee that the major reason for this was the poor type of evidence submitted by the sponsor. Whatever the cause, it takes about 7–8 years to market a drug after it has been developed. However, the FDA will approve a drug in a few weeks if the need for the drug is great.

After approval, the sponsor must report any new evidence for or against the drug every three months during the first year, twice during the second year, and annually thereafter. The drug is reviewed by the FDA at each of these times.

Supplemental NDA's are filed when any change is planned for the drug—manufacturing methods, dosage, components, or therapeutic claims. The FDA has a large backlog of these.

A study of the number of new drugs marketed each year shows that, after strict testing was required by the Drug Amendment of 1962 the number of new drugs marketed in the United States declined, but that the decline began before the Drug Amendment of 1962. There were slight rises in 1967 and 1968. However, the important therapeutic advances were almost the same for every year, three or four, except for 1962 when only one important new drug was marketed.

The development, application, and eventual withdrawal from the market of the drug thalidomide illustrates how close the people of the United States came to having a major drug-caused tragedy. In October 1957 a German firm marketed the sedative thalidomide which seemed to be completely safe. In fact it was so safe that it was almost impossible to kill a laboratory animal by injection of the material. Within two years physicians began to report adverse reactions: numbness in hands and feet, severe muscular pains, dizziness, and disturbance of coordination. A year later reports began about a rare kind of birth defect, small flipper-like arms and legs often accompanied by disfigured faces. During the same year the FDA was asked to register thalidomide for use in the United

States. Dr. Frances O. Kelsey postponed the necessary decision by asking for more information about the nerve symptoms. Pressure was put on Dr. Kelsey to permit the drug to be used in the United States; she refused. Late in 1961 the company informed Dr. Kelsey about the thalidomide babies and withdrew the drug application over three months later. By that time over 2.5 million tablets had been distributed to over a thousand physicians for use in gathering data. After the drug was withdrawn, the FDA tried to track down the doctors and their 20,000 patients who had taken the drug. The agency was never able to locate 99 of the doctors. There are a few thalidomide babies in the United States but this country escaped having the tragedy of the many defective babies that were born in the European countries and Japan. The system of drug regulation is not perfect but, in this case, it did protect the people of the United States from tragedy.

Labeling The FDA has the responsibility to regulate labeling and also package inserts and promotional material distributed to physicians and advertisements in periodicals.

The package insert and the promotional material are part of an NDA and must include the same information. They include information in substantially the format and order and with section headings as follows.

1. Description.
2. Actions.
3. Indications.
4. Contraindications.
5. Warnings.
6. Precautions.
7. Adverse reactions.
8. Dosage and administration.
9. Overdosage (where applicable).
10. How supplied.

Sections on animal pharmacology and toxicology, clinical studies, and references are optional.

The description must include both the generic name and the brand name with the generic name in letters at least half the size of those of the brand name. The chemical name is often long and hard to remember, so a shorter generic name is given to a drug. The brand name is usually a short, catchy name and belongs to a particular manufacturer. 4-dimethylamino-1,4,4a,5,5a,6,-11,12a-octahydro-3,6,10,12,12a-pentahydroxy-6-methyl-1,11-dioxo-2-naphtha-cenecarboxamide hydrochloride is the chemical name for the compound with the generic name of tetracycline hydrochloride. Five of the firms making this drug and their brand names are as follows.

Bristol	Polycline
Upjohn	Panmycin

Pfizer	Tetrabon
Lederle	Achromycin
Squibb	Steclin

Some promotional materials cover several pages of a periodical. The advantages of the drug may be in large print with beautiful illustrations. The disadvantages may be in fine print on the last page. Reminder advertisements need not contain dosages, conditions of use, contraindications, or warnings.

Drug information Doctors must be alerted if new information about a drug becomes available. An adverse reaction may not be evident in the limited, pre-marketing studies, but may be found when the drug is widely used. The doctor must also be alerted if the information in an advertisement is misleading. The FDA uses several methods to alert the nation's physicians.

1. A remedial or corrective advertisement.
2. A "Dear Doctor" letter (a letter sent by registered mail to all United States doctors).
3. Requires the drug producer to send a "Dear Doctor" letter.
4. Issues a *Current Drug Information Bulletin,* one topic covered on a single sheet mailed to every physician.
5. Alerts doctors through State and County Medical Societies.

All of these methods have disadvantages. Corrective advertisements may be run many months after the original. In the case of a drug called Fluonid the original advertisement was run in October 1969 and the corrective advertisement in May 1970, seven months later. The lag has been even longer in other cases. There is no assurance that the doctor who reads the first advertisement will read the second.

In the seven months between 1 December 1969 and 30 June 1970 the FDA wrote 28 warning letters about questionable drug advertisements, found five promotions (voluntarily submitted) defective, wrote two "Dear Doctor" letters, required two remedial advertisements, negotiated on two other corrective advertisements, supervised the correction of a monograph for the *Physician's Desk Reference,* and required the modification of a planned promotion for a specific drug, L-Dopa.

THE PATIENT What is the patient's responsibility for any bodily damage resulting from the use of drugs? Patrick P. McCurdy, editor of *Chemistry and Engineering News,* believes that the person who takes the drugs has equal responsibility with government, industry, and physicians:

. . . how about the share that rightfully rests with the people—the users—the consumers? Is there not a certain amount of risk implicit in the very word "patient." And isn't drug consumption a voluntary act? . . . almost any new product, even with stringent testing, involves a certain risk for the user. The risk may be specific and immediate or a long-term matter. Either way, given present knowledge, the world becomes a laboratory and all of us are human guinea pigs.[3]

If the patient is to share responsibility, he must be informed about the dangers involved in the use of the drug he is to take. This implies responsibility by the government, industry, and the doctor to supply the information the patient needs. The patient can only ask.

OVER-THE-COUNTER DRUGS

Prescription drugs are any drugs not found safe for self-medication. All others are over-the-counter drugs (OTC). No one knows how many nonprescription drugs are being sold, because there are no records of what drugs are sold or their components. Dr. Charles Edwards estimates that there are between 100,000 and 200,000 products made from about 200 significant active ingredients to treat about 30 symptoms (from testimony to Senate Subcommittee on Monopoly, 25 May 1971).

The same laws apply to the nonprescription drugs as apply to the prescription drugs: the Food, Drug, and Cosmetic Act of 1938 and its various amendments. In all of these there is the same grandfather clause exempting drugs marketed before 1938 and the same clause exempting all drugs generally recognized as safe. Any drug not covered by these clauses must file an NDA. The manufacturer has the right to decide whether or not the drug is new. If the FDA disagrees, it can seize the product as mislabeled and, probably, go to the courts eventually.

The FDA does not have the resources to force the manufacturer of each drug on the market to file an NDA. Even if the agency tried, it would be unsuccessful because a new combination could be marketed every week. The FDA could not keep up with the new drugs.

The FDA would like all OTC drug sponsors to file NDA's and to report any change in ingredients. A drug may contain components which are "generally recognized as safe" but the components may be in a new ratio which has never been tested for efficacy. Some of the drugs on the market are being advertised as new and reported in annual reports as new, but the manufacturer claims they are not legally new. The FDA hopes to solve these problems in the courts.

The FDA conducted a voluntary inventory of OTC drugs through the manufacturers and then grouped the drugs into 25 classes.

Antacids	Laxatives
Antimicrobials	Dentifrices and dental products
Sedatives and sleep aids	Sunburn treatments and preventives
Analgesics	Contraceptives
Cold remedies and antitussives (cough relievers)	Stimulants
	Hemorrhoidals
Antihistamines	Antidiarrheals

3. *Chem. Eng. News,* 51:1, 22 January 1973.

DRUGS AS PROBLEM SOLVERS

Mouth washes	Dandruff preparations
Anti-infectives	Bronchodilators and antiasthmatics
Antirheumatics	Antiemetics
Hematinics (blood improvers)	Ophthalmics
Emetics (causing vomiting)	Menstrual products
Antiperspirants	Vitamins and minerals

Each class has been or will be subjected to a guideline involving efficacy, safety, and labeling. Efficacy should include clinical evidence but it would relate to symptoms and not to a specific disease. The labeling (any statement included with the drug) should show when to take the drug, dosage for all levels, contraindications such as age or other drugs taken, and side effects.

Advertising of OTC drugs has been accused of over-promotiong nonprescription drugs and thus leading to needless consumption of such products. This, in turn, has contributed to drug abuse—the use of drugs for other than medical reasons or excessive use of drugs for medical reasons. There is no proof that over-promotion of OTC drugs leads to "pill popping", but many physicians and pharmacists believe that the idea of a pill for every problem has been influential in that direction.

Unlike prescription drugs, the FDA does not have jurisdiction over OTC drug advertising. Dr. Edwards has testified that he would like to see the same controls apply to OTC drugs as are used for prescription advertising; that is, the labeling would form the basis for the promotional advertising. He has said that, when drug promotion reaches the point where antacids are offered like martinis and laxatives are implied as essentials to everyday happiness, then the time has come to take a good hard look at the entire situation.

One company may make several drugs and advertise them with contradictory statements. A manufacturer advertises one product as an aspirin and claims that aspirin is the strongest pain reliever you can buy. They keep trying to improve it but they cannot. The same manufacturer advertises another product as extra strength with gentle buffers. Other extra-strength products are not buffered and other buffered products are not extra strength.

One study[4] comparing aspirin and a nonprescription sedative with a prescription tranquilizer found that the aspirin and the OTC sedative were no more effective than an inert sugar pill. In addition, the patients using the OTC drug reported as many side effects as those patients using the prescription tranquilizer.

One study of this kind is not definitive. Much more experimental work involving many nonprescription drugs is needed.

ASPIRIN Aspirin is the most commonly used medicine in the United States. It is advertised to be good for everything including the "blahs." The American

4. Karl Rickels and Peter T. Hesbacher, "Over-the-counter daytime sedatives," *JAMA*, 223:29–33, 1 January 1973.

public used about 37 million pounds of aspirin in 1971 or about 250 5-grain aspirin tablets for each person. Aspirin has many good points as a medicine: it reduces fever; it helps arthritics; it is a painkiller. However, it also has bad points about which every user should be aware. Aspirin causes three kinds of adverse reactions: (1) a rash, (2) asthma, and (3) gastrointestinal bleeding (bleeding from the stomach or intestine). There are some indications that the rash, at least, may be due to an impurity in the aspirin.

An asthma attack causes shortness of breath, wheezing, and gasping. It develops between 15 minutes and 3 hours after taking aspirin. Unlike asthma attacks due to hay fever, the attacks due to aspirin continue long after the person stops taking aspirin. Children do not usually develop asthma intolerance to aspirin, but during or after the teens a person may be affected. However, a person may take aspirin for years before developing asthmatic intolerance.

Most people who take aspirin lose about a teaspoonful of blood after the ingestion of two 5-grain tablets. The action of aspirin in the stomach is determined by the pH of the stomach. The stomach lining (the mucosa) is covered by a layer of tight columnar cells which in turn are covered with lipid (fat) and protein cells. Hydrochloric acid is produced in the mucosa and transferred to the stomach by tiny tubes. Ionic substances dissolve in the water in the stomach and nonpolar molecules may dissolve in the lipid cells covering the mucosa. Aspirin exists in the following equilibrium.

The form on the left is nonpolar and will dissolve in the lipid cells; the form on the right is ionic and will dissolve in the water solution of the stomach. In the acid solution of the stomach the equilibrium will be forced toward the nonpolar form, which will pass through the lipid cells to the mucosa where it will find a neutral solution. There the aspirin will become ionic. The ionic form damages the protective layer on the mucosa, allows hydrogen ions to get into the lining, and destroys tiny blood vessels. Hence bleeding into the stomach occurs. Normally the loss of blood caused by an occasional dose of aspirin is small, but the actual amount varies widely in individuals and also in the same individual at different times. There are a few people whose loss of blood becomes extensive. Varying levels of stomach acidity may explain the differing reactions to aspirin by different individuals.

Various estimates have been made as to the number of people who react to aspirin. One out of every 500 who take aspirin have some side effect. The number is between 8% and 20% for severe asthmatics.

A study carried out in Wales indicates that aspirin may be teratogenic. The study was conducted in such a manner that it is not completely reliable. However, women who are pregnant, or who think they may be pregnant, or who are trying to be pregnant have been warned by doctors and organizations such as the March of Dimes not to take aspirin during the first three months of pregnancy.

The question is not whether aspirin should ever be taken, but rather who should take it, for what, how often, and how much.

SOCIAL DRUGS

The middle-aged parents of a teen-aged son were told that their son had just been arrested for possession of illegal drugs. The mother took her "prescription" tranquilizer and the father had a drink.

Old Story

It is difficult to find a name to cover all the nonprescription and non-OTC drugs taken by Americans. There are the ones often called street drugs—narcotics, "uppers," "downers," and hallucinogens. There is alcohol, a drug accepted by society. There is tobacco, which is being questioned. However, there are others which are habit forming such as caffeine in coffee, tea, and colas. Dr. Yudkin of England thinks sugar belongs in the list.[5] He believes that the long-term dangers of sugar are great, although it does not have the immediate effect as do the street drugs.

Tobacco

Tobacco was suspected as a cause of illness and death for over 100 years, but it has only been during the last several decades that evidence has mounted about the degree of actual harm caused by smoking.

Smokers lose more work days than nonsmokers from bronchitis, influenza, and other symptoms which can be attributed to an infection. A study using animal cells in test tubes by Drs. Sorell L. Schwartz, Jano E. Lundin, and James C. Bond of Georgetown University Medical School found that the nicotine reduced the effectiveness of the macrophages, cells which act as the body's first defense system. An experiment with animal cells outside the body does not always apply to conditions inside the human body. However, it may explain the smoker's increased susceptibility to infections.

Not only is cigarette smoking hazardous to the health of the smoker, but it is also hazardous to those who are exposed to "second-hand" smoke. Experiments show that 30 min in a smoke-filled room significantly increases the nonsmoker's heart rate, blood pressure, and carbon monoxide content in his blood. Smoke from pipes and cigars as well as from cigarettes contains cadmium. Another study showed that cases of respiratory illness were twice as large among children whose parents smoke as among children of nonsmoking parents.

5. John Yudkin, *Sweet and Dangerous*, New York: Peter H. Wyden, 1972.

A fetus of a smoking mother is not exposed to second-hand smoke but statistics show that it is affected. Babies of smoking mothers have an average birth weight 8 oz. less than the babies of nonsmoking mothers. In some cases this one-half pound could be critical. Smoking mothers also have more miscarriages, stillbirths, and babies with congenital heart defects than do nonsmoking mothers. Long-term effects are more difficult to determine.

The smoker's body chemistry changes to adjust to the continued exposure to the products of smoking. When the smoking is stopped, the body has to make an adjustment to return to normal. Many smokers tend to gulp air when they stop smoking. This may be because they are no longer aware of the sensation of breathing hot air and pollutants. After a few days of not smoking former smokers may develop sore throats and mouths and coughs. A chronic irritation may have been present before, but the nerves of the mouth and throat were paralyzed so the smoker was not aware of the problem. As the cilia begin to operate again "gunk" is brought into the throat to be coughed up. Nicotine tends to cause blood vessels to constrict. When the nicotine is removed, the blood vessels expand and the tiny blood vessels become painfully congested. As the body adjusts, the pain stops. The most common symptom of nicotine withdrawal is weight gain. The reason for this is not understood but it affects about 60% of those who stop smoking. Efforts to lose weight are usually ineffective for about six months. All the physical symptoms will disappear in a relatively short time. The psychological need for smoking may be more difficult to conquer.

Alcohol Alcohol can be absorbed into the blood from either the stomach or the intestine, but absorption from the intestine is more rapid. An alcohol solution of about 15–30% is absorbed more rapidly than either more dilute or more concentrated solutions. The more concentrated solutions cause the opening into the intestine to close so the alcohol stays in the stomach where the absorption is slower. The alcohol is evenly distributed to all tissues according to their water content.

The actual mechanism of the metabolism and effect of alcohol on the human body is not known. Intense research is being done to answer some of the questions, and about 10,000 reports on this work are published each year.

In the liver, alcohol is changed to acetaldehyde and, subsequently, to acetic acid with the help of coenzyme NAD:

DRUGS AS PROBLEM SOLVERS

In a separate reaction $NADH_2$ is changed to NAD. However, this reaction is slower than the reaction which changes NAD to $NADH_2$. Thus the ratio of $NADH_2$ to NAD is increased. One theory is that the increase of $NADH_2$ at the expense of NAD is the explanation for the liver damage which often accompanies alcoholism.

Alcohol may interfere with the sodium-potassium balance in the nerve cells. One research group believes that the effect of alcohol on the cells is caused by a reaction of blood cells with alcohol to form a sticky compound. The compound may adhere to nerve cells and cause them to die.

Other researchers have worked with twins born to alcoholic parents but raised separately by alcoholic and nonalcoholic parents, as well as with twins born to nonalcoholic parents and raised by an alcoholic and a nonalcoholic parent. Their results suggest that alcoholism may have a hereditary basis.

Another group of physicians believe that low blood sugar (hypoglycemia) may be a contributory cause to alcoholism. They believe that the bodies of some people overreact to consumption of sugar by overproducing insulin which lowers the blood sugar below an optimum level. As a result the person becomes tired, hungry, and slightly groggy. Coffee, soft drinks, cigarette smoking, or an alcoholic drink may cause the blood sugar to increase to greater than normal amounts. Again too much insulin is secreted and the blood sugar is reduced too much. The person is on a "roller coaster." Dr. H. G. Roberts and other physicians estimate that there may be as many as 10 million people in the United States who react in this way. Other physicians and medical organizations believe that low blood sugar difficulties are much overemphasized. They think that there are people with low blood sugar but that they are very few.

The ingestion of alcohol produces a warming effect by dilating the blood vessels in the skin. Blood flowing through the vessels warms the skin. The skin feels warm but it actually is radiating heat to the atmosphere. The blood is warmed by the interior organs so the net effect is to take heat from the interior organs and transfer it to the atmosphere. Thus, the body is cooled.

Very little is known about the action of alcohol in the body after it has left the stomach and intestine. As new information becomes available, old theories will be sustantiated or disproved. Until then, there is no medical answer.

Whatever the cause, the results of alcoholism are tragic. Not the least tragic is the fact that hard-drug users often have a history of alcohol use by either themselves or their parents. Surveys of students have shown a significant correlation between hard-drug use and acceptance of alcohol in the home. Other surveys have correlated hard drugs with alcohol as a first-used stimulant. (Alcohol is commonly thought to be a stimulant, whereas it is actually a depressant.)

Narcotics

A *narcotic* is a drug which induces sleep and relieves pain. Morphine, a narcotic, is used as a painkiller but it also induces a state of euphoria. This narcotic is one of several compounds that is found in the opium poppy. At least 20 others have been isolated; two of these are heroin and codeine. Their chemical structures are shown on the next page.

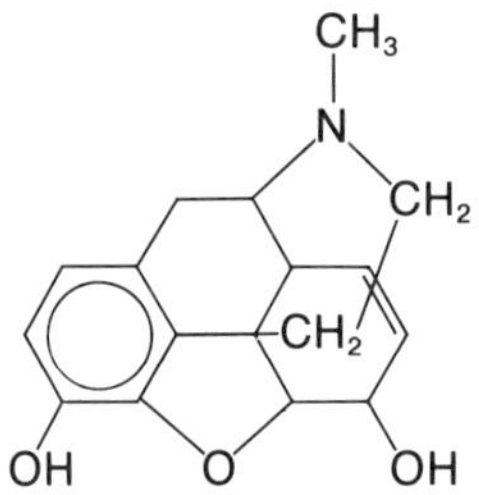

morphine

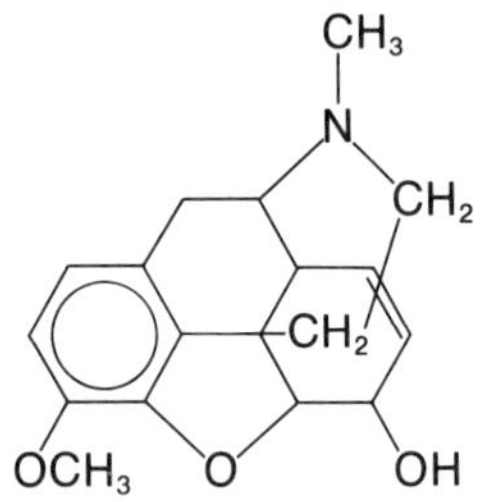

codeine

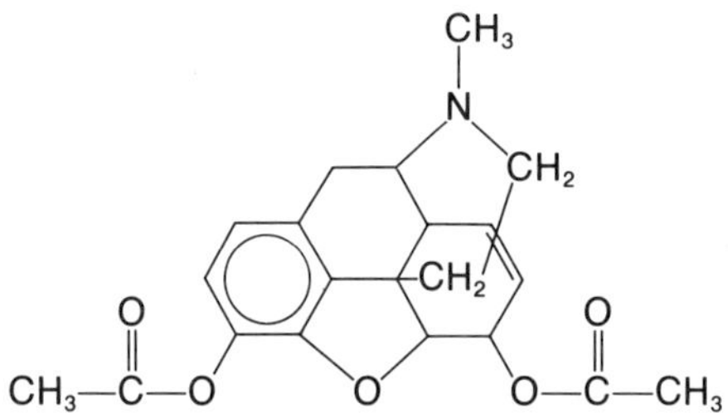

heroin

All of these drugs have similar structure, all are addictive, and all cause tolerance to develop in the user.

The complete mechanism of tolerance is not known. One theory is that the body produces enzymes which destroy alcohol, morphine, and heroin. As more of the enzyme is produced more of the drug must be used to give the desired effect. When the drug is withdrawn, the presence of excess enzyme produces *withdrawal symptoms.*

Chemical antagonists to narcotics are being studied. Two have similar structures to morphine.

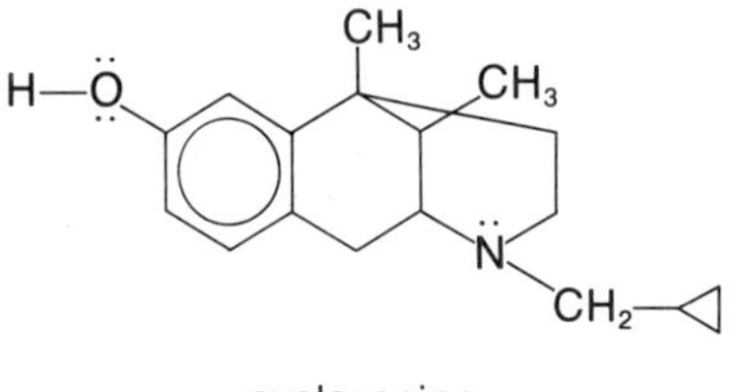

cyclazocine

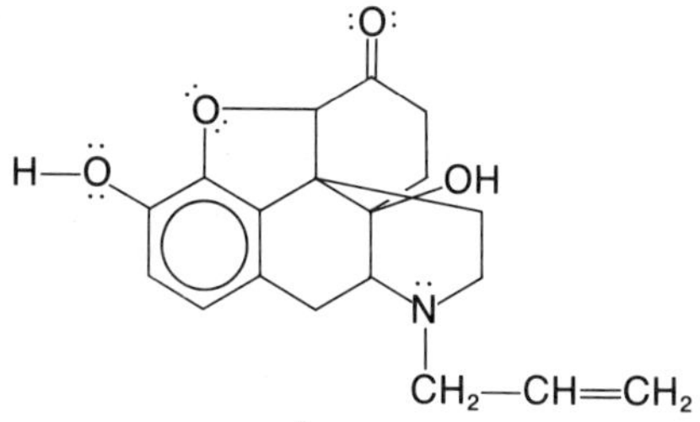

naloxone

It is thought that they attach to the receptor centers on the nerves and thus prevent the effects of morphine or other narcotics.

The two drugs shown above are experimental, but another, methadone, is being used to treat heroin addiction. Its structure is very different.

methadone

When methadone is substituted for heroin, the user becomes addicted to methadone but he is capable of functioning normally. However, withdrawal, although not as painful as that of heroin, lasts much longer and is more uncomfortable for some addicts. Methadone is given orally; thus there is not the danger of infection which results from the use of heroin injections. Even when clean needles have been used (for example, in England), difficulties with infections have risen. If a prescription for methadone for several days' supply is given to the addict, some tends to end up in the illegal drug market. Children have been killed by drinking methadone that was stored in a refrigerator.

Psychiatric treatment is the only other type of treatment for addicts. Often the two types of treatment, chemical and psychiatric, are combined. The methadone stabilizes the life of the addict so that he may try to solve his problems by psychiatric treatments. However, there are too few methadone clinics for all who wish treatment. Only 10% of the addicts in the United States are in any type of treatment program. In places, counseling is mandatory at a methadone clinic. Shortage of money and personnel to staff this type of program has limited the number of treatment facilities which have been opened.

England has a different system. Anyone can register as a heroin addict. Any time a registered addict needs the drug he may go to a doctor and have the heroin administered to him. Previously, the drug was given to him, but, because it could be sold, the number of addicts increased. Under the revised system, there seems to have been no increase in the number of addicts. The big advantage is the decrease in street crime. The addict no longer has to resort to illegal means to support his habit and organized crime can no longer profit from the sale of heroin. In addition, the maintenance dosage permits the addict to live a more or less normal life. England's system has been recommended for the United States but the suggestion has been received with horror. Methadone has also been recommended as a substitute for heroin in the same type of arrangement.

There are three classes of nonnarcotics: *stimulants*, *depressants*, and *hallucinogens*.

Nonnarcotics

STIMULANTS   The amphetamines are legal only by prescription. They are used for (1) obesity, (2) mild depression, (3) hyperactivity in school children, and

(4) a compulsive tendency to fall asleep (a rare condition). The first use has been largely discredited. Studies have shown that the obese person loses a few pounds when first taking the drug, but no more is lost unless diet and exercise are controlled. When the drug is discontinued, the lost weight often returns.

The amphetamines are the drugs often rumored to be given to athletes to make them more alert and to give them more energy. The pills stimulate the body to release stored energy. Excessive use can cause physical collapse, insomnia, high blood pressure, and brain damage. Amphetamines are not physically addictive but do cause emotional and psychological dependence.

DEPRESSANTS Barbiturates are probably the most dangerous drugs in the United States. Most drug deaths in this country are due to barbiturates. In New York City deaths due to drugs are the biggest cause of deaths in the age group 15–35. Alcohol mixed with barbiturates is particularly dangerous, because the action of the drug is enhanced 200 times. Barbiturates slow the action of the nerves, skeletal muscles, and heartbeat; blood pressure is lowered; the ability to work, think, and control emotions is impaired. Sudden withdrawal can cause convulsions and death.

HALLUCINOGENS Lysergic acid diethylamide (LSD) and marijuana are the most common hallucinogens, but peyote, mescaline, and hashish are also used.

The action of the hallucinogens is not known but the similarity of some of the naturally occurring drugs to serotonin should be noted. Serotonin has the

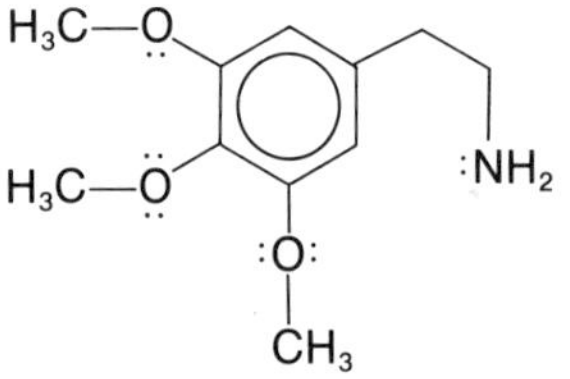

mescaline

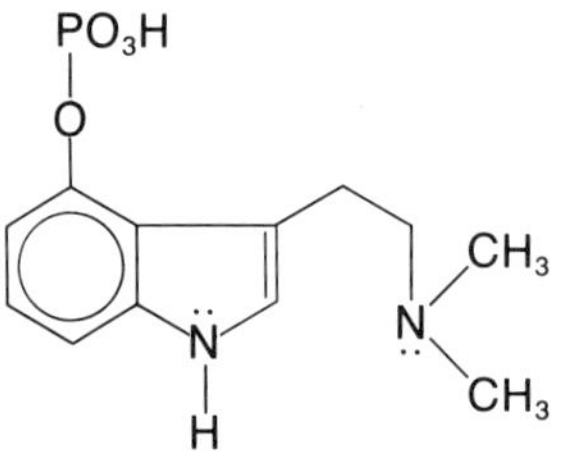

psilocybin

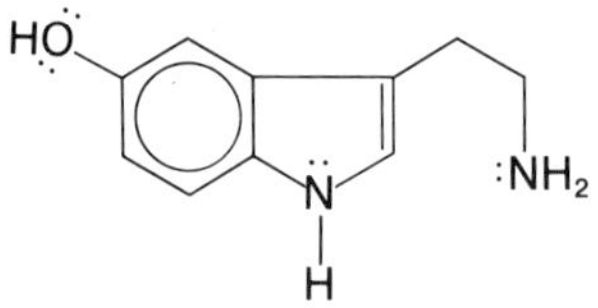

serotonin

same action as acetylcholine (see Chapter 5), that is, it carries a message from a nerve ending to a muscle, gland, or another muscle.

LSD, a man-made hallucinogen, has a structure similar to serotonin. However, the effects of LSD may or may not be due to interference with the action of serotonin. LSD is known to cause "bad trips" and the sensations may return repeatedly (flashbacks). The other accusations against LSD have not been proven; it may or may not cause birth defects and chromosome breakage. Since LSD is an illegal drug, the size and purity of the dose cannot be determined. When animal experiments are relied on, there seems to be an excessive number of defective fetuses born to animals given LSD.

Marijuana use has become widespread, but many things are claimed about marijuana and few are known. It took 40 years for the effects of tobacco to become known and even now new facts are being discovered. It should not take that long for the effects of marijuana to be discovered.

The following facts about marijuana are known.

1. Tetrahydrocannabinol (THC) is the active ingredient in marijuana.

tetrahydrocannabinol (THC)

2. THC will remain in the blood stream at least three days after exposure.
3. The metabolic breakdown products of THC will remain in the body for more than eight days.

A report by the Ford Foundation states: "There is presently little indication that marijuana causes physical harm but even persons who are sympathetic to marijuana use will be surprised if it is discovered that marijuana in large amounts over a long period of time is totally harmless."

A few indications of the harm marijuana can do may be emerging. Researchers have found that heavy users may undergo personality changes. The patients do not always revert to normal when use of the drug is stopped. Another area of concern is that male users may suffer a painful enlargement of the breasts. A whitish fluid may also be secreted. The same result may occur in female users but its detection would be difficult. One isomer of THC is similar to a female hormone, estradiol.

There are many unanswered questions about marijuana: Are personality and physical changes due to marijuana or to some other factor? Assuming they are due to marijuana, how often do bodily changes occur? How much marijuana would cause such changes? Would use of a small amount of the drug over a long period of time have the same effect as heavy use over a shorter period?

QUESTIONS

1. How is the action of antibiotics different from the action of antiseptics in killing bacteria?
2. What are some of the problems involved in the clinical evaluation of marijuana and LSD?
3. Should any of the presently illegal drugs be made legal? Explain your answer. Do you suggest any limiting conditions?
4. How should heroin addiction be treated?
5. Are all drugs toxic? Explain your answer.
6. Discuss the relationship, if any, between OTC drugs and advertising. What changes in regulations would you suggest?
7. What agency of the government should regulate OTC drugs?
8. Discuss the relationship between animal drugs and human health.
9. Through mutation intestinal bacteria of humans may become immune to antibiotics. What dangers may this pose with respect to pathogenic bacteria?
10. What suggestions can you make for the clearance and regulation of prescription drugs and OTC drugs?
11. The Right to Information Law requires governmental agencies to allow public access to all information in their files except trade secrets. How much information about drugs should be available to the public and to doctors?
12. Assuming that a substance causes only one type of effect, which of the following types of substances is the more dangerous? Explain your answer. (1) Teratogen; (2) carcinogen; (3) mutagen.

1. Brechet, E. M., and editors of *Consumers Reports, Licit and illicit drugs,* Boston: Little, Brown, 1972.
2. Dowling, H. F., *Medicines for men,* New York: Knopf, 1970.

Various Congressional committees hold hearings which provide much information about drugs. The following committees are apt to hold such hearings:
1. Senate Subcommittee to Investigate Juvenile Delinquency.
2. Senate Subcommittee on Monopoly.
3. House of Representatives Committee on Governmental Operations.
4. Senate Consumer Subcommittee on Commerce.
5. Senate Subcommittee on Alcoholism and Narcotics of the Committee on Labor and Public Welfare.
6. Senate Subcommittee on Health of the Committee on Labor and Public Welfare.

8 Energy and Its Effects

Virtually all of the benefits that now seem necessary to the "American way" have required vast amounts of energy.[1]

Peter Borrelli

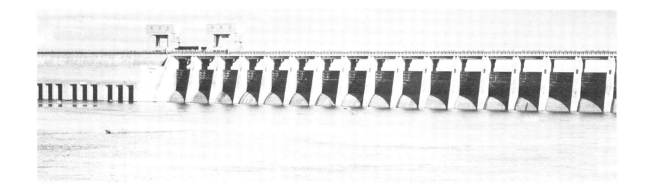

E nergy is a very difficult concept to define, but an understanding of energy is necessary to comprehend its importance to our society. Therefore, a short review of concepts and terms may help to explain the function and problems of the use of energy today.

Energy cannot be created or destroyed; it can only be transferred from one body to another, or from one form to another. This conversion is well illustrated by a teeter-totter, where energy is transferred from one body to another. The person at the top of the teeter-totter has *potential* or *stored* energy which he transfers to the other person as he descends and the other person rises. Industrial societies make great use of potential energy, for example, gravitational energy stored as water behind a dam, chemical energy stored in fossil fuels, and nuclear energy from uranium. Chemical energy from fossil fuels is the most important source. In order to be usable, the potential energy must be changed to another form, usually electrical or mechanical energy; the transformation is commonly accomplished by means of a heat engine, for example, a gasoline engine in a car, a steam power plant, or a diesel engine.

The energy in fossil fuels, i.e., coal, which contains other substances but is largely carbon (C), natural gas (CH_4), and oil ($C_{11}H_{24}$), is released by combustion:

$$C + O_2 \rightarrow CO_2 + \text{energy (heat)}$$
coal

$$CH_4 + 2O_2 \rightarrow CO_2 + 2H_2O + \text{energy (heat)}$$
natural gas

$$C_{11}H_{24} + 17O_2 \rightarrow 11CO_2 + 12H_2O + \text{energy (heat)}.$$
oil

Conversion of energy by a heat engine involves heating a fluid (e.g., water or a gas) to a high temperature in an enclosed space and then allowing the fluid to push against a movable piston or a set of propeller blades or vanes (Figure 8–1). In a turbine system the vapor is usually water (steam) but it may be other fluids such as ammonia (NH_3), propane, or isobutane:

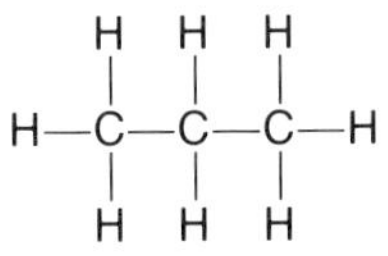

propane (C_3H_8) 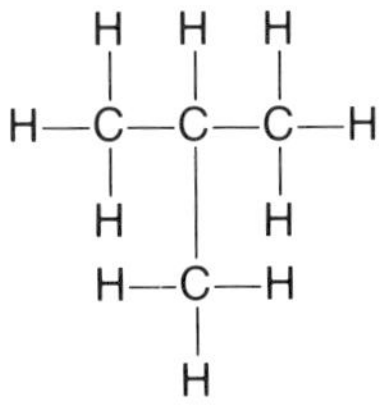   isobutane (C_4H_{10})

High-pressure vapor moves the vanes of the turbine; the vanes turn the generator which makes the electricity. The spent steam is passed through a condenser

1. Introduction to *Energy* by John Holdren and Phillip Herrera, San Francisco: Sierra Club, 1971, p. 10.

253

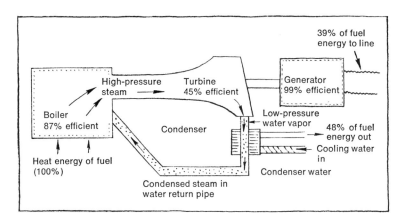

Figure 8–1. Diagram of a power plant. Overall efficiency 39% (.87 × .45 × .99 = .39).

to condense it to water, and then pumped back to the boiler to go through the cycle again.

All of the energy in the coal, oil, or gas is not converted into electricity or mechanical work. The maximum theoretical efficiency of any heat engine is given by the equation:

$$\text{heat efficiency} = \frac{T_{high} - T_{low}}{T_{high}}$$

where T_{high} represents the highest temperature of the gas of the heat system and T_{low} is the temperature of the exhaust gases in the case of an automobile engine or the temperature of the condenser in the case of a turbine. T_{high} is limited by the properties of the material in the engine. The formula shows that the greater the temperature difference between the highest temperature and the lowest temperature of the system ($T_{high} - T_{low}$), the greater will be the efficiency of the system. Thus, if the difference between T_{high} and T_{low} is small, the efficiency of the system will be low. Low efficiency can result if the high temperature is relatively low or if the low temperature is relatively high.

The temperatures are measured on the Kelvin scale (Appendix E). Zero on the Kelvin scale is approximately −273° on the centigrade scale. Thus, centigrade degrees can be changed into Kelvin degrees by adding 273 to the centigrade temperature value:

$$°K = °C + 273$$

for example,

$$363\,°K = 90\,°C + 273.$$

ENERGY AND ITS EFFECTS

The theoretical efficiency (absolutely highest possible) of a system operating between 473 °K (200 °C) and 303 °K (30 °C) is

$$\frac{T_{high} - T_{low}}{T_{high}} = \frac{473 - 303}{473} = 0.36 \text{ or } 36\%$$

Accordingly, 64% (100 − 36%) of the energy is lost as waste heat to the atmosphere to water, air, or to some other heat receiver. Actual heat engines cannot reach the theoretical efficiences given by the above efficiency formula. There are frictional losses, heat losses, energy transmission losses, and other losses which cause an overall decrease in efficiency compared with the theoretical value.

The efficiency of a power plant is reflected in the way in which power from a plant is expressed. A power plant might consume 1000 megawatts of heat energy, written megawatts thermal [MW(t)], but it may deliver only 300 megawatts of electrical energy, written megawatts electrical [MW(e)]. The overall efficiency of such a plant is, therefore, only 30%. The remaining 70% went out of the chimney with hot gases, warmed the water in the condenser, or was lost in other ways.

Not all uses of energy involve heat engines. A home heating furnace uses the energy from fossil fuel to heat space. It, too, loses heat, about 35% for an oil furnace and about 17% for a gas furnace. In this case no mechanical work is done and the measurement of efficiency is in terms of its transfer of heat from one body to another. Figure 8–2 gives the efficiency for common energy systems.

The ultimate source of energy, that is the primary source, is solar energy and materials from the earth. Fossil fuels, geothermal energy (hot gases and water from wells drilled in the ground), and the element uranium (nuclear reactors) are primary sources found on earth. Solar energy may be used as direct sunlight, wind, tides, and energy from the oceans, or by the use of plant and animal materials. All other sources of energy, such as batteries, fuel cells, and electricity, are secondary sources which necessarily are produced from primary sources. For example, a rechargeable battery is a secondary source which depends upon electricity for replenishing its energy; electricity is a secondary source of power which is usually derived from fossil fuels. Consequently, batteries cannot be considered to be a primary source of energy.

Secondary sources of power tend to be more efficient than the original heat engine energy conversion. Thus, a rechargeable battery is more efficient than the production of electricity used to charge it. However, no series of energy conversions can be more efficient than the least efficient step. If the efficiency of a battery is 95% and that of a steam plant is 40%, the overall efficiency is less than the least efficient conversion of 40%.

The inherent inefficiency of heat engines causes large amounts of heat energy to be discharged to the environment and results in what is known as thermal pollution, usually of a stream or lake, or of the ocean.

WASTE HEAT IN THE ENVIRONMENT

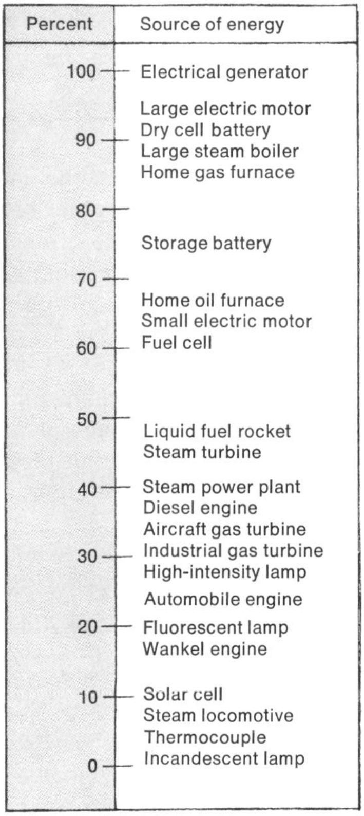

Percent	Source of energy
100 —	Electrical generator
90 —	Large electric motor Dry cell battery Large steam boiler Home gas furnace
80 —	
70 —	Storage battery
60 —	Home oil furnace Small electric motor Fuel cell
50 —	
40 —	Liquid fuel rocket Steam turbine
30 —	Steam power plant Diesel engine Aircraft gas turbine Industrial gas turbine High-intensity lamp
20 —	Automobile engine Fluorescent lamp Wankel engine
10 —	Solar cell Steam locomotive Thermocouple
0 —	Incandescent lamp

Figure 8-2. Energy efficiency. Adapted from "The Conversion of Energy" by Claude M. Summers. Copyright © 1971 by Scientific American, Inc. All rights reserved.

Compared with most other substances on a per gram basis, water requires relatively large amounts of heat to melt ice at its melting point of 0 °C, to heat it to its boiling point at 100 °C, and to vaporize it. (Conversely these same large amounts of heat are released to the surroundings when water is cooled from its vapor state to its liquid state to solid ice and to temperatures below its freezing point. Water, thus, moderates the temperature of land along its borders.) The thermal properties of water are summarized in Figure 8-3. Because of its properties, water is the ideal medium to absorb waste heat from electrical power plants.

The best fossil fuel plants convert 40% of the input energy into useful energy and discharge 60% of the input energy as waste to condenser water, stack, and other losses. Most fossil fuel plants are much less efficient; they average about 33%. Nuclear power plants are only about 30% efficient and discharge about 55% more waste heat for a given quantity of useful energy than the best fossil fuel plants. Fossil fuel plants discharge heat to both air and water, but nuclear

ENERGY AND ITS EFFECTS

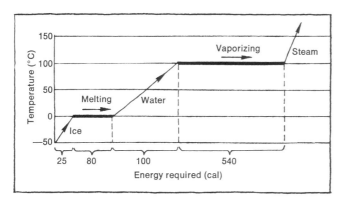

Figure 8–3. Thermal properties of water.

energy plants discharge waste heat only to water. If only the heat discharged through the cooling water is considered, the fossil fuel plant discharges 50% as much as that discharged from a nuclear plant of the same capacity.

The condenser coolant can be obtained from a natural body of water, an artificial pond, or a special cooling tower.

Cooling Systems

ONCE-THROUGH COOLING   The simplest condenser cooling system draws water directly from a natural body of water, passes it through the condenser unit, and immediately discharges it to the environment away from the cold water intake point.

A 1000-MW(e) plant requires 55 cubic meters (or about 2000 cubic ft, i.e., a space 10 ft × 10 ft × 20 ft) of water per second; the temperature of the water will be increased 5–10 °C (about 10–20 °F). It is expected that, by 1980, one-sixth of the average total runoff will be required to cool power plants. Much of the runoff occurs during the four months of flooding. During the remaining eight months, the flow is reduced and the plants would require a much larger fraction of the stream flow than the overall averages. Consequently, when the summer flow is lowest, the entire stream may be required for cooling purposes. The stream then becomes a hot-water stream at a time when it would normally be warmest. Biosystems may be adversely affected by the increased temperature of the water. The situation may be exacerbated by locating several plants on the same stream.

Formerly it was thought that a river would lose the added heat by the time the effluent water reached a point 15 km (about 10 miles) downstream. Recent studies have shown that the hot water stream extends 30 km downstream from the discharge point. In no case did the heat dissipation approach 50% in the 15-km distance.

COOLING PONDS   Heat may be kept out of natural waters by the use of extensive cooling ponds. Pond water is withdrawn from the bottom of the pond, passed through the condenser unit, and returned to the surface of the pond. The hot layer cools by radiation and evaporation of some of the water. Pond cooling is not entirely without effect upon natural bodies because it reduces the volume of natural waters. Since the evaporated water cannot be recycled, the water lost by evaporation from the hot surface of the pond must be replaced from natural sources.

Two to three acres of pond are required per megawatt of power. A 1000-MW(e) plant would require a pond covering an area of 4–8 square km (1.5–3 square miles). With a lower temperature requirement for intake water, 18–20 square km (about 7–8 square miles) would be needed.

WET COOLING TOWERS   Wet cooling towers, (Figure 8–4) with fan-induced draft are the most used in the United States. These are the least expensive to build but the most expensive to operate because they may require a 150-kW (about 200 horsepower) fan to create the necessary draft in the tower. Hot condenser water is sprayed into the top of the tower which is filled with corrosion-resistant strips to break the condenser water into fine droplets. The fan draws air in from the sides of the tower and across the cascade of water droplets. Some of the hot water evaporates from the droplets and thus cools the remaining droplets. The cooled droplets fall to a receiving pan in the bottom of the tower. The cold water is then recycled to the condenser of the turbine.

Figure 8–4. Diagram of a wet cooling tower.

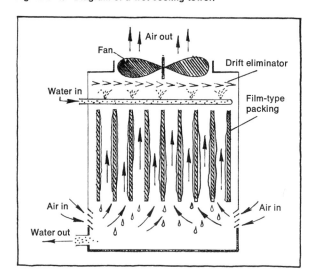

ENERGY AND ITS EFFECTS

An impact statement for a 1000-MW(e) nuclear power plant in Michigan stated that 14 cooling towers, each 73 ft wide, 400 ft long, and 60 ft high would be required to cool the condenser water. The towers would be spaced so that they would occupy 90 acres. The temperature to which the cooled water can fall is limited by the humidity of the air. The lower the humidity, the greater the amount of water that can evaporate into the air at a given air temperature and the lower will be the temperature of the condenser water. Usually, the temperature falls over a range of 5–20 °C (about 10–40 °F) and reaches a low temperature of 15–30 °C (about 60–83 °F). About 1% of the cooling water is lost per 5 °C (10 °F) decrease in condensate temperature.

By 1980, the Federal Power Commission (FPC) expects power plants of 2000–5000 MW(e) capacity to be built. For this large a station, water loss will be 35,000 gallons/min when operated at full capacity. Make-up water for a 1000-MW(e) nuclear plant cooling tower, up to 80,000 cubic meters (about 20 million gallons) per day, would irrigate 1000–1200 hectares (2500–3000 acres) of land.

An amount of water equal to the make-up water is lost to the atmosphere as vapor or small droplets. Serious problems of icing or dense, traffic-stopping fog can occur, especially in cold weather or high humidity. Ice from such a cooling system may cover several square km.

The cost of wet cooling towers adds 0.1–0.2 mills/kWhr (0.3–0.6% to the price of electricity). Because the tower requires electricity to operate the fan, the plant is able to deliver less electricity to the consumer.

NATURAL-DRAFT TOWERS   In Europe natural-draft cooling towers are used. These cost two-and-a-half to three times as much to build as a wet cooling tower but are cheaper to operate. They are hyperbolic in form (Figure 8–5) and may be 180 m (600 ft) in diameter and 150 m (500 ft) high. Fifteen hectares (40 acres) would be needed for a 1000-MW(e) power plant. The high cost of electrical power in Europe accounts for the popularity of the natural-draft cooling tower there. These towers also cool by evaporation of condenser water and require make-up water to replace the evaporation losses.

DRY COOLING TOWERS   Dry cooling towers work on the principle of a car radiator. Condenser water, corresponding to the water in the car motor, passes through radiator-type tubing where it is cooled by atmospheric air drawn through the radiator-type tower. Of course, the cooling effect is limited to the temperature of the cooling fluid, atmospheric air (Figure 8–6).

Dry cooling towers are more expensive to build than other types. They increase the cost of electricity by 33–50%. However, these towers are useful in areas which lack adequate cooling water or where the high-humidity effects of the wet cooling towers would cause unsafe conditions. The largest known operation is for a 200-MW(e) generator in South Africa.

Condenser water is treated with various chemicals to prevent scaling from occurring in the condenser system. When this water passes through cooling

Blow-down

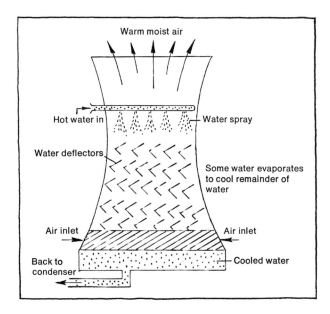

Figure 8–5. Diagram of a natural-draft cooling tower.

towers, some of the water evaporates and concentrates these chemicals to cause mineral deposits (scale) to form on the tower filling. Slime molds further add to the build-up on the filling. Generally the molds are destroyed using chlorine as a biocide. The total deposits may be removed by flushing with water containing additional treatment chemicals. These are added during two or three 30-min *blow-down periods* daily. This "blow-down water" is rather concentrated and may contain potent chemicals when it is discharged to waste.

Biological Effects of Heated Water

Each organism has an optimum range of temperature for carrying out its activities. Man's temperature is closely regulated near 37 °C (98.6 °F). If a man's temperature reaches 42 °C (107 °F), he is likely to die. If his temperature goes much below 98.6 °F, he becomes sluggish. Few people have survived having a body temperature lower than 10 °C (50 °F).

Man can adjust to a variety of temperature conditions by putting on or removing clothing and by adjusting the temperature of his buildings. An organism living in natural water has no such recourse; the temperature of the water fixes the temperature of the organism. If the temperature becomes too high, an aquatic organism may be harmed or killed.

Regulations usually state a maximum temperature for the edge of the mixing zone. This should prevent damage to the biosphere. However, many organisms,

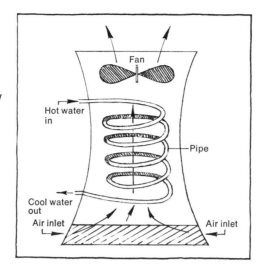

Figure 8-6. Diagram of a dry cooling tower.

especially those in tropical environments, have a very narrow range of temperature over which survival is possible. Any unusual condition might cause the regulation maximum to be exceeded. This might damage one or more organisms of a particular biosphere. Figure 8–7 shows the effect of temperature upon the survival characteristics of one organism.

Heating water reduces its capacity to dissolve oxygen (see Table 8–1). At the same time warmer water increases the activity and metabolism rate of the aquatic organisms. The metabolism rate approximately doubles for each 10 °C increase. Thus, as the need for oxygen increases, the available oxygen decreases. Under these circumstances, the oxygen supply is rapidly reduced and aquatic life dies. Warm water also increases the toxicity of poisonous substances, and the incidence of parasites and disease.

Heating water reduces the diversity and number of organisms that are present. Figures 8–8, 8–9, 8–10, and 8–11 show the effect of temperature upon the survival characteristics of aquatic organisms. Owing to the longer growing season

TABLE 8–1. Solubility of Oxygen in Water at Various Temperatures.

Temperature (°C)	Solubility (ppm)
25	8.4
15	10.2
5	12.5

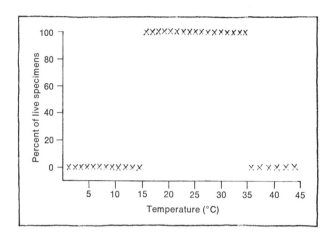

Figure 8-7. Percentage survival vs. temperature for *Periclimenes sp.* after 168 hours of exposure. Each point represents six organisms. From Anita Thorhaug, "Biologically allowable thermal pollution limits, Section II." (unpublished paper written for the Water Quality Office of the Environmental Protection Agency), September 1971, p. 34.

a larger biomass (total living systems) may be produced (Figures 8–8 and 8–9) in heated water than in a natural system, but often the heat-tolerant species are of little value. The new dominant species is determined by the amount of temperature change. If the change is moderate, a species like northern pike may substitute for trout or salmon. If the temperature change is larger, large-mouth bass may become dominant (see Figure 8–10). For some fishermen these changes might be considered desirable. However, if the temperature becomes high enough, worthless goldfish and creek shiners may replace the game fish. At high temperatures, green algae (Figure 8–9) grow apace, float to the surface on oxygen bubbles, die, decay, and pollute the water even without the addition of organic pollutants from external sources.

Any change of temperature is usually accompanied by simplification of the biosystem (Figure 8–11). Simplification leads to a loss of diversity which in turn makes the biosystem less stable.

Water which adult fish can tolerate may be too warm for reproduction. Large-mouth bass can live in water at 32 °C but do not reproduce if the temperature is above 24 °C.

In fall, spring, and winter fish may be attracted to the warm water, and fishing may be good in the heated channels where fish concentrate. This does not increase the number of fish or increase their growth rate. Many times fish have been killed when the electrical plant has been closed and the warm-water discharge discontinued. In summer, fish avoid the heated water.

ENERGY AND ITS EFFECTS

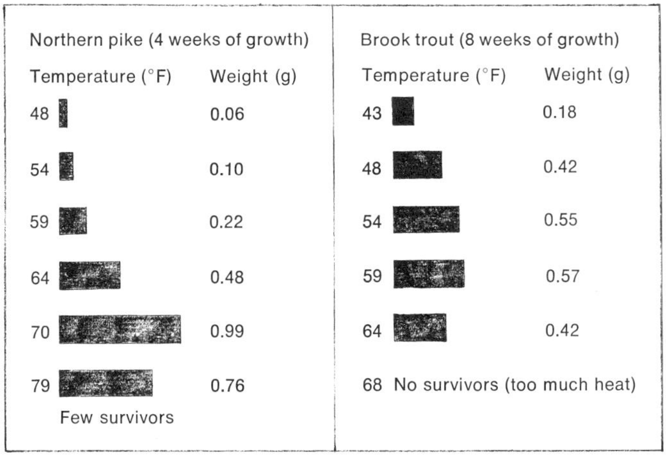

Northern pike (4 weeks of growth)		Brook trout (8 weeks of growth)	
Temperature (°F)	Weight (g)	Temperature (°F)	Weight (g)
48	0.06	43	0.18
54	0.10	48	0.42
59	0.22	54	0.55
64	0.48	59	0.57
70	0.99	64	0.42
79	0.76	68	No survivors (too much heat)
Few survivors			

Figure 8–8. Temperature and growth of fish. Courtesy of Donald A. Mount, Director, U.S. Environmental Protection Agency, National Water Quality Laboratory, Duluth, Minn.

Relatively small changes in normal temperature relationships may have subtle effects on the biota (living organisms) of a body of water. Normal natural waters undergo relatively small temperature fluctuations during a season. Temperature transitions from one season to the next are likely to be gradual. The behavior of organisms is tied to the natural ebb and flow of time and temperature;

Figure 8–9. Effects of temperature on types of phytoplankton. From J. Cairns, Jr., "Effects of increased temperature on aquatic organisms," *Industrial Wastes* 1(4):150, 1956.

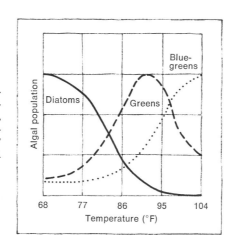

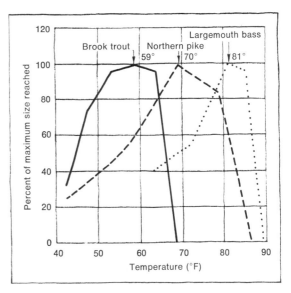

Figure 8-10. Shift in species with temperature increase. Courtesy of Donald A. Mount, Director, U.S. Environmental Protection Agency, National Water Quality Laboratory, Duluth, Minn.

survival depends upon time-honored sequences of events. When the time-temperature sequence becomes garbled, the organism does not follow its normal pattern of activities and may be destroyed. Any given organism may be capable of surviving the insults to its code of behavior, but if, in addition, its food supply chain is affected in some way, it may be eliminated.

Trout and salmon are especially sensitive to heat and will avoid warm water. River water becomes progressively warmer as it flows down to its outlet. It is possible for water in a river to be tolerable to trout near the outfall of a power plant yet be intolerable to the species some distance downstream. If the temperature of a stream is raised 1 °C (about 2 °F), 25 km (about 17 miles) of trout habitat may be lost (Figure 8–12); if the temperature is raised 3 °C (about 5 °F), 65 km (about 42 miles) of trout habitat may be lost. If the stream was originally a salmon stream, the upper thermal line for salmon would not intersect the line representing the temperature of the stream at any point in the stream. If the lines representing the temperature of the stream, after thermal additions, should intersect the upper thermal limit for salmon, salmon could not migrate upstream on spawning runs and the species would be exterminated in that stream. Cal Elling, director of the U.S. Fish and Wildlife Service's Biological Laboratory in Seattle, insists that if more power plants are placed on the Columbia, it will be the end of the salmon on the Columbia River.[2]

If the intake for cooling water is from the bottom of a lake and the discharge pipe is located at the surface, the thermal relationship of the top and bottom

2. From Ivan Bloch and Ben East, "Danger: Heat kills rivers, too," *Outdoor Life,* November 1968.

ENERGY AND ITS EFFECTS

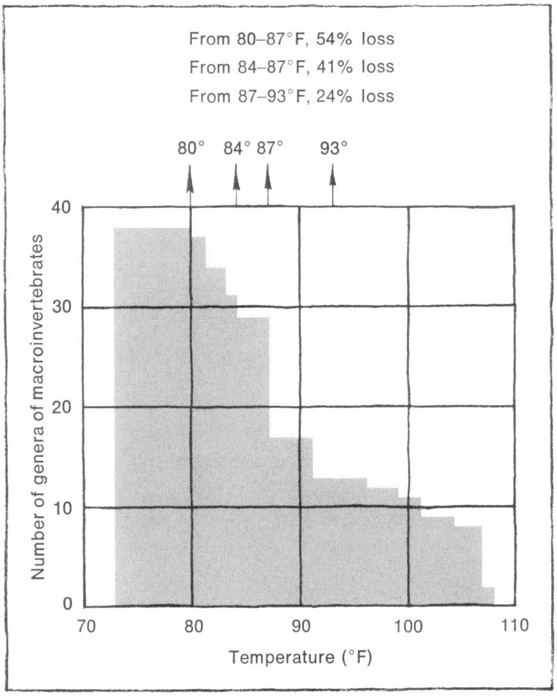

Figure 8-11. Relationship of temperature and number of invertebrates. From Bradford Owen, "Research project on effects of condenser-discharge water on aquatic life," *Progress Report 1960,* the Institute of Research, Lehigh University. Study funded by Pennsylvania Power & Light Company.

of the lake are changed. Most materials shrink in volume as they are cooled. Water decreases in volume until it reaches a temperature of 4 °C (39 °F), after which the volume increases again in going from a temperature of 4 °C to 0 °C, the freezing point of water. When water is being cooled to 4 °C, the dense cold water displaces warmer water from the bottom. As the warmer water rises, it carries with it the mineral nutrients which it acquired while in contact with the bottom. Overturning of water also occurs in the spring. Water transmits light and, if the body of water is not too deep, the light energy reaches the bottom where it warms the bottom layers and causes them to rise and carry nutrients to the upper layers. The effect of both overturnings of water is to increase the growth which can occur in the upper layers of water. Overturning also carries oxygen to the bottom for bottom-living fish. When cool water is taken from the bottom and replaced by warm water at the surface, the overturnings are delayed until later in the spring than normal and thus change the food and air relationship of the lake.

Overall, although changes have occurred in the type of aquatic life in bodies of water, no one knows just what actual damage has been done. A team of scientists from the Battelle Institute, Columbus, Ohio, studying thermal pollution of streams concluded:

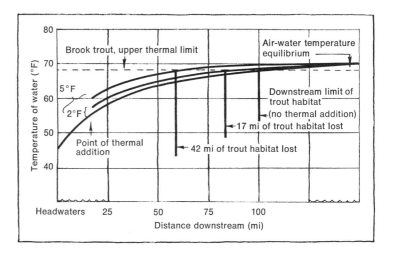

Figure 8-12. Effect of thermal additions on trout habitat. Courtesy of Donald A. Mount, Director, U.S. Environmental Protection Agency, National Water Quality Laboratory, Duluth, Minn.

Although there has been no apparent major damage to the ecosystem by cooling water discharge, there have been ecological changes. The complex interrelationships of species, populations, and communities in an ecosystem are the result of years of evolutionary trial and error. Therefore, although no major mortalities are noted, shifts in species diversity or abundance might upset delicate balances which exist, and results not be known for years.[3]

Productive Uses of Heated Waste Water

Some prefer to call the waste heat from power plants thermal enrichment rather than thermal pollution. They look at it as a resource out of place. A few power plants are built close to concentrated load centers in cities. The heated effluent of these plants could be used for domestic and industrial heating purposes.

Power plants reject enough heat to heat all the homes in the United States. This would be a huge saving in fuel resources, but not as much as at first seems possible. In order to have the temperature of the exit water high enough to heat space efficiently, the temperature of the exit steam would necessarily be higher than is most efficient in terms of electricity production. Extensive and expensive heating tunnels and lines to carry the heat would need to be built. It would be most efficient where industry or large apartment houses are located close to the utility.

3. A. A. Levin, *et al.,* "Thermal discharges: ecological effects," *Environ. Sci. Technol.,* 6:230, March 1973.

ENERGY AND ITS EFFECTS

Some power plants can supply process steam to industrial plants. However, if this is done, the efficiency of the conversion of fuel to electricity is reduced. For greatest efficiency the temperature of the condenser water must be as low as it is practical for it to be. Process steam is at a much higher temperature. Consequently, the loss of efficiency of the utility must be balanced by the benefits from the industrial process.

Agriculture and aquaculture cannot use water at high temperatures, so agricultural use of heated waste water would cause little interference with the efficiency of the plant. Warm water causes a more luxuriant growth of food material and extends the growing season. The growing season has been extended by this means in Oregon.

Many proposals have been made to use the relationship between warm water and food growth to develop artificial commercial fisheries in ponds or along the coast. At present this is largely a development for the future, although the Japanese have increased the production of seafood in this way. Heated waste water may contain noxious chemicals which could make the water undesirable for fisheries.

Waste heat could be used for heating greenhouses. There should be little problem about siting greenhouses near power plants, but it is unlikely that they would be extensive enough to absorb the enormous amounts of heat released as waste by the power plants.

Waste heat could be used to keep harbors open. Open water would reduce ice damage to pilings, docks, etc.

Desalination is often mentioned as the most advantageous use of waste heat. Here again the condenser-water temperature must be higher than that for the most efficient operation of the utility. At about $400 per 3 acre-feet, the present cost of desalinated water is too high for agricultural purposes. The utility must also produce enough energy to pump the water up on to high land where it can be used to grow crops. The enormous amount of energy that would be required for this purpose becomes apparent when it is remembered that we use water which collects on the highlands to produce electrical power as it falls over a dam to lower levels.

When the sun's energy, known as *insolation,* strikes the earth, some is absorbed and some is radiated back into space. The amount absorbed depends on the surface it strikes; the rough, black surface of soil will absorb more energy (heat) than the shiny, white surface of ice. Absorbed energy can be slowly released or it can be stored for long periods of time; energy is stored in vegetation and fossil fuels. Eventually, most of the insolation will be radiated back into space.

Over the centuries, insolation and radiation gradually developed a steady state which fluctuated slowly and only in small amounts. Industrial society is adding large inputs of energy and combustion products to the earth. The United Nations has estimated the global energy production as 5.5 million MW, or about $1/22{,}000$ of the solar energy reaching the earth. If use of energy increases by a factor of five before the end of the century, heat added by man's activities would amount to about $1/4000$ of the energy received from the sun. Dr. Alvin Weinberg has proposed building large *nuplexes* (groups of nuclear power plants together with various industries and farming) to supply the world's energy.[4] He estimates they would produce energy equal to $1/400$ of the solar insolation. The effect on the climate of present and future energy production is difficult to determine, since fossil-fuel combustion products and other factors also may cause changes in the heat balance. In any case, the climate of an urban area is different than that of a rural area (Table 8–2).

4. From A.M. Weinberg and R.P. Hammond, "Limits to the use of energy," *American Scientist,* July-August 1970.

TABLE 8–2. Changes in Climatic Elements Caused by Urbanization.

Element	Comparison with rural environment
Contaminant	
Condensation nuclei and particles	10 × more
Gaseous admixtures	5–25% more
Cloudiness	
Cover	5–10% more
Fog (winter)	100% more
Fog (summer)	30% more
Precipitation	
Totals	5–10% more
Days with less than 5 mm	10% more
Snowfall	5% more
Relative humidity	
Winter	2% less
Summer	8% less
Radiation	
Global	15–20% less
Ultraviolet (winter)	30% less
Ultraviolet (summer)	5% less
Sunshine duration	5–15% less
Temperature	
Annual mean	0.5–1.0 °C more
Winter minima (average)	1–2 °C more
Heating degree days	10% less
Wind speed	
Annual mean	20–30% less
Extreme gusts	10–20% less
Calms	5–20% more

Source: H. E. Landsberg, "Climates and urban planning," *Urban climates,* Geneva: Secretariat of the World Meteorological Organization, 1970, p. 372. © 1970, World Meteorological Organization.

ENERGY AND ITS EFFECTS

Insolation passing through the atmosphere may be absorbed or radiated into space by air pollutants. Energy from the sun hits particles and "backscatters" into space or is absorbed. Such energy never reaches the earth, and thus the earth is cooler than it would have been if the particulate matter had not been in the atmosphere. In addition, particles form a nucleus about which water collects to form the droplets that are clouds. Without particulate matter no clouds would form; with an excess of particulate matter the cloud cover and precipitation increase. Atmospheric turbidity (dustiness) has increased over the entire globe: 57% over Washington, D.C., in 60 years; 88% over Davos, Switzerland in 30 years; 30% over Mauna Loa Observatory, Hawaii, in 10 years. The relationship between turbidity and temperature is not known.

Carbon dioxide has the opposite effect to particulate matter. Carbon dioxide prevents the radiation of energy back into space. The resultant increase in temperature is called the *greenhouse effect.* By the end of the century, the carbon dioxide in the atmosphere is expected to increase by about 17%. An increase of 200% could lead to an increase in the overall global temperature of 2 °C. The exact effect of an increase of CO_2 and other mechanisms which would enhance or decrease that effect is not understood.

Every change in the surface characteristics of the globe causes a change in climate to some degree over a small or large portion of the surface of the earth. The changes may be small or large. Vegetation increases absorption and storage of heat (latent heat); thus, deforestation of the Amazon Basin would change the heat balance. Roads increase the reflectivity of energy. Irrigation causes increased absorption because of increased water surface. Dammed rivers increase the salinity of estuaries, cause less of the estuary to freeze in northern climates, and decrease reflectivity.

There is no doubt that the actions of mankind can affect the climate but how much and with what result is not known. Dr. Mikhail Budyko, a Russian meteorologist, believes we are in danger of overheating our planet. Increased heat from the production of energy and from an increase of carbon dioxide in the atmosphere will cause the boundary of polar ice to move northward about two degrees.

On the other hand, Dr. Reid Bryson, Director of the Institute for Environmental Studies at the University of Wisconsin, believes the weather patterns now considered normal are more advantageous than the weather patterns over the past few million years. At present, meteorologists do not know the cause of weather cycles or how the actions of man are affecting those normal cycles. The authors of *Inadvertent Climate Modification* have described the situation:

We have a conviction that mankind *can* influence the climate, especially if he proceeds at the present accelerating pace. We hope that the rate of progress of our understanding can match the growing urgency of taking action before some devastating forces are set in motion—forces that we may be powerless to reverse.[5]

5. Report of the study of man's impact on climate (SMIC), Cambridge, Mass.: MIT Press, 1971, p. 225.

At present man has an insatiable desire to use more and more energy; conditions in the future may or may not allow a continued increase in the use of energy.

Currently (1974) the population of the United States is increasing at a rate of less than 1%, while overall energy use is increasing at a rate of about 5% per year. Some energy sectors are increasing at a much higher rate; for example, electricity use is increasing by 9% per year. These changes represent explosive increases in energy use and consequently in primary energy resource consumption.

For most energy factors, the rate of use is accelerating. Between 1940 and 1965, energy consumption increased at an overall rate of 2.8% per year. Since 1965 an explosive increase to a 5% rate has occurred. The explosion further shows itself in the projections which various prognosticators have given for the year 1980. The results are summarized in Figure 8–13. However, the constraints of the energy crisis of 1973–1974 have slowed the rate of growth but have not stopped it.

A quantity increasing at a given rate each year is increasing under compound interest conditions and grows rapidly at what is called an *exponential rate.* Since any compound interest rate of increase leads to a definite doubling period of time for the quantity, the multiplication of bacteria provides a con-

Figure 8–13. Several forecasts of the 1980 energy demand. From "Time is short for government energy decisions," *Petroleum Independent* 42:4, July–August 1971.

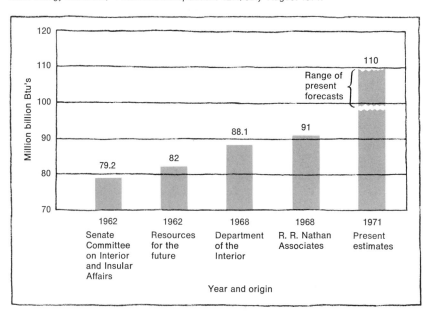

ENERGY AND ITS EFFECTS

venient model to demonstrate how quantities increase under exponential rates of increase.

Let us start with one bacterial cell and assume that each bacterium divides to produce two cells in the time period of one day and every day thereafter. The number of bacteria which exists at the end of each day can be plotted to give the form of a rapidly increasing quantity, an *exponential curve* (Figure 8–14). When the formula is applied to the quantities plotted in the graph the following quantities are found:

x	y	x	y
0	1	1	2
2	4	3	8
4	16	5	32

After a definite period of time, the consumption of the material will be doubled on a per year basis if the consumption of material increases at some uniform percentage rate of increase. The required calculation is a compound interest problem. Table 8–3 shows the length of time that it takes to double the amount of a quantity at different percentage rates of increase per year.

If oil consumption increases at a rate of 4% per year from the present time into the future, in 17.5 years the consumption will be double what it is now. Not only will the consumption be double what it is at present, but the amount that will be consumed during the 17.5 years will be equal to that which has been consumed up to the present time, if the growth has always been 4%.

An explanation may be found in the experience of a person who receives an inheritance of $16,383. He decides to use it conservatively by using only $1 the

TABLE 8–3. Percentage Rates of Increase and Doubling Time in Years.

Rate of increase (%/year)	Time to double (years)
1	70.0
2	35.0
3	23.0
4	17.5
5	14.2
6	12.0
7	10.2
8	9.0
9	8.0
10	7.3
20	3.8
40	2.0
50	1.7

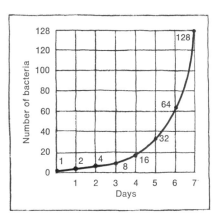

Figure 8–14. Increasing numbers of bacteria that double in population every day. The number of bacteria can be calculated by the formula $y = 2^x$ where y is the number of bacteria at each doubling period and x is the number of doubling periods.

first year, $2 the second year, $4 the third year, etc. The number of dollars he withdraws each year will be double the amount he used the preceding year (Table 8–4). At the end of seven years, it would seem he had enough resources to last 254 years based on that year's use instead of only seven more years. At the end of 10 years, his inheritance would last 30 years based on that year's use. After 14 years his entire inheritance would have been consumed.

In the model use of the inheritance was continued until it was completely exhausted. The exploitation of a natural resource cannot continue until exhaustion. Eventually, the mineral becomes more and more difficult to find and exploit, and other factors enter in. However, the model shows that a small initial consumption may be misleading in an overall view of the lifetime of the resource.

TABLE 8–4. Exponential Rate of Growth in Consumption of an Inheritance.

Years	Dollars Used per year	Amount Left
1	1	16,382
2	2	16,380
3	4	16,376
4	8	16,368
5	16	16,352
6	32	16,320
7	64	16,256
8	128	16,128
9	256	15,872
10	512	15,360
11	1,024	14,336
12	2,048	12,288
13	4,096	8,192
14	8,192	0

ENERGY AND ITS EFFECTS

1. Primary and secondary sources of energy and the methods of conversion from one to another.
2. Efficiency of energy uses.
3. Methods of disposal of waste heat, including productive uses.
4. Biological effects of waste heat.
5. Energy factors affecting climate.
6. Exponential growth.

1. What is energy?
2. What factors affect the efficiency of an energy system?
3. Trace a particular kind of energy from its source to its ultimate disposal.
4. What is the final form that energy takes when it is used?
5. List the factors which affect the theoretical efficiency of a heat engine.
6. Since marine life is abundant in warm tropical waters, why should the warming of waters in temperate zones pose any threat to the environment?
7. How can thermal pollution be controlled or reduced?
8. In what ways has man inadvertently changed the climate of the earth?
9. How may the discharges from a steel company stack affect the weather near the plant?
10. What could be the consequences of changing the ocean currents?
11. Assuming that water from northward flowing rivers in Canada and Russia were diverted to southern areas, how could these actions affect the seas and the climate of the world?
12. Apparently there will be no disastrous change in the climate for 20–30 years. What should we do before that time?

1. Bryson, R. A., "All other factors being constant . . . a reconciliation of several theories of climate change," *Weatherwise,* 21: 56–61, 1968.
2. Clark, J. R., "Thermal pollution and aquatic life," *Sci. Amer.* 220:18–27, March 1969.
3. Cole, L. C., "Thermal pollution," *Bioscience,* 19:989–992, 1969.
4. Gaucher, L. P., "Energy in Perspective," *Chem Tech,* pp. 153–158, March 1971.
5. *Inadvertent climate modification,* Cambridge, Mass.: MIT Press, 1971.
6. Morrison, W. E., and Reading, C. L., "An energy model for the United States, featuring balances for the years 1947 to 1965 and projections and forecasts to the years 1980 and 2000," Bureau of Mines Circ. 8384, Washington, D.C.: Government Printing Office, 1968.
7. Rasool, S. I., and Schneider, S. H., "Atmospheric carbon dioxide and aerosols: effects of large increases on global climate," *Science,* 173:138–141, 9 July 1971.
8. Woodson, R. D., "Cooling towers," *Sci. Amer.,* 224:70–79, May 1971.

9 Fossil Fuels—Energy from Ages Past

How many persons know that the prosperity of some modern cultures stems from the great flux of oil fuel energies pouring through machinery and not from some necessary and virtuous properties of human dedication and political designs?[1]

Howard R. Odum

During 1973, an energy crisis was a matter of great concern. Genuine, phony, or contrived, there was an apparent shortage of natural gas, gasoline, and fuel oil.

Consumer groups claimed that the so-called energy crisis was contrived by the energy (oil) companies to make it possible to extract higher prices for their products (Figure 9–1). Other groups claimed that United States oil and gas supplies are adequate to meet our needs for the next 20–30 years and that oil companies are concealing resource information. The oil companies claimed that all that is necessary to assure a continuing abundance of petroleum fuels is to give an economic incentive (higher prices) for drilling more wells.

Are either of these groups correct in their assessment of the crisis situation for the present and/or for the future? What is the true condition with respect to energy resources, and what does the future hold for the people of the United States and the world?

PETROLEUM

Because of its "bonanza-like" availability and overwhelming flexibility and convenience in processing and use, petroleum has captured about 75% of the energy market in the United States in the last 50 years. Forty-three percent of the energy used in the United States comes from oil and 32% from natural gas.

Figure 9–1. **"You give us what we want and we'll give you what you want."** Reproduced by courtesy of Wil-Jo Associates, Inc. and Bill Mauldin.

1. Howard Odum, *Environment, power and society*, New York: John Wiley, 1971, p. 6.

Figure 9-2. Bright Angel Trail into the Grand Canyon.

Deposition The primeval rocks of the earth were formed during the solidification of the original molten mass. Wind, water, heat, frost, and glaciers dissolved, cracked, and ground the rocks into small particles of sand and silt which were carried by flood waters down to quiet lakes or seas. Here the particles settled to the bottom and built up thick layers of material. The "ebb and flow" of geological forces deposited different materials at different rates at different times. When life appeared on earth, the organisms provided organic matter which mingled with the sediments. At times thick deposits of limestone-like material (rock containing calcium) was deposited upon the stream-fed deposits. From whatever source the deposits came, they often accumulated to a depth of many thousands of feet. As the deposits deepened the pressure upon the lower levels increased until they were compacted into hard sedimentary rocks: sandstones (from sand), shale (from clay and mud materials), and limestone (from shells and bodies of aquatic animals). Over a period of time, the organic matter which was trapped in the sediments was converted into petroleum compounds. These compounds were prevented from escaping upward by an overlying impervious layer of limestone.

FOSSIL FUELS—ENERGY FROM AGES PAST

Throughout its history, the earth has undergone many cycles of heaving, crinkling, and lowering of its surface. Rocks which once were deep beneath the seas may now be found 10,000 ft or more above sea level. The heavings of the earth frequently tilted the sedimentary rocks so that the layers were no longer horizontal. Many times the rock layers broke along a more or less vertical line (*fault*). Along a fault, rock layers can move relatively easily either horizontally or vertically with respect to each other. In Figure 9–2 a cross section of the Grand Canyon along the Bright Angel Trail is shown. Note the break in the rock formation that shows a movement between layers at a fault of about 200 ft in vertical distance. The thick layer of rock (limestone) is about 500 ft thick at this point.

If the rock layers on one side of a fault move upward with respect to the layers on the other side, a lower porous layer containing petroleum compounds may be brought up against an impermeable layer on the opposite side of the fault. Figure 9–3 shows how oil would move into and be trapped by faults and various

Figure 9–3. Geological structures that may trap petroleum. American Petroleum Institute.

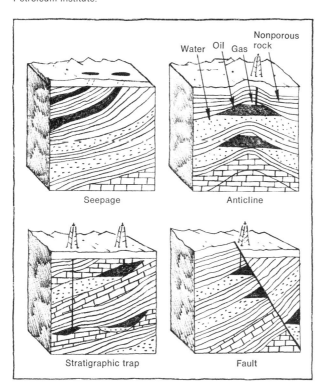

other formations. If the uplifted layers are inclined upward toward the fault, any petroleum materials which a pervious layer contains may move up along the incline under the overlying impervious layer and become trapped at the fault line against the face of the opposing impervious layer. Over eons of time petroleum may collect at the fault and eventually be recovered by man.

The deposition and collection of oil depends upon the slow work of many factors and circumstances. All contribute to placing a limit upon the amount of oil which man can recover and use.

Finding Deposits Often there is evidence at the surface that indicates geological structures which may contain petroleum. If there is no visible surface evidence, suitable underground conditions may be discovered from *seismic data*[2] acquired through the use of surface explosions or mechanical thumpers. An analysis of earth magnetic measurements taken near the surface may also indicate the presence of oil-bearing structures.

Sometimes oil and gas are found in nearly horizontal formations. The large 5-billion barrel East Texas field is an example of this kind of formation. Scientific seismic investigation is of little help in locating such a field; "crystal ball" drilling is necessary.

Oil When petroleum reaches the surface, the fractions with lower boiling points are stripped from it. The vapors of propane, butane, pentane, and 30–40% of the ethane are condensed to form natural gas liquids. The uncondensed gases, methane (CH_4) and some ethane (C_2H_6), are sold to customers as natural gas. The liquid remainder is *crude oil*.

UNITED STATES OIL HISTORY The United States is the most explored and developed oil-producing area in the world. Much data have accumulated about oil fields from their discovery to the exhaustion of their deposits. From the history of known fields, it is possible to make a reasonable estimate of the potentialities of new fields at various stages in their development. The aggregate knowledge about oil fields in the United States may be used to assess the ultimate amount of petroleum which is producible in this country. Similarly, it should be possible to estimate the ultimate amount of oil which is producible from the world taken as a unit.

Oil is not produced all at once but is withdrawn over a period of time. The amount of known petroleum which remains in the ground, and is producible, is called *proved reserves*. As more wells are discovered in an oil field, their proved reserves are added to those of the other wells. Together, these constitute the proved reserves of the field.

Development wells around a discovery well take some time to drill and bring to productive status. Eventually, the boundaries of the field are reached and

2. Earth vibrations caused by surface explosions reflect differently from different layers or formations. By a study of such "seismic" data, some idea of underground formations can be deduced, for example, presence of oil.

large additions to the proved reserves are no longer possible. As the oil is withdrawn from the ground, the reserves are reduced. Finally, the well and the oil field reach the point of exhaustion.

INCREASING THE AMOUNT OF RECOVERED OIL It is technically possible to increase the total production of a well by stimulating the flow by various means.

1. Water may be injected under pressure into wells surrounding a producing well.
2. Steam may be injected into a well in what is known as "huff and puff." As many as 20 cycles have been used, but each cycle is less productive than the previous one and the process finally becomes uneconomic.
3. Chemicals may be used to "unglue" the formation and make it easier for the oil to move to the producing well.
4. Hydraulic fracturing uses water at very high pressures to break up the formation so that oil may move through it more easily.
5. Conventional or nuclear explosives may be used to fracture the formations.

Additional oil recoveries made possible by these methods are added to the proved reserves and become a part of the cumulative discoveries that determine the ultimate production from the field.

Stimulation methods must be used with care. In the Baldwin Hills area of California, geologists traced an earthquake to the injection of brine into a formation. The earthquake ruptured a reservoir, and the resulting flood caused 12 million dollars damage and killed fived people. The oil company involved paid 3.9 million dollars in damages. Geologists also feel that such injections have caused earth tremors near the Rangely, Colorado, oil field.

Whatever methods are used to recover oil from a well or field, it is impossible to extract all of it. In 1967 it was estimated that about 30% of the oil in place was producible by the methods available at that time. The recovery rate has been increasing at about 0.5% per year, but the ultimate recovery is not expected to exceed 40% of the oil in place.

DISCOVERY-PRODUCTION-RESERVE CYCLES The graph of the history of cumulative discoveries of an oil field, of a nation, or of the whole world will follow the general form of the plot of the cumulative discoveries vs. time as given in Figure 9–4. The dates on this plot correspond to the situation for the United States. There is a slow beginning during the time of discovery. In the middle portion of the curve, the rate of cumulative discovery increases rapidly. After passing through a maximum rate of discovery (midpoint of curve), the discovery rate decreases with time. As the development becomes complete near Q_∞ the rate of discovery becomes negligible and little is added to the ultimately available petroleum.

The peak rate of discovery for the United States occurred in 1957. This year corresponds to the midpoint of the cumulative discovery. In 1957, cumulative discoveries amounted to 85.3 billion barrels of oil and the ultimate recoverable

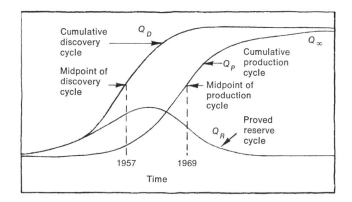

Figure 9–4. Cumulative discovery-production-reserve cycles. Adapted from *Energy Resources: A Report to the Committee on Natural Resources,* Publication 1000-D, M. King Hubbert, National Academy of Sciences-National Research Council, Washington, D.C., 1962. With permission of the author and the National Academy of Sciences.

oil, according to M. King Hubbert, should be twice this amount or 170.6 billion barrels, exclusive of Alaska and Hawaii.

The producible quantity discovered is not immediately produced and the amount not yet produced resides in the ground as proved reserves. Proved reserves increase over approximately the first half of the discovery cycle. When the discovery cycle reaches the last part of the plot, the rate of discovery falls from its maximum value and eventually becomes zero. At this point all the oil has been discovered and the discovery cycle has been completed.

When the discovery rate exceeds the production rate for oil, the quantity of oil in the reserve increases. When the production rate exceeds the rate of discovery, the proved reserves decrease. The complete cycle of these two effects produces the dome-shaped curve, Q_R (see Figure 9–4). Eventually, the rate of discovery becomes zero and addition to the reserves stops. At this point, all production must come from the reserves. Finally, the reserves become zero and production stops.

The experience of the industry is that the cumulative production curve has roughly the same shape as the cumulative discovery curve. Historically, the production curve has lagged behind the discovery curve by about 12 years. The quantity represented by any point of the production curve is equivalent to the corresponding point on the discovery curve. If oil discovery and production follow this pattern, the ultimate amount of oil produced must equal the cumulative amount discovered, or 170.6 billion barrels.

OIL LIFETIMES If past United States oil production is plotted as billions of barrels of oil per year against time, we obtain a curve like that shown in Figure

FOSSIL FUELS—ENERGY FROM AGES PAST

9–5 for the period 1900 through 1971. According to Hubbert the peak production of oil should have occurred in the year 1969. If this is true, the right-hand side of the curve should be a mirror image of the period from 1930 to 1969. Cumulative production up to January 1966 amounted to 81 billion barrels of oil, or almost half the producible oil. Enough oil has been produced since that time to bring the total to about 97 billion barrels up to 1 January 1972, or nearly 60% of the 165 billion barrels that Hubbert claims is producible from the conterminous 48 states.

A whole family of mirror-image bell-shaped curves can be constructed about various reference times for peak production, for example, 1980 and 1990. In each case the area under the curve represents the total cumulative production. The area under Hubbert's curve (lower curve) represents 165 billion barrels. About one-half as much more, 70 billion barrels, would be required to meet the requirements of the "bell" for the 1980 curve. A further additional amount of 70–75 billion barrels would be required to meet the requirements of the curve centered upon 1990. Thus, the 1990 curve would require a resource base twice as large as that projected by Hubbert, or about 330 billion barrels.

The plot of oil production since 1966 rises sharply above the peak projected by Hubbert. This does not necessarily mean that Hubbert was incorrect in his

Figure 9–5. Cycles of crude-oil production in the United States and adjacent continental shelves, exclusive of Alaska. Adapted from *Energy Resources: A Report to the Committee on Natural Resources,* Publication 1000-D, M. King Hubbert, National Academy of Sciences-National Research Council, Washington, D.C., 1962. With permission of the author and the National Academy of Sciences.

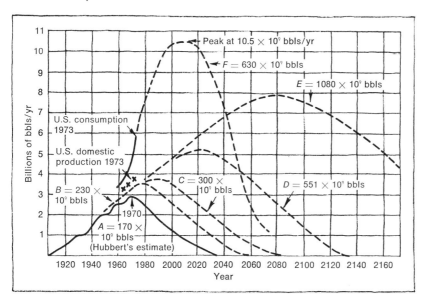

estimate. It is very possible that production could temporarily rise above the projected peak. However, if Hubbert is correct, any production above the curve must come out of the total volume of oil represented by the area under the curve. Consequently, at some future time production will fall precipitously inside the right-hand half of the curve. In this case the shape of the right-hand portion of the curve may change, but the total area under it must remain unchanged. Necessarily, such overshooting would exhaust the resource in a shorter time than shown by Hubbert's curve (see Figure 9–5).

Similar arguments apply to the curves plotted for the years 1980 and 1990 or any other peak reference year.

It is possible that the plotted production for 1970 and 1971 may be a part of a curve having a later reference year, 1980, 1990, etc. However, this is questionable in view of the fact that the number of wells being drilled and the amount of well pipe being used has decreased rather steadily since 1956 (Figures 9–6 and 9–7). Furthermore, it is likely that most of the larger and more productive fields have been discovered, and that any future discoveries will be smaller and less productive per foot of drill pipe used. Hubbert found just such a reduction in yield per foot over the period 1950 to 1966.

Even if Hubbert is wrong and one of the higher curves applies, the exhaustion of our oil energy base probably will not be delayed for more than 40 years. If this seems like a long time, reflect that the Great Depression occurred only 40 years ago and the first television stations were not built until about 27 years ago (1948). If one of the later curves does prove to be correct, it is possible that the present thrust of production could burst above the curves as represented.

Figure 9-6. Number of wells drilled from 1956 to 1971 in the United States.

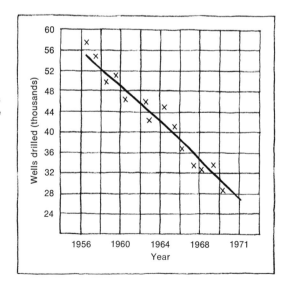

FOSSIL FUELS—ENERGY FROM AGES PAST

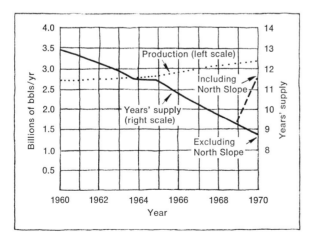

Figure 9–7. Amount of well-pipe used from 1956 to 1971 in the United States.

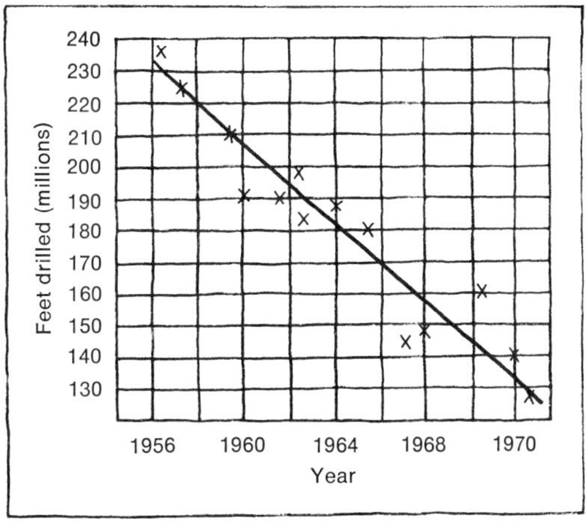

The consequences would be similar to those which applied to the rise of our present level of production above the Hubbert curve.

The United States has maintained production levels and even increased them, but this was done at the expense of proved reserves. Reserves dropped precipitously in 1969 by 1.1 billion barrels, or about one-third of that year's production. The reserve ratio is dropping rapidly (Figure 9–8). The smaller the ratio, the more serious is our energy problem. Other estimates are shown in Table 9–1.

Figure 9–8. Production and reserve-production ratio in the United States. Independent Petroleum Association of America.

Another source, Paul Meadow[3], quotes unpublished information from the United States Geological Survey to show that, if we extend the areas of the lower 48 states to include all off-shore areas under 200 m (660 ft) or less of water, our recoverable reserves would be 463 billion barrels of oil. If we include marginal and submaringal areas under 2500 m (about 8200 ft) or less of water, our reserves would jump to 2280 billion barrels. The present off-shore wells are drilled in about 200 m (about 600 ft) of water. Techniques are being developed to permit underwater drilling in 2000 m (about 6000 ft) of water.

Note the curve for the total consumption of oil in the United States (curve F, Figure 9–5). The vertical gap between the United States domestic production and total consumption is widening dramatically. Total consumption presently seems to be following the pattern of the curve from the 1972 value to the 1980 value estimated at 9 billion barrels by Thornton Bradshaw, president of Atlantic Richfield. It is difficult to say if total consumption will indeed reach Mr. Bradshaw's projected figure in 1985 or whether it will pass beyond it. After all, the projected value is only 1.5 times the 1973 United States oil consumption figure. Eventually, the exponential rise in consumption would meet resource resistance and the consumption curve would peak out and produce some form of a bell-shaped curve such as curve F.

For purposes of argument, it is assumed that consumption peaks out at a rate of 10.5 billion barrels per year in the year 2010, and that consumption then falls to produce the symmetrical curve as drawn. Relative to the area under curve A, the area under the consumption curve represents 630 billion barrels of oil. This amount is approximately four times the amount under curve A. Furthermore, this amount is about two-thirds the size of the total world reserves of about 900 billion barrels. It is noteworthy that world oil production is about four times the oil production in the United States and that world production is

3. *Mineral facts and problems,* Bureau of Mines Bulletin 640, Washington, D.C.: Government Printing Office, 1970.

TABLE 9–1. Some Estimates of U.S. Crude Oil Ultimate Production.

Billions of barrels	Source
190	Hubbert
353	Moore
433	Weeks
450	Elliott and Linden
432–495	National Petroleum Council
550	Hendricks-Schweinfurth

Source: V. E. McKevey, "Mineral resource estimates and public policy," *American Scientist* 62:36, Table 1, Jan.–Feb. 1972.

about three times the 5.5 billion barrels of oil that were consumed in the United States in 1971.

It is undoubtedly true that more oil reserves will be found to add to the totals of both the United States and the world, but it is highly improbable that the United States will be able to fill the consumption bell curve as detailed in Figure 9–5. United States oil consumption may indeed reach high above that value, but it is rather unlikely that it will follow the contour of the broad affluent curve F. As it is drawn, the United States will have returned to the present level of consumption (6 billion barrels of oil per year) within 60 years from 1973 and consumption should continue its steep decline as plotted. More than likely a much narrower bell will be formed and a steep decline will occur on the right-hand side of the curve.

The oil resources of the United States are inadequate now and in the future to support the projections given by curve F. Consequently, if we continue to depend on oil and if curve F is realized, massive imports of oil will be required. In those circumstances, if the foreign oil were to be cut off or reduced for any reason, the standard of living and lifestyle of United States citizens would be drastically changed.

ALASKAN OIL   The Alaskan oil has been ignored until now because the amount and transport are matters of controversy.

Estimates of the Prudhoe field run from 5 billion barrels to 10 billion barrels to as much as 40 billion barrels. There are eight other possibly rich, but as yet unexplored, areas. The greatest expectation should not amount to more than 320 billion barrels (1973). Even at the present rate of consumption, 6 billion barrels per year, this amount would last only for 50 years and the trend is to increase the rate of consumption. Most projections for production from the Alaskan oil fields do not approach 320 billion barrels.

The Humble Oil Company, in a television advertisement, said in part that the oil in Alaska will provide only a three-year supply for the United States at the present rate of consumption. "Present" (1971) United States consumption was about 5.5 billion barrels per year. A three-year supply would be about 17 billion barrels, which is approximately two-thirds of the 1970 proved reserves of 29 billion barrels for the lower 48 states. Hubbert estimates that 12 billion barrels of oil would be a fair amount for the Prudhoe field and 25 billion barrels for the whole of Alaska.

These estimates must be viewed in the light of a few facts: (1) the largest oil field in the 48 states is the East Texas field which had a producible oil content of 5 billion barrels; (2) the Cook's Inlet field in Alaska has an oil content of about 1 billion barrels; (3) the transport of oil from Alaska will be difficult. Thus, 35–40 billion barrels should be a generous estimate for the oil which may be producible from Alaskan fields. This amount is a little larger than the proved reserves of the 48 states (1970). Even if this amount is produced and brought to the lower 48 states, it can do little to delay the eventual energy crisis that

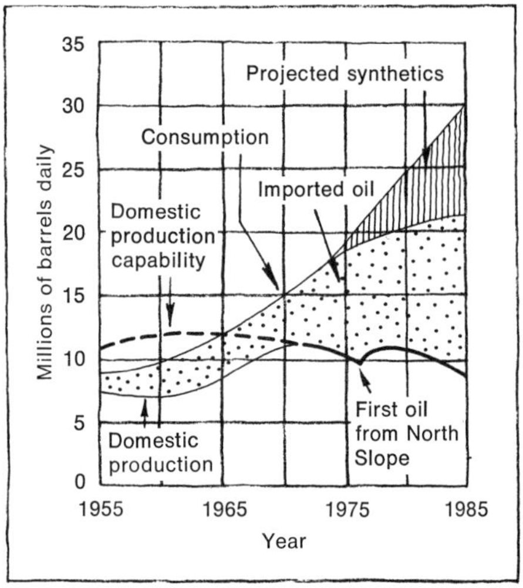

Figure 9–9. The petroleum gap in the United States. Courtesy of Professor Arthur M. Squires, Chemical Engineering Department, The City College of New York.

seems to be "just around the corner" for the United States. Figure 9–9 places Alaskan oil and gas supplies in perspective. Alaskan oil production is only expected to reach 2 million barrels per day. Consumption was 15–16 million barrels per day in 1972.

If Alaskan oil is of crucial importance to the continuance of our way of life, we are indeed in serious trouble. The oil really cannot save us and alternatives must be examined. On the other hand, if Alaskan oil is not of critical importance to us, there is no need to rush into production. Rather, we can wait until the problems involved in the production and transport of the oil are solved.

It is claimed that Alaskan oil is of great importance to our military security. However, if the oil is so important to our national security, why do we not save it rather than use it as rapidly as possible? Actually it can do little to make us secure. The field, the necessary pipeline, and the transportation system would be far from the centers of population, and with modern weapons thay would be about as vulnerable to cut off by a determined army as anything in the United States.

WORLD OIL   If the entire world were to attain the affluence of the United States, the consumption of oil would increase. Table 9–2 shows the amount of the increase. The world is not likely to attain this degree of affluence. If it should do so, the yearly consumption of oil would be one-third the known world reserves. Table 9–2 shows that there is not enough petroleum for the world's population to use at the same rate of consumption as the people of the United States (Figure 9–10).

FOSSIL FUELS—ENERGY FROM AGES PAST

Figure 9–10. "One of these days I'll be broke . . . then how will you support your habit?" Cartoon by le Pelley in The Christian Science Monitor, © 1973 TCSPS.

TABLE 9–2. Comparison of United States and World Consumption Based on United States Per Capita Consumption.

	1985	1970
United States		
U.S. population (millions)	250	200
Yearly consumption (billion barrels)	10	5.5
Per capita consumption (barrels)	40	27
World		
Population (billions)	5.5	
Per capita consumption based on U.S. consumption (billions of barrels)	40	
Yearly consumption based on U.S. per capita consumption (billions of barrels)	220	

Natural Gas   RESOURCES   In the 20-year period ending 1 January 1967, 6000 cubic ft of gas were discovered for each barrel of oil. Recently drilled wells are deeper and contain a larger amount of gas per barrel of oil. After 1 January 1967 it is assumed that the wells yield 7500 cubic ft of gas per barrel. In 1970, each barrel of oil produced corresponded to an actual production of 6,650 cubic ft of natural gas.

In terms of quantities of oil, Hubbert has calculated the original quantity of natural gas in place as 1298 trillion cubic ft. The cumulative production to date must be subtracted from this amount in order to find the amount that may be produced in the future (see Table 9–3)

The Potential Gas Committee says that 60% of future gas supplies will come from beneath the oceans bordering the United States and Alaska at depths greater than 15,000 ft. The Committee estimates that undiscovered reserves amount to 1179 trillion cubic ft, a quantity which is about four times the United States proved reserves and 53 times the 1970 production of 22.3 trillion cubic ft (see Table 9–4).

Arthur Warner, petroleum engineer of mineral studies with the Bureau of Mines, gives 1144 trillion cubic ft as the amount of gas to be produced after 31 December 1969.[4] We also quote H. P. Linden of the United States Geological Survey as placing our producible reserves at 2400 trillion cubic ft including off-shore areas to depths of 200 m. If we extend the offshore areas to include those under not more than 2500 m (about 8200 ft) of water, our producible reserves will jump to 4340 trillion cubic ft.

The different volume estimates can be used to find values for the lifetime of our remaining gas supplies. The lifetimes are found for a continuing consumption at the 1970 rate, 22.3 trillion cubic ft per year and for growth in production at a cumulative rate of 7.7% per year. The data can also be analyzed by use of the bell-shaped curve as was done in the discussion of crude oil. Figure 9–11 defines the prospects.

Curve A corresponds to Hubbert's assessment. Curve B represents 1.5 times the volume under curve A. Curve C represents the volume estimated by Linden, about 2400 trillion cubic ft, as being available in less than 600 ft of

---

4. *Mineral facts and problems,* Bureau of Mines Bulletin 640, Washington, D.C.: Government Printing Office, 1970.

TABLE 9–3. Gas to be Produced.

	Gas (trillion cubic ft)
Estimated producible gas	1298
Production 1 January 1971	561
To be produced (including Alaska)	737
To be produced (excluding Alaska)	599

FOSSIL FUELS—ENERGY FROM AGES PAST

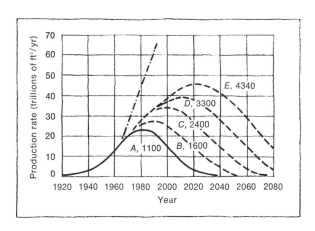

Figure 9–11. Cycles of natural gas production in the United States, adjacent shelves, and Alaska. Adapted from *Energy Resources: A Report to the Committee on Natural Resources*, Publication 1000-D, M. King Hubbert, National Academy of Sciences-National Research Council, Washington, D.C., 1962. With permission of the author and the National Academy of Sciences.

water. Curve E represents the gas supposedly available in all areas and under less than 8300 ft of ocean water, about 4340 trillion cubic ft of gas.

Hubbert's curve, curve A, peaks at the year 1980. This is odd because gas production is related to oil production. Early gas production was vented, and some of the vented gas may have been counted as being producible. The effect of this would tend to increase the apparent lifetime of the resource, that is, some gas is counted that is not there. However, Hubbert said that he had adjusted the volume for the amount vented. As the curve stands it projects about 775 trillion cubic ft as still producible and only 246 trillion cubic ft as having been produced by 1970.

TABLE 9–4. Lifetimes of Estimated Supplies of Gas.

Estimated supplies (trillion cubic ft)	Lifetime at uniform rate of 22.3 trillion cubic ft/yr (years)	Lifetime at 7.7% compounded (years)
4340 (Linden)	Less than 200	37
2400 (Linden)	Less than 110	30
1170 (PGC, 50 states)	53	22
737 (Hubbert, 50 states)	32	17
599 (Hubbert, 48 states)	27	15

According to the theory that gas production is related to oil production, the yield of gas should correspond to the amount of oil still to be produced as of 1 January 1972. According to Hubbert's curve and the production figures to 1 January 1972, only 63 billion barrels of oil remain to be produced, which is equivalent to 510 trillion cubic ft of gas or about 23 years supply at the 1970 rate of consumption of 22.3 trillion cubic ft per year. This compares with 35 years according to Hubbert's gas curve which centers over the year 1980.

An indication of the trend of our natural gas supplies is given in Figure 9–12. From shortly after 1950 until 1960 the reserves grew at a faster rate than production. After 1960 the rate of increase slowed and the reserve-production ratio started to fall (Figure 9–12). In 1967 the reserves began a rapid decline. Recently reserves have gone up again because of the Alaskan discoveries.

Possible reasons for the decline shown in Figure 9–12 include the following: (1) the outgrowth of a shift to explore offshore areas and neglect of onshore areas; (2) the fact that oil companies tend to work in different areas and, therefore, do not need to do protective drilling; (3) a changing pattern in supply and reserves with the reduction of the lag time between exploration and production; (4) the possibility that producers find it more economical to defer natural gas developments; (5) the gas is not available to be discovered.

It is interesting to note that, if the increase in consumption of natural gas continues at its present rate of increase, 7.7%, our natural gas will be gone by about the year 2000 regardless of the probable amount of reserve (see Table 9–4). As our supplies begin to dwindle, price relationships will force us to turn to other sources of energy.

WORLD RESOURCES World figures for natural gas production are unreliable. Much of the gas is produced in underdeveloped countries where there is little local demand for gas and where it is not feasible to transport it to consuming

Figure 9–12. Production and reserve curves for natural gas.

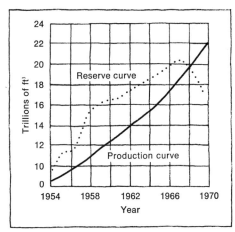

FOSSIL FUELS—ENERGY FROM AGES PAST

centers by pipeline. As a result large amounts of gas are flared (burned) near the producing wells. Of course, no records of gas production are kept or are even possible.

It is likely that the ratio of gas to oil in foreign deposits has approximately the same ratio as in the petroleum of the United States. If this is true, the flared gas represents a loss of about 40% of the energy that the petroleum originally contained.

Efforts are being made to recover the energy of remote natural gas resources. Refrigerated freighters are being built for transport of natural gas. The explosion hazards of such transport are very large but gas is being transported by this means. However, it is not expected to solve the natural gas shortage for the United States.

In Colorado, Utah, and Wyoming an area of 16,500 square miles contains 4000 **Oil Shale** billion barrels of oil (Figure 9–13). However, much less than 4000 billion barrels is economically recoverable. A recoverable shale oil resource must be (1) in deposits yielding 25–100 gallons per ton in beds a few feet or more thick and not more than 1000 ft below the surface, and (2) in lower-grade deposits yielding 10–25 gallons of oil per ton in units of 25 ft or more thick which are minable by open-pit methods. With these restrictions only about 80 billion barrels of oil are considered to be recoverable.

If, by the year 2000, the shale oil industry grows to 2 billion barrels per year, all reserves will have been used by the year 2030. Unless there are technical advances which would make it profitable to work lower-grade deposits, there would be no more oil from shale. Technological advances usually depend upon more intensive use of an energy resource. If shale oil must fuel its own exploitation, a point is reached where the invested energy equals the amount of energy obtained. At or before this point, exploitation of the resource must end. In fact, some experts think that the shale will be more valuable as a source of chemicals than as an energy resource.

The shale oil industry will cause two difficulties for the area where the rock is found. One is degradation of the water; the other is replacement of the vegetation destroyed by the industry.

The processing of the shale oil together with the water requirement for the municipal development which must accompany the industry will consume 70–138 gallons of water for each barrel of oil. If the industry develops, as hoped, to produce between 800,000 and 900,000 barrels per day by 1985, the amount of water consumed will be from about 60 to 120 million gallons per day.

In addition, surface pits left by mining shale will store water and lead to still more loss from the river. Underground mining will disrupt the flow of ground water. A small-sized oil shale refinery will remove the support from under 5–6 square miles of land. The resulting subsidence, in addition to the fracturing necessary for the mining, would interfere with the normal ground water drainage patterns. Deep mines would need to be pumped to remove water. This would lower the water table, destroy springs, and reduce the flow to streams.

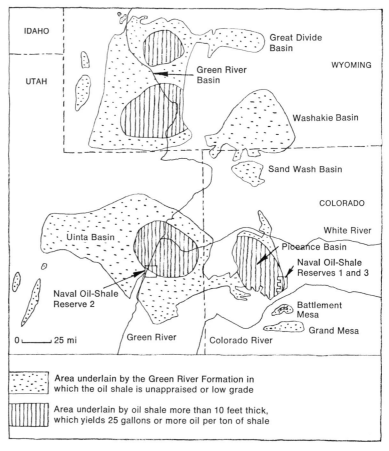

Figure 9–13. Map of the oil shale region.

The water table might be lowered as much as several hundred feet in one year. The water would be reduced in flow, which would increase the salt content to downstream users, especially those in Arizona and California. The shale wastes themselves would add increased salt loading to the water. The leaching of shale residues would add large amounts of sodium ion (Na^+) and sulfate ions (SO_4^{2-}) to the water, as well as lesser amounts of magnesium ions (Mg^{2+}), calcium ions (Ca^{2+}) and bicarbonate ions (HCO_3^-).

Large residues will be left after the oil is removed from the ore. One ton of spent shale must be disposed of for each barrel of oil. Because the shale rock is pulverized, it will occupy one-and-a-half times as much space as the original. Sixty percent of the residue can be used as minefill but 40% must be disposed of on the surface.

Dr. John Ward and George O. G. Lof, professors of civil engineering at Colorado University, Fort Collins, Colorado, found that growth of vegetation on spent shale is impossible under normal growing conditions. Grass has been made to grow in small areas by covering the shale with 4 in. of top soil, fertilizing twice a year, and irrigating with about 10 in. of water per growing season. In a region where the rainfall averages only 12 in. in the valleys and 20 in. on the mesa tops, that much additional water is not available.

Thus, not only will the water supply be reduced but the salt content will be increased by both the reduction in volume of flow and leaching of the spent oil shale. Colorado River water available for all purposes in the dry states of Arizona and California as well as in Mexico would be greatly reduced.

Oil shale may be mined by three methods. Surface mining will cause the same difficulties that are caused by surface mining of coal in the arid West. Underground mining will lead to interference with drainage and subsidence.

In situ burning (burning in the formation underground) of the oil shale has been tried. A total of 1350 gallons of propane was burned at the rate of 8 gallons/hr over a period of a week to heat the formation. The burning was self-sustaining for several weeks and gave a yield of 4.5 barrels per week. The yield from the first week recovered the energy used to start the burning. The efficiency of the process depends upon the length of the sustained burning. In order to obtain oil, the formation must be heated to about 900 °C. One of the problems of heating shale is that there are few natural passages through which oil or air can flow. Therefore, in situ burning is of limited usefulness.

A final problem is that shale oil belongs to a different family of hydrocarbons than does petroleum. Petroleum equipment cannot be used to process crude shale oil into useful products.

Fracturing the formation by conventional or nuclear explosions has been suggested as a way to make passageways in the deposits. Experiments using nuclear explosions have been used to stimulate the flow of natural gas from a tight formation in the Rangely, Colorado, gas field (Plowshare Program). These tests are still being evaluated for economic practicality and radiation danger.

When it is exploited, shale oil is projected to contribute 2 billion barrels of oil per year. In order to produce this amount, 50 plants, having a total capacity of 100,000 barrels per day, will need to be built. Each plant will cost about 300 million dollars to build (1971).

Oil shale seems to be a relatively inefficient source of energy compared with coal, even low-grade coal. Thirty-five gallons of oil—the production from a ton of the best shale—would produce about 4.7 million Btu while a ton of poor coal (lignite) would produce 14 million Btu, and a ton of ordinary bituminous would yield 23 million Btu. In addition, oil shale requires many processing steps, each of which requires energy.

Tar Sands

The Canadian tar sands have been evaluated to contain 300 billion barrels of recoverable oil. This is about two-thirds as large as the proved reserves of crude oil for the entire world (world oil resources stand at 454 billion barrels). By comparison it deserves to be designated a vast deposit and it is believed to be recoverable.

The oil has the consistency of a heavy crude oil and is so viscous that it does not flow through the sand. Ninety percent of the tar sands are too deep for surface mining; for example, Pan American's 105,000 acres of leases are 1000 ft below the surface. It will be difficult to devise an economical method of mining the oil deposits and removing the oil from the sand.

Eventually in situ recovery methods are certain to play a major role in the production from tar sands. The recovery process itself involves hydraulic fracturing of the underground formation, air injection into the tar, and displacement of the tar by a combination of air and water. The hot tar can be pumped from a well as in conventional petroleum recovery. The tars are from the same family of compounds found in petroleum and pose no great problems for processing in conventional petroleum refineries.

Even the most promising and easily worked deposits have economic oil recovery problems. However, it seems unquestionable that the tar sands will be worked profitably when competition from conventional petroleum production diminishes. The prospect of economic recovery of oil from the tar sands is much greater than from oil shale.

The implications for the United States are that there is a relatively large reservoir of oil in tar sands nearby, but the entire deposit will not be available to the United States. The tar sands would increase petroleum supply to an amount only four times that of the estimated future production of oil in the United States. Supposedly, the tar sands could add 80 years to our oil supply. However, there is no gas in the tar oil and it would need to cover the energy that we now receive from natural gas. Natural gas now supplies 32% of our present energy demands or 43% of the energy now obtained from petroleum sources. At most, at the present rate of consumption, petroleum supplies from Canada would extend our oil-based energy by only about 47 years. It is certain that we shall not obtain anywhere near that number of years of oil supply from Canada.

Petrochemicals

Only a small fraction of the petroleum recovered in the United States is used for chemicals and not as a source of energy. Even this small amount of petroleum produces 88% of the chemicals manufactured in the United States.

Petrochemicals reach into every phase of life in the United States. Fabrics with names like nylon, Dacron, Acrilan, Orlon, Fortrel, and Kodel are made from petroleum. Most natural fibers are mixed with synthetic fibers before use. All permanent press cottons contain some manmade fibers.

The usual house has many petroleum products in it. Fabrics in rugs, curtains, bedding, and upholstered furniture, as well as the cushions on the furniture and the mattress on the bed, may be made from petroleum. Vinyl siding, paint, and hard-surface flooring also come from petroleum.

Plastic bottles, boxes, and bags are made from petroleum. Milk cartons are coated with a plastic coating. Bubbles of plastic cover many packaged products. Plastic film is used for everything from wrapping leftovers to killing weeds in the garden. Other products from petroleum are drugs, both prescription and OTC, toys, pesticides, photographic film, dishes, synthetic rubber, and almost all products that have a benzene ring in their molecular structure. Indeed, plastics and other petroleum products are important in our society.

Some resource experts have said that oil resources should be saved to make chemicals and not used for energy. The Shah of Iran wants to reduce the use of oil so that it can be saved for future generations.

Chemical plastics are *polymers;* that is, they are made of repeating small units called *monomers.* For example, ethylene has the formula

$$\begin{array}{ccc} H & & H \\ | & & | \\ C & = & C \\ | & & | \\ H & & H \end{array}$$

Under proper conditions these small monomer molecules can be combined to form very large molecules:

$$\begin{array}{cccccccccccc} & H & & H & & H & & H & & H & & H \\ & | & & | & & | & & | & & | & & | \\ -C & - & C & - & C & - & C & - & C & - & C- \\ & | & & | & & | & & | & & | & & | \\ & H & & H & & H & & H & & H & & H \end{array}$$

The double bond of the ethylene opens and joins with other monomers to form indefinitely long chains. Masses of these molecules are formed into finished products such as polyethylene film, containers, and molded products. Monomers are polymerized by two methods, *addition* and *condensation.* Polyethylene is formed by addition.

Addition polymers require the presence of an initiator to start polymerization. Peroxides are often used as initiators since they easily form free radicals.

$$R:O:O:R \rightarrow 2R:O \cdot$$

Ethylene combines with the free radical to form another free radical.

$$R:O \cdot \; + \; \begin{array}{ccc} H & & H \\ | & & | \\ C & = & C \\ | & & | \\ H & & H \end{array} \rightarrow R:O - \begin{array}{ccc} H & & H \\ | & & | \\ C & - & C \cdot \\ | & & | \\ H & & H \end{array}$$

The peroxide-ethylene combination is also a free radical which can continue to react with other ethylene molecules to form a long chain. The chains become entwined to form the familiar products of polyethylene. If a hydrogen is displaced from a carbon, side-chains may form. This type of polyethylene is used to make bottles. All the monomers that form addition polymers are variations of ethylene where one or more hydrogens may be replaced by other groups.

Methyl group CH_3	Polypropylene	Carpet fibers, bottles
Chlorine atom Cl	Polyvinylchloride (PVC or vinyl)	Floor tiles, phonograph records
Phenyl group ⬡	Polystyrene	Toys, styrofoam
All H atoms by F atoms	Teflon	Coating for cooking utensils, valves
One H atom by a methyl group and one H atom by $O-\overset{\overset{\displaystyle O}{\|}}{C}-CH_3$	Lucite, Plexiglass	Windows, jewelry

Condensation polymers are usually produced from two different monomers reacting to produce a polymer and a small molecule, usually water. Polyester fabric is a well-known condensation polymer. An acid and an alcohol react to produce an ester and a molecule of water. The alcohol has a —COH group, and the acid has a —COOH group.

$$R-\overset{\overset{\displaystyle O}{\|}}{C}-OH + HO-R \rightarrow R-\overset{\overset{\displaystyle O}{\|}}{C}-O-C-R + H_2O$$
acid   alcohol   ester   water

If the acid has —COOH groups at both ends of the molecule and the alcohol has a —COH group at each end of its molecule, the two monomers may be polymerized to a polyester. Dacron is this type of polymer.

$$HO-\overset{\overset{\displaystyle O}{\|}}{C}-⬡-\overset{\overset{\displaystyle O}{\|}}{C}-OH + HO-\overset{\overset{\displaystyle H}{|}}{C}-\overset{\overset{\displaystyle H}{|}}{C}-OH \rightarrow -O-\overset{\overset{\displaystyle O}{\|}}{C}-⬡-\overset{\overset{\displaystyle O}{\|}}{C}-O-\overset{\overset{\displaystyle H}{|}}{C}-\overset{\overset{\displaystyle H}{|}}{C}-O- + H_2O$$

terephthalic acid   ethylene glycol   polyester, Dacron   water

Dacron forms cross-linkages which makes the fiber very strong. Generally such plastics are *thermosetting* plastics; they are strong, often rigid, and cannot be reheated and reformed. Plastics that form few cross-links between the chains of the polymer are *thermoplastic*. These plastics may be reheated and formed into new shapes without destroying the polymer (Figure 9–14).

There are many kinds of condensation plastics, depending on the particular compounds used as monomers. Polyamides form from an acid and an amide:

FOSSIL FUELS—ENERGY FROM AGES PAST

$$\underset{\text{acid}}{HO-\overset{\overset{\displaystyle O}{\|}}{C}-R-\overset{\overset{\displaystyle O}{\|}}{C}-OH} + \underset{\text{amide}}{H-\overset{\overset{\displaystyle H}{|}}{N}-R'-\overset{\overset{\displaystyle H}{|}}{N}-H} \rightarrow \underset{\text{polyamide}}{-\overset{\overset{\displaystyle O}{\|}}{C}-R-\overset{\overset{\displaystyle O}{\|}}{C}-\overset{\overset{\displaystyle H}{|}}{N}-R'-\overset{\overset{\displaystyle H}{|}}{N}-} + \underset{\text{water}}{H_2O}$$

If R is $(CH_2)_4$ and R' is $(CH_2)_6$, the polymer is a common nylon, nylon 66 (each monomer has six carbon atoms). There are other nylons with other carbon-hydrogen arrangements for R and R'. The polyamide forms hydrogen bonds with other chains and forms a strong polymer.

One of the earliest types of plastic was Bakelite, produced from phenol and formaldehyde:

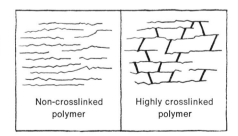

phenol   formaldehyde   phenol   Bakelite formica   water

These thermosetting plastics are extremely strong, since many cross-linkages are formed. Any hydrogen on the phenol can be lost in a condensation process.

A plastic similar to phenol-formaldehyde plastics is Melmac used for making dishes. It is made from the monomers formaldehyde and melamine:

formaldehyde   melamine $\rightarrow$ melamic plastic

Figure 9–14. Non-crosslinked polymers and crosslinked polymers.

Non-crosslinked polymer   Highly crosslinked polymer

Monomers for natural and synthetic rubbers are various derivatives of butadiene:

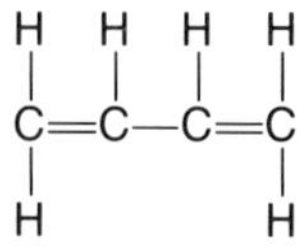

$$\begin{array}{cccc} H & H & H & H \\ | & | & | & | \\ C\!\!=\!\!C & - & C\!\!=\!\!C \\ | & & & | \\ H & & & H \end{array}$$

If one of the hydrogens on a single-bonded carbon is replaced by a methyl group (—CH_3), isoprene is produced; isoprene polymerizes to natural rubber. If the hydrogen is replaced by a chlorine atom, chloroprene is formed; chloroprene polymerizes to form neoprene, a synthetic rubber which is resistant to gasoline, oils, and fats. The most important synthetic rubber is a *copolymer* (two monomers adding to each other alternately) of butadiene and styrene:

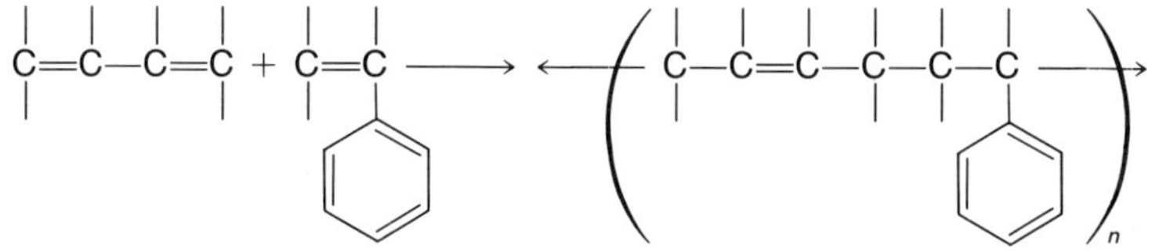

Thus, it is obvious that petrochemicals have become so important a part of our society that we are dependent upon them for the continuation of our present life-style.

COAL It is probable that petroleum resources will be exhausted rather soon, but we have large supplies of coal. Coal can and does provide both energy and raw materials for sophisticated products; oil, gas, electricity, and clothing.

Coal is formed from plant materials which accumulated over a long period of time. Plant materials have a formula that approximates $(C_6H_{10}O_5)_x$. Gradually the materials decay and form methane or marsh gas (CH_4), CO_2, and H_2O. Peat, the first usable form, still contains recognizable plant material and about 90% water. Further decay and loss of water produces brown coal and lignite, which contain about 40–50% water. Further decomposition yields subbituminous coal (which is about 25% water) and bituminous coal. If the coal is subjected to high pressures, more water and volatile materials are lost and anthracite coal is formed. Further heat and pressure may cause the anthracite coal to change to graphite, a form of pure carbon. Bituminous coal is the most common form of coal, representing about 45% of all coal resources.

Coal Resources Since coal occurs in stratigraphic beds in more or less uniform layers, it is relatively easy to map coal-bearing territory and make a fairly definite estimate of the amount of coal available in the United States and the world. For practical

FOSSIL FUELS—ENERGY FROM AGES PAST

purposes minable coal is defined as coal that occurs in seams at least 12 in. thick and at depths from 0 to 4000 ft. Coal below a depth of 4000 ft would pose expensive mining problems. Since it constitutes less than 10% of the total coal, deposits deeper than 4000 ft are ignored. Within these restrictions, the amount of original coal resources *in place* in the United States is estimated by M. King Hubbert to have been 2971 billion tonnes. Ordinarily only 50% of this is recoverable. This reduces the ultimate amount of recoverable coal to about 1468 billion tonnes. From this amount must be subtracted the amount already mined. However, if a little extra technology for recovery is assumed, we can round the value up to 1500 billion tonnes for convenience. This total includes all grades of coal —lignite, bituminous, and subbituminous. For the following discussion we shall assume that all the coal is bituminous. Such an assumption is somewhat optimistic, but the amounts of available coal are only approximations at best so the assumption will be adequate for our purpose of determining the maximum length of time that coal may be available to us.

Substitution of Coal for Petroleum Resources

The United States currently consumes about 600 million tons of coal per year. At this rate of consumption, using Hubbert's values, our coal would last 2500 years.[5] However, 600 million tons of coal supply only 20% of our current energy. When oil and gas are exhausted, coal is the prime candidate for assuming the energy burden presently carried by petroleum. This means that coal may need to be consumed at five times its present rate, or 3000 million tons per year, in order to supply all of the energy we now use each year. On that basis, at the present rate of total energy use the lifetime of our coal supplies becomes 500 years.[6] Total energy projections, however, are something like the projections in Table 9–5. If coal were to supply the total energy requirements at the rate given for the year 2000 in Table 9–5, the life expectancy of the energy in coal would be only 166 years.[7]

5. Lifetime coal years $= 1500 \times 10^9$ tons $\times \dfrac{1 \text{ year}}{600 \times 10^6 \text{ tons}}$
$\qquad\qquad = $ about 2500 years

6. $\dfrac{2500 \text{ years}}{5} = 500$ years

7. $\dfrac{170}{62} = $ about 3 (from Table 9–5), $\dfrac{500 \text{ years}}{3} = 166$ years.

TABLE 9–5.   Use and Projection of Energy.

Year	Use or projection (trillion Btu)
1968	62,000
1969	65,000
1980	74,000–97,000
2000	170,000

The energy content of the coal is not the only factor in the longevity of the resource. It is convenient to change coal into oils, gasoline, and pipeline gases. Energy is required for the processing of coal to form these upgraded products. In this processing 36–44% of the total energy may be lost. Some of that energy could be recovered if the processing is done where an electric plant or an industry could use the hot gases. In any case, approximately 60% of the energy will remain as useful energy in the upgraded material. Ignoring any possible recovery of heat, the coal resource as synthetic oil and/or gas now has a lifetime of 100 years.[8]

Professor Hoyt C. Hottel of the Chemical Engineering Department, Massachusetts Institute of Technology, told the American Association for the Advancement of Science, December 1971:

The probable size of the synthetic gas industry is indicated by the following: the United States consumed in 1970 some 23×10^{12} (trillion) cubic ft of natural gas. If 40% of that much gas were to be made synthetically by 1983 when the 11-year doubling time has elapsed and the synthetic gas then represents only 20% of the total, 100 gas plants of 250 million cubic ft per day each would have to be built, each requiring an investment of the order of 200 million dollars and each consuming 15,000 tons of coal per day—a total investment of 29 billion dollars and a total coal consumption of 0.5 billion tons, approximately our present total coal consumption.

Gasification There are four processes being investigated in the United States together with one which has been used both here and abroad to make "coal gas," a low-energy gas which contains more than 50% carbon monoxide and hydrogen. The aim of the experimental processes is to increase the percentage of methane (CH_4) in the gas and thus yield a higher energy gas.

All four processes are basically the same. Coal is subjected to steam at temperatures of 600–800 °C and pressures of 20–70 atm:

$$C + H_2O \rightarrow CO + H_2$$

The carbon monoxide then reacts with the steam to form more hydrogen:

$$CO + H_2O \rightarrow CO_2 + H_2$$

Hydrogen reacts with the carbon of coal to produce methane:

$$C + 2H_2 \rightarrow CH_4$$

The final mixture will contain 40–60% methane. The gas mixture is purified by removal of carbon dioxide, hydrogen sulfide, organic sulfides, and water. A catalytic methanation increases the percentage of CH_4:

$$CO + 3H_2 \xrightarrow{\text{catalytic}} CH_4 + H_2O$$

The final product, *synthetic natural gas* (SNG), is 95% methane with a heat content equal to that of natural gas.

8. 166 years $\times$ 0.6 (60%) = 100 years.

Although the basic process is the same in all systems, it is probable that different processes will be best for different types of coal. For example, the CO_2 Acceptor process seems best for the low-energy coals found in western United States. The reaction of CO_2, one of the by-products of the process, and calcined dolomite produces the heat necessary for the gasification process. Heat must be used to form the magnesium oxide-calcium oxide and since the process cannot be 100% efficient, energy will be required and lost in the process by which the dolomite oxides are formed. The equations are:

$$MgCO_3 \cdot CaCO_3 + energy \rightarrow MgO \cdot CaO + CO_2$$

$$MgO \cdot CaO + CO_2 \rightarrow MgCO_3 \cdot CaCO_3 + energy$$

Of the gasification processes under consideration in the United States, the HYGAS process produces the largest percentage of methane. However, a separate source of hydrogen is required, hence the name "hydrogen gas" or HYGAS.

The coal consumption at various percentage rates of increase in use is given in Table 9–6. For a given year, the first number listed is the number of tons which would be used in that year. The second number is the cumulative amount consumed to that date. The table provides a convenient reference for comparisons of different rates of increase in the use of coal.

Growth Rate and Coal Consumption

The 6% column in Table 9–6 gives the production performance of coal at the current rate of increase of consumption. Part of the increase in use might be caused by coal having to replace petroleum. Whatever the cause, if growth

TABLE 9–6. Consumption of Coal at Different Percentage Rates of Increase. (All values × 1 million tons.)

Year	6%	1%	0%
1970	600	600	600
	600	600	600
1980	1,070	663	600
	9,000	7,200	6,600
1990	1,920	732	600
	24,000	13,800	12,600
2000	3,440	808	600
	50,900	21,600	18,600
2010	6,170	892	600
	99,000	30,000	24,600
2050	63,400	1,330	600
	1,110,000	73,800	48,600
2060	114,000	1,460	600
	2,000,000	87,600	54,600

continues at a 6% rate, the energy of the coal used in the year 2000 may be larger than the total energy used in the year 1970 (the equivalent of 3000 million tons). If coal production could continue expansion at a 6% rate to the point of exhaustion, the resource would be consumed by about 2056, some 85 years from now.

Ninety years from now, straight-line coal production at the 0% rate (600 million tons per year) would result in "only" 54 million tons of cumulative production by 2060, approximately the cumulative amount which would be produced by the year 2000 at the 6% yearly compound rate.

Even at a 1% compounded rate of increase of production, cumulative production would be 60% greater than that for a 0% rate. The actual consumption for the year 2060 at the 1% growth rate is 1460 million tons compared with the 0% value of 600 million tons per year.

Assuming that coal consumption grows at the 6% rate until the year 2010 and then no longer increases its rate of production (0% growth rate after the year 2010), the production rate would be a constant 6000 million tons per year until exhaustion occurs some 280 years later (1970 to 2250). This is about 10% of the life expectancy of the resource at 0% rate of increase over 1970 production. Certainly, the growth rate and level of use of any resource greatly affects the length of time that it may be used.

Another interesting way of calculating the lifetime of coal resources is to use the relationship between coal resources and population and amount of coal used by each person. Table 9–7 shows the relationship. Various levels of coal consumption per person are listed at the left-hand side of the table. The population in hundreds of millions is given across the top of the table.

If the number of millions of people changes from 100 million to 200 million (doubles), while the consumption remains at 1 ton per person per year, the lifetime of the coal resource will be reduced from 15,000 to 7500 years. If the coal consumption increases from 1 ton per person per year to 2 tons per person per year while the population remains at 100 million, the lifetime will be reduced by the same amount. If both changes are made, the lifetime of the coal resource will be 3750 years.

Using the current level of consumption, 3 tons per person per year, and the population of 200 million, the lifetime is 2500 years. Coal *equivalent* of *total energy use* in 1970 is 15 tons per person per year. On this basis the coal lifetime for the current population of the United States is read from the table as 500 years.

Providing any of the projected energy demands will pose a pollution problem. Even the much smaller consumption of the past 30 years has caused serious environmental problems, such as air pollution and land degradation. Furthermore, the bulk of such energy additions must come from high-sulfur coal. Sulfur emissions from the combustion of coal are a serious problem at a consumption of 3 tons per person per year. What will happen when 15 or even 45 tons per person per year are burned?

FOSSIL FUELS—ENERGY FROM AGES PAST

The longevity has been calculated on the basis of the ultimate amount of recoverable coal, the full 1500 billion tons. Actual mapped recoverable coal is one-half this much or 750 billion tons. At present prices only 220 billion tons are considered to be economically minable. The longevity tables should be rechecked with this in mind.

The United States is relatively well off for coal compared with the world as a whole. It is estimated that the ultimate recoverable coal in the world is 7500 billion tons. Equally divided among the present 3.5 billion people, the coal per person becomes

$$\frac{7500 \times 10^9 \text{ tons}}{3.5 \times 10^6 \text{ people}} = 2100 \text{ tons/person.}$$

In the United States a comparable figure is

$$\frac{1500 \times 10^9 \text{ tons}}{200 \times 10^6 \text{ people}} = 7500 \text{ tons/person.}$$

The demands upon coal do not end with energy alone. Without petroleum, coal would be the prime chemical basis for clothing and the many chemical products which have become familiar.

TABLE 9–7. Lifetime of Coal in Years with Different Rates of Use and Different Populations Based on a Resource Base of 1500 Billion Tons.

A = ton/person-yr*	Population = B × 100 million				
	1	2	3	4	5
1 ⟶	15,000	7,500	5,000	3,750	3,000
2	7,500	3,750	2,500	1,875	1,500
3 ⟶	5,000	2,500	1,666	1,250	1,000
5	3,000	1,500	1,000	750	600
10	1,500	750	500	375	300
15 ⟶	1,000	500	333	250	200
20	750	374	250	188	150
30	500	250	166	125	100
40	375	188	125	94	74
50	300	150	100	75	60

*The arrow from #3 indicates the present U.S. consumption of coal (20% of the total energy consumed) is 3 tons per person per year. The arrow from #15 indicates that 15 tons of coal would be consumed per person per year if all our energy was obtained from coal alone.

QUESTIONS

1. Assume that curve A of the petroleum resource graph (Figure 9–5) is correct. What course should we follow in the immediate future?
2. Assume that there is twice as much petroleum resource as shown in Curve A (Figure 9–5). Does this change the direction which we should take? Explain your answer.
3. Assume that petroleum resources are 10 times those of curve A. What should we do now?
4. Assume that the supply of petroleum is essentially infinite in quantity. What course of action should we take?
5. What constraints are there upon how we use the oil supply available to us?
6. Maine has turned down a bid for an oil refinery along its coast three times. Are they wise or foolish? Explain your answer.
7. What can be done with the waste oil collected at gas stations? What do you recommend?
8. "The pipeline could cause welfare problems" is the possibility raised by the Alaskan State Housing Authority. What factors are involved in the possible welfare program?
9. What questions should be answered to determine whether an area now noted for fish, wildlife, and recreation should be leased for oil drilling?
10. Most of the coal companies hold "broad-form deeds" which mean they can take the coal by any means convenient to them and that they can take all the coal. What must be done to protect the land owner? How should it be done?
11. Suppose that the present internal combustion engine utilizing gasoline were abolished in favor of a steam engine using kerosene. What would happen to the petroleum industry? How would it change?

BIBLIOGRAPHY

1. Engler, R., *Politics of oil,* Chicago: University of Chicago Press, 1967.
2. Holdren, J. and Herrera, P., *Energy,* San Francisco; Sierra Club, 1971.
3. Hubbert, M. K., "The energy resources of the earth," *Sci. Amer.,* 224: 60–87, Sept. 1971.
4. U.S. Department of Interior, *United States petroleum through 1980,* Washington, D.C.: Government Printing Office, 1968.

Various petroleum companies and trade associations publish periodicals. Some of these are as follows.

1. *Lamp*, published by Standard Oil of New Jersey.
2. *Marathon World*, published by Marathon Oil.
3. *Oilways*, published by Humble Oil.
4. *Oil and Gas Journal*, published by The Petroleum Publishing Company.
5. *Petroleum Independent*, published by the Independent Petroleum Association of America.
6. *Petroleum Today*, published by the Committee on Public Affairs of the American Petroleum Institute.

10 Energy from the Core of the Atom

"On December 2, 1942, man achieved here the first self-sustaining chain reaction and thereby initiated the controlled release of nuclear energy."

Inscription at Stagg Field, University of Chicago.

A member of the faculty of the University of Chicago said ruefully, "We do not know for sure whether that is a boast or a confession."[1]

Richie Calder

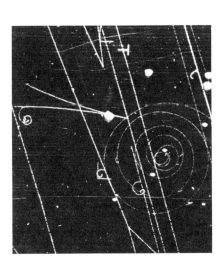

Nuclear energy is the result of changes which occur in the nucleus of the atom. The diameter of the core of the atom, the nucleus, is about 1/100,000 of the diameter of the atom. On this basis, if the nucleus were the size of a golf ball, the atom would be the size of a balloon 2.5 miles in diameter. Within the nucleus are the protons and neutrons which make up the weight of the atom.

The number of protons, each with a mass number of 1, is expressed by the atomic number for each element. The remainder of the mass is due to the neutrons, each of which has the same mass number as a proton. For example, lithium has an atomic number of 3 and therefore has three protons. If the total mass is 7, there are also four neutrons in the nucleus. The number of protons for a specific element is always the same but the number of neutrons may vary. Thus, the mass of the atom may vary. If an atom of lithium had only three neutrons, the mass would be 6. This is expressed as ^{6}Li or ^{7}Li. Each different kind of atom or nuclide (any atomic species) is called an isotope (see Chapter 2 for more information).

Symbols of the elements may be written to show which isotope is indicated.

$$\text{atomic mass } 7 \atop \text{atomic number } 3} \text{Li}$$

The symbol shows lithium with an atomic mass of 7 and with three protons in the nucleus, lithium-7.

The nuclei of some atoms are *radioactive,* that is, they are unstable and *decay* (change), ejecting energetic particles from the nucleus in order to go to a lower energy state and a more stable nucleus. *Alpha particles,* (symbol α), helium nuclei with two protons and two neutrons, are produced by *alpha decay. Beta decay* produces *beta particles,* which are electrons (symbol β).

Radioactive Elements

Uranium-238 undergoes alpha decay. The equation is

$$^{238}_{92}\text{U} \rightarrow {}^{234}_{90}\text{Th} + {}^4_2\text{He} \ (\alpha \text{ particle})$$

The superscripts represent atomic mass units. The total mass on one side of the equation is equal to the total mass on the other side of the equation:

$$238 = 234 + 4$$

Likewise, the subscripts represent the number of positively charged particles in the nucleus. The total number of these particles on both sides of the equation is the same:

$$92 = 90 + 2$$

Gamma rays are also emitted in the uranium-238 decay, as in most decay processes. Because the gamma rays have no mass or charge it is not necessary

1. *Living with the atom,* Chicago: University of Chicago Press, 1962, p. 1.

to include them in the equation. However, they are biologically important as we shall see later. Gamma rays affect chemicals in the same way as x rays, but are much more energetic (see Figure 6–21).

Strontium-90 undergoes beta decay. Beta particles are electrons and are represented in decay equations as $_{-1}^{0}e$ (−1 refers to a negative unit charge). The equation is

$$_{38}^{90}Sr \rightarrow _{39}^{90}Y + _{-1}^{0}e$$

mass numbers: $90 = 90 + 0$

charge: $38 = 39 - 1$

The beta and alpha particles emitted by nuclear decay processes are very energetic. They can break chemical bonds and cause ionization to occur in living tissue. These events may damage or kill the tissue. They can also initiate cancers and/or cause teratogenic or mutagenic changes. Thus radioactive materials pose many dangers to living things. It is important that they be carefully handled and stored.

A convenient measure of the rate of decay is the period of time required to change one-half of the original nuclide to the second substance, that is the half-life. (Chapter 5, p. 142) Half-lives range from much less than a second to billions of years. For example, uranium-238 has a half-life of two billion years; strontium-90, 28.1 years; and polonium-214, 0.000005 sec. Half-life is similar to exponential growth, except that the decay of an element is halving time instead of doubling time. After 10 half-lives, 0.1% of the original material is still present.

Fission Process

A few nuclides not only decay but are also capable of *fission,* that is, they split into two main, usually unequal nuclei plus a few neutrons (*fission products,* see Figure 10–1). Although uranium-235 atoms will split at a very low rate,

Figure 10–1. Distribution of fission products from uranium-235.

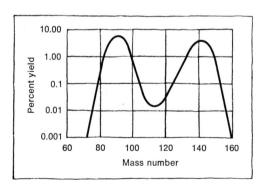

ENERGY FROM THE CORE OF THE ATOM

bombardment by neutrons increases the rate of fission. A typical fission reaction is shown by the following equation:

$$\underset{\text{atomic number}}{\overset{\text{atomic weight}}{}} \ _{92}^{235}U + _0^1n \rightarrow _{37}^{90}Rb + _{55}^{144}Cs + 2_0^1n + energy$$

The extra neutrons can act to trigger splitting of other uranium-235 nuclei. If a neutron is captured by a second uranium-235 nucleus for every fission of a primary uranium-235, a self-sustaining *chain reaction* results.

The ratio of neutrons to protons changes uniformly from the light elements to the heaviest elements as shown in Figure 10–2. Elements with low atomic numbers have a ratio of 1 neutron to 1 proton; the nuclides of highest atomic number have an "ideal" ratio exceeding 1.5 neutrons to 1 proton. Thus, the number of neutrons required by the fission products is less than those found in the nucleus of the uranium-235 atom.

The "extra" neutrons appear as either free neutrons, as shown in the above equation for the fission of uranium-235, or as more neutrons in the nuclei of the fission products than will form a stable nucleus. Thus, the nuclei of the fission products do not have the proper mix of neutrons and protons, are radioactive, and decay to some other nuclide, or *daughter element:*

$$_{37}^{90}Rb \xrightarrow{29\ min} {}_{38}^{90}Sr + _{-1}^0e \text{ (beta particle)}$$

$$_{38}^{90}Sr \xrightarrow{28.1\ yr} {}_{39}^{90}Y + _{-1}^0e$$

$$_{39}^{90}Y \xrightarrow{64\ hr} {}_{40}^{90}Zr + _{-1}^0e$$

Some of the excess neutrons from fission reactions may be absorbed by stable nuclei. This results in the formation of new isotopes which usually are radio-

Figure 10–2. Neutron to proton ratio in stable isotopes.

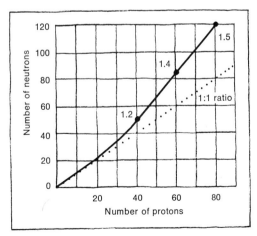

active and eventually decay stepwise to form a new element, for example

$$^{23}_{11}Na + ^{1}_{0}n \rightarrow ^{24}_{11}Na \xrightarrow{15\ hr} ^{24}_{12}Mg + ^{0}_{-1}e$$

Comparison of Decay and Fission Energies

The energy from fission is much greater than that produced by decay processes. Decay of a nuclide usually results in the production of a nearby element in the periodic table. The heat evolved by these transitions is small compared with a fission process (Figure 10–3 and the periodic table). On the other hand, there is a great difference in energy between uranium and its daughter elements, for example bromine-37. Iron is the most stable of all elements, that is, it contains least energy. Energy will be evolved by an elemental transition which changes in the direction of iron.

Mass-Energy Relationship

Nuclear equations using mass numbers do not show the mass loss which results from energy production. For example, a helium nucleus contains two protons and two neutrons for a mass number of 4. The mass loss which occurs in the formation of the helium atom from protons and neutrons is calculated as follows.

Mass of proton	1.0073
Mass of two protons	2.0146
Mass of neutron	1.0087
Mass of two neutrons	2.0174
Total mass of particles in nucleus	4.0320
Actual mass of a helium-4 nucleus	4.0015
Mass loss	0.0305

The mass loss represents the amount of mass that is converted to energy when the helium nucleus is produced from the primary particles, protons and neutrons. The evolved energy is known as the *binding energy*. Since each nucleus is different, the binding energy is given per *nucleon* (nuclear particle, i.e., proton or neutron). The amount of energy is found by Einstein's equation

$$E = mc^2$$

where E is energy, m is the mass that appears as energy, and c is the velocity of light (3×10^{10} cm/sec).

The amount of energy obtainable from fission is tremendous. One pound of uranium-235 is capable of supplying as much heat as can be obtained from the burning of 1500 tons of coal. Therein lies the promise of nuclear power.

NUCLEAR REACTORS

The *nuclear reactor* is a device to control the release of energy from the fission of nuclei, usually uranium-235 nuclei. Natural uranium consists primarily of the isotopes, uranium-238 and uranium-235. Uranium-235 comprises less than 1% of natural uranium but it is the isotope that will sustain a chain reaction.

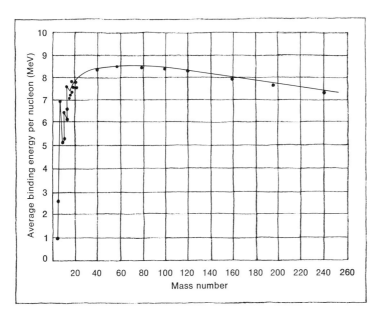

Figure 10–3. Relative stability of nuclei.

The nuclear plant is carefully designed to use uranium-235 to produce electricity.

The chain reaction takes place in the *core* of the reactor which is built inside a *containment dome*. The dome is a strong shell sometimes made of steel, sometimes of concrete, and sometimes of both. The shell is designed to contain the high pressures which may result from an accident involving the reactor contents and to prevent the escape of fission products. The relationship of dome, reactor, and energy transfer system for two types of reactors are shown in Figure 10–4.

FUEL AND FUEL RODS   In certain types of reactors, it is necessary to increase the proportion of uranium-235 to uranium-238 in the uranium mass. Since uranium-235 has the same chemical properties as uranium-238, physical methods must be used to improve the fraction of uranium-235 in the nuclear fuel. This is accomplished by converting the uranium isotopes to gaseous hexafluorides, UF_6, which have a boiling point of 56.2 °C. The hexafluorides of the isotopes uranium-235 and uranium-238 differ slightly in molecular weight (349 and 352), and, therefore, in the rate at which they diffuse through membranes. If a mixture of gaseous hexafluorides of uranium isotopes is made

NUCLEAR REACTORS

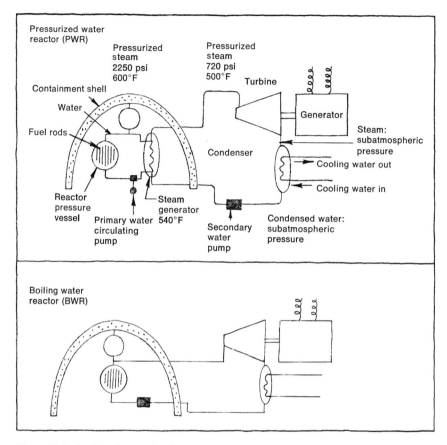

Figure 10–4. Light-water reactor diagrams.

to diffuse through a system of thousands of membranes, the uranium-235 molecules diffuse more rapidly than the uranium-238 molecules. Consequently it is possible partially to separate the uranium-235 compound from the uranium-238 compound. In this way the concentration of uranium-235 in the uranium fuel can be increased from the 0.71% of natural uranium to about 3%, or about 4 times the content of natural uranium. It is possible, but very expensive, to enrich the fuel to an assay of 98% uranium-235. Most nuclear power plants run on uranium enriched to about 3% uranium-235.

The enriched fuel is usually made into pellets the size of cigarette filter sections and packed into 10-ft-long sealed zirconium tubes called *cladding*. Zirconium best meets the requirements for fuel cladding. It does not capture many neutrons, it allows neutrons to pass through its internal structure without appreciable absorption of energy, it is extremely resistant to the corrosive environment inside the reactor, and it has suitable structural properties.

Commercial zirconium metal sponge was priced at $5 per pound at the same time that uranium oxide concentrate was priced from $8 to $15 per pound. Since the cladding for fuel rods weighs as much as the fuel pellets themselves, the cost of the cladding will be an appreciable part of the cost of the fuel rods.

Early reactors used stainless-steel cladding for fuel rods, but this relatively inexpensive material flaked and cracked under the high temperatures, neutron fluxes (flows), and corrosive conditions inside the reactor. As a result, the stainless-steel tubes leaked radioisotopes into coolant water.

The reactor holds the *fuel rods* or *pins* in place in a geometric pattern in an assembly which contains 200 rods (Figure 10–5). Each assembly weighs about 1000 lb. One hundred fifty or more such assemblies may constitute the core load of a reactor. Interspaced among the fuel assemblies are 50–100 *control rods.*

CONTROL RODS   When a uranium-235 nucleus undergoes fission, various numbers of neutrons may be freed, for an overall average of 2.4 neutrons. Only one of these neutrons need be captured by other uranium-235 atoms to sustain a chain reaction. If an average of less than one of these neutrons is captured, the chain reaction stops. If more than one neutron per fission event is captured, the chain reaction gets out of control, too much energy is released, and the reactor is said to "*run away.*"

In a nuclear reactor control rods containing cadmium or boron are used to absorb some of the neutrons and make it possible to control the rate of neutron capture by uranium-235 nuclei. When all the control rods are in place, the reactor is said to be *shut down*. When energy is desired, some of the control rods are slowly raised. This allows more neutrons to be captured with the evolution of heat energy and more neutrons that are capable of disrupting more uranium-235 nuclei.

MODERATOR   The neutrons must be *moderated* (slowed) because fast neutrons produced by the fission process are not easily captured by uranium-235 nuclei. Water flowing through the reactor core slows the fast neutrons by absorbing some of their kinetic energy when the neutrons collide with water molecules.

COOLING METHODS   The water not only acts as a moderator but also serves to cool the rods and to transfer the heat outside the reactor to heat exchangers or directly to a turbine. Each type of reactor has a slightly different cooling system.

In a *pressurized water reactor* (PWR) (see Figure 10–4) the water from the reactor gives up its heat to the steam line for the turbine through a heat exchanger. This arrangement helps prevent radioactive fission products (*radio-*

Figure 10–5. Bundles of uranium fuel elements for a nuclear power reactor. Courtesy of Samuel A. Musgrave, Atomic Industrial Forum.

nuclides) in the reactor coolant from getting into the steam of the turbine loop and from there into the condenser water which is discharged to the environment.

In a *boiling-water reactor* (BWR) the steam goes directly from reactor to turbine. This system increases the chance that radionuclides will get into the condenser water of the turbine and cause water pollution outside the plant.

The *high-temperature gas reactor* (HTGR), an uncommon type, uses helium gas as the coolant instead of water. Use of helium allows the reactor to run at a higher temperature than is possible with a water-cooled reactor, and therefore is more efficient in its use of heat. The higher temperature is possible because helium is inert and does not react with any of the reactor components. Helium does not absorb neutrons and thus does not become radioactive. It is relatively easily cleaned of the fission products which manage to get into it. These properties make it possible to eliminate an intermediate heat exchanger. Therefore it is a simpler and less expensive system. However, there are disadvantages: helium is a poor heat absorber and is in short supply (see Chapter 12); the HTGR is hard to control because the gas has a low heat capacity (carries little heat per unit weight) and does not moderate the reaction in the way that water does; some of the neutrons may be lost without causing fission to occur.

. . . a very low probability event coupled to a high consequence.[2]

Ralph Lapp

Excursions and Possible Effects

An *excursion* is a departure from the normal operating conditions of a reactor and is usually unplanned, uncontrolled, and ominous. The Atomic Energy Commission (AEC)[3] says that most reactors spontaneously return to normal operation. However, an excursion could lead to uncontrolled heating in which the fuel elements and the reactor in general may be damaged or melted. The reactor vessel may be ruptured and the containment dome breached. Such an accident was formerly considered an "incredible accident," but has now become a "maximum credible accident." In the event of dome breaching, the radioactive nuclides which have accumulated during the operation of the plant may be expelled and dispersed over the countryside.

A large amount of heat is evolved during the operation of a nuclear reactor. When a reactor is operating, the fuel pellets are at a temperature of 4000 °F. The cladding is held at a temperature of 660 °F by the flow of coolant fluid over its surface. If the flow of coolant is interrupted for any reason the temperature of the cladding and the fuel will increase rapidly. A loss of coolant accident (LOCA) is the most feared potential accident for all types of reactors. Even if the control rods were immediately lowered to shut down the reactor, a large amount of heat would still be evolved by some fission of the fuel and the decay of daughter radionuclides.

If the cooling water cannot reach the fuel rods in the core, the cladding may begin to fail in 10–15 sec and the fuel melt in 1 min. A melted core may sink deep

2. "A cooling threat to nuclear power," *Business Week,* 5 June 1971, p. 46.
3. On 1 January 1975, the functions of the AEC were divided between two new agencies: the Energy Research and Development Administration (ERDA) and the Nuclear Regulatory Commission (NRC).

into the earth, the so-called *"China effect."* The accompanying high temperature may vaporize quantities of daughter nuclides which have accumulated during the operation of the reactor along with any amounts of coolant which happened to be inside the reactor or the dome. If enough material is vaporized, the dome may be breached and the radioactive contents "subsequently dispersed to undesirable locations" as the AEC says.

An emergency core cooling system (ECCS) has been built into the plants in an attempt to ensure that the reactor will be cooled, even though a break occurs in the core cooling system and the water drains from the core; the water in the tank is expected to rush into the core and cool it. Unfortunately, when a 9-in. model was tested, the system failed in four tests out of four to cool the "reactor." Flashing steam[4] prevented the coolant from entering the reactor cavity or from contacting the reactor surfaces. Because of these failures, the entire reactor safety program has been questioned. Resolution of the problems posed by the ECCS failure depends upon the construction and testing of a system involving a small reactor which is scheduled to be built by 1976, but may not be ready until after that date.

The nuclear power plant is vulnerable to an effective loss of coolant accident without an actual loss of primary coolant in the reactor itself. The schematic diagram of a nuclear power plant (Figure 10–4) shows that the energy from the PWR reactor is piped to a heat exchanger where it is transferred to the pipes that lead to the turbine and condenser. Powerful electric motors drive large pumps that circulate the coolant in each of the pipe systems. If any of the pump systems fail (reactor core to heat exchanger, heat exchanger to turbine, or condenser to condenser cooling-water source), the removal of heat from the core would fail to take place. Consequently, heat would accumulate in the core and its contents. The pressures in the system could build up until the reactor ruptures, producing all of the effects of a loss of cooling event. The possibility of a pump failure is covered by a set of back-up pumps which go into action when the primary pumps become inoperable.

About one-tenth of the power produced by the plant is used internally to operate the plant (i.e., pumps, lights, etc.). If the power fails, none of the pumps can work. Therefore, a secondary power source in the form of a diesel generator is provided. It is arranged to snap into action in about 30 sec. In a test loss of power "accident" the back-up power system worked satisfactorily. If, however, the system did fail to work, loss of coolant actions would appear.

If for some reason a part of the coolant piping system should fail, it would be difficult or impossible to maintain cooling effects at the reactor. The pipe does not need to be connected directly to the reactor to initiate a loss of coolant accident. A break in any of the heat transfer pipes between the reactor and the turbine could cause a loss of heat transfer.

4. Flashing steam means that when water strikes a very hot surface it is immediately converted into steam. The steam produced prevents further contact of cooling water with the hot surface. This can be demonstrated by dropping or pouring water upon a red-hot piece of metal. Note how the liquid water seems to float over the surface.

An effective emergency core cooling system is unavailable. Meanwhile a set of criteria has been promulgated to limit the temperature of the fuel rods to 2300 °F except for the largest reactors. The core temperature of these was reduced to 2200 °F.

Critics say that temperature excursions may become uncontrollable at lower temperatures than the criteria allow. Moreover, tests conducted by the AEC show that fuel rods exposed to excessively high temperatures show no apparent deterioration, but later fail at a much lower temperature than rods which have not been overheated.

The United States has accumulated over 700 reactor-years of experience with commercial reactors. Therefore it is not likely that there would be one serious accident in 100 reactor years. However, one accident in 1000 years is a definite possibility. These statistics apply only to the small, presently operated reactors, and not to the big ones being built. If the accident rate does turn out to be 1 in 1000, and the 1000 reactors that are planned for 1990 are built, the United States will have a serious incident every year.

FUEL ROD DIFFICULTIES After a fuel rod has operated for a period of time, gaseous fission products accumulate and pressurize the rod. If a high-temperature excursion and depressurization occur, the gas in the fuel rod may cause the rod to swell and close the cooling-fluid channel. Without cooling fluid, the temperature of the core could rise rapidly.

According to a report filed with the AEC a photographic examination made in 1972 of 10,000 spent fuel rods from the Ginna reactor in Ontario, New York, showed that many of the rods were bowed and/or had collapsed cladding. In spite of the potential danger posed by the damaged fuel rods of the Ginna plant, it was allowed to operate at 83% capacity. According to one AEC source: "The choice was either to let the plant run or shut down the industry. We're playing the risk game. The probabilities of an accident are small although the consequences of an accident under these conditions might be worse."[5]

Several other Westinghouse reactors have suffered similarly damaged fuel rods. At first it was thought that the cause of the damaged rods was improper filling of the rods. It now appears that it is characteristic of the fuel rod itself. The fuel pellets may shrink in volume over a period of time and fall downward in the rod. Without the interior support provided by the pellets the cladding is crushed by the high pressures present inside the reactor. A bowed or broken rod may interfere with the flow of coolant through the coolant channels and increase the original effect.

A portion of the rod may come adrift and block some other channel or damage some other part of the reactor and its connecting pipe, pumps, or heat transfer system. Such an event would be similar to the breaking loose of a metal coolant deflector in the core of the Fermi nuclear power plant at Monroe,

5. Robert Gillette, "Nuclear safety: damaged fuel ignites a new debate in A.E.C." *Science* 177:330, 28 July 1972.

Michigan, which caused a partial melting of the core and, eventually, the decommissioning of the plant.

The collapse and other damage to fuel rods did not happen in earlier reactors. Dr. Ralph Lapp believes that the rod problems are caused by too rapid scaling up to larger-sized reactors. It is not simply that the reactors are physically larger, it is that the power density (amount of energy being produced in a given volume of a core) is much greater. As a result, the operating margin is narrower and the reactor is more subject to damage by excursions.

STRUCTURAL PROBLEMS   The breaching (rupturing) of a reactor may not be all that difficult. The bolts which secure the head of the reactor have a safety margin of only 13%, while uncertainty in the strength measurements is 20%. This hardly guarantees safe operation under normal conditions, much less excursions. In view of the fact that a PWR operates at 2150 psi (pounds per square inch)(more than a ton per square inch), if a reactor "flips" its 20-ton lid, nothing is going to keep it from penetrating the containment dome. Much of the reactor contents would follow the path of the lid.

The reactor itself is a heavy-walled vessel which may be 40 ft high and weigh 500 tons. The huge size of the reactor and the high pressures it must contain require thick cross sections of material for the structure of the reactor and its connecting pipes. Many of the parts must be welded together. It is difficult to produce good welds and to check the quality of welds if the cross-sectional area is large. Repairs are difficult because the core of the reactor is radioactive. Workmen making repairs on the core are exposed to high levels of radiation.

The operating experience with nuclear reactors is filled with examples of *downtime* because of faulty equipment. The Yankee Atomic Electric Co. plant needed a six-month, 6-million-dollar repair after some bolts failed in the core. The reactor of a Florida Power and Light Co. plant suffered a ruptured steam line.

THE HUMAN FACTOR   It is often difficult to tell what damage is due to improper materials and what is due to design faults. Many examples of claimed design faults in reactors have been the cause of shutdowns. For example, at the new Palisades plant in Michigan, "design deficiencies" led to a 44-day shutdown. Soon afterwards, it was shut down again for months for repairs.

Even routine operation is subject to human error. An operator in the Millstone plant in Connecticut extended the length of the plant downtime by his actions. The pipes carrying ocean water for condenser cooling corroded and leaked salt into the pure water. When the operator turned on standby demineralizers, the demineralizers were overwhelmed and the salt water spread throughout the plant.

A nuclear reactor is a complex technological instrument, as is a jet plane. A high degree of expertise is required to maintain and operate either of them; both require that quick decisions be made in emergency situations. The prevalence of human error is shown in a study of 148 jet crashes in which the plane was totally destroyed. BOAC found that 47% of the crashes resulted not from equipment failure but from simple human error. Nuclear reactor operation probably will not fare better and the potential for harm is enormously greater.

As the nuclear industry expands rapidly, many more highly trained technicians will be required. The present shortage of such personnel will lead to the necessity of using less highly trained people. Eventually the operation of reactors will become routine, and operators may become careless. It is impossible to make such a complicated system foolproof.

Safety cannot be engineered in. Dr. Hannes Alfven, Nobel Prize winner, has said:

> The reactor constructors claim that they have devoted more effort to safety problems than any other technologists have. This is true. From the beginning they have paid much attention to safety and they have been remarkably clever in devising safety precautions. This is perhaps pathetic, but it is not relevant. If a problem is too difficult to solve, one cannot claim that it is solved by pointing to all the efforts made to solve it.
>
> The technologists claim that if everything works according to their blueprints, fission energy will be a safe and very attractive solution to the energy needs of the world. This may be correct. Hence, they consider all objections to be due to "ignorance," "viciousness," or "hysteria." This is not correct. The real issue is whether their blueprints will work in the real world and not only in a "technological paradise."[6]

Although the nuclear industry has an enviable safety record, there have been incidents that show the impossibility of engineering complete safety. A tornado destroyed five separate emergency power lines at one plant, a mathematical impossibility. When an employee flushed the toilet at another plant, the malfunction of a valve led to a chain of reactions, eventually shutting down the reactor. Another reactor, a research reactor, underwent a series of 21 sequential failures (seven failures in three identical channels). The reactor was saved by a highly trained technician who switched to another system which was not being used because of unreliability.

Sabotage is always a possibility wherever there are materials which must be kept isolated for the safety of the public. In 1973 the "hijackers" of an airplane threatened to crash the plane into Oak Ridge National Laboratory where there is a small reactor. At one reactor, a disgruntled employee sabotaged the plant before it was operating. If these situations can happen, a nuclear plant can be breached any time the saboteur wants to make a great enough effort. There is always someone who can be "bought".

Not only is the plant itself a possible site for sabotage but any location where radioactive materials are being stored is also a possibility. If the material is being cooled, the destruction of the cooling system could lead to heat build-up that could lead to the breakage of the containment system and the dispersal of the contents. If the cooling system for pressurized cylinders or tanks should

6. Hannes Alfven, "Energy and environment," *Bull. Atom. Sci.* 28:6, May 1972.

fail or be destroyed, the containers could break explosively. Under these circumstances large amounts of radionuclides (nuclides which decay) could be discharged into a small space, creating extreme hazards to people in the vicinity.

Some concerned scientists have suggested that the building of nuclear plants around our Eastern cities and governmental center is an invitation to trouble from either a foreign enemy or a radical group within the country.

RADIATION AND ITS SOURCES

For every pound of uranium used for fuel purposes, at least a pound of radioactive wastes are formed. The resulting large accumulation of these wastes has the potential for great harm.

Radiation Measurements

There are two aspects to the measurement of radiation; one is the production of radiation and the second is the measurement of the effects of radiation upon some mass of tissue or other material. The rate of production of radiation is measured in *curies* (Ci) which is defined as 37 billion disintegrations per second from a radioactive material and which is the rate at which one gram of radium emits radiation. The curie is a measure of the potential for change or damage that may result from the disintegration of radioactive substances irrespective of the kinds of radiation emitted as gamma rays (a very energetic radiation, similar to x rays, that is produced at the same time that alpha and beta particles are produced during nuclear disintegrations), beta particles, or alpha particles. Each radioactive substance has its own unique mix of kinds of radiation, and since different radiations have different energies and different characteristics, the potential for damage varies with the radioactive substance even though an equal number of curies of each is considered.

The effect of radiation is measured in units of roentgens, rads, or rems. A *roentgen*, the amount of radiation from either x rays or gamma rays, will cause 2 billion ion pairs per cubic centimeter of air or about 1.8 trillion ions pairs per gram of tissue. Because a roentgen by definition applies only to the effects produced by x rays and gamma rays, a more general unit, the *rad* (radiation absorbed dose) is commonly used. One rad indicates the absorption of 100 ergs or about 0.0024 calories of energy from radiation by a kilogram of any type of material. If one gram of soft tissue is exposed to one roentgen of radiation from a moderately energetic gamma ray, about one rad is absorbed. For other types of tissue and other types of radiation, the values would be different. The most used unit, the *rem* (roentgen equivalent in man) reflects the difference in effects caused by different sources of radiation. For a beta particle or a gamma ray, the rad and rem are equivalent; for an alpha particle, the rem is ten times as damaging as a rad because an alpha particle produced within a tissue is much more damaging than a beta particle produced in a similar location.

The practical unit of radiation exposure is the *millirem* (mr), that is, $1/1000$ rem. The yearly background radiation (*natural radiation*) exposure has long been

ENERGY FROM THE CORE OF THE ATOM

accepted as ranging from 100 to 120 mr depending on the location. A recent study by the EPA indicated that 80 mr may be a more reasonable value. (A summary of radiation units is given in Appendix C.)

On 9 June 1971, the AEC published in the *Federal Register* a new set of guidelines for radiation doses to individuals from the emissions of a nuclear power plant.

Standards

1. 10 mr total dose for a year's time from noble gas emissions.
2. 5 mr as the maximum yearly dose from liquid waste discharges.
3. 5 mr as the maximum to any organ as result of release of long half-life nuclides (long half-life is defined as eight days or longer).

The AEC feels that the standards must be flexible enough to allow for some variations in the level of radioactivity in effluents. If the rate exceeds four to eight times the design objectives, the commission will take action to reduce the rate of release of radioactive material.

The population at the perimeter of the plant, i.e., within 2000-ft radius should not be exposed to more than 15 mr per year. However, dosage as high as 500 mr could be released if and when the AEC decided that the risk would be greater if a plant which was emitting excessively was shut down than if the people were exposed to the radiation.

The history of nuclear reactors, especially the large pressurized water reactor, is that of increasing emissions to both water and air. In four years of operation the total annual liquid waste discharged (less tritium) for the Connecticut Yankee reactor increased from 0.216 to 22.0 Ci in a period of four years. In a similar period the San Onofre reactor waste discharge increased from 0.32 to 3.8 Ci.

One group studied the pattern of iodine fallout from weather data and found that, by assuming that eight reactors were located between Washington, D.C., and Connecticut and that 0.1% of the produced iodine were to be emitted, the concentrations of iodine would exceed permissible values because of overlapping deposition.

Using the best advice available and considering various biological effects, such as ingestion and external and internal radiation problems, and the problems arising from a particular fission-product isotope having special biological importance, in 1957 the AEC adopted a range of exposures and effects (Table 10–1). Also in 1957, the AEC projected that a credible nuclear accident would kill 3400 people, injure 43,000 more, cause 7 billion dollars worth of damage, and contaminate 150,000 square miles of land. In 1965 the study was updated and it was projected that 45,000 people would be killed, 100,000 injured, and 17 billion dollars worth of damage would be done. Increasing prices have made the figure of 17 billion dollars for damages far too small. Locating reactors close to centers of population may have increased the number of dead and injured which would result from a credible accident.

Dangerous Levels of Exposure

The AEC also feels we shall "lose" a nuclear reactor occasionally. However, they think that the benefit to the world in general from the energy produced by the fast breeder reactor is greater than the risks involved. They state:

A 10% increase in mutation rate, whatever it might mean in personal suffering and public expense, is not likely to threaten the human race with extinction, or even serious degeneration.

The human race as a whole may be thought of as somewhat analogous to a population of dividing cells in a growing tissue. Those affected by genetic damage drop out and the slack is taken up by those not affected.

If the number of those affected is increased, there would come a crucial point, or threshold, where the slack could no longer be taken up. The genetic load might increase to the point where the species as a whole would degenerate and fade toward extinction—a sort of "racial radiation sickness."

We are not near this threshold now, however, and can, therefore, as a species, absorb a moderate increase in mutation without danger of extinction.[7]

Sources of Radiation   Radioactive materials are produced at every stage of handling nuclear fuel, from the mine to the final disposal of materials. Some are diluted and dispersed to surrounding air and water; the remainder, highly radioactive, must be completely sequestered for extremely long periods of time. Such wastes from the

7. Isaac Asimov and Theodosius Dobzhansky, *The genetic effect of radiation*, Division of Technical Information, Atomic Energy Commission, Washington, D.C.: Government Printing Office 1966, pp. 44–45.

TABLE 10–1.   Exposure and Effects of Radiation.

	Equivalent wholebody gamma radiation	Concentration of released fission products (FPs) to give equivalent exposures	
		Volatile FPs (Ci = sec/m³)	Gross FPs (Ci = sec/m³)
Lethal exposure	> 450 r	> 350	> 400
Injury likely	100–450 r	80–350	90–400
Injury unlikely, but some expense may be incurred; observation required	25–100 r	10–80	10–90
No injury or expense	<25 r	<10	<10

Source: "Theoretical possibilities and consequences of major accidents in large nuclear power plants," Bulletin No. 740, Atomic Engery Commission, Washington D.C.: Government Printing Office, 1957.

150 operating and planned reactors will produce more radioactivity than 130,000 bombs of the Hiroshima type. Waste nuclides accumulate at all stages of the fuel cycle and must be controlled:

(1) at the mine; (2) anywhere tailings from any operation may be stored or used; (3) at the ore mill; (4) at the fuel fabrication plant (facilities where uranium-235 is encapsulated and placed in rods); (5) at the reactor; (6) at the spent fuel reprocessing plant; (7) during transportation; (8) at the waste storage facility. The relationship of the various parts of the fuel cycle is shown in Figure 10–6.

REPROCESSING   As energy is produced in the core of the reactor, the concentration of uranium-235 atoms becomes too small to capture the necessary neutrons. The fuel rods are then said to be "poisoned" or "spent" and must be removed from the reactor. After removal, they are stored under cooling water at the power plant for several months until the decay of fission products

Figure 10–6.   Relationship of various factors of the uranium fuel cycle.

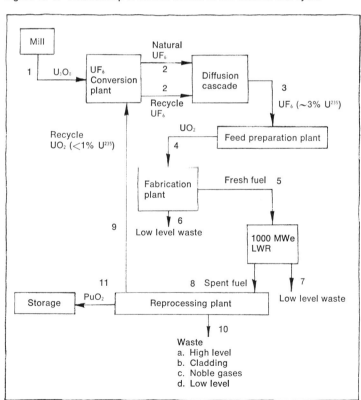

decreases sufficiently to allow the rods to be shipped safely to a reprocessing plant.

The reprocessing plant will recover the uranium-238 as well as a small quantity of uranium-235. In addition, the spent fuel rods contain plutonium (Pu) formed during the power-production cycle. Plutonium, a manmade element, results from the capture of a neutron by a uranium-238 nucleus.

It is necessary to separate and recover the plutonium because of its value as a potential fuel for reactors and because of its extreme toxicity. At present it is primarily used by the military for making nuclear warheads. For this purpose it commands a price of $10,000 per kilogram. Since only 5 kg of plutonium are needed to construct a simple plutonium bomb, these factors make it attractive for theft and blackmarket operations, and could contribute to international nuclear blackmail, sabotage, and terror tactics.

Treatment of fuel rods The radioactive spent fuel rods are mechanically stripped of their cladding and end boxes (seals at the ends of the rods) by remote control. The cladding material, about half the weight of the fuel rods, is itself radioactive and cannot be reused in the production of cladding for new fuel rods. The used cladding material is compacted and buried. Ten to fifteen tons of zirconium alloy cladding from one-third of the fuel rods of a reactor must be converted and buried each year.

The decladded material is dissolved in nitric acid (HNO_3) to give an aqueous solution of all substances present. In the process the radioactive gases krypton and xenon are released from the fuel pellets and must be trapped. Sometimes these gases are compressed and stored in heavy walled cylinders while they decay to a lower level of radiation.

WASTES More wastes are collected and/or discharged at the reprocessing plant than at any other stage of producing electricity from nuclear energy. Some are high-level wastes; all other wastes from the reprocessing plant and the wastes from other sources are low or intermediate wastes.

Low-level wastes The low-level wastes, liquids and gases, are stored for short periods of time to allow the shorter-lived isotopes to decay. Then the gases are vented to the atmosphere where they are diluted enough to be below the AEC radiation guidelines. The liquids are allowed to seep slowly into the ground water. Water sources have become contaminated in this way.

Some fission products are gases at the temperature of the reactor. Gaseous iodine and tritium can be scrubbed out of the gaseous emissions from a power plant but inert krypton is not chemically removable. These constitute the major radioactive effluents from a nuclear power plant, and provide the larger portion of the 5 mr of exposure which a person might experience at the boundary of a plant site.

Solids are buried in six commercial land burial sites in rural or sparsely settled areas in six states. The state must provide perpetual care and maintenance if the site is abandoned by the operator. A 1000-MW(e) plant will require about 0.2 acres to bury the wastes produced during a year.

Often radionuclides are isotopes of chemical elements essential for life. Living organisms preferentially extract these from the environment and concentrate them to far higher levels than exist in the environment. For example, iodine is preferentially extracted by the human body and deposited in the thyroid gland (see Chapter 6). "Benign" quantities of radionuclides from the environment can accumulate to high dosages through food chains. Thus, the nuclide may be nearly undetectable in the drinking water but easily detectable in the fish that feed in the water.

Nonessential elements may also be preferentially extracted. Strontium, in the same family as calcium, is stored in the bones along with essential calcium. Recent investigations indicate that tritium (^3_1H) may be preferentially attracted to the DNA base thymine.

The Russian ecologist G. G. Polykarpov said in 1966 that the oceans contained all the radioactivity that they can tolerate. Fish embryos show damage. Some species undergo physiological changes when the radioactivity level of water approaches or exceeds 100 pCi/liter or 100 trillionth Ci per liter. If Dr. Polykarpov is correct, what are the prospects if nuclear power generation is increased by the projected factor of 170 by the year 2000?

Intermediate wastes   In the United States, intermediate-level wastes are concentrated and stored at high-level wastes.

High-level wastes   The reprocessing of each ton of spent fuel leaves a residue of about 1000 gallons of high-level wastes. Each gallon emits at the rate of 1000 Ci. Thus each ton of fuel contributes a waste load of 1 million Ci. Each year a 1000 MW(e) plant requires a fuel load of 44 tons of fresh fuel. As a result the plant yields 44,000 gallons of high-level wastes containing 44 million Ci of radiation potential.

In a sense, the industry is in its infancy, but a huge expansion is planned for the immediate future. Table 10–2 shows the projections of spent fuel by several agencies whose estimates could be high if the recent controversies over plant siting continue into the future.

TABLE 10–2.   Forecasts of Quantities of Spent Fuel from Nuclear Power Plants (measured in tons).

Date	ORNL*	NFS†	AEC‡
1973	782	338	350
1975	1,351	1,288	870
1980	4,001	3,551	3,000
1985	17,697		

Source: W.A. Rodger and S.L. Reese, "Impact of large-scale plants on fuel reprocessing," *Reactor Fuel Process. Technol.*, 12:32, Winter 1968–69.
*Oak Ridge National Laboratory.
†Nuclear Fuel Service.
‡Atomic Energy Commission.

Storage of high-level wastes The AEC has set guidelines for the disposal of high-level wastes by reprocessing plants.

1. A reprocessing plant is limited to five years liquid storage capacity. Any excess must be solidified.
2. All high-level wastes must be transferred to Federal repositories as soon as possible with a limit of 10 years.
3. The Federal authorities will assume responsibility for the wastes at the repository. The industries will pay a single fee for disposal and perpetual surveillance.
4. Disposal can only take place on federal land.

In the past the wastes from nuclear weapons and the growing energy programs have been stored in huge tanks covered with earth. About 10 million gallons have accumulated at several AEC sites: Richland, Washington; Idaho Falls, Idaho; Savannah River, South Carolina. In 1969, the General Accounting Office (GAO) found that 227,400 gallons of wastes have escaped from 10 of 149 tanks which had no provisions for secondary containment. Later other leaks were found. Because the wastes must be stored for hundreds of thousands of years and because 18 tanks have failed in less than 25 years, the AEC is looking for a better technology for waste storage.

For 15 years the AEC through the Oak Ridge National Laboratory (ORNL), studied the possibility of disposal in salt mines. A large area near Lyons, Kansas, was purchased. The wastes were to be solidified and stored permanently in an underground salt mine. Dr. Alvin Weinberg, former director of ORNL, said in *Review, Oak Ridge National Laboratory* (Winter 1971):

Our decision to go to salt for permanent high-level disposal is one of the most far-reaching decisions we, or for that matter, any technologists have ever made. These wastes can be hazardous for a million years. We must, therefore, be as certain as one can possibly be of anything that the wastes, once sequestered in salt, can under no conceivable circumstance, come into contact with the biosphere.

Eventually the Kansas site was found to be dangerous; it was not watertight, the problems of heat flow were unsolved, and there was no way to retrieve the nuclides. Since then, the AEC has moved its investigation of salt storage to New Mexico. The agency is also studying other disposal methods. At the Savannah River site, deep-well disposal is being studied.

Another possibility is shooting the wastes into space. The cost (1971) is $1000 per payload pound to orbit a capsule. Even if the price could be lowered, the danger of shooting the wastes into space remains. Rockets are not foolproof. If a capsule loaded with radioactive wastes should fall to earth or burn in the atmosphere, the wastes would be spread worldwide.

Small power sources fueled by plutonium have been used in space capsules. In 1964 one burned up in the atmosphere and spread plutonium oxide over the entire globe. In 1967, an AEC official estimated that the chance of such failure occurring again was less than 1 in 1000. Between 1967 and 1972 three such

ENERGY FROM THE CORE OF THE ATOM

power sources have been orbited. One burned in the atmosphere and a second fell into the ocean.

Present plans are to build steel and concrete structures to store solidified wastes until permanent storage methods may be developed (Figure 10–7).

With the proliferation of nuclear energy, a worldwide waste problem is growing. England and Japan put low-level wastes in the ocean. England and France store high-level solid wastes "permanently" in cooled tanks. Russia pumps all wastes underground into deep disposal wells. A few countries put the wastes in steel containers and dump them in a deep part of the Atlantic Ocean. It is probable that these will eventually corrode and release radionuclides into the oceans. The United States is storing high-level wastes from Japan and several other foreign countries.

Reactors are expected to last 30 years. Because of the accumulation of radionuclides, they must be decommissioned with care. Three methods of disposal have been used.

1. The fuel is removed, all pipes are sealed and capped, and an exclusion area is established around the facility. The Piqua reactor, decommissioned by this method, is under the care of the city of Piqua for perpetual inspection, maintenance, and 24-hr surveillance. An estimate of the cost (1972) of decommissioning an average reactor would be 10 million dollars for the initial work plus $300,000 annually (about $800 per day).

2. In addition to the work described in method (1) the superstructure is removed and all radioactive portions which are above ground are encased in

Figure 10–7.   (translation) **"Presumably a shrine for one of their primitive religious cults."** Drawing by Richard Willson, used courtesy Friends of the Earth.

concrete. The Hallam reactor, decommissioned in this way, also requires "perpetual" surveillance.

3. In addition to removing the parts above ground, all contaminated equipment is removed. The ground is filled and graded. No perpetual surveillance is needed. The Elk River reactor was decommissioned by this method. Despite the fact that the reactor had operated for only a very short period of time, radioactive materials were discharged to the Mississippi River during the decommissioning operation. The contaminated equipment and facilities which are removed must be buried elsewhere.

TRANSPORTATION   Radioactive materials must be transported between each stage of the fuel cycle, but the most highly radioactive materials are shipped from the reactor to the processing plant and from the processing plant to the waste storage facility.

At present 95% of the shipments of radioactive material are relatively small packages of commercial items which involve low-level amounts of special nuclides. Many large shipments will be made in the future when the projected number of plants is built. The AEC says that one accident occurs for every 10,000 shipments. In the 30 accidents that occurred in 1970, the packages remained intact in 17 cases. Five of the packages were damaged with no material lost. In eight cases material was released. In five of these eight cases, the radioactive material was confined to the vehicle. In only three cases was material spread to adjacent land surfaces.

Thirty casks of spent fuel were shipped in 1970. Between 700 and 12,000 casks are projected to be shipped in the year 2000. For each 1000 MW(e) reactor about 32 truckloads of spent fuel casks or 10 railroad cars would be needed. An average of 60–100 casks would be in transit at all times. Each cask might contain 1.5 tons of fuel which could contain 75 million Ci of radioactivity. By contrast, today's casks contain about 7 million Ci. Even casks of today's size must be cooled. The casks themselves must be able to withstand a 30-ft fall and/or a 30-min fire. However, even with safeguards, an AEC study states "it is virtually impossible to design a package to survive any possible accident."[8]

In the future, highly radioactive solid wastes from reprocessing plants will have to be shipped to storage facilities. Today, this is not being done, because the reprocessing plants are government owned with storage for liquid wastes on site and because no technology for permanent storage has been developed.

MINING AND PROCESSING   The earth as a whole contains about 4 ppm uranium; large minable deposits may contain 0.1% uranium (2 lb per ton, i.e., 1 part per thousand). Therefore, large quantities of ore must be mined to obtain the desired uranium; for example, in 1969 5.9 million tons of domestic ore were

8. "The accident experience of the USAEC in the shipment of radioactive material," *Proceedings of the Second International Symposium on the Packaging and Transportation of Radioactive Material,* Oak Ridge, Tenn.: USAEC Division of Technical Information Extension, 1968, p. 204.

shipped and processed to yield 10,934 tons of uranium oxide. The residue of waste rock, called *tailings,* is radioactive. Only a small amount of the radiation comes directly from the uranium isotopes themselves.

Uranium-238 with a half-life of 4.5 billion years decays to isotopes of other elements which are themselves radioactive. These secondary isotopes accumulate in the ore body and supply the major portion of the radiation present in the mines. Eventually the decay series cascades down to a stable nonradioactive nuclide, lead-206 (Figure 10–8).

This is one of several more extended decay sequences. All radioactive changes toward stability require one or more steps. Since a subsequent step cannot occur before its predecessor, the mine and mill tailings will contain all the radioactive isotopes from the decay of both uranium-235 and uranium-238 as well as residues of the uranium. Roughly 85% of all the original radioactivity remains in the wastes. Of all the isotopes present in the tailings, radium is the most dangerous substance.

The uranium content of ore and, consequently, the radiation varies from mine to mine and from place to place in a mine. Work hours of miners are adjusted to the level of radiation in the mine so that the miner receives no more than a specified level of radiation. Radiation levels in the mine are reduced by forced ventilation to reduce the concentration of radon gas, a particularly dangerous nuclide (see Figure 10–8). Radon-222, with a half-life of 3.83 days, may decay while in the lungs and leave a metal, polonium. Polonium and the next three elements in the decay series have short half-lives. If it is assumed that all the atoms of an element will decay in 10 half-lives, then the four sequential steps in the series will occur in 10 hr. The lung tissue will be exposed to two alpha particles, two beta particles, and three gamma rays, in addition to the alpha particle and gamma ray from the decay of the radon, for each radon atom that decays. Some of the gamma rays are especially energetic and therefore extremely dangerous.

The incidence of lung cancer among uranium miners is greater than the incidence of lung cancer in the general public and in other miners. Smoking and mining uranium seems to have the same synergistic effect as smoking and working in the asbestos industry (see Chapter 6).

Figure 10–8. Decay pattern of uranium-238. The symbol (γ) represents high-energy gamma radiation (very high frequency electromagnetic radiation similar in nature to x rays).

$$_{92}^{238}\text{U} \xrightarrow[\text{alpha }(\gamma)]{4.5 \times 10^9 \text{ yr}} {}_{90}^{234}\text{Th} \xrightarrow[\text{beta }(\gamma)]{24.5 \text{ days}} {}_{91}^{234}\text{Pa} \xrightarrow[\text{beta }(\gamma)]{1.14 \text{ min}} {}_{92}^{234}\text{U} \xrightarrow[\text{alpha }(\gamma)]{233,000 \text{ yr}} {}_{90}^{230}\text{Th} \xrightarrow[\text{alpha }(\gamma)]{83,000 \text{ yr}}$$

$$_{88}^{226}\text{Ra} \xrightarrow[\text{alpha }(\gamma)]{1590 \text{ yr}} {}_{86}^{222}\text{Rn} \xrightarrow[\text{alpha }(\gamma)]{3.83 \text{ days}} {}_{84}^{218}\text{Po} \xrightarrow[\text{alpha}]{3.04 \text{ min}} {}_{82}^{214}\text{Pb} \xrightarrow[\text{beta }(\gamma)]{26.8 \text{ min}} {}_{83}^{214}\text{Bi} \xrightarrow[\text{beta }(\gamma)]{19.7 \text{ min}}$$

$$_{84}^{214}\text{Po} \xrightarrow[\text{alpha }(\gamma)]{0.00015 \text{ sec}} {}_{82}^{210}\text{Pb} \xrightarrow[\text{beta }(\gamma)]{22 \text{ yr}} {}_{83}^{210}\text{Bi} \xrightarrow[\text{beta}]{510 \text{ days}} {}_{84}^{210}\text{Po} \xrightarrow[\text{alpha }(\gamma)]{143 \text{ days}} {}_{82}^{206}\text{Pb} \quad \text{stable isotope}$$

Most uranium mines and a few of the mills are located in remote places, but many mills are in towns such as Grand Junction and Durango in Colorado and Salt Lake City in Utah. For a specified amount of uranium, 500 times as much waste is produced at a mill than at a mine, thus making the fine, sandy tailings available to many people. Since the tailings make a convenient fill-dirt and sand to mix with mortar, many homes and public buildings, including schools, have been built with the material. Since the tailings contain 85% of the radiation potential, the practice of incorporating the sandy material in buildings is dangerous, especially to children who are particularly susceptible to radiation and who are near the floor where the decay products would tend to collect.

Government agencies have been slow to accept responsibility for controlling the tailings and for replacing the material in buildings. However, the tailings are now fenced off and homes are slowly being made safe. Permanent protection of the tailings piles from weather is more difficult. The AEC spent $300,000 to cover and seed one tailings pile. The stabilizing action has a lifetime of about 20 years.

URANIUM RESOURCES The United States will need 250,000 short tons (1 short ton = 2000 lb) of U_3O_8 through 1980. In addition, the industry needs an eight-year forward reserve of about 650,000 short tons. Therefore, through the year 1988, a total of about 900,000 short tons of natural U_3O_8 will be required to be available for a certain cost per pound. The reasonably assured reserves of ore and the estimated additional reserves are shown in Table 10–3.

Table 10–3 shows that the reasonably assured and estimated additional reserves of U_3O_8 at prices between $5 and $15 per pound will be exhausted by 1988. The U_3O_8 available at less than $30 per pound, including the category "estimated additional ore," will be exhausted less than eight years later (1996). No expansion of productivity is expected after 1988. Thus, according to the Bureau of Mines information, all low-priced ore will be consumed before the year 2000, that is, in less than 25 years.

TABLE 10–3. Uranium Reserves of the United States.

Price (dollars)	U_3O_8 reserves	
	Reasonably assured ore (× 1000 short tons)	Estimated additional ore (× 1000 short tons)
5–10	300	350
10–15	150	200
15–30	200	440

Source: J.A. Decalo and C.E. Shortt. "Uranium," *Mineral facts and problems,* Bureau of Mines Bulletin 640, Washington, D.C.: Government Printing Office, 1970, p. 227.

ENERGY FROM THE CORE OF THE ATOM

The rate of discovery of uranium ore from 1948 to 1967 was 22,010 tons per year or 6.4 pounds per foot of exploratory drilling. Undoubtedly only the more promising areas with the more accessible ore were worked to find these deposits. Critics think that insufficient exploration has been done because the market has been "soft" much of the time. They contend that estimates are based on extrapolation of past production and not "estimation techniques standard in economic geology."

The United States does not rely solely on domestic sources. Uranium ores are widely dispersed throughout the world. Foreign ores supplied 43% of the United States demand in the period 1956 to 1958 and about 50% in 1969. Since other developed and undeveloped countries will need uranium, it is unlikely that the United States can continue to use 50% of the uranium consumed each year.

The AEC claims that nuclear power plants will not be competitive with fossil-fuel plants if the price of U_3O_8 rises much above $8 per pound (1970 dollars). If this relationship is correct, the nuclear power industry would consume all of its fuel supplies by the year 2000, even with continued importation.

However, the cost of U_3O_8 is a relatively small part of the cost of electricity from a nuclear power station. U_3O_8 at $8 per pound contributes only $0.00035 or 0.035 cents or 0.35 mills to the cost of a kilowatt-hour (kWh) of electricity. This is small compared with the cost of about $0.03 per kWh for electricity delivered to a householder in Michigan (1972 dollars). For each dollar increase of uranium, the cost to the consumer will rise about 0.043 mills or $0.000043. Other estimates are from 0.02 to 0.075 mills per kWh per dollar increase for a pound of U_3O_8. The costs per kilowatt hour due to various cost levels of mill-grade U_3O_8 are shown in Table 10–4. If uranium resources at prices up to $500 per pound are used in conventional reactors, there presumably would be enough uranium ore to fuel them for thousands of years at the rate of consumption of uranium projected for the year 2000, that is, 100,000 tons per year.

TABLE 10–4. Relationship between Cost of Uranium Oxide (U_3O_8) and Electricity Produced by Nuclear Energy.

Cost of uranium ($/lb)	Cost per kWh for fuel ($/kWh)	Mills per kWh for fuel (mills/kWh)	Total cost per kWh based on 3¢/kWh at $8/lb ($/kWh)
8	0.000349	0.349	0.03
10	0.000436	0.436	0.030087
15	0.000665	0.665	0.030316
30	0.00131	1.31	0.031066
50	0.00218	2.18	0.03194
100	0.00437	4.37	0.03413
500	0.0218	21.8	0.05156

Other conditions must be met besides cost to determine whether a certain grade of ore can be used to produce electricity. Energy is required to process the additional ore and to handle the large amounts of wastes. At some point more energy would be needed than would be returned from the power plant. At that point the ore would be uneconomical to mine.

NET GAIN FROM NUCLEAR ENERGY

The AEC and its critics do not agree on the net amount of energy to be produced from nuclear power plants. There are two areas of disagreement: (1) how much a power plant can produce from a given amount of uranium containing a certain percentage of uranium-235, and (2) the energy cost at all steps of the energy fuel cycle: mining, milling, conversion to UF_6, enrichment, fabrication, reactor operation, reprocessing, transportation, and storage of wastes.

The amount of energy produced by the plant is determined by the amount of uranium burned in a given period of time and the percentage of the time that the plant actually operates. Most of the present reactors have a history of large periods of "downtime."

Enrichment of the fuel in uranium-235 is the energy-intensive step. The energy needed depends upon the amount of uranium the plants process. During the processing, uranium hexafluoride is forced through thousands of membranes. Increasing the quantity of gases through the membranes increases the energy per unit of uranium required by the process. The AEC has prepared a summary of all the energy needed for all stages of the fuel cycle, except waste management and transportation. Dr. E. J. Hoffman of the Natural Resources Research Institute, College of Engineering, University of Wyoming, has found very different values, which do not include waste management, transportation, or energy for reprocessing. However, the latter is a low-energy process. The two sets of data are as follows.

	AEC	
Production MW-hr(e)/kg	210	29–43
Fuel cycle MW-hr(e)/kg	<10	18.7

Admittedly many figures involved in these calculations are approximations but they do question the efficiency of the nuclear industry. Much open investigation is needed.

Consumer costs do not accurately reflect industry costs because of the numerous subsidies involved. If all costs were internalized, it would be possible to arrive at a figure which might not only reflect the true costs but also the use of resources. Some of the unaccounted costs involved are the following.

1. Radon-induced lung cancer among uranium miners.
2. Mutagenic, teratogenic, and carcinogenic damage to the general population.
3. Cost of despoiled land.

4. Cost of proper disposal of millions of tons of solid tailings from uranium mines and mills.

5. Cost of disposal of nearly 500,000 gallons of radioactive liquid wastes from concentrating each ton of U_3O_8.

6. Cost of the 2.5-billion-dollar Oak Ridge gaseous diffusion plant (there are also two others).

7. Multibillion dollar research and development bill for the development of the industry.

8. Insurance risk borne by government.

9. If an accident occurs, the injured party will need to pay for most of his own loss under the Price-Anderson Act.

10. Cost of perpetual isolation of high-level nuclear wastes. Industry pays a fee, but how do you pay for perpetual surveillance?

11. Cost of artificially supported uranium price.

The *fast breeder reactor* not only produces electricity but also produces (breeds) more fuel for fission. The more common isotope of uranium, uranium-238, will absorb a fast neutron and then decay to plutonium-239, a fissionable nuclide:

$$^{238}_{92}U + {}^1_0n \rightarrow {}^{239}_{92}U \xrightarrow[\beta \text{ decay}]{\substack{\text{half-life} \\ \text{24 min.}}} {}^{239}_{93}Np \xrightarrow[\beta \text{ decay}]{\substack{\text{half-life} \\ \text{2-3 days}}} {}^{239}_{94}Pu$$

$$^{239}_{94}Pu + {}^1_0n \rightarrow \text{fission products} + \text{more than 2 neutrons}$$

The reaction will allow almost the entire amount of uranium to be used. In addition, thorium-232, a much more common element than uranium, can be bred to produce uranium-233.

$$^{232}_{90}Th + {}^1_0n \rightarrow {}^{233}_{90}Th \xrightarrow[\beta \text{ decay}]{\substack{\text{half-life} \\ \text{23 min}}} {}^{233}_{91}Pa \xrightarrow[\beta \text{ decay}]{\substack{\text{half-life} \\ \text{27 days}}} {}^{233}_{92}U$$

$$^{233}_{92}U + {}^1_0n \rightarrow \text{fission products} + \text{2 or more neutrons}$$

Over a period of seven to ten years an efficient breeder reactor may be able to produce enough fissionable fuel, plutonium-239 or uranium-233, to provide for its own operation plus enough to start a second reactor.

The diagram (Figure 10–9) of the fast breeder shows that its organization is similar to that of the pressurized water reactor (PWR). The reactor itself occupies a smaller volume because the fuel is more concentrated. Since liquid sodium is the coolant of choice for the fast breeder, an extra heat exchanger is introduced between the reactor and the steam supply to the turbine. This ensures that radioactive sodium will not irradiate the turbine steam with radioactive materials transferred to the condenser water.

Sodium is a good heat transfer medium and requires relatively small amounts of energy to pump it through the reactor at high rates. Sodium absorbs neutrons

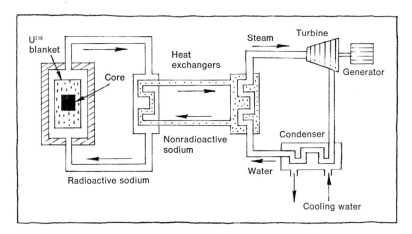

Figure 10–9. Model of the fast-breeder reactor.

and becomes radioactive but the radioactivity does not pass through the heat exchangers to the turbine. A disadvantage of sodium is that it is opaque and hinders observations inside the reactor, especially when fuel rods are being placed in the core. Another disadvantage is that sodium reacts violently with water to produce hydrogen:

$$2Na + 2H_2O \rightarrow 2NaOH + H_2$$

Enough energy may be evolved to start the hydrogen burning, and an explosion can result. At high temperatures with fast neutrons stainless steel becomes swollen and may react with the sodium. The fuel rods may need to be replaced frequently.

For maximum economy and performance, the fuel rods must accept neutron irradiation several times as intense as that common in a light water reactor (LWR). The power density of a proposed demonstration breeder (roughly one-third commercial size) is 400 kW/liter, some 12 times that of large commercial LWR's of the last few years. The heat output in the core would correspond to the heat evolved by 400 hand clothes irons all operating simultaneously in a space about the size of a quart milk bottle. By analogy, if an LWR is assumed to be the size of a cottage, the breeder of comparable power rating would correspond relatively to the size of a sofa.

The core of the LWR contains tens of kilograms of plutonium, but a breeder would contain a tonne of plutonium. The plutonium inventory in the fast breeder is concentrated, and is that quantity of radioactive material (in this case plutonium) which sustains a chain reaction. If the reaction proceeds at a neutron capture ratio greater than 1 neutron per fission event, the system may run away and perhaps explode. The critical mass for plutonium is only a few kilograms.

ENERGY FROM THE CORE OF THE ATOM

In normal operation there is no danger of plutonium concentrations reaching such a value. However, during a meltdown the possibility is great.

The high concentration of fuel makes the reactor harder to control. Although the control system may work as designed over long periods of time, it is expected that

Malfunctions of the automatic control systems . . . can reasonably be expected to occur within the lifetime of the demonstration plant . . . Among the more severe hypothetical accidents are reactivity insertions sufficient to cause the power level to rise rapidly beyond that for which the reactor was designed, leading to events which could damage the core before . . . inherent shutdown phenomena or normal control actions take effect . . . However for determination of environmental effects, such accidents should be considered on the basis that safety features function as designed.[9]

The AEC seems committed to the use of sodium coolant and stainless-steel fuel rods for its liquid metal fast breeder reactor (LMFBR).

Plutonium

Even with conventional reactors, it is expected that large amounts of plutonium will be moved about the country. If the breeder becomes a reality, much larger quantities will be shipped. If the AEC plans are followed, the inventory of plutonium will have the approximate values shown in Table 10–5.

The large amounts available and the high prices of plutonium constitute a great temptation to theft and conversion to weapons by subversive groups. Not only will much of the element be available at reactor sites, reprocessing plants, and fabrication plants, but huge amounts will be being transported at all times. It is estimated that by the year 2020, there will be 100 railroad cars loaded with casks of spent fuel in transit at all times. As indicated earlier in this chapter, nuplexes may be the answer to the problem.

Plutonium is a very toxic chemical. It can be washed off the skin, but, if ingested, inhaled, or deposited on a skin abrasion, 80% of the quantity that finds its way into the body will still be there 50 years later. One to 10% of the body

9. Joint Committee on Atomic Energy Hearing, *AEC Authorizing Legislation, Fiscal Year 1973, Environmental Statements*, Part 5, Vol. 1, pp. E866–E869, E871.

TABLE 10–5. Projections of Plutonium Inventory in the United States.

Year	Plutonium inventory (metric tons)
1945	<1
1980	45
1985	170
21st century	Thousands of tons

Source: Data from testimony of Milton Shaw to Joint Committee on Atomic Energy, *AEC Authorizing Legislation Fiscal Year 1973*, Washington, D.C.: Government Printing Office, pp. 1230, 1234.

burden is deposited in the bones. The maximum body burden has been set at 0.6 μg/kg, less than the size of a dust particle.

Plutonium forms an oxide which is a very fine material and can be widely dispersed. One pound of plutonium-239 has a potential for 9 billion human lung cancers. Even with 99.99% control, 1 million cancers are possible. Any time the element can be found by analysis, there is too much present for safety.

At present, the AEC cannot keep track of the plutonium produced by LWRs to much more than 99% (about a 1% loss). This does not imply that the plutonium is being stolen. It does mean that plutonium is being dispersed from the plants where it is processed or that the analytical methods are inaccurate.

FUSION ENERGY   The difficulties of devising an economical D-T fusion reactor are at least an order of magnitude greater [that is, ten times as great] than those involved in landing a man on the moon, while those of running a D-D fusion reactor might prove impossible. Fortunately, the time scale involved and the rewards of success are orders of magnitude greater in both cases.[10]

H. B. Hulme

Energy will be evolved by any process of fission or *fusion* (combination) of nuclear particles which results in the production of secondary particles having a higher binding energy per nucleon than that of the original nuclides. The relative amounts of energy which are possible from various nuclear changes are indicated by the graph of binding energy per nucleon (proton or neutron) vs. the mass number of the nuclide (Figure 10–3). The relative vertical distance between nuclides gives a measure of the relative amounts of energy which can be obtained in the change from one nuclide to a second. The figure shows that the conversion of hydrogen (atomic mass 1), deuterium (atomic mass 2), or tritium (atomic mass 3) into helium (atomic mass 4) or any heavier atom would evolve more energy per nucleon than is obtainable from any fission process.

A partial list of potentially useful fusion reactions is given in Figure 10–10. The quantities of heat produced seem very small but they are given for one atom in each case. There are many atoms in a mole. The equation for the second fusion reaction (D-D) illustrates the process.

$$\text{}^2_1\text{D} \quad + \quad \text{}^2_1\text{D} \quad \rightarrow \quad \text{}^3_1\text{T} \quad + \quad \text{}^1_1\text{P} \quad + 4.0 \text{ MeV.}$$

deuterium (D) + deuterium (D) $\rightarrow$ tritium (T) + proton + 4.0 MeV.

The energy yield from the combination of two atoms of deuterium is 15.2×10^{-14} calories. However, in the formation of 1 mole of helium (4 g) from deuterium the energy yield would be 91 billion calories, enough to heat 200,000 gallons of water from 0 °C to 100 °C. Certainly large amounts of energy are available from any of the fusion processes.

10. H. B. Hulme, *Nuclear fusion*, London: Wykeham Publications, 1969, p. 147.

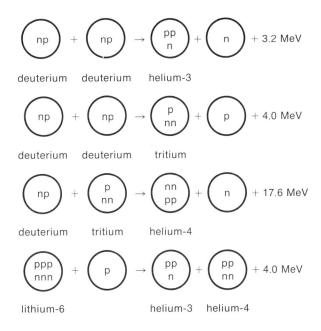

deuterium   deuterium   helium-3

deuterium   deuterium   tritium

deuterium   tritium   helium-4

lithium-6   helium-3   helium-4

Figure 10–10. Some potentially useful fusion reactions, involving protons (p) and neutrons (n). (1 MeV = 3.8 × 10⁻¹⁴ cal.)

For a fusion reaction to occur the velocity (*ignition temperature*) (a condition of matter in which the electrons and nuclei are separated from each other and true atoms no longer exist, i.e., it is merely a mixture of nuclei and electrons) of plasma particles must be large enough to overcome the repulsive force exerted between colliding particles having the same kind of charge. The two colliding particles must meet practically head-on for fusion, otherwise they are likely to be deflected from each other without fusion taking place.

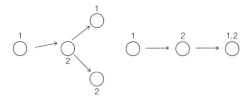

Many collisions must occur before a viable hit is made. These require a compressed *plasma*, a temperature greater than the ignition temperature, and enough time for particles to collide in just the precise manner required for fusion.

The simple deuterium-deuterium (D-D) reaction is the most attractive fusion system, because deuterium is cheaply available from the almost inexhaustible supply present in sea water. However, the ignition temperature for the D-D reaction is 100 million °C, while for a more attainable system, the deuterium-tritium (D-T) system, it is only 40 million °C.

$$_1^2D + {}_1^3T \rightarrow {}_2^4He + {}_0^1n$$

Consequently, experimental efforts are concentrated on D-T system.

The "conventional" method for containing and compressing the charged particles of plasma for fusion reaction is to use very intense magnetic forces. The magnetic "bottle" presents problems analogous to bottling watery Jello in a container of rubber bands. The system leaks. The magnetic bottle is created by the flow of large currents of electricity. Certain very cold materials (refrigerated by helium gas) have very low resistance and theoretically are capable of carrying "infinitely" large currents (see Chapter 12). These in turn create very intense magnetic fields which constitute the "bottle" for the plasma. The larger the magnetic forces, the greater the compression of the plasma and the greater the probability that a fusion reaction can occur.

The plasma may be heated to high temperatures by the compression effect produced by a magnetic field. Recently, powerful lasers have been used to heat pellets of fusion mixtures. A laser is an instrument in which a certain frequency or wavelength of light is stored temporarily until it is triggered to instantly release the energy as a narrow, nonspreading beam of light. The emitted light has some of the properties of a cohesive pellet and represents a very concentrated bit of energy that can be focused upon and absorbed by matter.

Dr. Raymond Baddour, chairman of the Chemical Engineering Department of Massachusetts Institute of Technology, told a House of Representatives Subcommittee that it would take at least 30 years before fusion could be commercially feasible. The first decade would be used to demonstrate scientific feasibility. The second decade would be needed to "solve problems such as the provision of intense specially shaped magnetic fields by superconducting windings bigger than any now in existence, provision of a molten lithium blanket surrounding the reactor to recover heat and convert neutrons to tritium, the attainment of useful equipment life under intense bombardment by heat, radiation, and neutrons, and efficient engineering of a complete power system whose individual components haven't yet even been invented.[11] The third decade will be needed to prove whether or not fusion is economically feasible. A series of progressively larger pilot plants would have to be built to give the answer.

Fusion reactors are large vacuum spaces, about 1 m in diameter into which the reactants are introduced, compressed, and heated (Figure 10–11). Surrounding the vacuum space are the conductors and/or magnets. Liquid lithium

11. From testimony to the House of Representatives Subcommittee on Science, Research, and Development, 9 May, 1972.

ENERGY FROM THE CORE OF THE ATOM

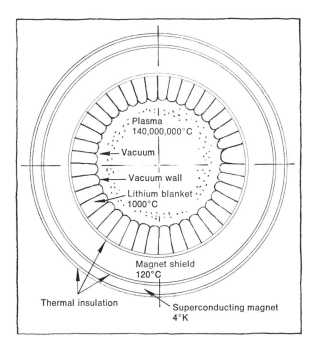

Figure 10–11. Model of the fusion reactor.

surrounds the vacuum space and absorbs the energy supplied by the neutrons that come from the reactor vessels.

The amount of radioactive nuclides from a fusion reactor would be negligible compared with the amount produced by a fission reactor. The fusion reactor requires positive action in order to make it work. Therefore, there is no possibility that the reactor can run out of control or explode in any way. Anything that goes wrong automatically stops the production of energy. Thus the fusion reactor is relatively safe.

Advantages of Fusion Power

Ultimately, the D-D reaction is the most attractive source of fusion energy because deuterium is inexpensively and abundantly available from sea water. If it becomes necessary to exploit only the D-T reaction, the situation will not be so "rosy." The necessary tritium must be produced from lithium-6:

Disadvantages of Fusion Power

$$^6_3\text{Li} + ^1_0\text{n} \rightarrow ^3_1\text{T} + ^2_1\text{H} + ^4_2\text{He}$$

Lithium-6 is a small fraction (7.42%) of the total amount of lithium isotopes found in nature and is in limited supply. Thus, fusion power rests primarily upon the feasibility of the D-D reaction.

Large fluxes (flows or currents) of highly energetic neutrons and gamma rays will be produced by fusion reactors. These will slash into the energy recovery coolant and the structural and shielding materials built into the reactor body. While the reactor is operating, it is estimated that each atom in the structure will be moved aside at least once each day. Furthermore, the construction materials may absorb neutrons over a period of time to become radioactive and decay into different elements which will weaken the structure. However, the isotopes formed are relatively short-lived. If the fusion power plant were to be isolated for a decade, the plant could be reused.

The hydrogen isotope tritium is the most dangerous substance produced by the fusion reactions. Chemically tritium behaves like hydrogen. If it becomes part of a water molecule, it will enter the human body along with other molecules of water. The tritium atom would be excreted by the body as water. Containing the tritium produced in the fusion reaction may be difficult. Hydrogen leaks through metal containers. Tritium is heavier than hydrogen but it would be expected to behave in the same way.

Helium will be needed to make possible the superconductivity required to produce the intense magnetic forces required for the confinement of the high-temperature plasma. Helium also has unique properties which make it useful for many other technical processes. The supply is definitely limited and may eventually place a limit upon the development of fusion power.

At one time fission power was touted to be so cheap that it would not be worthwhile to meter electricity produced by nuclear power stations. This assumption has proven to be false. Now fusion power is "just over the horizon" in the minds of many energetic and brilliant investigators. It is also touted to be very cheap and virtually inexhaustible. However, fusion power has not yet been proven experimentally, much less commercially. The evaluation of the ability of a fusion reactor to produce economical power in excess of its power requirements waits upon the actual construction and operation of a fusion power plant. Even if fusion does prove to be commercially feasible, it will not be costless.

KEY CONCEPTS

1. Decay and fission of nuclides.
2. Components and operation of a nuclear reactor.
3. Various causes of excursions.
4. Relationship of radiation guidelines and natural radiation.
5. Potential damage caused by nuclear accidents.
6. Operating and production of wastes at a reprocessing plant.
7. Disposal of the different types of wastes.
8. Potential for spills during transportation.
9. Dangers of radionuclides in mining and mining wastes.
10. Resource base of uranium.
11. Assessment of return from nuclear energy.
12. Operation and difficulties with a fast breeder reactor.
13. Operation and prospects of a fusion energy.

1. What are the types of damage to the body that can result from exposure to high-energy radiation? Are there any benefits? Explain your answer.
2. What are the essential parts of a nuclear fission reactor?
3. Is it reasonable to prohibit nuclear power plants from releasing any radioactive matter? Explain your answer.
4. Dr. Alvin Weinberg has stated that we will not need to be concerned about radiation when a cancer cure is available. Evaluate the usefulness of a cancer cure to the nuclear energy industry.
5. Given dangers of uncertain magnitude, should the public safety take precedence over the need of a nation to experiment and progress?
6. Is there any real difference between the accident risk accepted by society in the use of automobiles and the accident risk posed by atomic energy? Is one a "worse killer" than the other? Explain your answer.
7. People living in homes built on tailings in Grand Junction, Colorado, claim they feel fine. Comment on this.
8. It has been suggested that much of the furor over nuclear power plant siting problems can be eliminated by putting the plants out of sight, offshore. Evaluate the proposal in terms of the characteristics of nuclear energy and of the ocean.
9. According to industry, some AEC experts have excessive zeal for perfection in safety. The Russians have located atomic energy reactors in populated areas in former warehouses. They feel that too many safety devices make the reactors unsafe. Some industry people agree. Would you rather have safety devices or not?
10. Senator Gravel of Alaska has introduced a bill into the Senate calling for a nationwide moratorium on the building of nuclear energy plants until the problems have been solved. If you were a member of the Senate, how would you vote on such a bill? Give reasons for your answer.
11. What is the biggest problem for the atomic power industry? What solutions have been suggested for the problem?
12. In the conclusion of the chapter, the two views of the desirability of nuclear energy were given. Which point of view do you advocate? Give reasons for your answer.

1. Alfven, H., "Energy and environment," *Bulletin of the Atomic Scientists,* 28: 5–7, May 1972.
2. Benedict, M., "Electric power from nuclear fission," *Technol. Rev.,* 74: 32–41, Oct/Nov. 1971.
3. Forbes, I. A., Ford, D., Kendall, H., and MacKenzie, J., "Cooling water," *Environment,* 14: 40–47, Jan/Feb. 1972.
4. Gough, W. C., and Eastlund, B. J., "The prospects of fusion power," *Sci. Amer.,* 224: 50–64, Feb. 1971.
5. Novick, S., *The careless atom,* Boston: Houghton Mifflin, 1969.

6. Seaborg, G. T. and Bloom, J. L., "Fast breeder reactors," *Sci. Amer.,* 223: 13–21, Nov. 1970.
7. Shapely, D., "Radioactive cargoes: record good but the problems will multiply," *Science,* 172: 1318–1322, 25 June, 1971.
8. Weil, G. L., *Nuclear energy: promises, promises,* Washington, D.C.: George Weil, 1972.
9. Wood, L., and Nuckolls, J., "Fusion power," *Environment,* 14: 29–33, May 1972.
10. Three issues of the *Bulletin of Atomic Scientists,* 27 (7, 8, 9), Sept., Oct., Nov., 1971, are about the energy crisis.

11 Industrial Resources and the Environment

Mines bear no second crop. As new discoveries decrease there is only retreat to ever lower grades, imports, substitutes, synthetics, recycling, and eventually, exhaustion.[1]

Preston Cloud

The developed countries, especially the United States, use huge amounts of materials to produce the trappings of technological affluence. Modern man uses 88 minerals divided into four groups; 12 energy minerals, 12 ferrous minerals (iron and 11 others, such as chromium and nickel, which are alloyed with iron to produce a variety of products), 30 nonferrous minerals (metals such as tin, copper, and zinc that do not belong to the ferrous group), and 34 nonmetal minerals such as chlorine, asbestos, sand, and gravel.

All of the industrialized nations (the U.S.S.R. may be an exception) are net importers of most of the minerals or metals which they use. A country is considered deficient in a mineral if it imports 50% of its consumption. There are 13 basic raw materials which are required by an industrial society. In 1950 the United States was deficient in four—aluminum, manganese, nickel, and tin. Today, zirconium and zinc have been added to this list. By the year 2000, the United States will be deficient in eight more—copper, iron, lead, potassium, sulfur, and tungsten. Of the basic 13, domestic mines will supply over 50% of the requirements of only one, phosphates. Besides the basic minerals, many others are also in short supply. The United States supply of the platinum group of metals, very important as catalysts, would last only a few years if imports were stopped. Much or all of its supplies of cobalt, niobium, tantalum, asbestos, graphite, iodine, and many others are imported.

The international situation is more difficult to assess. Although the United States uses more minerals than any other country, all the industrialized nations use vast quantities. The leaders of the developing countries have stated their intentions of developing to the same level as the United States. In order to accomplish this aim, these countries must increase their use of minerals which are already heavily used by and committed to the industrialized nations. If the entire world, overnight, could, by some act of magic, reach the level of per capita consumption that the United States had in 1968, the lifetime of mineral resources would be shortened by a factor of 30–40. If these figures are calculated for the total consumption between the years 1968 and 2000, the resource base is shortened even more. For example, every person in the United States is expected to use about a half ton of copper between the years 1968 and 2000. If this were true of the entire world, 1.8 billion tons would be used instead of the projected 0.4 billion tons. The world reserves are only about 0.3 billion tons (Figure 11–1).

It is true that new discoveries and new technologies will make new resources available. However, new technologies generally require large amounts of processing materials and energy resources. It is probable that few new major discoveries will be made in the United States, but many areas of the world are not as well explored as the United States and major discoveries of new sources of raw materials will be made. However, if all resources are increased by a factor of 10 (an unlikely event), these will not last long at the present increasing rate

1. "Mined out!" *Ecologist*, 1:26, Aug. 1970.

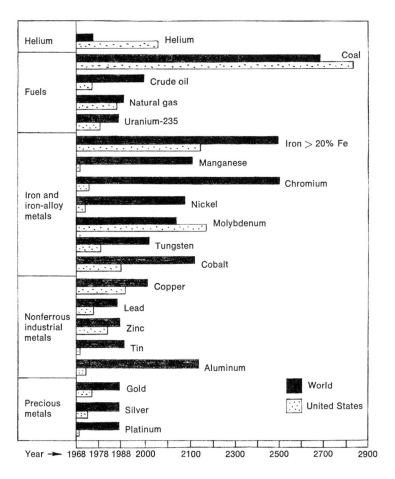

Figure 11–1. Relationship of reserves and consumption throughout the world.
Courtesy of Professor Preston Cloud, Department of Geology, University of California, Santa Barbara.

of consumption. Many of the new discoveries will likely be in remote areas and will be difficult to exploit.

The ocean is a source of all minerals used by man, but it is a lean source for most substances. Magnesium and bromine are recovered from the ocean; few others are likely to be recovered from the ocean water itself. On the ocean floor are manganese crusts and nodules containing nickel, cobalt, and copper. Industry is interested but has not been able to solve the technological problems involved in their recovery at competitive prices. It is likely that minerals, in addition to fossil fuels, will be found and exploited along the continental shelf

INDUSTRIAL RESOURCES AND THE ENVIRONMENT

and in land near to the shore. With the current exponential growth, these underwater resources can stave off shortages for only a few years. Underwater mining may affect or destroy fish and recreation resources. Adequate protection must be given to these.

Leaner sources of minerals are expected to become available if unlimited energy is available from fusion reactions. However, no one has ever proven a direct correlation between mineral production and energy input. If the extra energy is available, it must be absorbed by the earth and eventually radiated away.

There are many factors involved in mineral production besides energy input: labor, equipment to extract and transport, processing materials, and, most of all, the effect of vast quantities of waste on the ecosphere. As leaner and leaner ores are exploited, all of these factors may increase enormously per unit of useful product.

Present copper ores in the southwest United States are about 0.60% copper. For every ton of ore, 12 lb of copper could be extracted if 100% recovery were possible, which leaves at least 1,988 lb of waste. Ores containing 0.035% of the desirable metal are being considered for exploitation. These would yield more than 1,999 lb of waste per ton of ore. Not only must such large quantities of ore be discarded but ever increasing quantities of processing materials must be discarded. Often the volume of these wastes are larger than the volume of the ore itself.

Substitutions can and will be made for some of the scarce items, but usually at a higher cost or a performance penalty. For example, tantalum can substitute for niobium but the cost of the product will be more. Stainless steel may substitute for zirconium in nuclear reactors but the steel does not work as well. In many cases the substitutes are also in short supply. Nickel and cobalt can often substitute for each other, but both are limited resources.

INDUSTRIES

The iron and steel, aluminum, glass, and paper industries have been chosen to be discussed for two reasons: they produce the larger portion of useful products and cause the most evident disposal problems.

Iron and Steel Industry

Iron is the least expensive and most versatile of the metals that can be used for tool or structural purposes. It can be made into a material that is glass-hard or one that is soft enough to be twisted into spiral shapes. When alloyed with certain other elements, it makes very corrosion-resistant materials such as stainless steel. Industrial society depends upon the continuing availability of an abundant supply of iron.

MINING   In the United States, the iron-mining industry developed at the northern end of the Great Lakes. The lakes provided an economical transport system from the mines to the smelting centers lower on the lakes where relatively large amounts of coking coal are available.

BENEFACTION   *Benefaction* is any process that concentrates a desired mineral. When the rich hematite (40–60% iron in the form of Fe_2O_3) deposits of the Lake Superior region were exhausted, benefaction of the leaner taconite (25–50% iron in the form of Fe_2O_3 or Fe_3O_4) was developed. The ore is broken into pieces and ground into fine grains. When mixed with a large volume of water, the heavy Fe_3O_4 grains sink and the lighter impurities are skimmed off the surface. Two tons of solid waste are washed away for every ton of usable ore particles obtained. The finely divided waste causes a water pollution problem.

Taconite is a good example of the problems involved in processing lean ores. Large amounts of energy are required and large amounts of waste are generated. The ore particles are made into pellets that assay 65% iron. These pellets compare favorably with hematite ore that assays 50–60% iron. Foreign countries are beginning to make pellets of the iron ore that they ship to the United States. Many of these ores are higher grade than the taconite deposits of the Mesabi Range and their pellets are even more desirable than those produced in the United States.

A new magnetic benefaction process makes it possible to treat previously unusable ores. The process uses large, very powerful magnets developed for use in solid-state and high-energy research.

BLAST FURNACE   The purpose of the blast furnace is to reduce the iron ore to iron and partially to remove contaminating substances, mostly silica (SiO_2) and alumina (Al_2O_3), which are present in the ore (Figure 11–2).

When the furnace is operating, carbon monoxide is formed and proceeds to contact the ore and reduce (convert iron ore to metallic iron, i.e., gains electrons) it to iron while the ore is still in the solid state. The lower levels of the charge are consumed and melt to form a pool of slag and melted iron which collects at the bottom of the furnace. As the reduction and melting progresses, the upper reduced ore solids move downward and are themselves melted by the intense heat at the lower levels and collected at the bottom. The dense liquid iron settles below a less dense protective layer of liquid, glassy slag. Periodically the slag and molten iron are tapped from the furnace. Ninety-seven per cent of the iron charged to the blast furnace is recovered as molten iron. The limestone and gravel combine with the alumina and silica impurities to form the slag which protects the molten iron in the hearth from oxidation. The slag is discarded at a dump or sold to be made into cement or insulating materials.

Coke (coal heated without air to drive off gaseous impurities) is used as the fuel and to combine with the oxygen in the Fe_2O_3 instead of coal, because it contains less sulfur and does not form tarry materials which block the passage of gases through the charge. The low sulfur content is necessary because sulfur reacts with iron and makes the iron and steel brittle. Liquid iron dissolves some of the carbon from the coke as it trickles down through the blast furnace. The liquid metal falls rapidly enough through the oxidizing, air-blast region

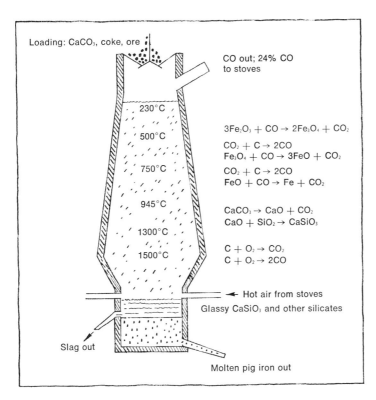

Loading: $CaCO_3$, coke, ore

CO out; 24% CO
to stoves

230°C

500°C

$3Fe_2O_3 + CO \rightarrow 2Fe_3O_4 + CO_2$

$CO_2 + C \rightarrow 2CO$
$Fe_3O_4 + CO \rightarrow 3FeO + CO_2$

750°C

$CO_2 + C \rightarrow 2CO$
$FeO + CO \rightarrow Fe + CO_2$

945°C

$CaCO_3 \rightarrow CaO + CO_2$
$CaO + SiO_2 \rightarrow CaSiO_3$

1300°C

1500°C

$C + O_2 \rightarrow CO_2$
$C + O_2 \rightarrow 2CO$

← Hot air from stoves

Glassy $CaSiO_3$ and other silicates

Slag out

Molten pig iron out

Figure 11–2. Blast furnace.

for the collected iron still to contain 4–5% carbon when it is removed from the furnace.

The molten iron is charged from the furnace into a large ladle which transfers the iron directly to a steel-making furnace or pours the iron into molds to produce *pig iron*. Pig iron may be remelted and cast into intricate shapes, sizes, and thicknesses. It reproduces the shapes of sand molds well and is useful in making rigid articles which do not have exacting size tolerance or require the casting to have great shock resistance. If the casting is cooled rapidly the casting may be as brittle as glass. Cast iron formed in this way and having these characteristics is called *white cast iron.* The fractures of white cast iron have a white silky sheen to them. If a cast-iron object is cooled slowly in the mold, most of the carbon separates out of solution in the iron and forms graphite particles which are uniformly distributed throughout the mass of the iron. It is called *gray cast iron.* It machines very well and is much less brittle than white cast iron. Automobile engine blocks, heads, and gear housings are cast from gray cast iron. Holes are bored to size and the rest of the block is drilled and machined to close tolerances.

Low-impurity, low-carbon irons which contain less than 1.2% carbon are known as *steel*. Structural steel contains about 0.2% carbon. It can be bent and hammered without breaking. Steels are more expensive but have properties which allow them to be used for many purposes.

STEEL-MAKING FURNACES   Molten iron from the blast furnace may be transferred directly to a steel-making furnace whose purpose is to burn out the carbon in the melt and remove other impurities. When this has been accomplished, a carefully measured amount of carbon and/or alloying metals may be added to the steel melt to give the resulting steel the desired set of properties.

Steels are superior to high-carbon cast iron in shock resistance and tensile strength. Cast iron is brittle but most steels can be deformed without breaking.

There are four types of steel-making furnaces: (1) Bessemer; (2) open-hearth; (3) basic oxygen furnace (BOF); (4) electric.

Bessemer furnace   In the Bessemer furnace air is blown through the molten iron to burn the excess carbon and other contaminants. The process requires only a few minutes but it produces a relatively poor steel. Less than 2% of present-day steel is made by this method.

Open-hearth furnace   The open-hearth furnace (Figure 11–3) is a large, fire-brick pan covered by a fire-brick roof. As much as 300 tons of molten iron and scrap may be heated by the oxidizing flame that arches between the roof and the pan. In this furnace the oxygen that removes the carbon from the furnace load must diffuse from the flame down into the melt, a slow process. Up to 8 hr of heating are required to remove the dissolved carbon. From charging the furnace to pouring the steel may require 9–13 hr. The process is subject to close control and the steel that is produced is of very high quality.

Figure 11–3. Open-hearth furnace.

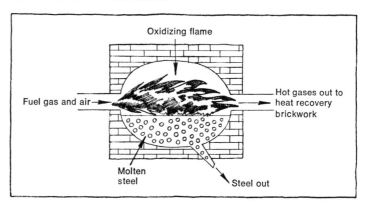

INDUSTRIAL RESOURCES AND THE ENVIRONMENT

Basic oxygen furnace (BOF) The basic oxygen furnace is the Bessemer furnace with oxygen added instead of air (Figure 11-4). It is a pear-shaped, refractory-lined vessel of 100–300 ton capacity. Oxygen at a pressure of 140–180 psi is supplied through the mouth of the vessel by a water-cooled lance. The supersonic stream of oxygen strikes against the surface of the charge and causes turbulence and mixing of the molten contents. In a period of 38 min to 1 hr, the carbon content and the impurities of the iron may be reduced to a satisfactory level, after which the alloying materials are added and the steel poured.

Since its introduction in Europe in 1954 and in the United States in 1963 the BOF has steadily displaced the open-hearth process and now produces over 50% of the steel made in the United States. It is expected that most steel will be made by this process by the year 2000.

At present the BOF cannot use more than 35% scrap iron in its charge; the solid scrap cools the furnace load too much. This difficulty could be removed by introducing fuel for a period of time until the scrap melts and then allowing the oxygen lance to complete the purification step.

Electric furnace The electric furnace has the shape of a large covered "bowl". The roof of the "bowl" carries the electrodes and can be removed so that the furnace can be loaded. The load may be a mix of molten blast furnace iron and scrap or a complete load of scrap.

Electric furnaces now produce 14–20% of the steel produced and they may continue to do so if electrical energy is available. The furnace has the advantages of speed, flexibility, and low capital cost, but its energy requirements

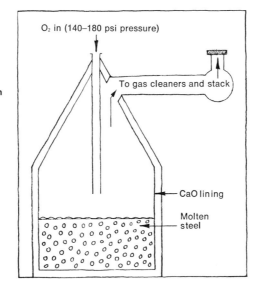

Figure 11-4. Basic oxygen furnace (BOF).

are large and expensive. On a fuel basis, it requires two to three times as much fuel to produce the electricity for electric-furnace steel as it would to heat the batch directly with the burning fuel.

POLLUTION FROM IRON AND STEEL PRODUCTION   Pollution in the industry starts with the mining of the ore. Taconite production produces large volumes of water contaminated with fine particles as well as dust from the pulverizing operation.

The production of coke causes more water pollution. The coke is heated in a closed container for 20–24 hr. At the end of the process the coke is pushed out of the oven and quenched in water. Heat is wasted and water polluted.

Steel-making furnaces cause air and water pollution. The air pollutants are mostly particles. Table 11–1 indicates that the BOF is especially bad in this respect. It not only produces a larger amount of particulate matter but 99.5% of the particles are less than 5 μm in diameter.

Much water is used for cooling. An integrated plant, that is, one with complete operations from blast furnace to final products, can use 10,000 to 50,000 gallons of water per ton of steel and raise the temperature of the water by 150 °F or more. One plant is designed to recycle water in a closed system and uses only 1500 gallons per ton of steel. Huge storage ponds have been built at many plants to allow the impurities to settle, but deep-well disposal is becoming the usual way to dispose of the most contaminated water.

ENERGY IN THE STEEL INDUSTRY   The direct use of fuel supplies most of the energy, but large amounts of electricity are also used. During 1967, 44.6 billion kWh of electrical power were used. This is equivalent to the continuous output of fifty-six 100-MW(e) power plants, but represents only about 35% of the total energy input to the industry.

It is very difficult to find exact data, but each pound of steel manufactured requires about 6–7 kWh of energy. On this basis, the energy from about 2 lb of coal is required for 1 lb of steel.

TABLE 11–1.   Particulate Emissions from Furnaces Producing Iron and Steel.

Process	Percentage of total particles in each of the size ranges					Emission factor (lb/ton)*
	< 5 μm	5–10 μm	10–20 μm	20–44 μm	> 44 μm	
Blast furnace	NA	NA	NA	NA	70.0	40–110 (60–90)
Open-hearth	46.0	22.0	17.0	10.0	5.0	12–20 (85–95)
Basic oxygen	99.5	0.5	0	0	0	46 (99)
Electric	NA	NA	NA	NA	NA	7–11 (97)

Source: Environmental Protection Agency, *Compilation of air pollutant emission factors*, Washington, D.C.: Government Printing Office, 1972, p. A2.
*The numbers in parentheses are the control efficiencies.

Aluminum is the most abundant metal in the earth's crust but it is possible to recover it economically only from the ore bauxite which contains 50–55% alumina (Al_2O_3). The United States has limited bauxite deposits in Arkansas. These deposits, while of excellent quality, produce only about one-tenth of the aluminum used in this country.

Extraction of alumina from bauxite is a chemical process. The alumina is dissolved out of the ore by sodium hydroxide. The alumina is then precipitated, recovered, and dried. Alumina will dissolve in another aluminum salt, called cryolite (Na_3AlF_6). A current is passed through the alumina-cryolite solution. Figure 11–5 shows how the reactions take place. One-half pound of carbon anode is consumed for each pound of aluminum produced. The carbon combines with the oxygen portion of the alumina.

POLLUTION   The red mud-like tailings produced from the production of alumina are a waste problem in the south-central states where 5.5 million tons are discarded annually. Some are dumped in the Mississippi River; most are stored in huge mud lakes near the plants.

Air pollution has long been a problem in areas adjacent to the electrolytic plants where formation of fluoride gases from the cryolite has killed vegetation and animals. Particulates are also produced by aluminum processing. Table 11–2 shows the relationship between primary and secondary (recycling) processes. While the secondary processing produces a larger quantity of small particles, the total quantities produced are such that, overall, the primary

Figure 11–5.   Aluminum production from alumina (Al_2O_3).

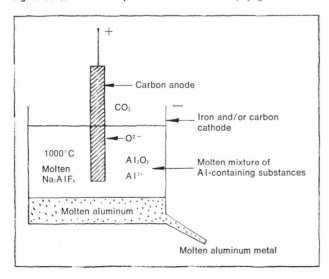

processing causes more pollution. Emission of particles less than 5μm in diameter varies from 3 to 18 lb/ton for primary processing and from 0.6 to 5 lb/ton for secondary processing.

ENERGY USED IN THE ALUMINUM INDUSTRY   Estimates for the gross energy used to produce a pound of aluminum are about 115,000 Btu/lb ($\pm$15%). At least half of this is used in the energy intensive step, the electrolysis of alumina-cryolite solution. At this rate, 10 lb of coal would be needed to produce the energy for one lb of aluminum. Therefore, the production of aluminum would use about 5 times as much energy per unit of weight as does the production of steel.

Two processes to reduce the energy consumed by the production of aluminum are under development. The Alcoa (Aluminum Company of America) process produces aluminum chloride from alumina and chlorine gas. Electricity is used to separate aluminum chloride into aluminum and free chlorine which is recycled to react with more alumina. This process is expected to use about 30% less energy than the present process and will completely eliminate the danger of fluoride air pollution from cryolite.

Another process by AARC (Applied Aluminum Research Corporation) changes the aluminum in bauxite or clay (found in the United States) to aluminum chloride and then frees the aluminum by chemical processes. Not only is less energy used in this process but it would make available the vast low-grade aluminum resources of the United States and end dependence upon imported bauxite or alumina.

Aluminum will always be more energy intensive than iron because large amounts of energy are needed to free the aluminum from combination with other elements in the ore. The aim of the developments is to reduce the amount of energy required to as close to this minimum as possible.

A comparison of energy costs of aluminum and iron must take into account how they are used. Aluminum is much less dense than iron. If the two metals are to be used for making 12-oz. cans, 1 lb of steel will make about nine cans while 1 lb of aluminum will make about 20. Thus, for this application the energy

TABLE 11-2. Comparison of particle emission in production of primary and secondary aluminum.

Process	Percentage of total particles in each of the size ranges					Emission factor (lb/ton)
	$<5\ \mu$m	5–10 μm	10–20 μm	20–40 μm	$>44\ \mu$m	
Primary	13	12	12	13	50	20–140
Secondary	34	20	23	10	3	1.9–14.5

Source: Environmental Protection Agency, *Compilation of air pollutant emission factors*, Washington, D.C.: Government Printing Office, 1972, p. A2.

INDUSTRIAL RESOURCES AND THE ENVIRONMENT

differential between the two metals is reduced from a factor of five to a factor between two and three. Other uses would result in other energy relationships.

Glass is a valuable, versatile material and one of the oldest made by man. It is made by cooling certain molten mineral mixtures so that they retain their liquid properties but become increasingly viscous until, for all practical purposes, they become solids. Glass may be used to make a delicate goblet or a hammer which can drive steel spikes into wooden planks. One type of glass can be dropped from great heights without breaking. Another can form a photographic image while yet another can become darker in sunlight and lighten again in shade (photosensitive glass).

PREPARATION   Sand (silica, SiO_2) can be used to make a glass but its high melting temperature and viscosity make it difficult to work. Silica glass is very expensive. If soda (Na_2O) is added to the sand, a glass is formed that is water soluble. If lime (CaO) is added to the mixture, the common type of glass is formed.

If lime (CaO) and soda (Na_2O) are fused with sand, the melting point of the mixture becomes low enough for the resulting fused glass to be relatively easily worked and formed into common glass articles. Cullet (crushed glass) is also added to the batch to lower the melting point of the mix and to shorten the heating period. In some cases, if sufficient cullet is not available, glass pieces are run and crushed to make the necessary cullet.

Other substances may be added to produce desirable properties. Iron produces a green tint in the glass. Addition of boron oxide (B_2O_3) produces glass which has a low coefficient of thermal expansion, Pyrex. Addition of lead oxide gives a high index of refraction, and addition of alumina adds strength.

Glass production is not a particularly polluting industry but the 2–3 lb/ton of air pollutants produced are all less than 5 μm in diameter.

ENERGY USED IN THE GLASS INDUSTRY   In making glass, energy is used in producing the raw materials, in transporting the raw materials to the manufacturing plant, and in the production of the glass. Less than 1 lb of coal is needed to produce the energy to make 1 lb of glass for containers. Other types of glass would require slightly different amounts of energy.

Paper is everywhere. It is cheap and convenient. There are 12,000 kinds of paper and 100,000 end uses for it.

The consumption of paper and paper products in the United States is about 575 lb per person per year. The next five largest consumers of paper use 200–300 lb less per year than the people of this country. The world average is about 72 lb per person. The people of the United States consume one-third of all the paper produced throughout the world. Domestic use of paper is increasing at the rate of 3% per year. Between 1961 and 1969 paper use increased by 45%.

Consumption is expected to rise from 58.2 million tons in 1969 to 74 million tons by 1980, and to 106 million tons by the year 2000.

FORESTRY Domestic production of pulpwood (pulp is the soft, moist mass produced from the wood and used to make paper) has been rising continuously in the United States. The 1970 production of softwood roundwood was 10% above that of 1969 and 45% above the level of 1960. Production of hardwood roundwood was up 3% over 1969 and 75% higher than 1960. Chip production in 1970 was 3% lower than in 1969, but the overall rise since 1960 was 11%. Sawdust is being increasingly used.

Pulpwood forests have a shorter turnover time than forests planted for lumber. New trees, better for pulp and faster growing, have been developed. A loblolly super pine will grow at the rate of 1 ft per month under the right conditions of fertilizer, water, and pesticides. Paper companies expect to produce seven times as much pulpwood per acre as the usual production.

A substitute for trees for pulpwood has been found in an annual plant, kenaf, which can be cultivated to yield even more pulp. Kenaf makes a good grade of paper.

A researcher from Maine has found that succession plants (plants which grow after a forest is cut) will produce paper pulp. Rights-of-way (electrical lines, fire breaks, etc.) are usually sprayed to kill the succession plants to reduce fire danger. He has been able to make more pulp per unit of time from the succession plants growing on such places than from the forest species. There are about 25 million acres of succession plants in the United States. He believes that they could produce 1.2 tons of wood per year. The wood is 41% fiber, while debarked softwood yields 45% fiber. The woody shrubs need only 30 min cooking while mature wood takes 120 min. The fibers of succession plants are shorter than fibers of mature plants, but are satisfactory for uses not requiring great strength.

With the tremendous increase in paper production that is projected for the next few decades, the pulpwood producers are becoming concerned that there will not be enough wood to supply the papermills. A shortage is possible by 1985. One source of pulp which has not been completely utilized is the waste from other forest industries. Although much lumber mill waste such as slabs, edgings, and cores, is being used, much more of these materials could be used. In addition, large volumes of fine wood materials, such as limbs and twigs, are available.

PRODUCTION OF PAPER Wood is first processed into pulp and then into paper. The production of wood pulp is one of the most polluting industries and one of the most difficult to control.

There are two methods of producing the pulp: (1) ground wood method and (2) sulfite method. In the first method the wood is held against grindstones to produce pulp for cheap, low-strength papers such as newsprint. The second is a chemical process where the pulp is freed from the wood by chemicals and

INDUSTRIAL RESOURCES AND THE ENVIRONMENT

washing operations which cause air and water pollution. The clean pulp is now ready to be made into paper.

POLLUTION IN THE PAPER INDUSTRY   From a distance the overwhelming pollution problem is an odor which has been described as a brew of "boiled cabbage and rotten eggs prepared by a skunk." The description is not unreasonable when the components of the gaseous effluents of skunks and pulp mills are compared. Recent research shows that a skunk produces

to notify you of his presence; a pulp mill will produce the close relatives, hydrogen sulfide (H—S—H, "rotten-egg gas"), methyl mercaptan

and dimethyl sulfide

These compounds result from the use of Na$_2$S and NaOH (sodium sulfide and sodium hydroxide) in the cooking process which dissolve lignin out of the wood to free the cellulose pulp fibers. Lignin is an addition polymer whose exact structure is not known. It adds strength to woody plants. In nature, lignin is resistant to complete decomposition, but it must be removed from pulp because it causes the paper to be low strength and to lose brightness. The sodium sulfide removes methyl groups

$$-\underset{\displaystyle \underset{H}{|}}{\overset{\displaystyle \overset{H}{|}}{C}}-H$$

from the lignin and produces the noxious gases.

Electrical precipitators can remove 99% of the particles from the effluent. Some of the odor-causing gases may be burned but sulfur dioxide is one of the combustion products. Other gases are removed at the point of production.

The waste water from the sulfite pulping process contains 100 g of solids per liter. The chemicals may be reclaimed from the black liquor by evaporation and by burning the organic (lignin) materials that are present. In most sulfite pulp mills, based on calcium bisulfite, the chemicals are not recovered. In this case, the chemicals and dissolved organics are discharged as a part of the waste water.

Large volumes of water are required to wash the pulp free of pulping-process chemicals. If the pulp is bleached, it is treated with chlorine and repeatedly washed. Some solids are lost in each operation and an additional burden is added to the waste stream. Appreciable efficiencies and savings can be effected by reuse of water. By using ponds, lagoons, tanks, bacteria, and settling agents, the waste water is not expected to damage the return stream or lake, but it has the color of tea. The coloring impurity is from bleaching the "grocery bag" color from the pulp. Both industry and the government are trying to find a process which will remove the color from the water.

Paper industries are in the lowest third on earnings of the 27 industries ranked by Forbes (1971). They are money-intensive industries. Since antipollution costs for paper companies are high, most capital expenditures will be depreciated and eventually earnings will be affected. It is claimed that antipollution controls add nothing to production or profit and will cause companies to fail. These are mostly the older plants which would have a relatively short lifetime left.

ENERGY USED BY THE PAPER INDUSTRY   There are many kinds of paper and paperboard so it is difficult to give a general figure for the energy needed to produce a pound of paper. Between 3 and 4.5 kWh are needed to produce a pound of paper. The required energy is equivalent to the heat content of a pound of coal.

DUMP, RECYCLE, REUSE   The choice among dumping, recycling, or reusing tends to depend on economics and convenience in our affluent society. In some cases, recycling would save resources; every ton of waste paper recovered saves 17 trees. In other cases, energy may be saved; processing secondary aluminum is much less energy consuming than producing aluminum from bauxite. In still other cases, reusing is the only way to save energy; recycling glass saves little if any energy but reusing glass containers reduces the energy required to one-third to one-quarter of the energy cost for throwaway containers. These relationships will be explored below.

The percentage of waste paper being recycled in this country has declined from 35% during the 1940's, to 27.4% in 1950, to about 18% in 1970. In 1971 recycled wastepaper increased to about 20%. Some countries have much higher salvage rates for wastepaper: West Germany, 50%; Britain, 25–45%; Japan, 30–40%. All Japanese newsprint must be 50% recycled paper.

Paper

A special kind of ink has been developed to make newsprint deinking a simple process. However, only a small portion of the newsprint used in this country is recycled back into newsprint. Other uses account for more than a quarter of the original paper.

The other big use for waste paper is in the manufacture of boxboard. The contaminants in highly coated paper, such as magazine paper, are not as important in boxboard manufacture as in the manufacture of better grades of paper. Cleaning highly coated paper is an expensive process and needs twice the pollution control equipment because of the "gunkier" nature of the waste. Small amounts of other types of paper are made from waste paper.

From an energy point of view, there is no question but that glass containers should be reused and aluminum cans should be recycled or banned. Returnable glass containers use less energy than throwaway containers or steel or aluminum cans.

Containers

There are many problems which must be solved if recycled glass is to be successful. Before recycling, the glass must be collected and sorted. Many sorting machines are in use and others are being developed. At this writing, information on energy relationships is available on only one, the Black-Clawson machine used in a pilot study at Franklin, Ohio. Efficiency in recovering glass is low, 50% for the separating process and 60% for the sorting process for a net efficiency of 30%. Energy use is high, many times the energy required to make the glass from raw materials. If the recovered glass is used for making asphalt or building materials, the energy is 60 times higher than using conventional methods. Each glass manufacturer has a slightly different formula for making glass. If the different kinds of glass are mixed, the product may be unsatisfactory.

Materials dumped as litter or as landfill are eventually recycled by nature. The exact lifetime in the environment depends not only on the material but also on the climate, humidity, temperature, and the type of soil. Paper is readily biodegradable. It will disappear in a few months. Steel or tin-coated steel may disappear in a year or more, or it may take over 50 years in an arid climate.

Aluminum is more resistant to degradation and probably would require about 500 years to disintegrate.

Less is known about plastics. Polyvinyl chloride (PVC), a plastic used to make bottles, has a half-life of 85 years if buried. In about 350 years 95% would have disappeared. On top of the ground, it would take longer. Many plastics contain poisons which kill the bacteria that attack them. Plastics are being developed that will biodegrade. Their use as bottles must be balanced against the amount of petroleum available and other uses for it.

Ordinary glass is a durable material; it might not break down naturally for millions of years.

The social, political, economic, and emotional side of the container controversy is more difficult to assess. The needs and desires of the producers, consumers, and environmentalists are in conflict. Will the American public buy returnables? Industry says, "No." The environmentalists say, "Yes, if they have a chance." If they buy them will they return them? Again industry says, "No" and the environmentalists say, "Yes, at least in some places."

There is no doubt that changes would be necessary in industry, but the overall effect is difficult to determine. Jobs in the glass and can industries would be reduced, but low-paying jobs in retailing and distribution would increase. Breweries and bottlers might be forced to decentralize. Even the possible effect of a decreased need for steel on the trade balance would have some effect on the economy. Because the subject is so complex, everyone can find arguments to support his position.

Throwaways are handled either by municipal garbage systems or by volunteer organizations. Environmentalists look upon the volunteer organizations as a subsidy for the industry. The industry looks upon them as a chance for the volunteer organization to make money. The handling of throwaways by municipal garbage collectors is looked upon as a subsidy or as a public service, depending on the point of view.

What ultimately is decided about the container dispute will be based on factors other than science.

Iron and Steel

Unmined ore is useful indefinitely; scrap deteriorates.[2]

There are three kinds of scrap: (1) *home scrap*, 60% of total; (2) *prompt industrial scrap*, 16% of total; (3) *obsolete scrap*, 24% of total. Home scrap is scrap which is used in the factory where it was produced. It is especially valuable because its chemical composition is known. Prompt industrial scrap is waste from fabrication processes. It is produced in one factory and sold to another. Obsolete scrap is iron or steel which has been used and discarded. Obsolete ships, railroad equipment, and manufacturing equipment supply the largest portion of this type of scrap. Cans, appliances, and cars contribute a small percentage of the total obsolete scrap.

2. U.S. Department of Commerce, *Iron and steel scrap, consumption problems*, Washington, D.C.: Government Printing Office, 1966, p. 40.

Scrap is valuable even when it costs more than an equal amount of iron ore. A ton of scrap saves three tons of raw materials, including the energy needed to reduce the ore. However, the freight rate for scrap iron is two-and-one-half times the rate for iron ore. The iron content of scrap iron is about 90% and for iron ore 60%, so to be economically feasible the freight rate for scrap iron would need to be one-and-a-half times the rate for iron ore.

Scrap does cause problems however, both in collection and preparation and in its use in industry. Automobile scrap is difficult to prepare. Burning cars to remove organic matter causes air pollution. Special incinerators have been developed, but they are expensive. Alloying elements and coatings cause undesirable effects in steel. For example, tin from tin cans builds up in steel when the steel is repeatedly recycled. Additions of tin cans at each recycling causes steel to become brittle. The tin can be removed and sold, but the process is not economically feasible. At present, most of the recovered tin cans are used to recover copper metal from copper ore in the southwestern United States.

Copper from cars produces undesirable effects if present in steel in quantities larger than 0.2%. It is possible to engineer copper removal into the design of the automobile. Many alloying materials cannot be removed from the iron. When scrap cars are used in steel making, molybdenum and nickel, among other metals, progressively increase in the steel. Most steel makers refuse to use any junk automobiles in their steel. If cans are made from the steel obtained from junk automobiles, the cans may contain trace elements which can dissolve in food placed in the can. Cadmium is one of the elements which can leach into food from cans made from recycled automobile bodies. Some uses are not sensitive to the trace elements found in scrap.

The average car uses about 31,000 kWh of energy, or the energy from 3 tons of coal, for its construction. Dr. R. Stephen Berry of the University of Chicago has calculated that maximum recycling of car materials would save about 10% of the energy used in making a car. However, extending the lifetime of the car might reduce its energy use by a factor of 5, 10, or more. Extending the lifetime of the car might make the car cost more in dollars but, if the car lasted twice as long, it could logically cost twice as much without increasing the cost of transportation.

The secondary materials industry takes scrap iron, scrap metals, paper stock, secondary textiles, rubber, and plastic scrap, and recycles and reclaims recoverable materials. On an annual basis, it is a 5–7 billion dollar industry.

In 1968 the industry produced 45% of the copper, 20% of the aluminum, 40% of the lead, 18% of the zinc, and 15–20% of the nickel used in the United States. The recovered nickel and copper represents 31% and 1.1%, respectively, more than the domestic production of the metals.

The industry feels that it could reclaim more materials if it were given the opportunity. Zoning, air pollution equipment, urban renewal limitations, highway construction, and beautification regulations are shutting the industry out of the most favorable locations.

Secondary Materials Industry

1. Minerals: demand and resource base.
2. Energy, pollution, and processes of the iron and steel, aluminum, glass, and paper industries.
3. Recycling and reusing: difficulties and prospects.

QUESTIONS 1. Discuss the problems of recovering minerals from very lean sources.
2. What are the prospects of substituting one substance for another which is scarce?
3. What are the advantages of the basic oxygen steel-making furnace?
4. What factors determine whether it is economical to recycle glass bottles?
5. What factors enter into the recycling of paper?
6. Distinguish between the terms "reuse" and "recycle."
7. Fertilized loblolly pine forests can produce seven times as much pulpwood as an unfertilized plot. Assess the long-term prospects of this practice.
8. It is proposed that reuse of containers be controlled by use of a deposit charge. What problems arise if the deposit is (a) low, for example, at 2¢ per bottle, and (b) high, for example, at 15¢ per bottle?
9. (a) What kind of development should the developing countries undertake?
(b) What should be the role of the industrialized countries in these developments?
10. What are the advantages of a tax related to the lifetime of the goods (the longer the lifetime, the lower the tax)?
11. Who benefits from the use of throwaways? Who benefits from the use of returnables?

BIBLIOGRAPHY 1. Cloud, P., "Mined out!" *Ecologist*, 1: 25–29, Aug. 1970.
2. Hannon, B. M., "Bottles, cans, energy," *Environment,* 14:11–21, March 1972.
3. Makhijani, A. B., and Lichtenberg, A. J., "Energy and well-being," *Environment,* 14:10–18, June 1972.
4. Meadows, D. H., *et al., The limits of growth,* New York: Universe Books, 1972, pp. 54–69.
5. *Mineral facts and problems,* Bureau of Mines Bulletin 640, Washington, D.C.: Government Printing Office, 1970.

12 Energy in the Future

The nation's energy problem is more than the search for more oil and coal, the hope of the breeder and fusion reactor, and the pursuit of more efficient energy converters.[1]

Although the exact amount of available fossil fuels is controversial, supplies are finite. In the short term, the amount immediately available to us in the United States depends upon governmental action by the United States and by other countries throughout the world. It also depends upon the amount demanded by other countries. The supplies will need to be shared.

Nuclear energy has many problems. If fusion can be made to work commercially, it is a certain energy source for the future. However, if the development of fusion is found to be impossible, reliance now upon its future development could be disastrous.

There are several courses of action available: (1) technological developments, (2) alternative sources of energy, and (3) energy conservation.

Technology can help reduce the amount of energy needed during energy production, energy transport, or energy use. More efficient air conditioners and automobiles which use less energy are probable technological developments of the future. Because electricity may be the energy of the future, any method which can produce it or transport it more efficiently is important. Three developments involving electricity are: (1) superconductivity, (2) magnetohydrodynamics (MHD), and (3) fuel cells.

Considerable power is usually lost in the transmission of electricity from the generating plant to the consumer. The loss is due to the *resistance* which the conductor has to the passage of the electrical current. The resistance of the wire to the flow of the current causes the wire to be heated. As the wire becomes warmer, the resistance of the wire increases and a larger amount of heat is produced for a given amount of current. In an overhead line the heat produced is dissipated to the air; the temperature of the conductor is kept low and the resistance of the conductor is kept relatively low. On the other hand, an underground line cannot dissipate the heat as rapidly; its temperature rises and its resistance is increased. On the average, an overhead line loses about 10% of the electrical energy that it carries as heat to the air. Underground lines lose twice as much because they operate at a higher temperature where the resistance to current flow is greater.

In a wire at normal temperatures, some outer-shell electrons are rather loosely held by the metal conductor. During the passage of an electric current only a very few electrons are passed along the wire. When the temperature of a wire is increased, the random motions of atoms and electrons are increased and it is more difficult to force the electrons to flow along the conductor. The overall effect appears as resistance to the flow of electrical current. Conversely, cooling the conductor leads to less resistance (greater conductivity). The maximum effect occurs at *supercooling* temperatures.

It is possible to improve the conductivity of certain conductors by cooling them to a temperature of 5–18 °K (−450 to −428 °F or −268 to −255 °C). These temperatures are near the boiling point of liquid helium. At these low

1. "We are all part of the problem . . .", *Technol. Rev.* 75:52, July–Aug. 1972.

temperatures (supercooled) niobium-tin and niobium-copper bimetal combinations are capable of carrying 10 times as much current as an ordinary copper conductor of the same size. Such high conductivity (*superconductivity*) allows transformers and electric motors to be made much smaller than would normally be possible.

Supercooling of conductors is achieved by refrigerating a conductor with liquid helium. If the system is to be effective, outside heat energy must be prevented from entering the system. This calls for nearly perfect insulation, otherwise the refrigeration system would rapidly lose its low temperature and the conductor would not be superconductive. A very good insulating material has been developed which allows liquid helium and hydrogen to be transported by tank car. Such insulation should be adequate for a helium-refrigerated superconducting line. Helium is the best refrigerant. However, helium resources are limited.

HELIUM RESOURCES   The United States has most of the helium resources of the world. There are small recovery plants in France and Canada. The Soviet Union recovers about 70 million cubic ft per year. The scarcity of helium is shown by the high percentage of helium that is recycled by foreign nations.

Helium occurs in most natural gas deposits, but only a few wells contain more than 0.3%. Below this level it is not economical to recover the helium. It is estimated that our reserves of helium in natural gas deposits which contain more than 0.3% helium amount to 165 billion cubic ft. A total of 8.5 billion cubic ft of helium is being exhausted each year. Eight per cent of the helium reserves occur in natural gas of low heating value. For this reason, these reserves are not being processed. They remain stored underground where they are accessible for recovery at a later date when they are needed.

The major field is in the Oklahoma-Texas area, although there are some wells in Arizona. No new wells are expected to be discovered. The last helium producer was drilled in 1943.

It is expected that the United States will exhaust its helium reserves and stored supplies by the year 2000. In 1967, 907 million cubic ft of United States helium was used, including 25 million cubic ft that was exported. In the year 2000 it is conservatively estimated that the demand will range from 1400 to 3600 million cubic ft.

Unless we undertake strict recovery and reuse of helium, we will find it necessary to use unsatisfactory or expensive substitutes such as hydrogen and argon. Because of the high price of helium, other countries are already practicing conservation techniques.

ALTERNATIVES TO HELIUM-COOLED ELECTRICAL TRANSMISSION   Nitrogen is being suggested as a substitute for supercooling. It does not produce a true superconductive state but does improve the conductivity of a line at less cost. Since nitrogen constitutes almost 80% of the air, there is no supply problem. It may also be possible to discover alloys or metal combinations which will provide superconductive effects at higher temperatures.

Some experts say that refrigerating electrical lines would make it economical to transmit current over long distances. Others say that it will cost more energy for refrigeration purposes than is saved by the superconductivity that is produced. The United States government has been reluctant to give research grants for superconductive systems.

Conventional overhead lines cannot carry more than 500 kW per line. If the voltage in the line is large, energy is lost because electrons are lost from the wire by arcing between the wires. If the voltage is relatively small, a much larger electrical current is required to transport a given amount of energy. The movement of a larger amount of electrons requires a larger conductor. Ten overhead lines, each with three cables, would be needed to carry as much electricity as a 4-in. underground, supercooled cable. The entire area above the underground cable could be used, while only parts of the area under the overhead line can be used. These advantages must be balanced against the cost of supercooling the wire. The esthetics of tearing up the land for the cable and cooling stations must be balanced against the esthetics of the huge towers needed to hold the lines.

Magnetohydrodynamics (MHD) holds the promise that electrical power may be provided more efficiently than is possible by a steam power plant which is 40% efficient at best. If MHD systems can be made to produce electricity at a heat efficiency of 60%, it would save 50% in fuel, produce 50% less air pollution, reject 50% less heat to the environment, and perhaps not produce any thermal pollution of water.

Magnetohydrodynamics

An MHD device produces high voltage direct current. A potassium salt is introduced into a burner (Figure 12–1) where it is ionized by the high temperature and blown downstream from the burner through an intense magnetic field. The magnetic lines of force act at right angles to the axis of the channel and to the direction of the movement of the ions. The fast moving ions cut across the magnetic lines and are forced sideways; the negative ions move toward one side and the positive ions move toward the opposite side. Thus, oppositely charged ions are separated and collected at opposite electrodes.

Work is required to separate the charges and to force them to the collecting electrodes. The energy for this work is extracted from the hot gases which attempt to force the ions through the channel and out the exhaust end. The kinetic energy of the gas is thus transferred to the electrodes. When the electrodes are connected by wires to an external electrical load, work is done in the external circuit where the power is used by an electric motor or other electric device. If no load is applied across the electrodes, energy is not used and charges accumulate on the electrodes. When the charges build up sufficiently, the electrodes repel incoming ions and force them to remain in the gas stream and no useful work is done.

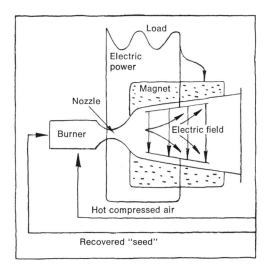

Figure 12–1. Magnetohydro-dynamic (MHD) generator.

It is necessary that a MHD unit operate at a temperature near 2760 °C (5000 °F) to dissociate potassium compounds into ions which would provide the conductive medium in the channel. The potassium ions are called the *working fluid*. Since conductivity is halved for each 132–182 °C (270–360 °F) lowering of the temperature, the temperature must be maintained as high as practicable. The higher the conductivity of the gas stream, the greater the amount of power that can be produced. Furthermore, the higher the temperature, the more efficient the system.

In order to attain the high temperature, the input air to the burner must be preheated to about 1093 °C (2000 °F) and compressed to 20–30 atms. Sometimes oxygen is used in place of air. If air is used for combustion, large volumes of gases must be compressed. If oxygen is used, a considerable amount of energy will be required to separate the oxygen from the air. In either case, some of the energy produced by the unit will be consumed in providing the air supply, thus reducing the net energy available for sale.

The hot gases may or may not be vented to the atmosphere. If they are vented, the system is relatively inefficient, probably less than 20%. However, the system using vented gases may be used as a *topping unit* for a conventional steam power plant or gas turbine, that is, the hot gases are run through an MHD unit before they operate a conventional turbine. Here, of course, the efficiency of the system is increased.

Magnetohydrodynamics holds promise of greater efficiency in use of energy but its commercial feasibility is in doubt. There are no commercial units in the United States. A Russian pilot plant has encountered technical problems.

ENERGY IN THE FUTURE

DIFFICULTIES WITH MHD SYSTEMS   All MHD systems must be run at as high a temperature as is practical. The high temperatures put severe demands upon structural materials. Channels erode rapidly under the hot blast conditions. Zirconium dioxide is the preferred material for electrodes. It is temperature resistant and conducts electricity at high temperatures. However, it does erode and fuse with the potassium seed which collects on it. Perhaps the electrodes and channels can be made of disposable materials and thus reduce costs.

The conductive seed for the MHD system costs several times as much as coal fuel would. It is necessary to achieve 99% recovery of the seed if the process is to be economical. Cesium is two to three times as conductive as potassium at a given temperature, but is so costly that it would be necessary to recover 99.9% to make it economical. Such a high degree of recovery is not probable.

Most tests of MHD prototypes use clean gaseous (methane) or liquid (petroleum) fuels. Since coal is the fossil fuel with the largest resources, a coal-fueled MHD system would be most desirable from an economical standpoint.

The abrasive fly ash from coal would erode the electrodes. However, the potassium content of the ash would supply an appreciable amount of conductive seed and make recovery of seed more economical. Perhaps an answer to the abrasion problem would be to use gasified coal.

The higher the combustion temperature (as in automobiles) the larger the amount of nitrogen oxide air pollutants becomes. There is some thought that the proportions of nitrogen oxides may be enough to make it economical to process the exhaust gases and recover nitric acid together with sulfuric acid from SO_2.

An MHD system is capable of fast (1 sec) start up. There in no inertia, that is, no heavy equipment to start moving. Therefore, MHD would be valuable for supplying power for peak loads and this may be its main field of usage. It will be less useful for continuous operation as a base-load generator. With all of its problems MHD is not expected to be commercially available until at least the year 1985.

Fuel Cells

A *fuel cell* is a device which changes a fuel directly to electricity. The most common fuel cell is the hydrogen-oxygen (air) cell. Hydrogen gas (H:H) reacts at one catalytic electrode (anode) to lose electrons and produce hydrogen ions (H^+). The removed electrons are transported (Figure 12–2) through an external circuit (wire and load) to the cathode (opposite electrode) where they are removed by the O_2 and oxide ions

$$: \overset{..}{\underset{..}{O}} :^{2-}$$

are formed.

Thus the catalytic action of the electrodes and the strong electron-holding ability of oxygen atoms allows oxygen to remove electrons from hydrogen

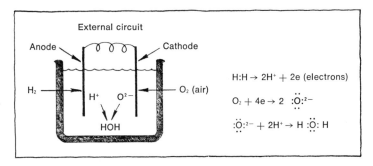

Figure 12-2. Diagram of a fuel cell.

atoms by way of the external circuit. The end product formed by this catalytic battery-like process is the same as that formed by the direct molecular reaction of hydrogen and oxygen:

$$H_2 + \tfrac{1}{2}O_2 \rightarrow H_2O + energy$$

Electrical energy can be obtained directly from fuels without the use of a heat system such as steam or hot gases. Theoretically, fuel cells can be 100% efficient; practically, they may be more than 60% efficient. The efficiency of a hydrogen-oxygen fuel cell can never exceed the efficiency of the energy needed to produce the fuel. If the hydrogen is produced from electricity which is 40% efficient, the overall efficiency of the fuel cell is 40% or less.

Hydrogen may be obtained by other means. Organic compounds may be decomposed to yield hydrogen gas. The efficiency of this system is suspect because fuel energy would be consumed in the decomposition of the organic compound. The nonhydrogen part of the compound would be wasted. It is very likely that more useful energy would be obtained from complete combustion of the organic fuels instead of going through a fuel cell unit.

Hydrogen-oxygen fuel cells may be useful if the hydrogen could provide a convenient storage system for energy which is produced intermittently and used at times when power is not being produced. This situation applies especially to the diffuse energy systems such as the sun, wind, and tides. A further advantage is that the hydrogen could be transported great distances, if necessary, by use of conventional gas-line networks.

Several other substances may substitute for hydrogen as the source of fuel. Natural gas has been used and is very efficient as a producer of electricity. Other sources, carbon monoxide (CO), hydrazine (N_2H_4), and zinc or aluminum metals, must be manufactured before they can be used in the fuel cell. They can only be as efficient as the energy source required to make them.

If fuel cells could be developed that would completely consume petroleum, or even better coal, in a fuel system, then a very viable arrangement would exist.

Under these circumstances the full efficiency of the energy source would be available. Fuel cells have a future only if primary fuels are consumed directly or if the fuel is produced, because the manufactured fuel is the most efficient energy storage system available.

Hydropower—flood control—irrigation—recreation—transport; a river is many things to many people, each of whom see the river as providing the maximum of benefits to himself.

A man living on the flood plain thinks of the river as "that blasted river!" Every spring it delays planting and if a crop is planted the river often floods it out: "The river must be controlled." A man living on arid land sees the river as a source of water. What he needs to make himself wealthy is water, cheap water. It is a shame to let all that beautiful fresh water flow uselessly into the sea. A river barge captain fights flood waters and snags on sand bars. The river must be regulated. A river is fine for boating and fishing but you really could speed around if it were wider. There is power in that water; it should be harnessed. Power is desperately needed—cheap power, nonpolluting power.

All of these people see a common solution—dam the river. Dammed it is. The water is ready to perform its new tasks. Land is drowned to form a large lake and water laps high on the hills. The recreational boater has room to roar around, the river is kept away from the door of the river-flats dweller, and the barges have a regulated flow. The turbines turn relentlessly and the farmer obtains irrigation water.

However, no one gets all that he wants. During certain seasons the water may be drawn down to reveal mud flats. The water that is diverted to irrigation cannot be used for production of power or increasing stream flow. The water that produced power cannot be used for irrigation except as it is used to pump water to farms across the mountain. The erosive power and the sediment-carrying capacity of the river is reduced by the new placidity of its waters. The amounts of fresh water and dissolved nutrients which reach the sea are reduced and changed over a period of time. The balance of sea life at the mouth of the river is changed and fish catches are reduced. The lake behind the dam collects and eventually is filled by the silt carried into it. For example, Santa Ynez River has provided water for the city of Santa Barbara in California:

To create a reservoir . . . Santa Barbara built a dam. Alas, they found that the reservoir quickly built up silt behind the dam, until they faced imminent possibility of a flat plain of silt over which the Santa Ynez would flow to turn the dam into a waterfall. So Santa Barbara built another dam. Same problem. Now they have built a third dam. If we are spared death by nuclear war or by depredations of Engineers, some future explorer will locate a strange river flowing to the sea in California, over an odd series of flat alluvial plains, one above the other. They will probably grow vegetation eventually, but they will probably never be as pretty as the original Santa Ynez River bed.[2]

Two thousand dams in the United States are completely silted. Lake Powell on the Colorado River will be silted in 200 years.

Dammed water creates problems for fish. Water held in a lake behind a dam becomes warmer than a river. The oxygen content of the water is reduced. When the water spills from the dam, it entraps nitrogen and causes nitrogen narcosis and bends in fish downstream. The dam effectively blocks spawning runs of fish. Fish ladders (a series of ascending pools arranged to allow fish to swim around or over a dam) are not adequate answers to the problem. Fish follow the current upstream, and the lake behind a dam does not have a current. If the fish are able to reach the lake, they lose direction and do not find their way to the spawning areas at the head waters of the stream.

A river is expected to be a bountiful horn of plenty to all. The benefits are proclaimed to exceed the costs, but almost always the costs exceed the benefits. Robert Haveman of Duke University studied every Corps of Engineers project in 19 states. He used five separate accepted accounting methods and found that 63 of 147 projects did not pass any of the cost-benefit evaluations and none of them met the requirements of all tests. He found that flood control and reclamation projects ruin more land than they protect. These failures did not take into consideration the effects upon fish, streamside economics, or soil fertility. The story is told by the Aswan dam and the Nile, the Grand Coulee dam and the Columbia, the dams of the Colorado, and many others.

Grand Coulee was to produce 5575 MW(e); years after erection it produces only 2000 MW(e).

Lake Nasser behind the Aswan dam is not yet full of water, and probably never will be, but its lake is full of choking water hyacinths. The fish catch is disappointing. The soil of the flood plain of the Nile is being salted to death (see Chapter 4). The lack of water and volcanic silt has destroyed the prolific fishery at the mouth of the Nile. The fertility of the soil has decreased because of lack of silt. One-and-a-half million acres have been added to production, but now Egypt imports pesticides and fertilizer instead of food. The irrigation canals of the lower Nile have been invaded by a snail which infects the people with bilharzia. This is a debilitating disease caused by a parasite. There is a drug which can cure the disease, but the drug is almost as dangerous as bilharzia. Even if cured, the people will be reinfected as soon as they work in the irrigation water. In some areas up to 80% of the people are affected. The potential for damage by a mosquito from the Sudan is even greater. In 1942 the mosquito invaded a small area of Egypt where it killed 100,000 out of 1 million affected before the World Health Organization (WHO) could eradicate it. Now, with Lake Nasser reaching within 50 miles of the mosquito's habitat, it would be impossible to eradicate.

2. Gene Marine, *America the raped,* New York: Simon & Schuster, 1969, p. 159.

As economist Kenneth Boulding has said:

The only way you would explain the water policy in this country was the religious explanation that we worship the water goddess, and hence had to build all those dams and temples. There is no other conceivable rational explanation.[3]

Tidal Power

Man has long wanted to harness the energy in tides. In order to do this it is necessary to build a dam across a coastal basin where a two-way turbine can be turned by the twice-daily filling and emptying cycle. During President Kennedy's term of office, the development of such a power plant was discussed but never built. France has the largest operating power station, a 240,000 kW(e) installation. There are relatively few places which are suitable for tidal power development. If all were to be developed, only 13 million kW(e) could be produced, in the opinion of M. King Hubbert.

It may be that it is safe to exploit tidal power. If so, it is there to be used. However, up to the present (1973) tidal power has not been considered to be economically feasible in the areas which would be served by the power.

Geothermal Energy

In Yellowstone Park steam and hot water gush forth. These phenomena are common or possible in volcanic or earthquake-prone regions of the world where earth heat may be available near the surface. In some places, man is harnessing this heat to provide electrical power.

The total amount of heat stored in the earth is very large; removing enough heat to cool the earth a mere half a degree centigrade would provide enough energy to supply electricity for 2 million years at the present rate of use. The heat is thought to be essentially inexhaustible.

Heat is bleeding from the depths at the rate of 1.5 millionths of a calorie per square centimeter per second. When a hole is bored into the crust of the earth, the temperature of the rock rises about 5 °C for each 1000-ft increase in depth. At 20,000 ft the temperature is high enough to boil water; at a depth of 20–40 miles the temperature may be 1100 °C. Rock is plastic (like wet modeling clay) at this temperature and can flow from place to place.

The more accessible earth heat is found where earthquake and volcanic actions occur: California, Mexico, Alaska, Japan, New Zealand, Italy, and Russia. In these places earth slippage faults extend several hundred kilometers deep into the globe. Molten magma (rock) circulates upward along the earth fractures and carries heat close to the surface. Here it may meet ground water which is converted to high-temperature water and/or steam. The hot water may be trapped underground by an impervious rock layer or by hydrostatic pressure such that it can be heated above its normal atmospheric boiling point, just as water in a pressure cooker or steam boiler can be heated to a higher temperature than its boiling point at atmospheric pressure.

3. F. F. Darling and J. P. Milton (eds.), *Future environments of North America*, Garden City: Natural History Press, 1966, p. 198.

The geothermal heat reservoir can be reached by drilling through the overlying rock layers to a depth of 500–7000 ft. However, it is unusual to drill down more than 6000 ft. The temperature of the resource may be from 80 to 3000 °C and may be hot water or dry steam. Twenty hot-water wells are discovered for each dry-steam well. When a hot-water well nears exhaustion it changes into a dry-steam well. The temperature of the steam somewhat compensates for the lower flow by being more efficient because of its higher temperature, as high as 700 °C.

Steam is a lean resource (not rich; in this case, steam does not contain large amounts of energy) and geothermal water requires large-diameter wells to produce a sufficiently large flow of relatively low-pressure steam to flow through the turbines. The lower the temperature of the steam, the larger the equipment required. In order to provide large flows, steam wells are usually 12–24 in. in diameter.

The geothermal water may be a brine containing as much as 33% solids. As it rises in the drill pipe it may flash into a steam and leave a residue of solids in the pipe. Eventually the accumulation of solids may become great enough markedly to reduce the flow or completely block the passage. When this occurs, the well must either be drilled or replaced by another well. At a price of $58–170 per meter of well, this can be an expensive operation. In fact, the wells are the major expense in exploitation of geothermal resources.

Geothermal steam is acclaimed to be pollution-free power. However, each well in the Geysers development in California vents 1000 lb of high-density H_2S gas each day. In addition, ammonia gas escapes and boron and other mineral salts pollute the waters of the area.

When water, oil, or any other material is removed from the ground some of the support for the overlying layers is removed (Chapter 4). Water or steam supports the surface in a way analogous to the manner in which a water bed supports a person or an inflated tire supports a car. When the water or steam is removed from a cavity, the soil subsides. The sinking may be countered by injecting water or waste brine into the formation, probably through a second well. It is possible to inject so much fluid that, instead of subsiding, the land surface is lifted, an occurrence which may be as undesirable as subsidence.

POWER PLANT   Steam flashing from a hot brine in a well may entrain some of the solids and carry them into the power plant. The solids must be removed from the steam flow before it passes through the turbine, where the solids will damage the blades. For this reason, solid particles are removed by a cyclone separator (Chapter 3, Cleaning Stack Gases). In a noncondensing power plant, cleaned raw steam is passed directly through the turbine and immediately vented to the atmosphere. This system is very wasteful but it is frequently used for small installations in the 500–600-kW range.

Larger plants make more efficient use of geothermal energy by condensing the exhaust steam. This lowers the low-temperature factor of the efficiency equation (see Chapter 8). Large amounts of cooling water from a natural source or cooling tower are required for the condenser unit, but the increased efficiency pays for the cost of the installation.

The energy in the low-temperature geothermal water can be recovered by using a secondary liquid with a low boiling point to turn the turbine. A secondary liquid, such as Freon or isobutane, receives the geothermal heat at an intermediate heat exchanger. The fluid boils and the vapor passes through the turbine. The exhaust vapors, of course, are condensed and pumped back to the heat exchange boiler to repeat the cycle.

LIFE OF FIELD   Each well or field has a different energy potential. At present there is not enough information to predict the lifetime of a geothermal structure. In the United States a well usually lasts an average of 20 years, in Japan, 10, and in Iceland, 7.

In the beginning a well may produce 7–15 MW but tails off to 1–3 MW toward the end of its life. When production becomes small it is necessary to redrill the well or replace it. Italian experiences indicate that a steam field lasts for 30 to 60 years. Estimates for other fields range from 50 to 100 or even 300 years. There really is not enough information upon which to base a judgement. However, from the decrease in production from a field it can be determined that energy is being withdrawn from fields at many times the rate at which it is being replenished by natural heat flow from beneath. In New Zealand this factor is 4 times; in Iceland, 9 times; in Lardello, Italy, 10 times; at Geysers, California, 170 times.

The geothermal potential of the Imperial Valley in Southern California is about 20,000–30,000 MW; for the entire United States it is perhaps 100,000 MW. Fully developed, these resources could supply 5–10% of the power demands of the Western states.

Geothermal power is economically attractive. It is being actively pursued by the "energy" companies, such as Union Oil, as part of their trend toward horizontal expansion into all forms of energy. The companies have broad experience in dealing with exploration and drilling operations.

The sun powers the winds, the ocean currents, hurricanes, and tornados (Figure 12–3). It supplies the energy with which plants synthesize the foodstuffs for themselves and parasites including humans. Over a period of millions of years the sun pumped in the energy now stored in coal and oil. The sun powers the earth.

The amount of solar energy supplied to a surface depends upon the location of the surface (Figure 12–4). Outside the atmosphere of the earth 1.4 kW of energy would fall upon 1 square meter of surface. In passing through the earth's atmosphere, 0.4 kW (30%) of the sun's energy is absorbed and only 1 kW (70%) falls on 1 square meter. Since the sun is not always overhead during the day, the amount of energy received averages about 0.83 kW per square meter for an 8-hr sun day. Thus, a maximum of 6.64 kWh of energy would be recovered each 24 hr. However, over most of the surface of the earth, the sun never reaches the

Solar Energy

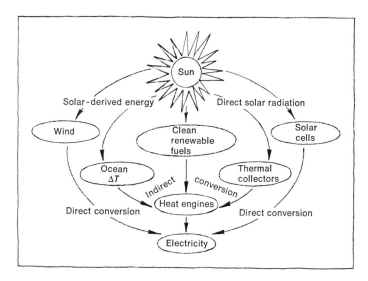

Figure 12–3. Solar energy.

zenith. For example, at Boulder, Colorado, on the longest day of the year the sun at noon still passes 17° below the zenith, and on the shortest day of the year the angle is 62° below the zenith. Assuming an average declination from overhead for the sun of 45° throughout the year, a square meter of horizontal surface will receive energy at a power rate of 0.585 kW or a maximum of 4.68 kWh of energy each 8-hr day. The power rating is sufficient to light six 100-W bulbs for the 8 hr that the sun supplies power; currently only about 10% of this can be recovered. A large surface area would be needed to collect enough of this diffuse energy to yield the energy equivalent of a 1000-MW power plant.

An informative estimate of the sun's power potential is given by calculating the amount of solar energy which would fall on a football field at Boulder using the 0.585 kW per square meter average energy input. Taking a yard to equal the length of a meter, the area of the field would be 50 m by 100 m or 5000 square meters. Thus, the energy falling on the field would be equivalent to 23,400 kWh of electrical energy each 8-hr day, enough to supply 100 families for a month.

Natural inputs of energy to the earth, such as natural sunlight, are invariant additions or sources of energy. Thus, sunlight, the slow seepage of heat from the depths of the earth, wind, tides, and water power are invariant sources of energy. Any source of energy which adds to the natural equilibrium inputs of energy is a variant source. Fossil and nuclear fuels, geothermal energy, and energy from space stations are variant sources of energy.

The invariant sources tend to have a natural balance over centuries of time. However, over eons of geological time, the heat balance of the earth has

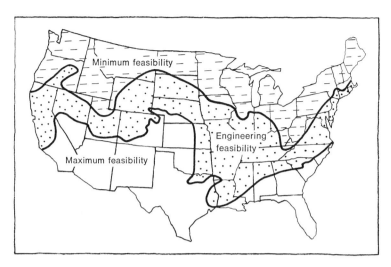

Figure 12–4. Zones indicating the feasibility of solar heating in the United States.
Courtesy of Presstech Design, Inc., from "Space heating with solar energy," *Heating and Ventilating*, September 1950, pp. 88–90.

changed as is evidenced by the glaciers. Variant sources would tend to change the natural balance. The effects may be negligible or significant.

SOLAR COLLECTORS   The perfect collector of solar energy would trap all frequencies of radiation and would not permit radiation to escape from the receptor system. Depending on the collecting system, the efficiency of collecting and concentrating solar energy varies from 2% to 70%. A 2% efficiency does not necessarily mean that the system is impractical, nor does a 70% efficiency mean that the system is practical. Cost of equipment and special circumstances may determine the economic value of solar energy trapping systems.

The collectors and/or concentrators of radiation may be flat-bed collectors, inclined-bed collectors, specially coated surfaces, large natural areas of land or sea, converging mirrors or lenses, or solar cells. Whatever the method, the receiver must intercept the rays from the sun and must not interfere with or shade other receptors.

Flat-bed black absorbers (black absorbers trap all color and all frequencies) serve to trap solar energy where relatively low temperatures are required, such as greenhouses, house heating, and domestic hot-water heating. A greenhouse is warmer inside than (Figure 12–5) outside because glass is transparent to the high-frequency rays of sunlight. Visible radiation is converted to invisible lower-frequency, lower-energy infrared rays and heat (molecular motion). The glass does not allow all of the longer infrared rays to escape. When infrared

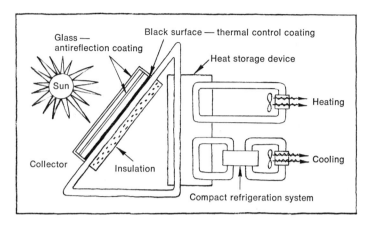

Figure 12–5. Flat-bed collector of solar energy for heating and cooling buildings.

rays are absorbed, some of the energy is converted to molecular motion (heat). Therefore, the heat builds up inside the greenhouse.

Tilted beds are flat-bed absorbers which are inclined at an angle to make it possible for sunlight to fall more nearly perpendicular to the surface. Simple flat-bed or tilted-bed systems are useless for collecting and concentrating the large amounts of energy required for the production of commercial electric power. The concentration of energy is too low. However, flat-bed collectors will collect energy under cloudy diffuse sunlight conditions.

In the past the efficiency of solar energy collection and conversion to electricity has been less than 10%. Recently, Aden and Marjorie Meinel[4] have suggested a collection and energy storage system which may be 30% efficient overall. Their method depends upon recently developed surface coatings which have high absorbance for solar radiation and low emittance in the infrared region of the spectrum. High-frequency energy enters from the sun and is changed to lower-frequency, infrared radiation. The coating prevents the escape of the infrared energy which appears as heat in the coating. The coating is thin, made of molybdenum or aluminum oxide, and can withstand heatings to 540 °C (1000 °F) on a continuous basis for 40 years. It is proposed that the heat be recovered by passing liquid metals through channels in the collectors. The collected energy could be stored at 540 °C (1000 °F) in a molten salt for use at times when the sun is not shining.

The Meinels propose that industry and the United States government erect a pilot plant covering 1 square mile of Arizona to test the concept. They estimate that a 1000-MW plant would cost 1 billion dollars, which is four times the cost of

4. "Is it time for a new look at solar energy?" *Bull. Atom. Sci.* 27:32–37, Oct. 1971.

ENERGY IN THE FUTURE

a fossil-fuel or nuclear plant of comparable size. However, there are no fuel costs. The Meinels believe that such a plant, with an operating lifetime of 40 years, should produce power at an average cost of 0.5¢/kWh. Fossil-fuel plants now produce electricity for 1.5–5¢/kWh.

The location of land-based solar energy plants such as these would be restricted to desert regions fo the southwest United States where clear skies and reliable sunlight are most available. It is estimated that only 14% of the area of Arizona, or about 14,000 square miles, would be required to produce the total electrical energy requirements for the United States. The required area seems large and wasteful of land, until it is considered that surface mining for fossil fuels is projected to disturb 71,000 square miles of land.

Southern Arizona is far from eastern population centers. It is not usually practical to transport electricity more than 500 miles because of the large energy losses over long lines. A possible solution would be to use superconducting lines. Alternatively, water could be electrolyzed to produce hydrogen and oxygen, and the gases distributed by pipeline to consuming centers, where they would be converted to electricity by fuel cells or conventional power plants.

Focusing Lenses and Mirrors

Nearly everyone has at some time used a lens to focus the sun's rays upon a piece of paper and thereby caused it to char and burn (Figure 12–6). Large lenses are capable of causing very high temperatures in an object. The higher the input temperature of a heat system the more efficient it will be.

Two University of Massachusetts scientists have suggested the use of large lenses to collect solar energy to produce hydrogen and oxygen gases from water.[5] The lens system would heat a boiler to 1500 °C (2700 °F) which is a sufficiently high temperature to slightly dissociate water into hydrogen and oxygen. Hydrogen would diffuse through a palladium metal membrane into a second chamber where it would be pumped out. Oxygen would be recovered from the residual gas by condensing out the water. The lenses would be made of light-

5. N. C. Ford and J. W. Kane, "Solar power," *Bull. Atom. Sci.* 27:27–31, Oct. 1971.

Figure 12–6. Concentration of the sun's rays by converging mirror and lens.

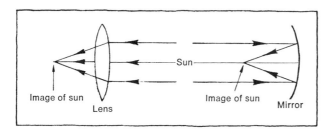

stable plastic and, together with the associated equipment, the system is expected to cost about $33 per square meter. About 500,000 lenses each of area 10 square meters would be required to collect enough solar energy to power the equivalent of a 1000-MW electrical energy. The lenses must move to track the sun across the sky in order to keep the sun's image focused upon the unit where the thermal dissociation of the water occurs. The lenses must be sufficiently far apart that no lens will interfere with or shade another. For the equivalent of 1000 MW of energy, the plant would cover a square area 1.4 miles on a side or about 2 square miles.

SOLAR CELLS   Anyone who has used an exposure meter for a camera has used a solar cell. The greater the amount of light that falls on the cell, the greater the reading given by the exposure indicator.

Present solar cells are largely hand-crafted and cost about $200,000 per kilowatt of power output. This is 500–1000 times the cost of a fossil- or nuclear-fuel plant. In addition the cells have a relatively short lifetime. At present the cost of clean power from solar cells is prohibitive. However, there is some hope that production can be made into a continuous, large-scale, automatic process through the use of an automatic multilayer-coating machine. If this becomes a practicality, it is hoped the cost of solar cells could be reduced to about 50¢ per square foot, or less than $100 per installed kilowatt.

A low-priced solar cell has not yet arrived, but cell output can be improved by using reflectors to increase the concentration of light impinging upon the cell. By this means, Eugene Ralph has increased the output of a silicon solar cell by a factor of 2.5.[6] Further work with reflectors may increase the output by a factor of 125. If this is possible, then even the use of the present high-cost silicon cells could prove to be economically viable.

If the price of solar cells can be reduced so that they are practical to use, it is estimated that 1 acre of solar cells could give a profit of $2000 per acre per year. An area of 1 square mile could provide 60,000 kW of power for an installed price of 100 million dollars, including maintenance over a period of 20 years. The installed price per kilowatt would be about $1600 or about four to eight times the present cost of fossil-fueled power plants. The high price per installed kilowatt is offset by the fact that the solar plant would require no fuel and would produce no pollutants.

SOLAR POWER FROM SPACE   Peter Glaser of Arthur D. Little, Boston, has suggested a space version of a solar power plant. He would deploy a 5-mile square (25 square miles) solar cell receptor (Figure 12–7) in synchronous orbit 22,300 miles out in space. The cell would always face the sun and would be connected by a 2-mile-long cable to a microwave converter which would change electric current to microwaves which would be beamed to a 6-mile square microwave

6. E.L. Ralph, *Large-scale Solar Electric Power Generation*, a paper presented at the Solar Energy Society Conference, Greenbelt, Md., 10 May 1971.

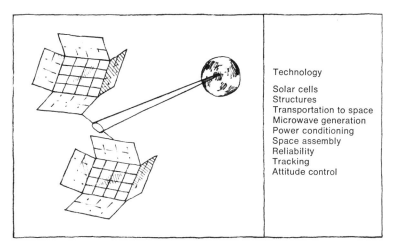

Figure 12-7. Energy from a solar space station.

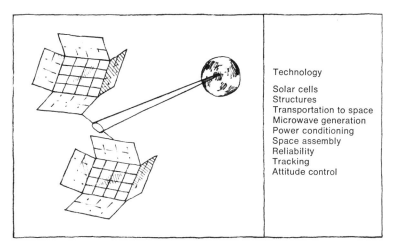

receiving antenna on earth. The receiving station would convert the micro-wave energy to commercial electricity. Power would be supplied 24 hr a day all the year around. There would be no problems about night and day, clouds, or angle of sun from the zenith. The solar cell would continuously receive the full flux of the sun's energy in space, that is, 1.4 kW per square meter 24 hr a day. Also the energy would transmit through dense clouds.

The efficiency of the system on the earth is 70–90%. The efficiency in space (sunlight to microwaves) is much less, 5–8%. This is unimportant when con-sidering the effect of waste heat, but it is important when considering the amount of material that must be boosted into orbit.

The system is not without dangers. Because of the great distance of the space station from the earth receiver, a slight error in the direction of the beam would cause the beam to miss the receiving station. The radiation would be 1 W per square centimeter (see Chapter 6).

It is estimated that 250 space installations could supply the electrical needs of the United States for the year 2000. The implementation of these stations would require the production of cheap (50¢ per square foot) solar cells as a long-lasting film about 1/10,000 in. thick. Placing the station into space requires a capability to launch a 5-million-pound unit into space at a price of $50 per pound of pay load. Placing a satellite in synchronous orbit now costs about $4000 per pound of payload. The Glaser concept is intriguing and exciting and in tune with the space age. However, can it become a practical device?

WIND   The power that is in the wind originated in the sun. Obtaining energy from the wind is an indirect way of trapping the sun's energy.

Wind power brought the Pilgrims to our shores and wind power provided much of the commercial power of the Netherlands. In the 19th century more than 30,000 windmills faced the winds across Denmark, northern Germany, and the Netherlands. There they provided a billion kilowatt-hours of power. Rounding the number of hours in a year to 9000, gives a continuous power rating of 110 MW. This was done with relatively primitive technology. We can make the wind yield power more efficiently with large sophisticated aerogenerators located in the more advantageous places. However, only about 6% can be collected from any one place.

In 1940, an aerogenerator station was established on Grandpa's Knob, Vermont, in an attempt to produce relatively large amounts of power from wind. The 1.25-MW aerogenerator was powered by a propeller with 100-ft stainless-steel blades. The plant was operated successfully and, for a time, supplied power to the commercial power grid in Vermont. In 1945, a fatigue-type failure in the blade root of the propeller caused the loss of a blade. It was impossible during wartime conditions to obtain repair materials. The generator unit was dismantled. It was not reactivated because it was felt that nuclear energy would soon produce cheap electricity.

There are a few large aerogenerators in operation in Europe; a 100-kW unit is operating in Denmark and a 640 kW unit is in use in France.

Little has been done in the United States in recent years to test the feasibility of aerogenerator systems, but proposals have been made. Professor Voight and other engineers from Salem, Oregon (in a personal communication to Senator Mike Gravel, 7 April 1971) have proposed the building of a 740-kW aerogenerator. It would take three years to bring into operation and would cost about 1 million dollars, or about four times the installed cost per kilowatt for a conventional power plant. However, the fuel cost would be zero and the plant would cause no chemical pollution. Because the units could be used to supply local areas and would not require expensive high-voltage transmission lines, line losses would be small.

A study by Oklahoma University shows that the average wind energy in Oklahoma is 18.5 W per square foot. This is equal to the average of the sun's energy falling on 1 square foot of Oklahoma soil. Both figures are averaged over 24 hr throughout the year. Sixty to 80% of the wind's energy can be converted to electricity by aerogenerators. At this efficiency, Oklahoma wind should be able to supply an average of about 1 kW of power per 100 square feet of propeller sweep area or 24 kWh of power per day. With proper storage and energy conversion systems, this should be sufficient energy to supply an individual home.

The average velocity of wind in the arc from Texas across the plains to North Dakota and east to New England is between 12 and 20 mph. In certain areas on the west and east coasts the average velocity exceeds 20 mph.

The greater the height above the earth's surface, the higher the velocity of the air. At a 500-ft height the velocity of the wind is approximately 1.45 times as great as it is at a 100 ft height. As a result, the higher the supporting tower, the

ENERGY IN THE FUTURE

greater the velocity of the wind striking the propeller, and the more efficient the system will be. The higher tower allows the use of longer blades which will make possible the use of larger generator capacities.

Suggested capacities for single commercial units vary from 2 MW to 7.5 MW. The Grandpa's Knob unit was a 1.25-MW installation with 100-ft propeller blades. The blades for a 2-MW unit would be 140 ft long, and those for a 7.5 MW unit, 250 ft long. Present-day units should be lighter and cost less than those which were installed on Grandpa's Knob in 1940. The propeller vanes would incorporate de-icing units and be capable of being feathered and adjusted to give constant velocities of turning regardless of impinging wind velocity.

One to three million aerogenerator units of 2-MW capacity could supply the entire electrical demand in the year 2000 when the total demand may be 2 million MW (current installed capacity is 350,000 MW). In order to attain this amount of generation the generator units would be spaced on a grid as close as a mile apart in favorable locations.

Two hundred fifty tons of steel were required for the 1.25-MW Grandpa's Knob unit. On this basis, approximately 220–440 million tons of steel would be required for the generator units. It is possible that today's technology could reduce the amount of steel required, but it would require careful planning to obtain it.

It has been suggested that the power be used to electrolyze water into hydrogen and oxygen. This system would give considerable flexibility to the energy supply and the resources of different areas could be pooled by the use of a pipeline and its storage centers.

Dr. William E. Herronemus, Professor of Engineering at the University of Massachusetts, has proposed an offshore wind power system for the east coast.[7] It should be able to produce 159 trillion kWh of electricity in 1990 at a total revenue of 2.51¢ per kWh while a nuclear, fossil-fuel, or hydroelectric alternative system would require a revenue of 2.72¢ per kWh.

Not only is wind useful for producing electricity, it may also be used directly. A recent study showed that, if fossil fuels increase in price only very slightly, vessels built to use wind power will be competitive for ocean shipping.

Wind energy poses problems but it does not thermally or chemically pollute or require fuel. It makes few demands upon resources. Aerogenerators should have a long lifetime and be essentially maintenance free. Furthermore, they would have little effect upon the climate of the earth; the energy which is absorbed from the wind in one place will only be released at another point or points on the earth's surface.

SEA POWER   The seas contain tremendous amounts of heat. The water acts as a solar heat receptor over 70% of the earth's surface. The Gulf Stream carries

7. W.E. Herronemus, *The U.S. Energy Crisis: Some Proposed Gentile Solutions*, a paper presented at the joint meeting of A.S.M.E. and I.E.E., West Springfield, Mass., 12 Jan. 1972.

the heat received by the Carribean Sea water and is transported northeast to provide Europe with a "hot-water" heating system. This is rather effective, since southern France is at the latitude of central Michigan and Norway spans the latitudes occupied by Alaska.

The warm Gulf Stream water flows to the Arctic, cools, sinks to the bottom of the ocean and returns to the place of its origin in the south, that is, it is a convective system. The warm Gulf Stream passes directly above the cold stream and within 2000 vertical feet of it. The James Hilbert Andersons, senior and junior, have plans to trap some of the energy carried by the Gulf Stream system.[8] The heat content of the Gulf Stream could provide 200 times as much energy as the total energy requirements of the United States. It is available on a continuous 24-hr-day, year-round basis. The problem is to devise a method of economically extracting the energy contained in the water. The Andersons believe that they have the solution to that problem.

They propose to drop a 35–40-ft diameter, corrugated, thin-walled pipe down to the cold water against the condenser side of a turbine powered by a propane vapor system (see Figure 12–8). Warm (79–87 °F) water from the surface would be pumped against a boiler system containing propane. Propane boils at an effective temperature of 74 °F to produce a boiler pressure of 133 psi. The high-pressure propane vapor would pass through the turbine, be cooled to 54 °F, and condensed by the cold water supplied to the condenser. The liquid propane would be pumped back to the boiler where it would be reconverted to vapor. The efficiency of the system would be rather small because of the small temperature difference between the boiler and condenser sides of the turbine (Chapter 8). Theoretically, the thermodynamic efficiency is 3.7%. Theoretical efficiency is not obtainable. The actual useful efficiency is likely to be more like 2% or 3%, if allowance is made for heat losses, including the energy used for pumping, and nonequilibrium conditions.

The Andersons propose to submerge almost the entire unit so that the pressure inside any component of their system will be balanced by an approximately equal external pressure. Therefore, the boiler section would be submerged about 290 ft below the surface where the pressure slightly exceeds 133 psi.

All waste water would be discharged at the depth of the respective units. The power station would be anchored firmly in place and stabilized by strategically located propellers on a surface platform. The flowing streams of cold and warm water would continually replenish the boiler "fuel" water and the condenser coolant water. It would be like being anchored over rivers flowing in opposite directions and removing desirable materials as they flow past.

The Andersons suggest that sea-power plants could be used to produce cheap desalinized water, oxygen at one-third the cost of that produced directly from air, and could nourish fisheries by bringing nutrients to the surface waters along with the cold water that is used in power production.

8. J.H. Anderson, *The Sea Plant: A Source of Power, Water, and Food Without Pollution*, a paper presented at the Solar Energy Society Conference, Greenbelt, Md., 12 May 1971.

ENERGY IN THE FUTURE

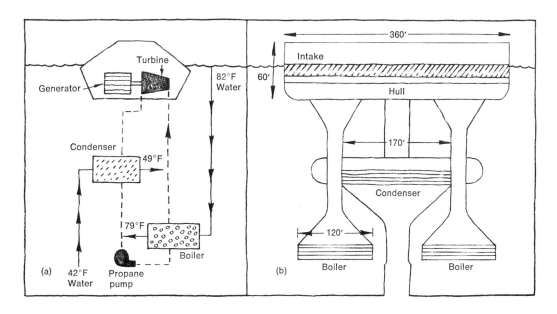

Figure 12–8. Diagrams of a sea power plant: (a) schematic diagram of parts and processes, and (b) diagram showing dimensions. From Sea Solar Power, Inc.

The sea is a lean but large source of stored solar energy. It has the advantage that it is chemically, thermally, and aesthetically nonpolluting. The Andersons may have a solution to economical recovery of the energy in sea water. However, as with any system, small changes in the environment may produce large results. The effects of the system must be examined to determine how much, if any, energy may be removed from the ocean currents without triggering widespread, disastrous results. As Dr. Jacques Piccard told the Air and Water Pollution Subcommittee on 16 June 1971, "Please do not touch the ocean currents."

BIOCONVERSION Bioconversion is the growing of plants to convert the energy of the sun into fuel energy in the form of dried plant tissue. In the past, trees have been the vehicle for bioconversion.

However, trees are of limited availability and are slow growing. On a sustained basis, forests can provide only between half a cord and a cord (4 ft × 4 ft × 8 ft pile of wood) of dry wood per year per acre. On this basis, about 10 acres of woodland is required to supply continuously the heating requirements of a 1200-square-foot home in the northern part of the country. We just do not have that much wood available.

Algae are one-celled water plants which are relatively efficient energy converters. In order to grow, they need metal salts, phosphates, carbon dioxide, and ammonia as a source of nitrogen. Outdoors they only utilize about 5% of natural incident light. Indoor ponds under electric lights may convert 15–25% of the incident light to energy. The efficiency of the production of the electricity from dried algae would make the overall efficiency much lower than 15%. There is a possibility that extracts of the necessary enzymes would be able to produce methane at even higher conversion rates.

The luxuriant growth of sugar cane is a possibility for bioconversion for energy purposes. Indeed sugar cane wastes are the fuel used to produce most of the electricity used in the Philippines. A disadvantage is that sugar cane does not grow in northern climates, and, therefore, is of limited usefulness. Growing sugar cane for fuel would necessarily take land that could be used for food production. A choice would have to be made.

CONCLUSION There is sufficient energy from the sun to supply the needs of the United States. The average energy from the sun that falls on Lake Erie would be more than enough to supply all the energy consumed in the United States. However, the energy is extremely diffuse. Thus, the problem is collection of the energy.

The difficulties lies in the technology necessary to exploit the energy. As usual, when the future is concerned, there are differences of opinion as to when such technology can be available commercially and how fast it can be incorporated into the nation's use of energy.

The Solar Energy Panel, a group organized by the National Science Foundation and the National Aeronautics and Space Administration, has given the following times for commercial availability of the use of solar energy (early 1973): building heating, within five years; building cooling, 6–10 years; synthetic fuels from organic materials, 5–8 years; electrical production, 10–15 years. The group found that by the year 2020, solar energy could provide up to 35% of the total building heating and cooling requirements, 30% of the fuel requirements, 10% of the liquid fuel requirements, and 20% of the electrical requirements. These estimates are based on the conclusion that, although the cost of solar energy is now too high to be competitive, it will be competitive in the near future.

There are several individuals trying to develop methods of using the sun's energy as well as the possible academic and industry developments (summer 1973). A man in Washington, D.C., has built several houses heated almost entirely by solar energy. A family in New Mexico has a house completely supplied with energy by the sun directly or indirectly, but the cost of this house is prohibitively high for the average person. Another inventor has built a wind generator for electrical energy which costs about $400. Several individuals are marketing systems which convert wind energy into electricity. These are relatively expensive.

Solar energy looks promising and it may be in use before the Solar Energy Panel expects.

Considerable quantities of organic wastes are produced each year in the United States. A 1971 Bureau of Mines report estimates that 2 billion barrels of oil could be processed from the agricultural wastes and another 400 million barrels could be obtained from the organic matter in urban wastes. This is 40–50% of our present crude oil needs. In addition some gas would be obtained.

The amount of energy produced by burning a substance depends upon the heat involved in the formation of the substance and also the heat of formation of each of the products of the combustion. For example, the equation for the combustion of glucose is

$$\begin{matrix} & H & H & H & H & H & H \\ & | & | & | & | & | & | \\ H- & C- & C- & C- & C- & C- & C=O + 9O_2 \rightarrow 6CO_2 + 6H_2O \\ & | & | & | & | & | & \\ & O & O & O & O & O & \\ & | & | & | & | & | & \\ & H & H & H & H & H & \end{matrix} \qquad (1)$$

The heat of formation of glucose molecules is represented by the equation:

$6C + 6H_2 + 3O_2 \rightarrow C_6H_{12}O_6 + 300$ kcal

This means that 300 kcal of energy were produced during the formation of glucose from its constituents (*heat of formation*). The heat of formation of carbon dioxide is 94 kcal per mole or 564 kcal for the six moles of carbon dioxide in equation (1):

$C + O_2 \rightarrow CO_2 + 94$ kcal

The heat of formation for water is 68 kcal per mole or 408 kcal for the six moles of water:

$H_2 + \frac{1}{2}O_2 \rightarrow H_2O + 68$ kcal

Thus, the net energy produced during the burning of one mole of glucose (180 g) is the difference between the total heat of formation of the products and the heat of formation of glucose, or 672 kcal:

$564 + 408 - 300 = 672$

Not only is this the amount of heat produced by the burning of glucose but it is also the amount of heat produced by the decomposition of glucose by aerobic bacteria.

Decomposition of glucose by anaerobic bacteria is a different reaction:

$C_6H_{12}O_6 \rightarrow 3CO_2 + 3CH_4$

Methane (CH_4) has a relatively low heat of formation, 18 kcal per mole or 54 kcal for three moles. The energy produced is the difference between the total heat of formation of the products (54 kcal for the 3 moles of methane + 94 kcal × 3 for the 3 moles of carbon dioxide) and the heat of formation of glucose:

$$282 + 54 - 300 = 36$$

Thus the net energy produced by the reaction is 36 kcal, much less than that from the oxidation (burning) of glucose.

If the methane is burned,

$$3CH_4 + 6O_2 \rightarrow 3CO_2 + 6H_2O$$

the energy produced is 636 kcal per mole. Thus the amount of energy produced from a mole of glucose equals the sum of the energy produced by the anaerobic decomposition of glucose plus the energy from the burning of methane.

Anaerobic decomposition may have been the process by which natural gas may have been formed. The gas would have been held long enough to be trapped by the consolidation of impervious layers of sediments above it. This reaction also takes place in a cow's first stomach, and is the source of the methane in the cow's flatulence.

There is no doubt that a fuel can be produced by the anaerobic decomposition of glucose. Other carbohydrates such as starch would also produce methane under anaerobic decomposition. The question is whether this is the most favorable way to dispose of the wastes. Except where very large numbers of cows are fed and kept, not enough waste would be produced to supply a plant without transportation of the wet, heavy material.

Another source of organic material is urban waste. Most of the energy in urban waste is from paper which may be of more use as a source of raw material for paper.

After the organic material is decomposed a black liquid remains. The fertilizing substances nitrogen, potassium, phosphate, and other minerals are in the black liquid. Whether the liquid also contains the important humus colloids apparently has never been investigated. This question should be answered.

Conclusion   Energy is available in several places—underground, tides, sea, wind, and sun. Man needs to learn how to tap this energy for his use. In doing so there are two precautions that he must remember: (1) how much energy he can take from the earth's systems without causing changes which would be detrimental, and (2) how to manage the necessary technology so that it is ecologically as harmless as possible. Presently, much of man's technology has been developed and used with little question about the harm it might do to the environment.

ENERGY CONSERVATION   Energy has been so cheap in the United States that we have regarded it as being available in unlimited quantities. Accordingly, we have developed bad habits in using energy. In our use of tools, we have used energy-intensive methods rather than capital- and labor-intensive methods. For example, automated machines substitute energy for labor. In fact, the automobile industry recently produced more cars while using fewer employees. Each substitution of energy for labor increases the demand for energy and increases the energy cost per unit of goods or service.

A study[9] indicates that all goods and services now used can be provided for as little as 62% of the present per capita energy. No new technology is needed. All that is required is a shift to more energy-efficient methods which are available now.

Energy-efficient technologies are available in all phases of life. Transportation is one of the areas where most energy is expended and also where the opportunity for energy savings is great.

Modern man is characterized by his great desire and need for transportation of goods and himself. Since energy has been relatively cheap and available, man has used energy-intensive methods of transport because they are convenient and save time.

Transportation

The shipping of intercity freight has become increasingly energy intensive. Railroad use has steadily decreased during the last 30 years. The shipping of freight by airplane (54 times as energy intensive as railroads) and truck (about three-and-a-half times as energy intensive as railroads) has increased in the same period of time.

The energy cost of moving an average-sized passenger is about five times the cost of moving a ton of freight. More luxurious accommodation, higher speeds, and greater vehicle weight per unit carried accounts for the higher energy cost.

Although it takes less energy to move a given mass over rails than it does to move the same mass with rubber-tired vehicles, buses have a net propulsion efficiency (N.P.E., the number of passenger-miles per gallon achieved by the carrier) of 125, while the N.P.E. of railroads is only 80. The discrepancy results from the fact that a much larger vehicle weight is required or used per rail passenger than is required per bus passenger. With an N.P.E. of 32 for automobiles and 14 for airplanes it is obvious that these carriers are much less efficient. In general urban-area transit is less efficient than inter-city passenger traffic using the same mode. For example, an automobile has an average N.P.E. of 32 between cities but only 26.9 for urban traffic. Walking and bicycles are even more efficient, 450 for walking and 756 for bicycles on an equivalent energy basis.

Different modes of transport show wide ranges of energy efficiencies. The larger the vehicle weight per passenger or per unit weight carried, the more costly it is in terms of energy. A Volkswagen bus carrying seven passengers has outstanding energy efficiency because it is light and loaded to capacity. Conversely, the huge transatlantic liner *Queen Mary* was very energy inefficient because of larger per person weight which included a swimming pool, ballroom, and spacious cabins of heavy steel construction.

9. A. B. Makhijani, and A. J. Lichtenberg, "Energy and well-being," *Environment*, 14:5–18, June 1972.

The degree of loading of a vehicle affects the energy efficiency of the vehicle. The average loading of a B747 jet plane is about 210 passengers. If the plane could be loaded to its capacity of 350 passengers, its energy efficiency would be increased by at least 50%. Conversely, if the Volkswagen microbus carries only one person, its energy efficiency drops from 180 passenger-miles per gallon of fuel burned to 25.5 passenger-miles per gallon, a value which equals the N.P.E. of an average B747. An average automobile would be even less efficient, with an N.P.E. of 14 for a single passenger.

Each vehicle has certain speeds where it is most efficient. In general a vehicle moving very rapidly consumes more energy than a slower-moving one. The decrease in the N.P.E. of automobiles from about 15 passenger-miles per gallon in 1950 to about 14 in 1968 is partly due to the increase in average speed from 48.7 mph in 1950 to 60.4 mph in 1968.

Motor vehicle energy efficiencies are cut further by any device on the vehicle that uses energy. The EPA expects that automobile gasoline mileage will decrease by 20–40% as a direct result of air-pollution control devices. Other devices which consume more energy than standard equipment are air conditioners, power steering, power brakes, automatic transmissions, and "Christmas tree" lighting. Each necessary or unnecessary device has an energy cost.

You do not get "something for nothing."

TOTAL ENERGY COSTS OF THE AUTOMOBILE   Much more energy is involved in automobile transport than is contained in the gasoline which is burned directly. Energy is used for mining, processing of raw materials, direct manufacture, transport to saleroom, selling costs, etc. More elusive are the indirect and variable energy costs involved in repairs, maintenance, replacement parts, accessories, oil, insurance, parking, tolls, and tax-supported highways. Average dollar costs can be given to these items and an energy cost calculated on the basis that so many Btu cost so many dollars. At present, 72,000 Btu are approximately equivalent to $1 of gross national product. About 51% of the energy assignable to cars is burned as gasoline. Consequently, if a car has a gas mileage of 13.9 miles per gallon (mpg) of actual, direct gasoline consumption, the net value of the mileage in terms of total energy consumption becomes about 7.1 mpg.

Thus the indirect energy costs for an automobile are approximately equal to the direct energy cost measured as actual consumed gasoline. If this is true, the energy equivalent of automobile transport corresponds to double the energy content of the actual gasoline consumed on the road, or about 25% of the total energy consumption of the United States. Direct consumption of gasoline by automobiles is about 12.5% of the total energy consumption of the United States.

BATTERY-POWERED CARS   Battery-powered cars are often suggested as an alternative mode of transport, especially in urban areas. The source of energy for charging the batteries would be a conventional steam plant which is, at most, 40% efficient. The battery, itself, is only about 70% efficient and the motor somewhere between 63% and 92% efficient. The overall efficiency cannot be greater than the lowest efficiency, 40%. Actually the overall efficiency is about 15%.

The overall 15% efficiency of the battery-powered car compares unfavorably with the 25% energy efficiency of the conventional automobile. In addition, the large weight of batteries required for the energy storage would cause a further erosion of the efficiency of the electric car. Thus almost twice as much energy would be consumed to provide the same carrying capacity as is supplied by the conventional gasoline-powered automobile.

TOTAL TRANSPORT ENERGY   Automobile transport consumes about one-half of the energy required for all forms of transport: car, truck, bus, rail, air, etc. Thus, if other forms of transport also have nonfuel costs essentially equal to direct fuel costs, 50% of the energy consumed in the United States can logically be assigned to the transport sector of the economy. These relationships are plotted in Figure 12–9. Consequently only 50% of the total energy must provide all other goods and services.

Figure 12–9.   Transport energy.

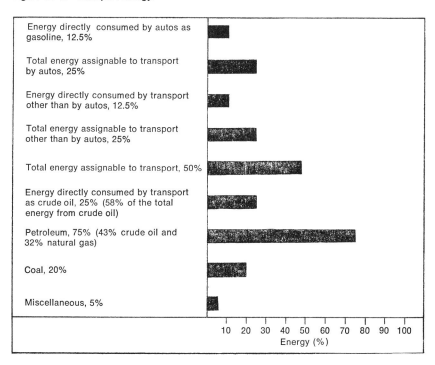

CONCLUSION Because of the large percentage of energy used by the transportation sector, transportation is a very suitable place to curtail energy use. Mass transit is less energy intensive than the familiar automobile.

The situation now is quite different from the period during which the change from mass transit to private transport occurred. At that time mass transit was a thriving business. As people became more affluent, it was easy to desert mass transit and buy their own car. However, mass transit was available until it was bled to near extinction in the 1960s. Even if mass transit is desirable or necessary, it is not available or is extremely inconvenient.

The United States Department of Transportation says that it will take at least two decades to change automobile transport to mass transport. It is also necessary to overcome the attitude expressed in the following quote:

Whenever someone talks about the glories of mass transit, the rights of the individual person who may prefer to drive his automobile are completely ignored or trampled on.[10]

H. Dillon Winship

Residential Heating and Cooling

In 1967 approximately 10.8% of the total energy consumed in the United States was used for household space heating.

GAS If it is available, natural gas is the fuel of choice; it is clean, efficient, convenient, and relatively inexpensive. Recently, however, gas supplies have become tight and it is likely to become difficult to obtain natural gas service in the future, yet the Detroit Edison Company contracted to use natural gas for one of its power plants. The plant will consume enough natural gas to heat about 48,000 homes. Detroit Edison will solve its air pollution problem, but will also exacerbate the natural gas resource problem.

ELECTRICITY Electricity is the most expensive space-heating mode because it is so inefficient. It is less efficient than the least efficient stage, production of electrical energy. Electric heat requires two-and-one-half to three times as much fuel energy input as does a direct gas heating system.

However, electrical heating has been used in speculatively built housing because it is flexible and the installed cost is much less than for an alternative system of comparable heating capability. The builder is able to offer a building for sale or rent at a lower price, but the owner or occupant will pay excessively large bills for the privilege of having "clean" electric heat.

For the ultimate in energy conservation, both good construction and conservative habits are needed. In comparing similar homes in Chicago, a study showed that the cost of gas for the largest user was 47% greater than that for the smallest consumer. For electrically heated homes, the cost spread was 120%. Since the price of heat decreases with increase in consumption, the

10. Vice Chairman, American Trucking Association, in "Closing Quote" *Detroit Free Press,* 23 May, 1973.

ENERGY IN THE FUTURE

actual energy spread would be still greater. Because of the high cost of electrical heating, those who use it tend to use a lower quantity of heat in terms of Btu than do gas consumers. Nevertheless, electric heat consumers pay much more for heat.

HEAT LOSSES, DEGREE DAYS   Heat is lost through ceilings, walls, floors, windows, doors, and general infiltration. The amount that is lost depends upon the location and the construction of the building. Heating need is measured in terms of *degree days.* Degree days are calculated from the following type of information. The inside temperature is assumed to be 75 °F; if the average temperature outside is 35 °F during one day, the number of degree days would be 75 − 35 (i.e., 40) for that day. The sum of the degree days throughout the year is a measure of the heating need. In fact, knowing the number of degree days, fuel suppliers can accurately estimate fuel consumption even by individual fuel users.

There are many factors in house planning and construction which can reduce the use of energy for heating. The greatest saving of energy centers around the windows. In a study of a house built to the Federal Housing Administration's minimum property standards, it was found that the windows covered about 14.5% of the sidewall area. However, this window area lost about as much energy as the sum of the energy loss from the sidewalls, ceiling, and floor. Windows with storm windows lose less heat than double-glassed windows, and double-glassed wooden windows are 22% more efficient than double-glassed aluminum windows. Generally the type of exterior finish does not affect the rate of loss from the house. Insulation in the ceiling and walls reduces heat loss.

Modern housing emphasizes openness and spaciousness. Past systems emphasized limited room heating. Unheated rooms were shut off from the heated area. The latter system was partially derived from the necessity of heating each room with its own limited heating system. Older heating systems were very inefficient. By limiting the volume heated, the heating cost could be kept within reasonable bounds. Centralized modern heating systems can heat large volumes efficiently. However, if fuel is "short" and likely to be "shorter," a shift to a system in which only a limited area is heated could save fuel.

AIR CONDITIONING   The amount of air-conditioning energy required can be calculated from the energy which may seep into a building.

Again it is the window system which is the most important factor in the energy required for comfort. Limiting the window area would result in a saving of energy for both heating and air conditioning. Many protests have been made against the use of window walls, particularly sealed window walls. There is only one way to cool such a building and that is with an energy-consuming air-conditioning unit.

Air-conditioning units require large amounts of power. When the air conditioner is in operation, that amount of energy is added to the heat outside and further increases the outside temperature. The increased outside temperature increases heat infiltration and the necessity for cooling.

PEOPLE HEAT   People evolve energy at a rate of about 225 Btu/hour, about the same as a 70-W light bulb. Large buildings serving large numbers of people sometimes need to be cooled in order to maintain a comfortable temperature even in cold weather. During the energy "crisis" of 1973, stores were accused of running heating units when they had only turned off their air conditioners to conserve energy. People heat was heating the building.

ECONOMICS OF INSULATION   Insulating a building costs money. However, the additional investment is almost returned in savings in the cost of energy. Most modern houses use 40% more energy for heating and air conditioning than would be needed if they had been planned and built more carefully.

SOLAR HEATING   Solar heating is usually discussed in terms of production of electricity. However, solar heating of homes may be more immediately attainable. Together with other proposed economies of energy use, it should be possible to heat a well-insulated house by using solar energy. The better the insulation, the more feasible solar heating will be. It should be possible to heat homes even in the northern climates with a minimally fueled, back-up system.

Lighting   Household lighting consumes about 4.7% of the total energy used. Figure 8–2 shows that fluorescent lights are more than four times as efficient as incandescent lights. A conversion to fluorescent lights for most lighting purposes would reduce the energy required for this purpose. There have been further protests that it is unnecessary to have as high light levels as we are now inclined to use. Any reduction in excessive lighting would provide energy savings.

Many savings in energy use could be found if they were investigated. Insulated cooking vessels and simpler advertising signs have been mentioned as possible areas to effect savings. Many uses would afford only small reductions in the use of energy but many small reductions could result in important conservation of energy. Savings of energy equate to savings in coal, oil, gas, and nuclear fuel—and less pollution.

KEY CONCEPTS   1. Superconductivity: advantages and difficulties.
2. MHD: method and prospects.
3. Water power (rivers and tides): risks, costs, and benefits.
4. Geothermal energy: usefulness and difficulties.
5. Ways of exploiting energy from the sun.
6. Places where energy can be conserved.

QUESTIONS   1. What problems do MHD energy systems have?
2. Why may hydrogen fuel cells be important to any solar energy plant in Arizona?
3. Some fuel cells are 80% efficient. Why are they not more used?

ENERGY IN THE FUTURE

4. What ecological and environmental changes may be caused by the damming of a river?

5. Why is a silted-in dam useless as a source of water power or irrigation water?

6. What questions would you want answered before you would agree to an ocean-energy plant like that proposed by the Andersons?

7. There is energy in the tides. Assume that all available tidal power sites are used. What difficulties may occur?

8. Why is helium important to fusion power?

9. Is geothermal power nonpolluting power? Explain your answer.

10. Why is geothermal steam an inefficient source of power?

11. Peter Glaser has suggested setting up solar-cell receptors to collect the sun's energy. What factors stand in the way of this system becoming a reality?

12. The Meinels propose a system of ground-based solar receptors which would eventually cover at least 14,000 square miles in Arizona. What problems are associated with their system of producing and transporting electrical power?

13. Converging lenses concentrate light rays. Why are they not likely to be used in solar power production?

14. How would you set up a solar heating system for a house?

15. What questions would you wish to be answered if a windmill power plant was proposed for a site near your home town?

16. Organic agricultural and urban wastes may be processed into natural gas or oil. Evaluate the prospects of these processes becoming useful realities.

17. In what ways can an automobile be made so that it will be more energy efficient than present-day cars?

18. More and more four-lane freeways are being built. Evaluate the validity of building these roads.

19. What can be done to reduce the amount of energy consumed by transport without changing the volume of passenger and goods transport?

20. Evaluate the energy impact of power steering.

21. How may the fuel requirements for cooking be reduced?

22. What part of a house loses the greater amount of heat? What can be done to hold the heat loss to a minimum?

23. It is proposed that algae be grown in 5 million acres of ponds. What problems can you foresee in this suggested bioconversion method?

24. Compare small decentralized solar energy systems with huge installations.

25. List all ways in which you can reduce the use of electricity by direct methods (for example, turning off lights), and by indirect methods (for example, recycling aluminum cans).

BIBLIOGRAPHY

The *Scientific American,* vol. 224, September 1971, was completely devoted to energy. The following articles from that issue are especially pertinent to this chapter.

1. Cook, E., "The flow of energy in an industrial society," pp. 134–144.
2. Gates, D. M., "The flow of energy in the biosphere," pp. 88–100.
3. Luten, D. B., "The economic geography of energy," pp. 164–175.
4. Summers, C. M., "The conversion of energy," pp. 148–160.
5. Starr, C., "Energy and Power," pp. 36–49.

Other publications are:

6. Bowen, R. G., and Groh, E. A., "Geothermal—earth's primordial energy," *Technol. Rev.* 74:42–48, Oct.–Nov. 1971.
7. Ford, N. C., and Kane, J. W., "Solar power." *Bull. Atom. Sci.* 27:27–34, Oct. 1971.
8. Hirst, E., *Energy consumption for transportation in the U.S.,* Oak Ridge, Tenn.: Oak Ridge National Laboratory, 1972.
9. Lessing, L., "New ways to more power with less pollution," *Fortune* 32:78–81, 131–136, Nov. 1970.
10. Makhijani, A. B., and Lichtenberg, A. J., "Energy and well-being," *Environment,* 14:10–18, June 1972.
11. Marine, G., *America the raped,* New York: Simon & Schuster, 1969.
12. Meinel, A. B., and Meinel, M. P., "Is it time for a new look at solar energy?" *Bull. Atom. Sci.* 74:32–37, Oct. 1971.
13. Moyers, J. C., *The value of thermal insulation in residential construction: economics and the conservation of energy,* Oak Ridge, Tenn.: Oak Ridge National Laboratory, 1971.
14. Rex, R., "Geothermal energy—the neglected energy option," *Bull. Atom. Sci.* 74:52–56, Oct. 1971.
15. Rice, R. A., "System energy and future transportation," *Technol. Rev.* 75:31–37, Jan. 1972.
16. Sterling, C., "Aswan Dam," *National Parks and Conservation* 45:10, August 1971.
17. Weinberg, A. M., and Hammond, R. P., "Limits to the use of energy," *Amer. Sci.,* 58:412–8, July-Aug. 1970.

13 Human Egoism and Ecology

If the earth must lose that great portion of its pleasant-ness which it owes to things that the unlimited increase of wealth and population would extirpate from it, for the mere purpose of enabling it to support a larger population, I sincerely hope, for the sake of posterity, that they will be content to be stationary, long before necessity compels them to it.[1]

John Stuart Mill

The previous chapters have established that all resources are limited, and that technology likewise is limited in its ability to provide solutions to our environmental and ecological problems.

The present chapter deals particularly with the nontechnological factors which may produce effects upon the environment: awareness of time, attitudes and philosophies of people, sociology, social and political organization, economics, and human desires and foibles. This egoism is the quality of thinking or acting with oneself and one's own interests in mind. Any discussion of these topics is likely to be subjective and biased. However, the solutions to our ecological problems necessarily must be found in these areas.

HISTORY

A look at the recent past may put the present conditions in perspective and provide some guidance to the direction in which we must move in the future. The authors have been privileged to have lived through and experienced many of the changes that have occurred within the last 50 years. However, nearly everyone, regardless of age, has seen some changes take place—a new road, a new building, earth satellites, B747s.

There is a feeling in all of us that we have always possessed our present style of life. Visualization of the life of the past is as difficult as it is for the parents of a teenager to realize that at one time the teenager was a baby. Similarly, it is difficult for anyone to visualize the "shape" of the future. For most people the future is merely an extension of the style and thrust of the present. It is hoped that a short discussion of the past will help establish a frame of reference in time and circumstances.

Frontier Psychology

The United States was born as a frontier society. There were few people and large expanses of untilled soil, huge forests, and large amounts of undiscovered oil, coal, and other minerals. The resources were almost free for the effort of taking. Waste could be dumped anywhere. There was no need to be careful. The exploiter was unaffected by the exhaustion of any resource at any one place. Over the hill or over the horizon there was always more to be taken.

Most of the industrial development in the United States has occurred in the last 50 years and certainly within the last 200 years. Over the combined life expectancies of three men (about 210 years), the United States has changed from a continent held by Indian societies to the highly industrialized state that now exists.

Exploitation of the riches of the United States was and is regarded as an unqualified good. The government promoted exploitation. Pioneer farmers were granted 160-acre homesteads (later 320 acres). Railroads were granted wide swaths of land across the continent. Miners obtained mineral rights for the cost of staking out a claim and paying a small fee. Tax laws were enacted to allow fast write-offs, depletion allowances, and other financial incentives. All were subsidies to encourage development and extraction of all resources (Figure 13–1). The subsidies accomplished their purpose, rapid growth in the

1. John Stuart Mill, *Principles of political economy*, Vol. 2, London: John W. Parker, 1857.

Figure 13–1. "... And that's what they called 'a flower' ..." Cartoon from Het Parool, Amsterdam.

use of resources occurred and along with it a growing sense of well-being and affluence on the part of the people of the United States.

The frontier psychology of abundance and potential growth is still with us in a period of growing depletion. Worse still, other nations envy our affluence and want to be like us.

Scientific and Technological Development

Using the resources of the nation, science and technological development has made possible the affluence of the United States—the automobile and its highways, the color television sets, the variety of food, and the electrical slaves so common in the homes of the nation.

TRANSPORTATION   In 1848 (125 years or two lifetimes ago), the only way to go from the Eastern states to California was by prairie schooner or sailboat. In the East there were a few wood-burning steam engines but the railroads had not yet extended their lines into the West. Henry Ford drove his first car in 1896. In 1903, within the lifetime of people alive today, the Wright brothers flew their first gasoline-powered aircraft. In the horse economy of 1915, people traveled

HUMAN EGOISM AND ECOLOGY

only an average distance of 200 miles a year. By contrast, the average annual distance traveled today amounts to upwards of 10,000 miles.

From 1915 well into the 1930s there was a transition period from the horse economy to an oil-powered economy. In the early 1920s there were relatively few main roads between cities and towns. Intercity travel was by steam train or electric interurban rail cars. If one wished to go to another city, one took an electric street car to the rail station and there boarded a train for one's destination city. Upon arrival one rode street cars and/or walked to one's final destination. The lack of cars in the early 1920s is shown by the fact that there were no traffic lights. Instead a policeman stood at the center of main intersections and directed traffic by blowing a whistle and changing the direction of a stop-go sign.

By 1936, the more flexible and efficient buses displaced the electric street cars. At the same time automobiles had taken some traffic away from intercity trains. However, it was still convenient to make a 25–100-mile trip by train. Interestingly, at least as late as 1944 presidential candidates campaigned from the rear of a steam-powered passenger train.

During the turmoil of World War II in the 1940s propeller-driven airplanes more or less regularly crossed the oceans from land to land. On the Atlantic run, stops were made at Gander in Newfoundland and Shannon in Ireland. Regular commercial transatlantic flights were begun in 1950 and the first commercial jet aircraft went into service in 1952.

Although passenger trains were still a much used mode of travel in 1959, they rapidly fell victim to the personal automobile and jet plane. The decline was so rapid that now, in the early 1970s, passenger trains are practically extinct.

Thus, in the short span of less than 70 years, we have come from horses, steam trains, and kites, to automobiles and jets.

In the changing horse economy of the early 1920s, milk was delivered by horse and wagon, gravel was transported by special wagons, and house foundations were dug by horses pulling a scoop. Horses even pulled steam-powered fire-engine pumpers to fires. Snow-covered roads were not plowed but horses pulled simple triangular wood plows to clear the sidewalks after a snowfall. This in itself indicates the relative importance of different modes of travel; feet were still important.

COMMUNICATIONS   In 1922, there were only 60,000 radio sets in the entire United States and they were probably battery-powered sets that howled and whistled. Important late news was dispensed by newspaper extras that were sold by newsboys who hurried up and down the streets, wailing, ''Extra, extra, read all about it.'' Eventually, radio made extras unnecessary and unprofitable.

More recently, the first TV picture was broadcast in 1948. It is difficult to believe that it has not always existed. Nevertheless, it is a relatively recent arrival on the scene.

ENTERTAINMENT   Silent black-and-white movies were the rule until the 1930s. The dialog was interspersed with action and appeared as printed matter on the screen. Mood music was played by a small (about five-piece) orchestra or a single piano or organ in front of the stage. Film changes and intermissions were covered by vaudeville acts usually performed in front of the stage curtain.

FARM LIFE   Throughout the 1930s most of the farm work was done by horses. There were a few small tractors. Steam-powered tractors hauled threshing machines from farm to farm to separate the grain from the sheaves stored in stacks. Hay was loaded on wagons in the fields by the use of pitch forks. There were no balers to help the farmer with his harvest.

Rural mail was delivered by horse and buggy. Houses were lighted by kerosene lamps and water was pumped by hand or windmill. Limited living space was heated by wood-burning kitchen stoves, while other rooms were heated by barrel-shaped stoves. One roasted on the side facing the stove but was definitely cool on the back side.

CHANGES IN ENERGY SOURCES   Before 1850, wood was the common fuel, even for the few steam trains that existed at that time. Coal displaced wood and was the main fuel source until the early 1940s. Petroleum began to become increasingly important after 1920. By 1950 oil had taken over so much of the market that even the president of the coal union heated his home with oil. A 24-in. natural gas pipeline, built during World War II, signaled the emergence of natural gas as the preferred domestic and industrial fuel. In the early 1970s, oil and gas supplied upward of 75% of all energy used in the United States. Coal is still available and, in fact, is our largest remaining store of energy. However, the temporary availability and convenience of oil and gas makes them the prime energy resource.

Up to the present, the energy to fuel man's activities has been progressively available; coal replaced wood, and oil and gas replaced and supplemented coal. We have had the "energy dollars" that have made our present high standard of living possible. Eventually nuclear energy is projected to replace oil. Ultimately, upon exhaustion of all mineral fuels, the sun is expected to carry the energy burden, unless nuclear fusion becomes commercially feasible.

In the past the transition from one source of energy to another was smooth. The new energy resource was available and the technology for its use was already developed. Furthermore, the new energy resource phased in as the old resource phased out. Oil and gas have not phased out as yet, but there is a danger that they may phase out before a replacement energy source, if there is one, phases in. The nuclear replacement for petroleum has not phased in as yet. Massive problems must be solved before nuclear energy can be considered to be useful. Even if nuclear energy were phasing in, it would be of little help in the energy crisis of this decade. It takes many years to plan and construct nuclear power plants. If conventional uranium fuel is used as required to cover our projected energy demand, the uranium fuel will be consumed in less than

30 years or by about the year 2000. In view of the fact that fossil fuels are projected to last at least that long, nuclear energy does not provide the answer to our energy difficulties. Fast breeder, fusion, and solar energy systems are more or less in the nebulous dream state of development. Most future systems are beset with monumental problems for implementing their use. As it now stands, we do not have a visible energy replacement for our fossil fuels.

A lack of resources inevitably will force a slowdown in economic activity and force a reduction in the standard of living upon the people of the world and of the United States. Furthermore, the standard of living will be still further decreased by any increase of population. The amount of resources per person is decreased thereby, and necessarily the overall standard of living is decreased.

URBAN LIVING   In cities in the 1920s a family often had a 60 ft × 90 ft lot with a house, a privy, a chicken house, a few fruit trees, a small garden, shade trees, and a small lawn. Indeed most of the space was used. Food was grown locally, consumed locally, and waste was disposed locally.

Transport was sufficiently difficult for only the more valuable and relatively nonperishable produce to be transported and sold away from the farm.

Even in the late 1940s, the major portion of food purchases was made at local, individually owned neighborhood stores. The central business district was important for supplying most other needs. Since that time, with the expansion of the number of cars and the building of more roads, more and more of the functions provided by the neighborhood grocery stores and the central business district have been taken over by huge outlying shopping centers. As a result, the central business districts have become relatively less used and many are decaying.

The individual mobility provided by the automobile has made possible the suburbanization of the countryside around the edges of the city. The suburbs of nearby cities reach out and fuse with each other. In many places it is possible to travel long distances without really leaving one city or suburb before you enter another. For example, essentially an urban megalopolis extends between Washington, D.C., and Boston. Automobile mobility is so great that people drive long distances to work and may travel considerable distances each weekend to a recreation home. In so doing, they may not have an enduring feeling for any place.

Since 1920, the gasoline engine and associated machinery has had a drastic effect upon the farm population. Tractors and farm equipment have surely increased the productivity of the individual farmer. Consequently, fewer farmers are needed to produce the necessary food and fiber. The unneeded workers have migrated to the cities to seek employment and have helped to swell the populations of urban areas.

The effect of mechanization and the increase in individual automobile transport has at once gutted our cities and bled the countryside. While these changes have been occurring between the 1920s and 1970s, the population has more than doubled, increasing from 100 to 210 million.

Over this same period real estate property, resource ownership, and industrial capacity have been increasingly concentrated into the hands of fewer and fewer individuals. The rationale of growth has produced larger factories, more automated production, larger corporations, larger holding companies (conglomerates), and large industrial-type farms. As a result, an increasingly larger portion of the population have become wage earners, instead of owning and running their own private enterprise.

IMPORTANCE OF ENERGY AND OTHER RESOURCES

We are inclined to brag about our technological and scientific achievements. However, our ability to enjoy our resulting affluence depends upon a reliable energy source. In a very real sense energy resources provide us with the "dollars" which allow us to do those things that we now do. If coal had not been discovered and available we would never have emerged from the horse-and-buggy age, and, if oil and gas had not been available, we would not now be riding in jet planes. The quotation from the beginning of Chapter 9 expresses this view:

How many persons know that the prosperity of some modern cultures stems from the great flux of oil fuel energies pouring through machinery and not from some necessary and virtuous properties of human dedication and political designs.[2]

In the past energy resources have been abundantly available.

Since the 1940s more oil has been consumed in the United States than was produced from wells in the 48 states. In the future the difference between domestic production and consumption is expected to increase at a rapid rate (Figure 13–2). A simplistic solution is to increase supplies by massive imports. Thereby the problem can be concealed. Under these circumstances, all the consumer knows is that for the immediate future he can drive his car and read by electric light. The long-term prospects are not considered.

The amount of Arabian oil may in truth be massive compared with the United States reserves, but ultimately it, too, is exhaustible. It is estimated that world oil resources will be exhausted between the years 2010 and 2025—truly a pitifully short time.

The situation for oil and most other resources is detailed elsewhere in this text. Gas and oil have been selected for special consideration here because they are the key to our present standard of living, whether it involves transportation, food, or any number of other goods and services.

If we buy time by importing oil, we buy it at the expense of a balance of payment deficit. In 1968, for the first time ever, the United States had a trade deficit. It was relatively small—only 2 billion dollars—but still a shock. Some economists project that the yearly deficit could grow to 25 billion dollars. We are importing more goods from abroad than we are exporting.

2. Howard R. Odum, *Environment, power and society,* New York: John Wiley, 1971, p. 10.

HUMAN EGOISM AND ECOLOGY

Figure 13–2. Drawing by Richard Willson, used courtesy Friends of the Earth.

"ALARMiST!"
...THERE'S STILL 500FT TO GO

Over a period of 10 years, extensive importation of oil could cause our cumulative negative balance of payments to amount to 130 billion dollars,[3] or about 10% of the value of all business stocks and all bank deposits in the United States. Rocks and Runyon speculate that, since the producing countries cannot absorb this many goods, it is likely that they would invest in American business

3. L. Rocks and R. P. Runyon, *The energy crisis,* New York: Crown, 1972.

concerns and gain appreciable control of them. In the past we have used our energy resources to acquire foreign assets. If we follow the energy importation route, it may be our turn to be "taken over" by foreign investors.

Not so incidentally, the figure of 130 billion dollars mentioned above represents oil paid for at near present prices. As foreign supplies become depleted, the price is likely to rise. Any increase in prices will increase the trade-deficit problem.

Upon exhaustion of world oil we would be in the same or a worse condition with respect to energy than we are now. In the process, we may have lost control of a large section of our economy to foreign investors.

If domestic or imported oil is not the solution, what can be done? Why not use our "vast" stores of coal or turn to nuclear energy? Again the situation with respect to them is documented elsewhere in the text. They, too, offer at best 100–300 years of energy consumption and a host of problems for ourselves and for our descendants. We can ill afford solutions which provide such small short-term benefits. As of now there is no resource or technology available. It is doubtless heresy in this scientific age, but the authors refuse to believe in uncertain technological solutions until the proposed system works. They have seen too many "wonderful" failures and apparent successes which were actually failures because scientists and others did not assess all of the subsequent effects of the material or system.

CHANGES IN SOCIAL ORGANIZATION

Science and technology can help solve the resource deficiencies but they are not sufficient. Social changes may be necessary.

Many individuals and groups have suggested changes to preserve the amenities of civilization. Some want to slow, or even stop, growth; some want to change to a simpler life style; others want to modify the life style of the middle class and extend the pattern to everyone. A simpler life style does not mean going back to a past culture; a return to the past is not possible even if it were desirable. However, we can take what was good from the past and combine it with what is desirable in the present to assure a safe, comfortable future. None of the suggestions may be the best solution. All should be given a fair hearing.

California Plan II

California is a rapidly growing state and has serious problems involving land use and growth. A nonprofit education organization founded and led by Alfred Heller has published the California Plan II, which is a comprehensive plan for dealing with the environmental and human problems of California. It proposes that the state be divided into regional units such that no region would cut across any existing county boundary. Land would be zoned as agricultural, conservation, urban, or regional reserve, and would be taxed according to its category. Zoning would be directed toward containing the sprawl of cities and preserving agricultural and other open land. Under this plan a city would abruptly stop at the boundary of the area zoned as urban. The following proposals are also made.

1. Universal medical care.
2. Minimum income of $6000 per family of four per year.
3. Zero population growth.
4. Changes in election laws to prevent the powerful economic interests from overwhelming the electorate. There would be tax credits for individual contributions to election campaigns, equal free time for TV exposure, and free distribution of information on the candidates. It is further proposed that there would also be free postal and other subsidies for the candidates.
5. A mass transit system be developed as an alternative mode of transport.
6. A coordination of national, state, and local policies so that California would not suffer increased immigration because of its liberal handling of minimum income and other benefits.
7. Tax on packaging materials.
8. Tax on automobiles with cars limited to 65 hp.
9. Oil depletion tax rather than depletion allowance.
10. Water development and transport costs be charged to users of the water (no subsidies).
11. Reuse and multiple use of existing structures.
12. Inclusion of curricula in general ecology (both classroom experience and practical experience) in all schools.
13. Capital gains benefits on profits from sale of raw land be outlawed.
14. Tax on consumption of electricity.
15. Amenities such as high air and water quality, space, and privacy.
16. Solar energy use encouraged.

The plan does not propose great changes in the present urbanization pattern except to limit it by firm zoning. There is no change of life style required. What exists now becomes more regulated, but under local control so that amenities are improved and/or maintained.

The plan proposes the construction of some new expressways along with mass-transit modes of travel. Some expansion of energy production in the form of electrical generation is also included in the plan. The plan also proposes a planning council which will consider the effects of all decisions upon other areas of concern.

Rand Report to the California Assembly

The Rand Corporation is often described as a "prestigous think tank." It describes itself as "a nonprofit public service corporation engaged in research and analysis on problems of national security and public welfare."

Rand was commissioned by two California agencies, the Committee of Planning and Land Use of the State Assembly and the California Resources Agency, to prepare a report on California's energy and growth problems. The studies were cosponsored by the Rockefeller Foundation and the National Science Foundation. In general, Rand's comments on energy resources, nuclear fuel, and growth apply to all states and nations, and not merely to the state of California.

The following are excerpts from Volume 3 of the three-volume report.[4] They could be said to be a summary of the points of view that are presented in Chapters 9 through 13.

Technology offers no short or medium term solutions to the energy crisis . . . so demand for power must be curtailed.

Resources on our spaceship are finite and must ultimately be conserved and recycled. . . . As the matter now stands, the problem of perpetual storage of high level radioactive wastes is unresolved and present plans call for above ground temporary storage in concrete and steel vaults. Thus while research goes on, reactors continue to be built, radioactive wastes accumulate and the severity of the problem multiplies . . . the consequences are serious and raise questions about the wisdom of future expansion of nuclear power . . . Perhaps a "go-slow" nuclear policy for California would be more prudent until some of these basic difficulties with nuclear power systems are closer to resolution.

Rand proposes certain tax approaches and, if necessary, proscriptive regulations to control the use of energy. It is in favor of reduced growth, but does not envisage a no-growth society stabilized at some lower level of resource use. It depends upon legal means to manipulate the status quo—reduce the growth but do not stop it. Except for a trend to more multiunit housing, there is little to indicate changes in life style.

The Rand Corporation has made the following specific suggestions which would accomplish the goal of reducing growth to what they feel is an acceptable level.

1. Tax and/or proscribe inefficient operations; such action would raise electrical prices but would also reduce undesirable growth.

2. Label appliances to show electrical efficiency.

3. Reduce residential lighting load.

4. Change building designs to reduce the ratio of exposed surface to usable volume.

5. Build more multiunit housing.

6. Improve thermal insulation of buildings.

7. Push development of solar water and space heaters.

8. Substitute natural gas appliances for electrical appliances. They point out that using gas for space heating, water heating, air conditioning, and clothes drying in 1970 would have reduced the residential electrical load by 27%.

9. Finance a consumer education effort on energy conservation by utilities, appliance manufacturers, and/or state government.

10. Prohibit counting promotion expenses of gas and electrical utilities (promotional advertising, builder rebates, free consumer services, etc.) as legitimate business expenses.

11. Encourage neighboring states to follow similar energy conservation policies.

4. The Rand Corporation, *California's electricity quandary,* Vol. 3, *Slowing down the growth rate,* 1972.

HUMAN EGOISM AND ECOLOGY

Professor Daly, economist at Louisiana State University, wants to control growth by placing constraints upon resource availability. He suggests that pollution and resource depletion are best controlled by regulation of the input of resources into the economic system. Under this plan, optimum quotas of such resources would be determined and placed on the market for open bidding. The restriction on the amount of a resource available at any one time would conserve the resource and at the same time would effectively limit the amount of pollutants which could result from the processing and/or use of resource.

A fine adjustment for the control of a resource would be the application of a pollution tax upon the emissions which result from the processing and on the use of a resource. The pollution tax would channel the resource into the less polluting uses and would cause the price of the articles to reflect as nearly as possible all external costs in addition to the normal production costs. Accordingly, the combination of quotas and emission taxes would automatically divert resources into the most efficient uses and into the production of more durable and useful materials.

In addition, Professor Daly would fix a lower limit of income and, more importantly, would establish an upper limit on income. In a society based on limited resources, the higher the lower income limit, the lower the upper limit must be. Any income above the fixed upper limit would be confiscated. Thus, an effective limit would be placed upon acquisition. Under these conditions the total population could possess private property and thus would be as free and independent as possible.

He suggests as a starting point a limit on upper income of twenty times the lower income limit. After a period of time, experience might show that the lower income limit should be raised and the upper income limit lowered. He does not think that the lowered upper income would discourage people from entering professions with long and expensive training.

Professor Daly also advocates the granting of a share of the nation's resources to every individual when he comes of age. The individual might do as he wished with the resource. However, if he lost it, it would not be replenished. He may have lost his capital by poor management, but he would still have his guaranteed income each year.

Malcolm Slesser of the University of Strathclyde, Glasgow, Scotland, suggests that every person be issued an energy ration card. Every purchase would be charged against the energy ration as well as being paid for in money. If each individual were allotted the per capita energy used in the United States, he would be allowed 350 million Btu. A 2-lb loaf of bread would cost 1200 Btu, feed-lot beef would cost 12,000 Btu/lb while grass-fed beef would be only 5000 Btu/lb. A gallon of gasoline would require 140,000 Btu to fuel a car costing 150 million Btu. Convenience foods would cost more than fresh foods, which

Professor Herman Daly

Energy Rationing

would cost more than foods grown in a garden. Professor Slesser would allow a white market in energy units, that is, the units could be bought and sold.

If the system were to be applied worldwide, the individual ration would have to be far below the 350 million Btu used by the American people. The world is not capable of producing the needed 12×10^{18} Btu. Even if production of that much energy were possible, the earth could not sustain such a production.

The Blueprint of Survival

The editors of the British periodical *The Ecologist* have proposed a plan called the Blueprint of Survival which adapts society to the constraints of its resources. Under the plan, society would be decentralized and organized in neighborhoods of 500, communities of 5000, and regions of 500,000. The goal would be to create community feeling and global awareness and to eliminate dangerous nationalism. In the case of Britain, it is proposed that the population be stabilized at 30 million (one half the current population). It is hoped that by 2075 a network of self-sufficient, self-regulating communities will exist throughout Britain and the rest of the world.

The Blueprint for Survival emphasizes durability of goods, and the expenditure of a minimum amount of energy and other resources. Every possible material would be recycled to the maximum possible extent, including the return of sewage and waste water to the land. A resource-materials tax would be imposed to penalize resource-intensive industries and to encourage labor-intensive ones. Durability of goods would be encouraged by an amortization tax. For example, a 100% tax would be levied on products which last a year, and a 0% tax if the product is designed to last 100 or more years.

The authors of Blueprint for Survival recognize that it is going to be difficult to convince politicians, business leaders, and the general public of the desirability of their plan. The necessary changes in human attitudes would be accomplished as much as possible through educational processes. In order to accomplish the objectives, citizens must understand the necessity and urgency of the proposed changes. It is proposed that the changes take place over a period of about 100 years. At the end of that time it is hoped that an eternally sustainable steady state economic and social system can be attained.

Other Cultures

If newspaper accounts can be trusted, China has some of the organizational and attitudinal characteristics which are required for the success of a plan such as the Blueprint for Survival. Apparently, the emphasis in China is for everyone to look after everyone else. It may be worthwhile to observe the Chinese system and adapt those parts which seem to apply to our problems. The interest here is to seek a system which is equitable to all people and sustainable indefinitely into the future. If the American Indians, the Chinese, or the head hunters, if any, of Borneo can contribute valuable experience and systems, let us adapt them to our own situation. Probably no culture can be substituted for another, but perhaps some parts of a culture can be adopted by another society.

Perhaps a more palatable model system would be that displayed by the Scandinavian countries. Denmark's policy is "that few have too little and few

Figure 13–3. Cartoon by Richard Willson from *The Ecologist*, October 1972.

have too much." The balance is attained through high estate taxes among other things. Denmark also controls land use through strict zoning laws. For example, cities are not allowed to expand into the country.

There are many other suggestions. Most include stabilizing population, because an increase in population will increase the need for the use of more resources and put more stress on the environment. Other suggestions to solve our problems include the following.

Other Suggestions

1. A de-development of the highly industrialized countries while the developing countries are encouraged to continue developing.
2. Material possessions should be made with long life times.

3. Advertisements should be severely limited to decrease consumption of resources.

4. Closer cooperation is needed between members of different disciplines. William Longgood[5] writes of interviewing many professionals about the future prospects of the world. He found that the engineers were confident that every problem could be solved. On the other hand, the biologists were pessimistic. The only difference between the various biologists was how long man had before a catastrope hits, what form it will take, and where it will hit. One biologist thinks 10 years is the limit but a consensus seems to be 30 years at the most (Figure 13–3).

CONCLUSION No one questions the desirability of using resources or the need for technology. The question is: How much resources are needed? How are they to be used? What kind of technology is best?

Thomas Jefferson stated that no generation has the right to use the resources which belong to the next generation. If this means cutting back on the use of resources, it does not mean a dreary, physically exhausting, primitive life. John Stuart Mill expressed the opinion:

It is scarcely necessary to remark that a stationary condition of capital and population implies no stationary state of human improvement. There would be as much scope as ever for all kinds of mental culture, and moral and social progress; as much room for improving the Art of Living and much more likelihood of its being improved.[6]

KEY CONCEPTS 1. Historical development of the effects of technology.
2. Importance of energy resources.
3. Suggestions for future social organization.

QUESTIONS 1. Give the advantages and disadvantages as you see them of
(a) the recommendations of the California Plan II;
(b) the report of the Rand Corporation;
(c) Professor Herman Daly's recommendations;
(d) Professor Slesser's energy ration plan;
(e) the Blueprint for Survival.
2. How could a guaranteed job with a 30-hr work week affect the economy? Consider possible lowered earning power, lower taxes, and welfare expenses.
3. Carry Professor Daly's suggestions on income to the ultimate conclusion— same income for all. What effect would this have on our society?

5. William Longgood, *The darkening land,* New York: Simon & Schuster, 1972.
6. *Principles of political economy,* Vol. 2, London: John W. Parker, 1857.

1. Editors of *The Ecologist, Blueprint for survival,* Boston: Houghton Mifflin, 1972.
2. Burch, W. R., Jr., *Daydreams and nightmares,* New York: Harper & Row, 1971.
3. Daly, H., "How to stabilize the economy," *Ecologist,* 3:90–96, March 1973.
4. Falk, R. A., *This endangered planet,* New York: Random House, 1971.
5. Longgood, W., *The Darkening Land,* New York: Simon & Schuster, 1972.
6. Meadows, D. H., *et al., The limits of growth,* New York: Universe Books, 1972.
7. Santa Monica: The Rand Corporation, *California's electricity quandary,* Vol. 3, *Slowing the growth rate,* Doctor, R. D., Anderson, K. P., *et al.,* 1972.
8. Rocks, L., and Runyon, R. P., *The energy crisis,* New York: Crown, 1972.

The following book presents the opposite view, namely that the ecological situation is overblown:

9. Maddox, J., *The doomsday syndrome,* New York: McGraw-Hill, 1972.

Appendix A. Elements, Symbols, Atomic Numbers, and Atomic Weights

Name	Symbol	Atomic number	Atomic weight
Actinium	Ac	89	227
Aluminum	Al	13	26.98
Americium	Am	95	243
Antimony	Sb	51	121.7
Argon	Ar	18	39.9
Arsenic	As	33	74.9
Astatine	At	85	210
Barium	Ba	56	137.3
Berkelium	Bk	97	249
Beryllium	Be	4	9.01
Bismuth	Bi	83	208.9
Boron	B	5	10.8
Bromine	Br	35	79.9
Cadmium	Cd	48	112.4
Calcium	Ca	20	40.08
Californium	Cf	98	251
Carbon	C	6	1201
Cerium	Ce	58	140
Cesium	Cs	55	132
Chlorine	Cl	17	35.45
Chromium	Cr	24	51.99
Cobalt	Co	27	58.9
Copper	Cu	29	63.5
Curium	Cm	96	247
Dyspropsium	Dy	66	162.5
Einsteinium	Es	99	254
Erbium	Er	68	167
Europium	Eu	63	151.9
Fermium	Fm	100	257
Fluorine	F	9	18.99
Francium	Fr	87	223
Gadolinium	Gd	64	157
Gallium	Ga	31	69.7
Germanium	Ge	32	72.5
Gold	Au	79	196.9
Hafnium	Hf	72	178

Name	Symbol	Atomic number	Atomic weight
Hahnium	Ha	105	260
Helium	He	2	4.00
Holmium	Ho	67	164.93
Hydrogen	H	1	1.00
Indium	In	49	114
Iodine	I	53	126.9
Iridium	Ir	77	192.2
Iron	Fe	26	55.8
Krypton	Kr	36	83.8
Kurchatovium	Ku	104	257
Lanthanum	La	57	138.9
Lawrencium	Lr	103	257
Lead	Pb	82	207.19
Lithium	Li	3	6.9
Lutetium	Lu	71	174.97
Magnesium	Mg	12	24
Manganese	Mn	25	54.9
Mendelevium	Md	101	256
Mercury	Hg	80	200
Molybdenum	Mo	42	95.9
Neodymium	Nd	60	144
Neon	Ne	10	20
Neptunium	Np	93	237
Nickel	Ni	28	58.7
Niobium	Nb	41	92.9
Nitrogen	N	7	14
Nobelium	No	102	253
Osmium	Os	76	190
Oxygen	O	8	15.99
Palladium	Pd	46	106
Phosphorus	P	15	30.97
Platinum	Pt	78	195
Plutonium	Pu	94	244
Polonium	Po	84	210
Potassium	K	19	39.1
Praseodymium	Pr	59	140.9
Promethium	Pm	61	145
Protactinium	Pa	91	231
Radium	Ra	88	226
Radon	Rn	86	222
Rhenium	Re	75	186
Rhodium	Rh	45	102
Rubidium	Rb	37	85.47

ELEMENTS, SYMBOLS, ATOMIC NUMBERS, AND ATOMIC WEIGHTS

Name	Symbol	Atomic number	Atomic weight
Ruthenium	Ru	44	101
Samarium	Sm	62	150
Scandium	Sc	21	44.9
Selenium	Se	34	78.9
Silicon	Si	14	28
Silver	Ag	47	107.8
Sodium	Na	11	22.98
Strontium	Sr	38	87
Sulfur	S	16	32
Tantalum	Ta	73	180.9
Technetium	Tc	43	97
Tellurium	Te	52	127
Terbium	Tb	65	158.9
Thallium	Tl	81	204
Thorium	Th	90	232
Thulium	Tm	90	168.9
Tin	Sn	50	118.6
Titanium	Ti	22	47.9
Tungsten	W	74	183.8
Uranium	U	92	283
Vanadium	V	23	50.9
Xenon	Xe	54	131.3
Ytterbium	Yb	70	173.3
Yttrium	Y	39	88.9
Zinc	Zn	30	65.4
Zirconium	Zr	40	91

Appendix B. Periodic Table of the Elements

1 **H** 1																	2 **He** 4
3 **Li** 7	4 **Be** 9											5 **B** 11	6 **C** 12	7 **N** 14	8 **O** 16	9 **F** 19	10 **Ne** 20
11 **Na** 23	12 **Mg** 24											13 **Al** 27	14 **Si** 28	15 **P** 31	16 **S** 32	17 **Cl** 35.5	18 **Ar** 40
19 **K** 39	20 **Ca** 40	21 **Sc** 45	22 **Ti** 48	23 **V** 51	24 **Cr** 52	25 **Mn** 55	26 **Fe** 56	27 **Co** 59	28 **Ni** 59	29 **Cu** 63.5	30 **Zn** 65	31 **Ga** 70	32 **Ge** 72.5	33 **As** 75	34 **Se** 79	35 **Br** 80	36 **Kr** 84
37 **Rb** 85.5	38 **Sr** 88	39 **Y** 89	40 **Zr** 91	41 **Nb** 93	42 **Mo** 96	43 **Tc** 97	44 **Ru** 101	45 **Rh** 103	46 **Pd** 106	47 **Ag** 108	48 **Cd** 112	49 **In** 115	50 **Sn** 119	51 **Sb** 122	52 **Te** 128	53 **I** 127	54 **Xe** 131
55 **Cs** 133	56 **Ba** 137	57 **La** 139	72 **Hf** 178.5	73 **Ta** 181	74 **W** 184	75 **Re** 186	76 **Os** 190	77 **Ir** 192	78 **Pt** 195	79 **Au** 197	80 **Hg** 200.5	81 **Tl** 204	82 **Pb** 207	83 **Bi** 209	84 **Po** 210	85 **At** 210	86 **Rn** 222
87 **Fr** 223	88 **Ra** 226	89 **Ac** 227	104 **Ku** 257	105 **Ha** 260													

58 **Ce** 140	59 **Pr** 141	60 **Nd** 144	61 **Pm** 145	62 **Sm** 150	63 **Eu** 152	64 **Gd** 157	65 **Tb** 159	66 **Dy** 162.5	67 **Ho** 165	68 **Er** 167	69 **Tm** 169	70 **Yb** 173	71 **Lu** 175
90 **Th** 232	91 **Pa** 231	92 **U** 238	93 **Np** 237	94 **Pu** 244	95 **Am** 243	96 **Cm** 247	97 **Bk** 247	98 **Cf** 251	99 **Es** 254	100 **Fm** 257	101 **Md** 256	102 **No** 254	103 **Lw** 257

Appendix C. Metric and Conversion Units

In the metric system, prefixes are used to show multiples and fractions of a base unit. These prefixes are listed in Table C–1 with abbreviations and the prefixes used with the *gram*, the basic unit of mass. Various other basic units are the *meter* (m), unit of length; the *liter* (l), unit of volume; the *watt* (w), unit of energy; and the *curie* (ci), unit of radiation. All prefixes are not commonly used with every base unit. For example, the prefix hecto for 100 is not commonly used with the meter (hectometer) but it is a common expression for land area with the base unit "are" (pronounced air and equal to 100 square meters)—hectare (100 ares or 10,000 square meters).

In the text most measurements are given in both metric and English units, except for engineering units which are generally given in the English system. However, it may be desirable to convert some measurements to the other system. The more commonly used conversion factors are given in Table C–2.

Energy is measured in various units. Conversion factors are given in Table C–3 together with the quantities of energy sources needed to supply the United States and to supply one person with energy for a year. Table C–4 shows the relationship between radiation units. These are used mainly in Chapter 10 of the text.

Environmental pollutants are often measured in parts per million (ppm) or even in parts per billion (ppb). One ppm is equal to 1 mg/kg. However, a more qualitative relationship is helpful, as shown in Table C–5.

TABLE C–1. Prefixes of the Metric System, their Abbreviations, and Combinations with the Base Unit, the Gram.

Prefixes	Abbreviation	Factor	Prefix with gram unit
pico	p	1/1,000,000,000,000	picogram (pg)
nano	n	1/1,000,000,000	nanogram (ng)
micro	μ	1/1,000,000	microgram (μg)
milli	m	1/1,000	milligram (mg)
centi	c	1/100	centigram (cg)
deci	d	1/10	decigram (dg)
the base unit		1	gram (g)
deka	dk	10	dekagram (dkg)
hecto	h	100	hectogram (hg)
kilo	k	1000	kilogram (kg)
mega	M	1,000,000	megagram (Mg)

TABLE C-2. English-Metric Conversion Factors.

English unit	Metric equivalence
inch	2.54 centimeters
yard	0.914 meters
mile	1.609 kilometers
pound	454 grams
ounce	28.4 grams
ton	0.907 tonnes (metric ton)
quart	0.946 liters
cubic feet	0.0283 cubic meters
gallon	0.00379 cubic meters

TABLE C-3. Energy Relationships.

Energy units and their relationship:

Btu (British thermal unit)	252 calories (.252 Calories or kc)
Btu	0.00293 kilowatt-hours
calorie	0.00116 watt-hours

Units of alternative sources of energy needed to supply the United States for one year:
210×10^{12} (trillion) kilowatt-hours
70×10^{15} (quadrillion) Btu
18×10^{18} calorie (18×10^{15} Calories)

Amounts of alternative sources of energy needed to supply the United States and each consumer annually:

Source	Requirement (approximate)	
	United States	per capita
natural gas (cubic feet)	70×10^{12} (trillion)	350×10^3
oil (barrels)	13×10^9 (billion)	60
coal (tons)	2.7×10^9	13
wood (cords*)	2.8×10^9	14

*A pile of wood 4 feet by 4 feet by 8 feet.

TABLE C-4. Radiation Units.

Unit	Definition
1 curie	3.7×10^{10} disintegrations
1 roentgen	2.1×10^9 ion pairs
1 rem	1 roentgen equivalent man
1 millirem (mrem)	1/1000 rem
1 rad	100 ergs/gram

*1 rad and 1 rem cause approximately the same effect.

TABLE C–5. Parts per Million (ppm) Defined.

1 ppm is equal to 1 inch in 16 miles
1 ppm is 1 minute in 2 years
1 ppm is a 1-gram needle in a ton of hay
1 ppm is one penny in $10,000.00
1 ppm is 1 ounce (30 grams) of salt in 62,500 pounds (28,374 kilograms) of sugar
1 ppm is one large mouthful of food when compared with the food we will eat in a lifetime
1 ppm is the theoretical concentration that 1 teaspoon of DDT will impart to the hay when spread on 5 acres of alfalfa
1 ppm is one drop in 16 gallons

Source: W. B. Deichmann and H. W. Gerarde, *Toxicology of drugs and chemicals*, 4th ed. New York: Academic Press, 1969.

Appendix D. Unit Conversions

Curiosity or necessity may make it desirable at times to convert a quantity from one system of units to another. This process is most expeditiously done through a unit approach to the calculation. The process depends upon the following mathematical facts.

1. No matter how many times a quantity is multiplied by a number equal to one, it is still the original amount. For example, one inch multiplied by one is still the quantity one inch.

2. Any quantity divided by the same quantity equals the number one. Twelve inches and one foot represent the same quantity. Therefore, 1 ft/12 in. or 12 in./1 ft are both equal to one.

3. Units are treated as numbers and, therefore, are subject to mathematical operations.

Since mathematical principles apply to units of measurement, it is possible to convert from one unit to another if an adequate table of equivalents is available. For example, consider the following problem which is easily set up and solved mathematically: How many centimeter (cm) units are there in a distance of 1.685 miles (mi)? Stated in equation form the question in the problem becomes

$$? \text{ cm} = 1.685 \text{ mi}$$

The mile unit must be changed to the centimeter unit. No other units must remain. This is accomplished by multiplying 1.685 miles by numbers equal to one (see principle 1 above). Thus,

$$? \text{ cm} = 1.685 \text{ mi} \times \frac{5280 \text{ ft}}{1 \text{ mi}} \times \frac{12 \text{ in.}}{1 \text{ ft}} \times \frac{2.54 \text{ cm}}{1 \text{ in.}}$$

$$\text{(A)} \qquad \text{(B)} \qquad \text{(C)}$$

Each of the multiplying fractions (A,B,C) is equal to one and is obtained from a statement of equivalence by dividing both sides of the equivalence equations by the same number:

$$1 \text{ mi} = 5280 \text{ ft} \qquad 12 \text{ in.} = 1 \text{ ft} \qquad 2.54 \text{ cm} = 1 \text{ in.}$$

$$\frac{1 \text{ mi}}{1 \text{ mi}} = \frac{5280 \text{ ft}}{1 \text{ mi}} = 1 \qquad \frac{12 \text{ in.}}{1 \text{ ft}} = \frac{1 \text{ ft}}{1 \text{ ft}} = 1 \qquad \frac{2.54 \text{ cm}}{1 \text{ in.}} = \frac{1 \text{ in.}}{1 \text{ in.}} = 1$$

In the original equation, the mile, foot, and inch units divide out and only the centimeter unit remains. Finally, the distance in centimeters becomes

$$? \text{ cm} = 1.685 \times 5280 \times 12 \times 2.54 \text{ cm}$$
$$= \text{about } 271{,}200 \text{ cm}$$

Similarly, it is possible to calculate the number of cubic centimeters (cm³) in one cubic mile (mi³) of space:

$$? \text{ cm}^3 = 1 \text{ mi}^3 \times \frac{5280^3 \text{ ft}^3}{\text{mi}^3} \times \frac{12^3 \text{ in.}^3}{1 \text{ ft}^3} \times \frac{2.54^3 \text{ cm}^3}{1 \text{ in.}^3}$$

Conversely, it is possible to calculate the number of mi³ in one cm³:

$$? \text{ mi}^3 = 1 \text{ cm}^3 \times \frac{1 \text{ in.}^3}{2.54^3 \text{ cm}^3} \times \frac{1 \text{ ft}^3}{12^3 \text{ in.}^3} \times \frac{1 \text{ mi}^3}{5280^3 \text{ ft}^3}$$

When the mathematical statement is detailed in this way (all units written in fractions), it is easy to check the numerical values and the thinking process involved. When only the desired unit remains, the problem is solved, except for the arithmetic involved.

The necessary equivalences for a calculation may be found in a conversion table such as is found in the *Handbook of Chemistry and Physics*. They may be theoretical information obtained from a chemical equation, or they may be empirical relationships derived from experimental work. All may be used to solve a problem.

Appendix E.   Interpreting Graphs

Graphs are often used to show how one quantity changes with respect to changes in another quantity. The apparent rate of change shown by a graph is highly dependent upon the way in which the values are measured (that is, scaled) on the graph.

Graphs a, b, c of Figure E–1 plot the same data on different scales; each plot gives a different impression of the rate of change which is occurring. Graph a in Figure E–1 shows an apparent small increase from 2% to 3% (actually a 50% increase) between the years 1900 and 1970. The same relationship is shown in graph b, but in this case only that part of the graph between 2% and 3% is shown. The rate of increase in graph b appears to be much greater than the increase in graph a. Graph c shows the same relationship but the years are given in a smaller space. The rate of increase in graph c seems greater than in either graph a or graph b even though the same data has been graphed in each case.

If the values of one quantity involve a wide range of values, a logarithmic graph may be used. Here the scale is made by plotting 0, 10, 100, 1000, etc. in each step instead of the usual numerical scale. Graph a in Figure E–2 is plotted in logarithmic units. Graph b in Figure E–2 is the same relationship graphed on the more usual scale. If the graphs were extended only one more step, the next number would be 10,000. On graph b this would be several page lengths beyond the plotted graph; on graph a, the same value would be the highest point on the graph.

Thus we find that whether a small or large increase is desirable can be determined only from the factors involved.

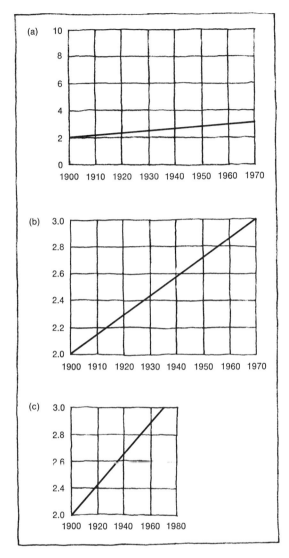

Figure E-1. Three ways to graph the same data.

Figure E-2. Graphing of exponential data.

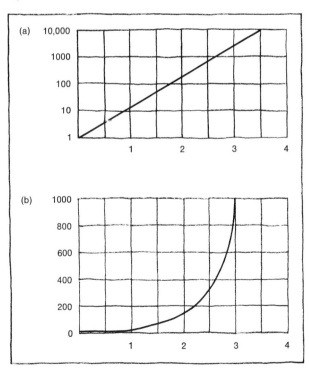

INTERPRETING GRAPHS

Appendix F.   Temperature Scales

°K	°C	°F
1073	800	1472
973	700	1292
873	600	1112
773	500	932
673	400	732
573	300	572
473	200	392
373	100	212
273	0	32
0	⁻273	⁻460

$$°C = \frac{5}{9} \, (°F - 32)$$

$$°K = °C + 273$$

Art Credits

Figure 3–5. Data from U.S. Department of Health, Education and Welfare, Public Health Service, *Air Quality Criteria for Particulate Matter*, Washington, D.C.: Government Printing Office, p. 57.

Figure 3–8. From U.S. Department of Health, Education and Welfare, Consumer Protection and Environmental Health Service, *Air Quality Data*, Washington, D.C.: Government Printing Office, 1967, p. 18.

Figure 3–9. From U.S. Department of Health, Education and Welfare, Public Health Service, *Air Quality Criteria for* SO_x, Washington, D.C.: Government Printing Office, 1969, p. 13.

Figure 3–11. From U.S. Department of Health, Education and Welfare, Public Health Service, *Air Quality Criteria for* SO_x, Washington, D.C.: Government Printing Office, 1969, p. 64.

Figure 3–12. Data from U.S. Environmental Policy Division, Congressional Research Service of the Library of Congress, *Energy—The Ultimate Resource*, Washington, D.C.: Government Printing Office, 1971, p. 141.

Figure 3–14. From U.S. Environmental Protection Agency, *Air Quality Criteria for Nitrogen Oxides*, Washington, D.C.: Government Printing Office, 1971, p. 6–2.

Figure 3–16. From U.S. Department of Health, Education and Welfare, Public Health Service, *Control Techniques for Carbon Monoxide, Nitrogen Oxides, and Hydrocarbon Emissions from Mobile Sources*, Washington, D.C.: Government Printing Office, 1970, p. 1–1.

Figure 5–2. From U.S. Department of Agriculture, *Two-thirds of Our Land: A National Inventory*, Washington, D.C.: Government Printing Office, 1971, p. 15.

Figure 6–9. From a graph prepared by the U.S. Senate Select Committee on Nutrition and Human Needs, *Poverty, Malnutrition and Federal Food Assistance Program: A Statistical Summary*, Washington, D.C.: Government Printing Office, 1969.

Figure 6–14. From U.S. Food and Drug Administration, Leaflet No. 10, *What Consumers Should Know About Food Additives*, Washington, D.C.: Government Printing Office, 1969.

Glossary

acid a substance that donates protons (hydrogen nuclei) to another substance called a base

activated carbon carbon that adsorbs other substances

adsorb to collect on the surface

adverse reaction serious reaction to a drug other than the desired reaction

aerobic pertaining to or caused by the presence of oxygen

alcohol a carbon compound with the structure R_3COH; R can be either a carbon group or a hydrogen atom

alpha particle a helium nucleus with two protons and two neutrons

amino acid a substance with an amine group (NH_2) and an acid group (—COOH) on the same carbon

anaerobic pertaining to or caused by the absence of oxygen

antibiotics any of a large group of substances produced by microorganisms and having the property of destroying other microorganisms

antioxidants compounds used to prevent oxidation from occurring; often found in rubber, food, fats, and oils

aquifer underground layers of sand, gravel, or rock that contain usable amounts of water

aromatic compounds any compounds that contain a benzene ring

asymmetric carbon a carbon atom with four different groups; it can form molecules having two different structures (mirror images of each other)

atom a small, discrete particle of matter that cannot be further divided by chemical reactions

atomic mass unit a unit of weight (amu) based on 1/12 the mass of carbon-12

atomic number number of protons in an atom

atomic weight average relative weight of all isotopes of an element based on carbon-12 as exactly 12.00

base a substance that attracts protons (hydrogen nuclei) from another atom

benefaction any process that concentrates a mineral

beta particle an electron which may be ejected from a nucleus

biodegradable that which can be broken down by bacteria or other microorganisms

biorefractories substances that are not biodegradable

BOD, biological oxygen demand a quantitative measure of the oxygen required for the biological decomposition of organic matter in water

body burden a deleterious substance carried by the body

brackish salty water with from 1000 to 35,000 ppm dissolved solids

branched chain compounds carbon compounds with a second chain of one or more carbons attached to a main chain

brine a concentrated salt solution

broad-spectrum any substance, such as a drug or a pesticide, that acts on a wide range of organisms

carcinogen that which causes cancer by acting on the reproductive process of any nonreproductive cell

catalyst an agent that affects the rate of a chemical reaction without apparent change in itself

chain reaction a reaction where the products of the reaction act as initiators to start a succeeding reaction

chelation the process by which a complex organic compound (chelating agent) holds a metal ion by several bonds to form a cage

chromosome DNA bonded to a protein

clearcut complete removal of all forest growth

climate the total weather over a region

coenzyme a stable, organic molecule that must be loosely associated with a certain enzyme in order for that enzyme to function

colloid a particle ranging in size from that of molecules to visible particles

compost a mixture of decaying organic matter

compounds substances whose molecules are of only one kind

copolymer a polymer made from a mixture of usually two monomers

covalent bond the attraction of a nucleus of one atom to the electrons of another atom, which results in a pair of electrons being shared by the two atoms

DDT, dichlorodiphenyltrichloroethane a persistent chlorinated hydrocarbon pesticide

degradation the breaking down of organic substances into simpler substances

depressant that which reduces biological or physiological activity

desalination the process of removing minerals from brackish or sea water

desulfurization the process of removing sulfur

detergent any substance used for cleaning

distillation the process of purification by which substances are heated, and vapors are collected and liquified

DNA, deoxyribonucleic acid the chemical of the cell that controls inheritance

ecology the relationship between organisms and their environment

effluent a discharge from any source

electrolysis the process of separating the elements of a compound by use of an electric current

electrons negatively charged particles that orbit around the nucleus of an atom

elements those substances whose atoms are of only one kind

energy-intensive industry an industry which uses large inputs of energy. Conversely, any industry that uses large inputs of labor instead of energy is a labor-intensive industry.

enzymes huge, high molecular weight compounds that are part of or attached to a protein molecule; they act as catalysts in living organisms

equilibrium a state in which the forward and reverse reactions involving the same chemicals are proceeding at the same rate at the same time

erosion the process by which land is worn away by action of water, wind, glaciers, etc.

ester a compound with a double-bonded oxygen and an OR group on a carbon the result of the combination of an acid and alcohol

estuary the lower part of a river where it mixes with the sea

eutrophication stimulation of the growth of algae by the addition of nutrients to a body of water

evapotranspiration a combination of processes in which water evaporates from a field and transpires from the plants

excursion a departure from the normal operating conditions of a nuclear reactor, usually unplanned and uncontrolled

fallowed land land where no crop is planted for a crop year but which is cultivated to prevent growth of weeds

fast-breeder reactor a reactor that not only produces energy but also "breeds" or produces more fuel than it uses

fats esters resulting from a long, straight-chained acid and a three-carbon alcohol: CH_2OH, $CHOH$, and CH_2OH. If the acid has no double bonds, the fat is saturated.

FDA, Food and Drug Administration the federal agency that regulates the sale of foods and drugs

fission the process where certain heavy nuclei split into two main nuclei plus a few neutrons

food additives substances added to food in small amounts to improve storage capability or consumer acceptance

food chain a series of organisms, each of which feeds on the preceding one

fossil fuels fuels that were formed millions of years ago from organisms whose matter has changed into oil, oil shale, natural gas, tar sands, and coal

fractional distillation a process in which substances with different boiling points are collected separately

free radical an element or group of elements which have an unpaired electron, indicated by a raised dot (·) after the formula

fuel cell a device that changes fuel directly to electricity

fused melted

fusion the process whereby two small nuclei combine to form a larger nucleus with the evolution of energy

gene unit of inheritance in a chromosome

genetic wealth total genetic material of all kinds

geothermal energy energy from hot water and steam from within the earth

gram-atomic weight atomic weight of an element expressed in grams

gram-molecular weight molecular weight of a compound expressed in grams

greenhouse effect an increase in temperature that results from the trapping of shorter wave radiation which is changed to long wave radiation and does not escape as easily

Green Revolution the development of hybrid seeds which, with the addition of large amounts of fertilizer and pesticides, may increase food production

half-life the period of time it takes for one half of something to be changed

hallucinogen anything that induces false perceptions which have a sense of reality

hard water water that contains multiple-charged ions such as Ca^{2+} or Mg^{2+}

heavy metals those five times as dense as water

herbicides substances used to kill plants

highwall the high side of a cut made in a hill to reach a mineral deposit

humus decaying organic matter that is a normal and desirable component of soil

hydrocarbons compounds of hydrogen and carbon

hydrogenation the process of adding hydrogen to a compound with double bonds, usually carbon–carbon double bonds

hydrogen bonds a proton from one molecule attracting an electron from another molecule to form a weak bond

hydronium ion a proton attached to several water molecules, written as the formula H_3O^+

incineration to consume by burning in furnaces, usually with air pollution devices

insecticides substances used to kill insects

insolation incoming solar energy

Ion an atom which has lost or gained one or more electrons, or a group of covalently bonded atoms which carry a charge; e.g., SO_4^{2-}, NH_4^+.

ion exchange the process whereby an ion in a solution is exchanged for another ion held by a solid

ionic bond the attractive force between a negatively charged ion and a positively charged ion which holds the ions together

ionization removal or addition of electrons to an atom

isomer two or more substances with the same number and kind of atoms but with different arrangements of the atoms

isotope an atom of a given weight and kind

leach the removal of soluble constituents by percolation of water; e.g., minerals may be leached from the soil

lean resource low grade

legumes plants whose roots have colonies of bacteria that change atmospheric nitrogen into a form usable by the plant

mass number the sum of the protons and neutrons in the nucleus of an atom

micronutrients nutrients needed by plants in small amounts

mole 6.02×10^{23} particles

molecular weight the sum of all the atomic weights of the atoms found in a molecule

monomer small molecule or unit that may unite with many other similar molecules to form a much larger molecule

mutagen an agent that changes the genetic material of a sperm or egg cell

narcotic   a drug that induces sleep and/or relieves pain

neutrons   uncharged particles about the same weight as the proton and located in the nucleus

nitrogen fixation   the process whereby nitrogen gas of the air is changed to an ionic form which plants can utilize

nonspecific   that which attacks a large number of organisms

nucleus   the heavy center of an atom where the protons and neutrons are located

nuclide   any atomic species

nuplex   groups of nuclear power plants together with various industries and farming

octane number   an arbitrary number indicating the tendency of a gasoline to cause an engine to knock

orbital   places that electrons may occupy

organic acid   a carbon compound with a COOH group

organic chemistry   the chemistry of carbon compounds

osmosis   the process by which fluids pass through a membrane

overburden   soil and rock above a mineral layer that is being mined

oxidation   loss of electrons; a reaction with oxygen where oxygen takes the electrons away from another atom. Oxygen is the oxidizing agent.

ozone   three atoms of oxygen combined to form a molecule

PCB, polychlorinated biphenyl   one of a group of organochlorine compounds that has two phenyl (C_6H_5) rings

persistence   long lasting

pesticides   general term referring to any substance used to destroy plants or animals

petrochemical   a substance related to petroleum

petroleum   liquid fossil fuels

pH   a number that indicates the concentration of protons present; that is, the acidity of a solution. A pH of 7 is neutral; above that is basic; below that is acidic.

photochemical   referring to a chemical reaction triggered by light

photosynthesis   the process by which plants change light energy into chemical energy and produce food

plankton   the microorganisms that live in the ocean—phytoplankton are plants; zooplankton are animals

polar   referring to a molecule which has its atoms distributed in such a way that it has a center of negative charge and a center of positive charge. Molecules whose charges are distributed uniformly are said to be nonpolar.

polymer   a huge molecule that is made of small units called monomers

potable water   drinkable water

potential energy   stored energy

predator   any organism that lives by preying on others

protein   a complex organic molecule resulting from the combination of 50 or more amino acid molecules (a polymer)

protons   positively charged particles that are located in the nucleus of an atom

pyrites   lumps of an iron-sulfur compound (FeS_2) in coal and other rock formations

pyrolysis   a process of breaking down organic substances by heating them to 590 °C–760 °C in the absence of oxygen

radiation   energy in the form of light, waves, heat, sound, or particles

radioactive   the property of a few elements that are unstable and decay (change) by ejecting energetic particles from the nucleus to form a new and different element

radionuclides   nuclides that undergo radioactive decay

RDA, recommended daily allowance   daily amounts of various vitamins and minerals considered essential by the FDA

reduction   gain of electrons, e.g., $Fe^{3+} + e^{1-} = Fe^{2+}$

renovated water   water returned to a ''clean'' condition by removal of organic and mineral matter

resistance   certain characteristics which allow organisms to live in the presence of a chemical that formerly killed others of the same kind

saline   salty (containing at least 1000 ppm of soluble mineral matter)

salts   compounds resulting from the combination of a positive ion, other than a hydrogen ion, and a negative ion, other than a hydroxide ion

saturated fat   a fat with no double bonds (an unsaturated fat has at least one double bond)

semipermeable membrane   a membrane such as a cell wall which allows some ions and molecules to pass through but stops others

sludge   semi-solid matter from a sewage treatment plant

smelting   a process whereby ores are separated into metallic components by melting; sulfur oxides are often produced

smog   any visibility-reducing mixture of liquid and solid particles in the atmosphere. A ''London'' type smog is caused by sulfur oxides and particulates. A photochemical smog is caused by nitrogen oxides and hydrocarbons.

soap   a cleaning agent with a nonpolar end from a fatty acid and polar end (acid)

spoil   layers of overburden that have been piled in a convenient place or dumped down the side of a hill

stimulant   anything that arouses or heightens biological or psychological activity

substrate   a substance being acted upon by an enzyme

superconductivity   the characteristic of conducting materials when cooled to very low temperatures

syndet   a man-made detergent

synergistic   two substances whose effects together are greater than the sum of the separate effects of each

tailings   waste produced at a mine or an ore-processing plant

teratogen   something that causes a birth defect

thermal pollution the addition of unwanted heat to the environment, sometimes called thermal enrichment

thermoplastic plastics plastics that may be reheated and reformed

thermosetting plastics on polymerization these plastics form a rigid structure that cannot be melted without decomposition.

threshold a level of safety or no effect

tolerance a capacity to accept certain allowable amounts

vitamin a complex organic compound that is essential to the human body in small amounts

water softener that which removes the positive ions which cause water to be hard

weight a measure of the gravitational pull on an object

Index